S0-ATH-301

East Asia and the Western

d the
Western Pacific
1996 29TH EDITION

PATRICK M. MAYERCHAK, PH.D.

STRYKER–POST PUBLICATIONS

HARPERS FERRY, WEST VIRGINIA

NEXT EDITION—AUGUST 1997

Patrick M. Mayerchak . . .

Professor of Political Science and Director of International Studies, the Virginia Military Institute. He received his doctorate from the School of International Service of the American University. Author of *A Scholar's Guide to Southeast Asian Studies*, co–author of *Linkage or Bondage: United States–ASEAN Trade Relations*, he is a regular contributor of book reviews on Asia for *Studies in Conflict and Terrorism*. Since 1987, Professor Mayerchak has served as study group leader for the Smithsonian Institution's "Far East Adventure."

First appearing as a book entitled
The Far East and Southwest Pacific 1968,
revised annually and published in succeeding years by

Stryker-Post Publications
P.O. Drawer 1200
Harpers Ferry, WV. 25425
Telephones: 1–800–995–1400
    From outside U.S.A.: 1–304–535–2593
    Fax: 1–304–535–6513
    VISA–MASTERCARD

Photographs used to illustrate *The World Today Series* come from many sources, a great number from friends who travel worldwide. If you have taken any which you believe would enhance the visual impact and attractiveness of our books, do let us hear from you.

International Standard Book Number: 0–943448–98–0

International Standard Serial Number: 1043–2140

Library of Congress Catalog Number 67–11540

Cover design by Susan Bodde

Chief Bibliographer: Robert V. Gross

Cartographer: William L. Nelson

Printed in the United States of America
by Braun–Brumfield, Inc., Ann Arbor, Michigan

Typography by Stryker–Post Publications
and Braun–Brumfield, Inc.

Table of Contents

Gold dragon on the roof of the Happiness and Long Life Temple at the Chinese Emperor's summer palace

UNIFORMS . . . lifesize clay warriors, 4000 strong, somberly guard a Chinese emperor's tomb near Xian (roughly, *She-yan*), while Japanese baseball ("Yah-kyu") players thrill their screaming fans in Tokyo.

The United States and Asia in 1996: The Pacific Century Rolls on

A card party on an old street in Beijing, China

Photo by Miller B. Spangler

In 1993 and 1994, the Clinton Administration recognized the advent of the "Pacific Century," and attempted to initiate a new foreign policy which recognized a new importance of Asia for the United States. Unfortunately, in 1995, that policy was in disarray. Relations with two major regional actors, China and Japan, were on the skids. Washington's commitment to regional economic cooperation was in question. And there was also concern about America's commitment to regional security. Should President Clinton win re–election in November 1996, a mid–course correction would be possible.

A Dole presidency would almost certainly bring forth a new policy. However, by then, the course of events could progress in such a way that U.S. participation in the most important region of the world will be cast aside. America was correct in recognizing the Pacific century. Now, it must understand what needs to be done to share in its benefits.

While Washington fumbled from one issue to another, the Asia–Pacific region was becoming more secure with its continued economic prosperity. Leaders of certain Asia–Pacific states were redefining their place in the world and that of the West, especially the United States. By 1996, the nature of the Asia–Pacific challenge was no longer purely economic in nature. It had also become a challenge of ideas.

A Year of Policy Blunders

By April 1996, one could look back at what appeared to be a number of serious policy miscalculations on the part of several nations in the previous year. Fortunately, none led to irreparable damage. In November 1995, President Clinton failed to show for the third Asia Pacific Economic Cooperation (APEC) meeting in Japan. This after Assistant Secretary of State Winston Lord stated that there was no way Clinton wouldn't attend. The President's absence not only hurt Washington in Asia's eyes, it also made the Japanese look bad. The meeting presented Tokyo with a golden opportunity to establish its regional credibility, regarded as essential as a counter–balance to China. The opportunity clearly was dimmed by President Clinton's absence. This narrowed the strategic options for Tokyo and Washington as they face the question of what to do about economically emerging China.

Japan and the United States also had to endure tough talks on automobiles. At one point Washington threatened a 100% tax on Japanese luxury cars. An agreement to open the Japanese market was reached prior to the June 30, 1995 deadline. The relationship was further strained as a result of the rape of a 12 year old Okinawan girl by three U.S. servicemen which could not have been anticipated. In April 1996, it was announced that there would be a 20% reduction in the amount of land occupied by U.S. bases on Okinawa. The Administration seems unable to understand that economic and security issues cannot be separated. Strains in one area inevitably spill over into the other. The U.S.-Japanese security arrangement will survive. A series of consultations organized by Assistant Secretary of Defense Nye were useful, and this example should not be forgotten in the future.

Washington–Beijing relations turned sour in 1995. The serious deterioration in relations escalated when President Clinton reversed his own advisers, caved

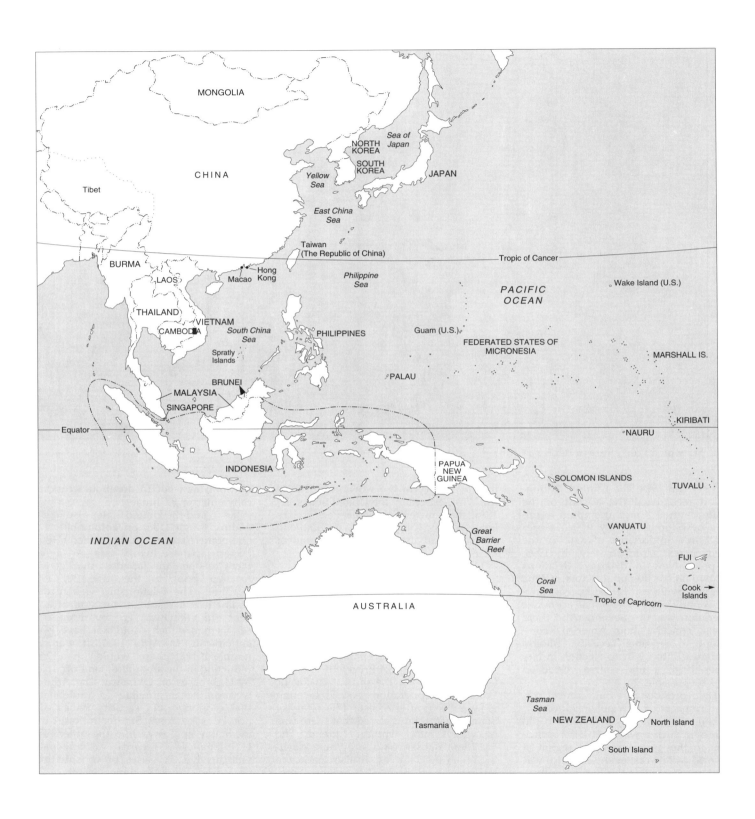

U.S. Trade With Key East Asian and Pacific Countries*
(In millions of U.S. dollars)

Country	U.S. Exports			U.S. Imports		
	1992	1993	1994	1992	1993	1994
Brunei	453	472	376	29	30	45
Indonesia	2,777	2,770	2,811	4,526	5,434	3,523
Malaysia	4,385	6,064	6,984	8,293	10,563	13,977
Philippines	2,753	3,529	3,888	4,357	4,893	5,720
Singapore	9,623	11,678	13,021	11,317	12,798	15,380
Thailand	3,962	3,766	4,861	7,528	8,541	10,307
ASEAN tot	23,953	28,280	31,822	36,053	42,261	51,934
Australia	8,912	8,276	9,780	3,691	3,297	3,199
New Zealand	1,307	1,248	1,503	1,219	1,207	1,420
Papua N G	71	50	65	63	97	108
Fiji	59	26	113	73	68	97
Cambodia	16	15	7	0.1	0.7	1
Laos	1	1.5	5.7	5.9	8.6	8.8
Vietnam	4	7	172	0	0	50
Burma	4	12	11	38	46	67
Japan	47,786	47,891	53,480	97,181	107,246	119,149
China	7,489	8,762	9,286	25,729	31,539	38,781
Taiwan	15,204	16,167	17,077	24,601	25,701	29,710
Hong Kong	9,069	9,873	11,445	9,799	9,554	8,697
S. Korea	14,630	14,782	18,028	16,690	17,118	19,857
Macao	18	27	21	721	668	791
Other EAP	373	307	119	60	73	78
EAP Total	128,893	135,748	153,057	215,935	238,324	271,781
World Total	448,156	465,091	512,669	532,497	580,669	663,761
EAP as % of World	28.7%	29.1%	29.8%	40.5%	39.6%	40.9%

*Abstracted from U.S. Department of Commerce data

in to a congressional resolution, and allowed President Lee of Taiwan to visit the United States. This was a terrible miscalculation which would better not have occurred. Hopefully, the U.S. Congress will have learned something from this episode. However, with an abundance of ideologues in the House, this is not likely.

U.S. policy toward Korea was more successful. North Korea made a clumsy attempt to force Washington into negotiations without including South Korea. North Korea still refused to admit that South Korea exists. The North even declared in April 1996 that it no longer would recognize the demilitarized zone between the two countries. If the country would simply indicate that it is ready to join the international community, it would be welcomed—though grudgingly—at this point. Instead, its policy has been to force acceptance by the international community. Thus far, it has failed in this ambition.

An agreement was recently signed with the Korean Peninsula Economic Development Organization (KEDO) allowing the construction by South Korea of two light water nuclear reactors in the North. It can be assumed that further delays and mini–crises will occur. Eventually, the program will go forward.

If Washington and Pyongyang were guilty of miscalculations in foreign policy as outlined above, Beijing made even more mistakes. Military exercises conducted off the coast of Taiwan in March

1996 were an overt threat to discourage voters from supporting what Beijing saw as pro–independence candidates in the first ever Republic of China (Taiwan) presidential elections. Predictably, the intimidation failed as pro–independence candidates won about 75% of the votes in a four way race. President Lee was re–elected with a huge margin and China was humiliated.

North Korea has little experience in diplomacy. Beijing and Washington do. This is not a blanket criticism. It is disconcerting, however, to think that both are capable of unnecessary miscalculations. Relations will be repaired. However, time will be lost and opportunities missed. China and the United States must move through the Pacific century together. This will be difficult even with good relations which don't appear probable in the future. As of May 1996 both sides were engaged in delivering threats of increased tariffs, creating the danger that both sides will blunder into a full–scale trade war.

The basic difficulty lies with Chinese piracy of copyright–protected artistic, intellectual and technological items originating elsewhere. The is not a matter of easy choice for the Chinese government, which is under tremendous pressure from the new class of Chinese businessmen. President Clinton threatened confiscatory tariffs on Chinese goods to end this piracy (at the request of the powerful Microsoft and others). But Clinton is also under pressure from U.S. businessmen

doing billions of dollars in trade centered on Chinese–produced articles who oppose tariffs. In May 1966 he gave in to the latter and announced he would propose continuation of China's Most Favored Nation status, under which higher tariffs would not be charged.

The basic question remains unsolved. How long should China be allowed to operate outside accepted standards of international law and trade? To allow this to continue threatens the stability of the whole structure of world trade.

A Year of Small Steps Forward

While relations did not go smoothly for the three major regional actors—China, Japan and the United States, there were some positive events to report.

National elections in Thailand and the presidential election in Taiwan both served the interests of democracy. The same can be said for the arrest, trial and conviction of two former presidents in South Korea.

The second meeting of the ASEAN Regional Forum (ARF) witnessed the successful transformation of the South China Sea dispute from bilateral to multilateral status. In agreeing to this, China accepted the position of the ASEAN states (Brunei, Indonesia, Malaysia, Philippines, Singapore and Thailand. This could give a substantial boost to the security concerns of the Southeast Asian states, which continue to be centered on Washington's future commitment to the region.

The inclusion of Vietnam in ASEAN and the establishment of full diplomatic relations between Hanoi and Washington also added to the collective accomplishments throughout the region. All in all, the positives were more likely to be lasting while the blunders will be overcome.

The New Challenge of the Pacific Century

In last year's edition of this volume, the suggestion was made that the rapid economic growth characteristic of the Asia–Pacific region, and especially of the NIC's (Newly Industrializing States), could be explained.

Recently, Asians themselves have come up with their own answer. They argued that their economic miracle results from a superior set of fundamental values. A coherent statement of this position was put forward by Kishore Mahbubani, in "Go East Young Man," published in *The Washington Quarterly*. Mahbubani is permanent secretary in the Ministry of Foreign Affairs, Singapore, and will undoubtedly be Foreign Minister someday.

Essentially, he argues that we could learn much from the values of the East, which tend to lean more toward order instead of personal freedom. The article is brilliantly written and offers more than one provocative thought. Mahbubani is not, however, anti–American in his approach. He is arguing that we have something very important to learn from the East.

In the view of this author, the arguments of Kishore Mahbubani, right or wrong, signal a basic change in the way East looks at West. Asia can now look at the West, knowing that its success is not entirely the result of Western thought and technology. And of course it never was. To the extent that the new leaders of the Asia–Pacific region understand this, their confidence will allow them to be more direct in seeking the interests of their own societies in their international relations.

This does not mean that the West has lost a monumental struggle of ideas. Time will prove that much of what we in the West believe is primarily for the well–being of man. But we may also realize that some of what we practice has betrayed our own values. There has been a change in the psychology of the East–West relationship. Knowing this will allow both sides to make that relationship better.

P.M.M.

Lexington, Virginia, June 1996.

China opens to U.S. business

The People

The origin of the various people of East Asia is obscured by the veils of unwritten history; it is difficult and virtually impossible to trace the ancestry of the inhabitants of any nation or area with accuracy. The scattered remnants of skeletons and tools which have been preserved in the rocks of the region, and the physical appearance of the majority of the people in any given area, are the only sources of guidance.

The most striking characteristic of the vast majority of the people of eastern Asia is their basically Mongol appearance. This is seen in the eyelid fold, sometimes and incorrectly described as "slant eyes;" other identifying features include a broad nose, straight, often coarse black hair and little facial or body hair even among the males. The Chinese and most other Asians tend to be shorter than Europeans and Americans.

The Japanese and Koreans come originally from a branch of the Mongols which lived a nomadic existence in the remote parts of Central Asia; the Japanese have some characteristics which come from intermarriage with the Caucasian Ainu people who occupied the island prior to the arrival of the "newcomers" from the mainland.

The people of Mongolia, Xinjiang (China) and Tibet (now part of China) all have similar appearances and live a rugged life in some of the most inhospitable areas of the world. The basic Mongol blood has often mingled with Turkish strains over the centuries; the eyelid fold is present to a slightly lesser degree than among the Chinese, and the complexion also tends to be darker than found in China.

The major people south of China in Burma, Thailand, Cambodia, Laos and Vietnam originated for the most part in what is now Southwest China or Tibet; their partial Mongol heritage has been modified by intermarriage with people living in Southeast Asia for countless centuries. The modern inhabitants of Malaysia, Indonesia and the Philippines are described as being of Malayo–Polynesian ancestry. Also short in stature, they tend to be somewhat darker–skinned than the Chinese.

The continent of Australia and the islands of New Zealand are the only countries in the region with a majority of Caucasians, almost all of whom are descended from British colonists. A few aborigines, known as Bushmen, survive in Australia. New Zealand has a minority group of Polynesian origin, the Maori.

Religious Beliefs

Confucianism:

The moral and ethical thinking of Confucius, later expounded upon and formalized by other Chinese philosophers, constitutes the main indigenous philosophy in East Asia. Confucius lived from about 551 to 479 B.C., and developed a system of thought that was more a social philosophy than a religion. The basic ideal was a form of self–discipline and network of social and political relationships that would tend to preserve order and harmony. Education and moral influence enabled the ideal man to guide the lesser people around him with patience, justice and a benevolent and fatherly attitude. A later Chinese philosopher, Mencius, modified and developed this system of belief, stating that by maintaining and creating an ever higher level of public welfare through exemplary conduct, it would be possible for China's emperors and princes to peacefully govern those around them.

This system of morality was very influential in China for many centuries and became the basis for the existence of a class of civil servants and administrators who performed the functions of day–to–day governing for several dynasties of emperors. Confucianism migrated from China to Korea, Japan and Vietnam. This system of belief was never formalized into something administered or taught by a church; it was preserved by the Chinese state which found it a useful tool to legitimate its authority.

Buddhism:

At the same time that Confucius lived in China, Buddhism was founded in Nepal by Gautama (c. 563–483 B.C.). It actually was, in some ways, a protest against the teaching of Brahmanisn, or Hinduism, which was then emerging in India. The *Buddha,* as Gautama is called, taught the concept of repeated rebirths to the hardships of life, in human and animal forms, the belief that fate could be controlled by human efforts and the idea that a good person moved upward through successive existences to an ultimate reward. The greatest reward possible, according to this belief, was the attainment of *Nirvana*—a state of nonexistence which ended the painful rebirth into a succession of burdensome lives. These teachings, which urged withdrawal from the world for meditation, created monastic communities in the ensuing centuries; the stress on personal religious experience made this much more of a missionary religion than Hinduism, contributing to its spread in East Asia.

The form in which it migrated to Southeast Asia is known as *Hinayana* ("the Lesser Vehicle"), *Theravada* ("the Way of the Teachers"), or simply, the Southern School of Buddhism. This school had its major home on the island of Sri Lanka (Ceylon) which was converted to Buddhism in the 3rd century B.C.

Hinayana countries in Southeast Asia— Vietnam, Laos, Cambodia, Thailand and Burma—all have large communities of monks devoted to the daily practice of Buddhism. In recent times, these communities have been influential and increasingly active in national and political affairs. Although the *Hinayana* Buddhists share the same central beliefs, there is no system of central authority regulating the monks, and almost every country has its own individual sect.

Buddhism spread north and northeast from India in the first centuries of the Christian era in the form known as *Mahayana* ("the Greater Vehicle"), which entered Tibet, China, Korea and Japan. This form of religion places less emphasis on good works and monastic withdrawal for contemplation, and greater weight on elaborate scriptures and faith. The canon (authorized texts) was printed in China in the 10th and 11th centuries, using some 130,000 wooden blocks on which characters had been carved. It was widespread in Central Asia until almost eliminated by the Turks, who had been converted to Islam.

Although *Mahayana* Buddhism became widespread in China, its prevalence was rather brief. It lost much of its following and influence after a few centuries because of persecutions at the hands of the Confucian civil administrators and because of its unsuitability to the Chinese temperament, usually preoccupied with the world of the present.

A form of Buddhism developed in Tibet known as *Tantrism*, which was heavily influenced by a type of Hinduism that engaged in demon worship and varieties of magical practices. It still exists today, particularly in eastern Tibet, but has been largely replaced by a newer form known as *Lamaism*, or "The Yellow Sect" to distinguish it from *Tantrism*. This is a combination of a purer form of Buddhism similar to *Mahayana* with an elaborate monastic organization common to *Hinayana*, but actually even more highly formalized. Lamaism, of which the Dalai Lama is the leading figure, spread to Inner and Outer Mongolia in the 16th century.

The teachings of Buddhism have changed over the centuries, and have been modified by many varied external influences, particularly local beliefs of a basically animist nature. It does not contain established churches in the manner of Judaism or Christianity. The Buddhists

Part of the Grand Palace, Bangkok

Courtesy: Bruce Terry Howe

retain the attitude that the teachings of their faith are always subject to further illumination, which may be in the form of minor variation or fundamental change.

Islam:

An Arab prophet living in what is now Saudi Arabia founded *Islam* in the 7th century A.D. This faith preached the belief in one God, revealed through the last of his prophets, Mohammed (Muhammed), a last judgment, the duty to donate to the poor and observance of the holy month of Ramadan. Mohammed personally stressed the need for daily and systematic prayer. Conquerors spread the faith eastward into India, and Arab missionaries, traveling by sea, spread their beliefs to Indonesia as well as attracting sizable numbers of believers in China, Malaysia, Indonesia, the Philippines and Central Asia.

Other aspects of Islam include the concept of a resurrection into heaven and a system of predestination which is supposed to decide the fate and the behavior of man by divine decree. In part, Islam is derived from Judaic and Christian concepts and beliefs. The resurgence of mil-

itant Islam in the Middle East has had its effect in such Southeast Asian countries as Indonesia and Malaysia. Here, it has taken the form of increased wearing of the traditional dress, stricter dietary rules, and the establishment of Muslim banking operations. Though Islam is more strictly adhered to in Malaysia, religious resurgence in this country or in any other part of Southeast Asia does not approach that which is found today in the Middle East. None of the Muslim states in the region—Brunei, Indonesia, Malaysia or the Philippines (the latter has only a small Muslim minority)—is threatened by religious extremism.

Hinduism:

There are few people in East Asia who are followers of Hinduism. This religion is actually the same as Brahmanism, the set of beliefs of most Indians with a history dating back to several centuries prior to the Christian era; as with Buddhism, it is also native to India. Because this system of belief is heavily dependent upon the historical Indian culture it did not spread as widely as Buddhism; the only countries in which it is significant in

Asia are Cambodia, where it is overshadowed by Buddhism, Indonesia, particularly in Bali, and Malaysia.

Christianity:

In spite of efforts to convert Asians to Christianity during the period of Western exploration and colonialism, there are comparatively few Christians in the region. The only nation with a predominantly Christian population is the Philippines, where Spanish missionaries had a relatively longer time to convert the people. Korea also has a sizable Christian community, as do a few other areas, such as Hong Kong, where Western influence has been unusually strong.

In southern Vietnam there are a substantial number of Roman Catholic Christians who are descendants of the educated upper class of the period of French colonial rule. Their number was swelled by refugees when communist control became final in North Vietnam, but in spite of their number, they are a minority when compared to the remainder in a predominantly Buddhist country.

A major cause of the failure of Christianity to attract larger numbers in Asia has been the fact that Asia has other established, sophisticated religions. Another factor is the inconsistency in the minds of the people between Western colonial military conquest and the religion professed by the intruders.

Shinto:

Shinto emerged in the early period of Japanese history and originally was an animistic religion which gives human form to the various gods that ruled the forces of nature. This evolved into an organized system of mythology in which the sun goddess was paramount. As *Mahayana* Buddhism entered the islands, the two beliefs tended to influence each other. At minimum, it was possible to profess the ideologies of both without feeling inconsistent. Buddhism in Japan split into numerous sects, and for several centuries Shinto beliefs were somewhat dormant, although not forgotten. In the late 19th and the early 20th century, the Shinto heritage became the state religion; it was claimed that the Emperor was a descendant of the sun goddess and possessed her divine powers. This revival of Shinto beliefs corresponded with a rise of militarism in Japan, culminating in World War II. After defeat by the allies, Japan renounced the idea of the divinity of the Emperor and Shinto lost its official status. The people who follow Shinto today often also subscribe to Buddhism and other faiths.

Inside the Liu Rong Buddhist temple (479 A.D.) in Guangzhou, China

Photo by Miller B. Spangler

Central Asian Conquerors

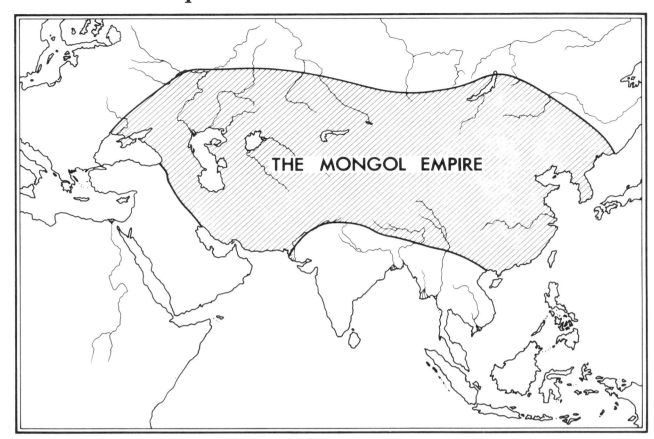

THE MONGOL EMPIRE

Before the coming of Buddhism, which is an essentially humble and peace–loving religion, the remote areas of Central Asia and Mongolia were the birthplace of mighty conquering empires. A combination of factors, such as a great leader, weakness among the richer and more settled states of Central Asia or possibly the drying up of pasture lands, gave rise to powerful nomadic empires from time to time during the "Middle Ages."

These empires were temporary unions of many nomadic tribes of various ethnic origins into a powerful force that could overrun Asia and part of Europe. The aggressive Mongols and Turks, born cavalrymen with great stamina, accustomed to riding for great distances, and fierce warriors, were able to subdue any opposing force with little difficulty. The Huns, who were more Turkish than Mongol, overran parts of North China, Central Asia and Eastern Europe during the leadership of Attila (445–453 A.D.) and in the succeeding decades.

A leader of Outer Mongolia, Temujin, renamed Chingis Khan (often misspelled Genghis Khan), was able to create an empire in the early 13th century. The name he took means "Very Mighty King." His Mongol Empire, as enlarged by his heirs, included China, Central Asia, most of Siberia and southern European Russia. His ability to conquer such a vast territory, which was usually defended by armies and populations that heavily outnumbered his forces, was based on the great mobility and horsemanship of his men. These talents enabled them to move rapidly from place to place, shift quickly in battle and to catch the enemy by surprise.

On the other hand, the nomadic peoples knew almost nothing of the arts of civilization and government administration, and had to call upon local inhabitants to help them run their empires. Their numerous empires usually lasted no longer than the needs and factors which produced them in the first place, and never more than a few generations. While they lasted, after initial massacres, they often provided a surprisingly efficient and humane government. The Mongol power faded to the extent that it only remained a threat to the Chinese, and they invaded the lands of others for the last time in the 17th century, when the Manchus, who were related to the Mongols, became paramount in China. Even these last Mongolian rulers were eventually all but assimilated into the Chinese population they ruled.

The Impact of the West

The countries of early modern Western Europe, especially Spain, Portugal and the Netherlands, tried to reach East Asia and the Western Pacific in order to acquire certain commodities, especially spices, to gane converts to Christianity and to acquire new territories for their respective governments. The first European to lead an expedition to the region was Magellan, a Portuguese in the service of Spain, who was killed in the Philippines in 1521.

Half a century later, Spain, operating from bases in the New World, began to colonize the Philippines, which it held for three centuries before losing it to the United States. In the late 19th century, a number of educated Filipinos were moved by modern nationalist ideals to declare independence and cooperate briefly with the United States in expelling the Spanish during the Spanish–American War of 1898.

In the 16th century, Portuguese explorers, traders, missionaries, etc. spread similarly from the Indian Ocean to Southeast Asia and the coast of southern China. They were not strong enough, however, to make much of an impact on the region, and most of their holdings soon fell to the Dutch.

The Dutch East India Company was the strongest European influence in East Asia and the Western Pacific in the 17th century. Its main theater of operations was the Dutch (or Netherlands) East Indies (now Indonesia), the richest in the region in natural resources then in demand in Europe (spices, coffee, etc.). The Dutch government took control of the East Indies in the 19th century; its rule was distinctly paternalistic and did little to develop the islands from either an economic or a political point of view.

The British impact on the region was less than on the Indian Ocean and South Asia, but it was still significant. In the 18th century the British East India Company became a major commercial force along the South China coast, its main interest being Chinese tea, silk and porcelain. Private (non–East India Company) merchants brought opium, usually bought from the Company in India, to the South China coast and sold it in defiance of an official ban. Machine-made British textiles became a major Chinese import in the 19th century, especially after the British East India Company lost its legal monopoly of the British side of the China trade early in the century. The British government used armed force at intervals to compel China to lower its barriers to expanded foreign trade (including opium imports) and residence (including missionary activity). Before the end of the 19th century, the

other western powers (including the U.S.) and Japan had established important commercial and cultural presences in China and were introducing the Chinese to the concept, and the difficulties, of modernization as it was understood at the time.

The U.S. and Britain similarly spearheaded the western entry into Japan, beginning in the mid–19th century. The Japanese, being better organized than the Chinese, were much better able to control the process, and Japan never became a "semi–colony" of the west as China was sometimes denominated. In effect, Japan chose what it wanted to borrow from the West (mostly technology and organization) and combined it with the essentials of its own culture as it saw fit. In the process, it became a military and imperial power strong enough to defeat China (in 1895) and Russia (in 1905).

In Southeast Asia, the British colonial presence began first in Burma. For the British, expanding control was usually a response to growing commercial interests. In Burma, territorial disputes and issues of sovereignty arose in the late eighteenth century. Anglo–Burmese relations deteriorated until 1823, when British forces captured Rangoon. By the end of the 1860's, the British had integrated all of the Burmese provinces into British Burma and into the Indian empire.

By 1826, the British had established what was known as the Straits Settlements along the coast of Malaya (today, Malaysia). These settlements consisted of the island of Penang, just off Malaya's north coast, Malacca, formerly a Dutch possession on the central coast, and Singapore at the southern tip of the Malay peninsula. Over the next fifty years the British established their control over all of Malaya. Their presence yielded vast quantities of tin from the interior and commerce from the straits settlements. The Anglo–Dutch Treaty of 1824 recognized British dominance along the Malay coast and also acknowledged Dutch interests to the south. This resulted in the effective splitting up of the old Malay world. The Dutch eventually established their control over all of Sumatra and Java, and became the colonial masters of the future Indonesia. The British controlled Malaya and Singapore until their independence.

The Treaty of Saigon of 1862 established the French colony of Cochinchina in southern Vietnam. The conflict leading to this treaty was in response to several decades of tension as a result of inroads into Vietnamese society by French Catholicism. The French seemed to be as much interested in the spread of their own religious ideology as the potential

for economic gain. Vietnam's leaders wanted the benefit of western technology but were not prepared to accept western thought. This eventually led to their total subjugation. French control of Cambodia and Laos followed and, with Vietnam, became French Indochina. The Laotians and Cambodians were more favorably disposed toward the French, having been under the authority of both Siam and Vietnam previously. For Vietnam, the period of French domination was culturally much more difficult.

Sandwiched between the British colonies of Burma and Malaya, and the French in Indochina, Siam (now Thailand) was able to survive under its own monarchy without being colonized by any European power. This was partly because the British and French were more interested in penetrating Southwest China from their bases in Southeast Asia than in colonizing Siam and because they both saw the benefit of Siam as a buffer between their respective territories. Siam also benefitted from a highly talented monarchy that earlier saw the need to learn about western institutions and governing methods. When the British did come, the Siamese showed considerable diplomatic skill in meeting the challenge.

An important aspect of western colonial rule in Southeast Asia was the coming (from about 1850 to 1920) of large numbers of Chinese immigrants, driven by poverty and chaos at home and drawn by the economic opportunities created by colonialism. These "overseas" Chinese have tended to be resented by the indigenous peoples and have never been allowed a share of real political power (except in Singapore, where they are the majority), but their economic activity and influence have been very great.

After the Spanish–American War, the United States proceeded to take over the Philippines, mainly in order to prevent some European country (which would probably have been Germany) from doing the same. After crushing a spirited Filipino resistance, the U.S. set up a reasonably efficient colonial regime and did a good deal to prepare the Filipinos for self–government, but like the other colonial powers in the region it did not qualitatively develop the economy, which remained essentially an extractive (mining) and plantation one.

Major political and military trends of the twentieth century, culminating in Japan's launching of the World War II in the Pacific (see Japan), were to sweep away Western colonial rule in Southeast Asia, make its restoration after the war a practical impossibility, and largely eliminate Western influence in China and contribute to a Communist seizure of power.

Nationalism, Communism and Revolution In Twentieth Century Asia

One of the principal and predictable results of Western influence, which contained the inherent threat of domination because of advanced technology, has been resistance to the idea of external control in Asia. The desire to be independent of such influence is part of the structure of modern Asian nationalism. As long as Western political control over colonial Asia seemed unshakable, there was little basis for the emergence of nationalism. When Japan defeated Russia in 1905, however, the myth that the Western powers were invincible was shattered.

Japan also showed by its example that it was possible, however difficult, for an Asian country to modernize itself along the lines of Western nations. During the brief period that it controlled substantial portions of Southeast Asia, Japan gave active aid and encouragement to revolutionary nationalists in the hope that they would join in opposing Allied military efforts.

Next to the influence of the West itself and that of Japan's successes, the third great external influence on the emergence of modern Asian nationalism was the example of Soviet Russia. Before 1917 Marxism had almost no following in the area, but many Asian leaders became impressed with the seemingly rapid success of Lenin's *Bolsheviks* in seizing power within Russia in 1917. Of even greater importance was the loudly declared determination to modernize Russia along socialist lines, and to help the people of the non–Western world to throw off alien influence. The communism of Marx, prescribed for industrial nations of Europe and America, was billed as the medicine which would allegedly cure the ills of the poor, non–Western countries.

Lenin attracted great attention with his theory that the main obstacle to progress in the non–Western world was Western "imperialism"; he urged that local nationalists, supported by Soviet Russia, could make progress toward expelling this imperialism. This would be, according to him, a preparation for the day when "proletarian" parties, in other words, communist parties, organized along the disciplined and apparently effective line of the *Bolsheviks,* could emerge and seize power. The combination of the concept of *imperialism,* the exploitation of existing nationalism and the triumph in Russia of a communist party has had an enormous influence in Asia as well as elsewhere in the world. These ideas have become part of the mental equipment of many, although by no means all, Asian nationalists, whether or not they consider themselves communists. Stated otherwise, many Asian nationalists have adopted some communist ideas and techniques without becoming communists—or find it politically useful to act as though they have.

The result is a complex series of combinations of nationalist and communist elements, in which it is often difficult to see where the nationalistic spirit ends and the communist aims begin. The obvious communists are not hard to identify; Ho Chi Minh was certainly a communist and also a Vietnamese nationalist and probably saw no conflict between these two sides of his political personality. Ho was a founder of the Nanyang (South Seas) Communist Party in the 1920's, which was responsible for introducing Marxist–Leninist ideas into Southeast Asia.

Anti–colonial movements began to assume importance in the colonies of Asia about 1920. The spread of Western education and political ideas, the limited measure of self–government granted by the colonial powers, the influence of Woodrow Wilson's doctrine of self–determination—the idea that every people has the right to choose the form of government under which it will live—and the Bolshevik Revolution in Russia all played parts in the spread of nationalism.

The Chinese communities living in Asian countries other than their homeland (the "overseas Chinese") were stimulated to nationalist activity by the revolutionary forces then at work within China, but usually preferred a continuation of Western political rule to the possibly oppressive rule of the native majorities where they lived. Non–Chinese nationalists usually resented the Chinese for their hard–earned wealth and economic influence, to the same degree that they also opposed the political control of the Western powers. As a result, their agitation was usually directed against both groups of outsiders.

Prior to World War II, there were no nationalist movements in Southeast Asia able to challenge the well armed colonial governments. Nationalists were unable to gather sufficient support for the independence cause.

Communist challenges arose in the Philippines, in the form of the Huk rebellion in the early 1950's; in Malaya, under the "emergency" declared from 1948 to 1960; and in Indochina and Indonesia. Burma, Thailand and even Singapore also experienced Communist activities. In Indonesia, the movement was strongest in Central Java. The Indonesian Communist party met its bloody demise in 1965.

Today, Vietnam is the only surviving communist regime in the region, and that will be increasingly debatable as reforms move ahead. Laos no longer qualifies as a bonafide Marxist state. Laotion politics was for decades a family affair, and with the opening of the country in recent years, economic change will easily overcome the remnants of the past.

It is difficult to find a uniform explanation for the Asian experience with communism. One thing is clear, the remaining communist states, the People's Republic of China and Vietnam have been among the poorest in the region. If the ideology contributed to the spirit of nationalism, it certainly did not do much for the economic well being of those who were subjected to its rule. In Southeast Asia it was often difficult for committed Marxist/Leninists to recruit from the indigenous peoples. Often, the communists found their most fertile ground in the overseas Chinese communities. However, this population was easily identified and thus could be isolated, in the case of Malaya, and eliminated in the case of Indonesia. Communism may have been an essential ingredient in the emerging nationalism of the region. In some cases, it forced colonial and then newly independent governments to address social problems which they might have otherwise ignored. It can be argued that the region would be vastly different if those opposing colonialism had never heard of Marx.

6

Democracy and Economic Development

The Daehan Life Insurance (DLI) Building in Yoido, Korea's business district, one of Asia's tallest at 63 stories

As the new states of East and Southeast Asia began to emerge after the demise of colonialism, hopes were high, especially in the West, that many new democracies would emerge. In fact, many new states attempted to emulate the West. Burma, Indonesia, Malaya (Malaysia), Philippines and Singapore were all born as democracies. Singapore and Malaysia survive as single party dominated systems, while the Philippines continues to struggle with an imported democratic model from the United States which has been grafted onto a Spanish–Asian culture. Indonesia, and Burma to a much greater extent have tempered democracy with the military. Thailand has not yet resolved its political future and also mixes its military with elements of democratic rule. The communist states of course detoured in a different direction, to try a different kind of experiment, while the East Asian Newly Industrialized Countries (NIC's) went through an extended period of strongman governments. In Japan, democracy as understood in the West was modified by the distinctive and strong local culture.

It is easy enough to explain the initial failures of democracy in Asia. Governmental systems were imposed on cultures lacking the traditions of the West where the governmental forms were first fashioned. Burma is a prime example. In addition, in some cases preparation was inadequate. Even those who welcomed Western ideas in many cases were not prepared for their arrival. And, in some cases, the departing colonial powers did little to assist in the changeover.

Today, it can be argued that modified democracies have succeeded in East and Southeast Asia. Most lack the strong opposition found in Western democratic systems, i.e. Malaysia and Singapore, and even Japan until recently. Nevertheless, there are Asian political systems where elections are fairly conducted and where the ruling elites accept the results. There are systems where the press is free to print the news if not to editorialize. There are of course a number of political systems where even limited democracy is not yet a reality. As economic development goes forward, how will these states fair?

The argument put forward here for consideration is that, regardless of the current status of any government in the region, all, whether quasi–democratic or still authoritarian, will face the ultimate prospect of becoming more democratic if they are to survive as functioning states. The reason is straightforward. East and Southeast Asia are now experiencing unprecedented region–wide economic growth. This is true for the remaining communist states as well as the most democratic. Even Burma, the hermit state, is opening to the outside world and seeking economic benefits. Most governing elites tend to subscribe to the idea that they can manage their domestic political environments in spite of outside influences. Singapore's leaders continue to resist a more open and democratic society. China's leaders will soon be faced with Hong Kong in their midst not to mention the already out of control southern provinces. Both the old authoritarian state and the modern, developed quasi–democracy struggle to maintain their old political ways and to justify them by proclaiming the need for political order. Something must give, and it will. A mini–state like Singapore may have the best chance at putting off the inevitable. A mammoth state like the People's Republic of China doesn't stand a chance. Authoritarianism will be overwhelmed by complexity and distances too great for any military or ideological leadership to cope with.

What about the states in between? Japan is beset with growing unrest among its own elites over the standard pattern of political behavior which regularly includes bribery, payoffs and inside deals. Cultural characteristics peculiar to Asian societies may have delayed the final confrontation. However, it appears that peoples throughout the region desire a legitimate opposition over a paternalistic elite which legitimizes itself with the trappings of democracy. Furthermore, the technological advances required for sustained economic development and which, themselves, demand a higher level of education, can only hasten the final confrontation. No one can predict when this fascinating drama will be concluded. However, the final act has begun.

Australia

Aberdeen Angus cattle on the Hunter River, New South Wales

Australian Information Service

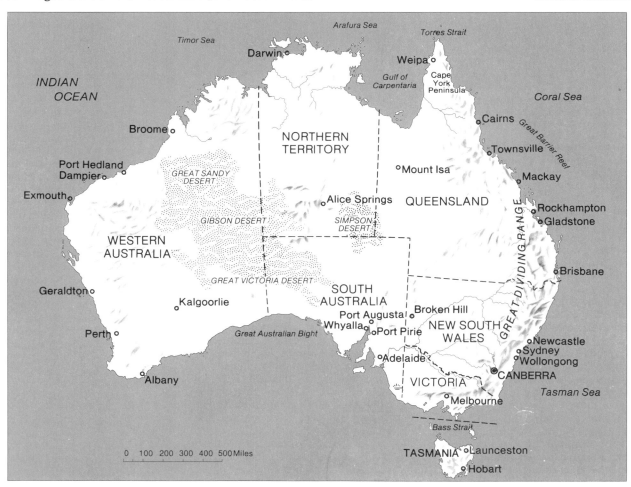

Australia

Area: 2,970,000 sq. mi. (7,692,300 sq. km.), slightly smaller than the continental U.S., the "lower 48" states.

Population: 18.3 million (estimated).

Capital City: Canberra (Pop. 265,000, estimated).

Climate: Tropical to subtropical in the north, temperate in the south; the interior is highly arid.

Neighboring Countries: Indonesia, Papua New Guinea lie to the north; New Zealand to the southeast.

Official Language: English.

Ethnic Background: British, other European, Asian, indigenous aborigines and aboriginal–European mixed ancestry.

Principal Religion: Christianity.

Main Exports: Coal, gold, wool, meat, iron ore and aluminium ore.

Main Imports: Automobiles, computers, petroleum and telecommunication equipment.

Currency: Australian Dollar.

Former Colonial Status: British dependency (1788–1900).

National Day: January 26 (anniversary of the first British settlement at Sydney in 1788).

Head of State: Her Majesty Queen Elizabeth II, represented by Sir William Deane, Governor General.

Head of Government: The Rt. Hon. John Howard, Prime Minister.

National Flag: A blue field with the Union Jack in the upper left quarter, a seven–pointed star in the lower left corner, and five stars at the right side.

Per Capita Income: US $20,720.

The Rt. Hon. John Howard

The enormous island called Australia is so immense that it is classified as a continent—at 2.97 million square miles it is almost the size of the continental United States. Its 12,000 miles of coastline is relatively smooth with few harbors, but in the northeast the sandy coast is in the lee of the Great Barrier Reef, a 1,200 mile chain of coral reefs and islands extending north almost to Papua New Guinea. With its vivid coral and a profusion of other marine life, the reef is one of the world's natural wonders and a magnet for scientists and tourists.

Australia is one of the oldest of the continents and also one of the flattest and driest. Its few mountains have been worn with the passage of time and the highest peak today is Mt. Kosciusko at only 7,300 feet. The largest chain of mountains is found in the east and is called the Great Dividing Range; in the southeast they are known as the Australian Alps. They divide the narrow crescent of land along the coastline from the vast interior. It is in the fertile eastern coastal area that the great majority of Australians live and their largest cities are located.

To the west are large lowlands and plateaus which begin the vast interior region known to Australians as the Outback. This is the region containing the two–thirds of Australia classified as desert (fewer than 10 inches of rain annually) or semi–desert (fewer than 15 inches). The region's "rivers" often are chains of waterholes and flow only following infrequent rains. Most never reach the sea, but instead widen into areas called lakes which most of the time are actually mud flats encrusted with salt. By drilling to great depths it is possible in some parts of this region to locate limited amounts of ground water, making possible the raising of livestock. However, large areas are needed to support even small numbers of animals—some Outback cattle ranches in Australia are larger than the smaller European countries. Apart from mining settlements, population is scattered and averages fewer than two persons per square mile.

Australians many years ago introduced the Royal Flying Doctor Service, utilizing two–way radio and light aircraft to bring medical services to those living in this isolated environment. Outback children also use the radio system as students of the School of the Air, working through their daily lessons with a teacher in a studio–classroom in the nearest township hundreds of miles away. Large parts of the region are not inhabited at all. An occasional thunderstorm moistens the thirsty land, and grasses and wildflowers rapidly spring up, flower, wither and die,

dropping their seeds to the ground to await the many months before the next rainfall. To the southeast, in the regions of the Murray and Darling Rivers, the land becomes more moist, but the need for water is still so great that these rivers are dammed for irrigation.

Apart from its dry center, Australia has a widely varied climate. It covers more than 30 parallels of latitude and more than a third of the country is in the tropics. Normally snow falls only on the southeastern ranges during the winter as Australia's position surrounded by sea and the absence of marked physical features give a more temperate climate than other land in corresponding latitudes. Because of the low humidity in many places, the high summer temperatures are not as enervating. The North is subject to tropical cyclones (hurricanes), and the city of Darwin was almost completely destroyed by Cyclone Tracy in 1974.

Isolation from other countries by wide expanses of water has affected Australia in many ways from its plant and animal life to its contemporary culture. Australia has many wildflowers found nowhere else. The main native trees are 500 varieties of eucalyptus and 600 species of acacia (known to Australians as *wattle* and akin to the mimosa of North America). About half of Australia's native mammals are marsupials—animals which produce their young in embryo form which is a tiny fraction of the adult weight of the parent. The newborn offspring finds its way miraculously to the adult's pouch where it continues its development; the mammary glands on which it suckles are located within the pouch. Only when it is the equivalent of a three to five year old human does it leave the pouch, returning for nourishment as needed until even more mature. Marsupials include members of the kangaroo family, the koala, the wombat and possums. Australia is also the home of another of nature's oddities—the duck–billed platypus, a cross between bird and mammal. It lays eggs, but then nurses its young after they have hatched, yet its body is covered with fur and it lives in a water habitat. Australia's 800 bird species include the ostrich–like emu and many brightly colored parrots.

History: During the many centuries of development of the western world, Australia was thinly populated by an estimated 300,000 Aborigines, a nomadic, tribal hunting and gathering society. (Strangely, they bear a striking resemblance to a similar people found in southern Africa.) About 160,000 Aborigines remain today, but many have embraced a largely Western life style; some later ra-

This painting by Algernon Talmage shows the unfurling of the British flag at Sydney Cove. Captain Arthur Phillip and his men drink to the health of King George III.

cially intermixed with the European settlers. They now are a disadvantaged and increasingly assertive minority.

Ships of the Dutch East India Company touched on the Australian coastline in the early 17th century; the Dutch explorer Tasman circumnavigated the continent in 1642–43. The first real penetration was by the British, led by Captain James Cook, who claimed the eastern portion of the island in 1770 in the name of the British Crown.

The principal interest of Britain in Australia was initially as a penal colony where its criminals could be exiled or held in prison. The first settlers, numbering 270 soldiers and sailors and 760 convicts, landed on the present site of the city of Sydney in 1758 to establish the colony of New South Wales under the royally appointed Governor, Captain Arthur Phillip.

The Crown later permitted non–convict settlers to emigrate from the British Isles to Australia. Most of them became

interested in sheep raising, to which the island was ideally suited. A close social organization quickly emerged among these free settlers; they dominated the New South Wales Corps, which was a special military police force. They became very influential and struggled with a succession of royal governors, sometimes gaining the right to use the services of convict labor at a low wage, and to expand their sheep raising activities. They also sought control over internal and external trade.

The notorious Captain Bligh, the former commander of HMS *Bounty*, struggled with the New South Wales Corps when he was governor in 1805 and lost. The next governor, Macquarie, was much more respected and successful. He curbed the power of the police force, set limits on land grants and organized and permitted rapid economic development. No more convicts were sent to Australia after 1868.

The discovery of gold in 1851 gave a

great boost to the Australian economy and was accompanied by disorders in the mining camps, similar to those in the American West during the same period. In the succeeding decades, additional immigration of free settlers, exploration of the eastern and later the western parts of the continent, and with general economic development, took place at a steadily accelerating rate.

Six British crown colonies were successfully established in Australia from 1788 through the first half of the 19th century. All had been granted self–governing independence by the end of that century. In 1901, the colonies became the six States of an Australian Federation under the title Commonwealth of Australia. This status continues today.

Although an independent, self–governing nation, Australia, along with other countries of the British Commonwealth, recognizes the British sovereign as the head of state, symbolizing historical links with Britain. The Queen (or

King) is represented in Australia by a Governor–General. Australia's chief executive is a Prime Minister elected by members of the majority party in the Federal Parliament. The Parliament consists of a Senate and a House of Representatives functioning under a written constitution which borrows from both British and American experience. There is no elected President. Cabinet officers must also be members of Parliament.

Australia sent volunteer units that fought bravely on the Allied side in the Middle East and on the Western Front during World War I. The demands of the British war effort benefited the Australian economy. During the period between the two World Wars, it continued to experience growth, as well as the emergence of a powerful labor movement pressing for benefits for workers. It was gripped by the worldwide depression, with a sharp drop in trade in 1931 and the following years.

Prior to World War II, the foreign policy of Australia was one of comparative isolation from the community of nations. In spite of this, Australia responded to the outbreak of World War II by coming to the aid of the British in the European War in 1939, and after 1941 joined the Allied war effort in the Pacific. For Australia, the war was made much more complicated and dangerous because of the closeness of Japan.

Japanese troops quickly conquered most of Southeast Asia by mid–1942. Australia became the base for the headquarters of General Douglas MacArthur after the fall of the Philippines. The main concern of the Australians was that they also might be invaded next. Darwin, the northern seaport, suffered heavy Japanese bombing raids. However, Allied victories in the Pacific and fighting by Australian troops in New Guinea prevented a Japanese invasion.

The *Labor Party*, led by Prime Minister John Curtin, had come to power in late 1941 and was responsible for major changes in Australian international thinking during World War II. After such close cooperation with the United States in achieving ultimate victory, Australian strategic thinking turned towards the United States after the war.

The end of World War II brought another period of growth and prosperity. Substantial immigration, encouraged by the government, resulted in a larger population, primarily Caucasian. Until 1966 Australian immigration policies discriminated against non–Europeans and in earlier years this had been known as the "white Australia" policy. Since 1966 successive governments have removed discriminatory restrictions. However, the overall rate of immigration was reduced during the 1970's. Today, one in every three Australians was born overseas or is the son or daughter of an immigrant. The influx of newcomers has brought marked changes in Australian society, lifestyle and culture.

The country was governed by a coalition of the *Liberal Party* and the *Country Party* between 1949 and 1972, for 17 years under its leader, the colorful Sir Robert Menzies, then Harold Holt, John Gorton and William McMahan. All maintained steady support for U.S. policies and efforts in Southeast Asia. Australian troops took part in the war in Korea, the campaign against communist terrorists in Malaya (1948–1960) and the Vietnam war.

Elections in 1972 returned the *Labor Party* to power. The new Prime Minister, E. Gough Whitlam, a tall man of strong personality and intellect, recognized the People's Republic of China and established diplomatic relations with North Vietnam, North Korea and East Germany. He withdrew the remaining Australian troops from South Vietnam and moved to establish closer economic relations with Japan, while placing some restrictions on foreign investment which had been pouring into Australia's mineral–rich economy. He abolished the draft, lowered the defense budget, instituted fairer treatment of the Aborigines and introduced ambitious domestic social programs.

The opposition *Liberal* and *Country* parties held a narrow majority in the Senate and blocked some of Whitlam's more controversial domestic measures. Australia also began to feel the impact of the world economic recession with inflation and increased unemployment. Faced with these problems, Whitlam called an election in April 1974 which reduced his majority in the House of Representatives but enabled him to continue in office.

By late 1975, the continuing poor state of the economy and controversy over *Labor Party* programs and the performance of some cabinet ministers prompted the *Liberal* and *National Country Party* (previously known as the *Country Party*) opposition to again press for new elections. When Whitlam refused, the opposition took the unprecedented action of using its Senate majority to block the government's budget appropriation bills, leaving it without authority for funds to pay its creditors, including Federal employees and recipients of social security and other benefits. As the government's reserves of money ran out, the constitutional crisis intensified. It is at this point that one of the more peculiar features of Australia's government became apparent.

Politics and Government: Australia is a parliamentary democracy whose political institutions and practices follow the Western democratic model, reflecting both the British and American experience. The Australian federation has a three–tier system of government: the national government consists of the Parliament (House of Representatives with 148 seats and the Senate with 76 seats) and the Government (the party or parties with a majority in the lower house constitute the government, controlling all ministries); six state governments, the Capital Territory and Northern Territory (similar to states; and some 900 local government bodies at the city, town, municipal and shire level. Senators in the Federal Parliament serve six year terms (Senators for the two territories serve three year terms), and Representatives serve for three years..

Australia has a written constitution which came into force on January 1, 1901, when the colonies federated to form the Commonwealth of Australia. The constitution is amended by referendum if a majority of voters in a majority of states as well as an overall majority approve the proposed change. Proposed changes must be passed by absolute majority in both houses of Parliament. If an amendment is passed twice by one house but fails in the other, the Governor–General may submit the amendment to the electorate.

Australia pioneered the secret ballot in parliamentary elections and has used the

Kangaroos cavort on a reserve near Melbourne   Australian Information Service

11

Barbecued chicken on Christmas Day at Sydney Harbor   Australian Information Service

system since 1879. Voting is compulsory at the national level. The franchise extends to everyone over 18 years of age except criminals and the insane.

The Australian system of law resembles the British system from which it was taken. Australian law places great importance on the rights of the individual. The law provides for habeas corpus (which prevents arbitrary arrest or imprisonment without a court hearing), bail, trial by judge and jury, the presumption of innocence until proven guilty, and prevention from double jeopardy.

The High Court resembles the American Supreme court and deals with federal and state matters. It has original jurisdiction in important areas, including interpretation of the Constitution, determination of legal disputes between the federal Government and state governments, suits between state governments, and suits between citizens of different states. The Court has one Chief justice and six other justices. The Federal Court is a specialized court dealing with matters such as copyrights, industrial law, trade practices, bankruptcy, and administrative law; appeals from territory supreme courts and tribunals administering federal laws. The other specialized court is the Family Court which deals with divorce, custody of children, and associated matrimonial property disputes.

All states and territories have supreme courts and magistrates' courts and several have intermediate district or county courts which deal mainly with state laws, federal criminal offenses and federal income tax. The supreme courts have the same role at the state level as the High Court does federally. Magistrates' courts

deal summarily with most ordinary offenses and preliminary hearings to determine whether sufficient grounds exist in more serious offenses to be tried before a judge and jury. The capital territory and external territories of Norfolk Island, Christmas Island and the Cocos islands have court system similar in general to the states. Australia has independent federal, state and territory police.

Because the country is part of the British Commonwealth, the Head of State is Her Majesty Queen Elizabeth II, represented by Governor–General Bill Hayden, who took office in February 1989. The Governor–General position is a holdover from the British empire. In late 1975, a crisis between the major parties (described above) over a budget appropriation bill could not be resolved. The Governor–General then stepped in, dismissed the sitting Prime Minister and asked J. Malcolm Fraser to form a new Liberal government. The party, in coalition with the National Party, won the next election and controlled the government until March 1983. Thus, a representative of a foreign nation was able to substantially interfere in Australia's domestic political process.

Today the two major political parties are the *Australian Labor Party (ALP)* and the *Liberal Party*. The *ALP*, under the leadership of Prime Minister Robert Hawke controlled the government from 1983 to December 1991 when Paul Keating replaced him as head of the party and Prime Minister. Mr. Keating was returned to office in the March 1993 elections. It is probably correct to characterize the country as having a multi–party system. In addition to the two major parties,

other parties represented in the parliament are the *National Party, Australian Democrats, Northern Territories Country Liberal Party*, and the *Western Australia Greens. Labor* controls 80 of 147 seats in the House and 30 of 75 seats in the Senate.

Political Issues: The *Liberal Party* selected its fifth leader since 1983, when 42–year–old Alexander Dower replaced John Hewson, who had taken the blame for 1993 election losses. *ALP* continued to rule with 80 of 147 seats in the House and 30 of 75 seats in the Senate. The *Liberal–National* opposition coalition controlled 49 and 16 seats and 30 and 5 seats respectively in the House and Senate. Andrew Peacock, former *Liberal* foreign minister and party leader, retired from politics. This left the party without a major person in the area of foreign affairs.

Prime Minister Paul Keating, on the other hand, remained atop the ALP in spite of a scandal involving Roslyn Kelly, who allegedly doled out sports grants for political purposes prior to the 1993 elections. Brian Burke, former Western Australia *Labor* premier, was sentenced to prison for misuse of government and party funds. Internal squabbling in the ALP was also a problem in 1994. This was exacerbated by the release of the memoirs of former Prime Minister Robert Hawke.

There were other serious issues arising during the year including the question of the future role of women in the *ALP*, and declining support for the party among unions, which comprised only about 37% of the membership.

In March 1995 the fortunes of the *ALP* began to change when the party's Bob Carr narrowly defeated *Liberal Party* candidate John Faye for the premiership of New South Wales. However, the *Liberals* defeated the *ALP* in the Nappa Valley by-election with an 18% swing in the vote from the previous election, one of the worst defeats in a by–election in recent Australian history. A 2% rise in the interest rate was apparently a major issue. In July the *ALP* retained control of Queensland with a 16 vote margin. In addition to high interest rates, a significant increase in the cost of welfare, and a decline in real estate values provided strong ammunition for the *Liberals*.

Nationally, the *Liberal Party* experienced a resurgence. John Howard was selected as the new party leader and throughout the year he gained popularity, especially among older Australians. However, Howard did not appear to be a strong leader, having tried once before, in the late 1980s, to guide the *Liberal Party*. He did manage to moderate some of his views, for example, calling for a referendum on the question of whether the country should become a republic (he had been a monarchist). In the end, however, the economy and the personality of the two contenders, Howard and Keating, proved decisive.

On March 2, 1996, the *Liberal–National* coalition won a landslide victory in national elections which gave the new government a 40 seat margin in the lower house of Parliament. The victory ended 13 years of *ALP* rule.

Analysts predicted that any move toward republic status will be slowed by the new government. In foreign policy it looked as though there would be some revision in the country's move toward Asia.

Foreign Relations: In 1995, relations with the states of East and Southeast Asia were good despite the predictable temper tantrums by Malaysian Prime Minister Mahathir who charged at one point that Australia didn't understand Asian values. Southeast Asia is especially important to Australia, and because of its proximity, Indonesia, the world's fourth largest country, is the top priority in the region. The two countries have had

strained relations in the past over human rights issues and especially East Timor. In September 1994, the Indonesian Vice–President, Try Sutrisno, visited Australia. The meeting seemed to smooth over relations at least for the time being. In March 1995, the government issued a statement calling for a reduction of Indonesian forces in East Timor. Australia also took a strong public stance against Chinese nuclear tests in May 1995. Relations had been good with Australia looking for significant trade between the two countries.

In March 1995, relations with Cambodia were negatively affected when the Phnom Penh government granted amnesty to Khmer Rouge General Tuk Rin. The problem centered over the fact that the general may have had a part in the killing of David Wilson who was kidnapped while on vacation in Cambodia. Kellie Wilkinson, another Australian, was killed in Cambodia earlier in 1994. A Khmer Rouge field commander, Paet, is believed to be the one directly responsible for Wilson's death. The Australian government indicated that am-

nesty for the commander was not acceptable.

Prime Minister Keating spoke out strongly against French nuclear tests in the latter half of 1995, at one point charging that it "defied common sense." On October 2, Foreign Minister Gareth Evens called for new international controls on nuclear weapons production and stockpiling in a speach at the UN.

Australia was one of the more vocal countries speaking out prior to the third Asia–Pacific Economic Cooperation (APEC) forum held in Osaka, Japan on November 1. The prime minister made clear on many occasions that for APEC to succeed, member states must be willing to come forward with an "Action Agenda" by the next meeting to be held at Subic Bay, Philippines. Australian officials were particularly concerned that countries not exclude, or protect, sectors of their economy. This applied especially to agriculture, which is important to the country. Many states are under significant pressure to protect their agricultural sector.

In early 1995, the foreign minister, Ga-

Aerial view of Canberra with Lake Burley Griffin in the background

Australian Information Service

reth Evans, indicated an increased emphasis on the country's relations with Asia when he called for "full partnership" with the region. There was also a re–emphasis on the fact that Australia did not look toward the United States as a guarantor for the security of the area. In early 1996, there were indications that the new government intended to re–state the country's foreign affairs position to emphasize that Australia still valued its relationships with Europe and the United States even with the newer emphasis on Asia. The government was backing away from the notion that Australia was part of Asia.

Culture: Apart from its small minority of Aborigines (who are beginning to assert themselves politically) and Asians, Australia is Western in population and culture. Education is free and compulsory through the secondary school level. There are no tuition fees at the 18 government–funded universities and many colleges offering diploma, degree and post–graduate studies. Eminent artists, writers, scholars and scientists are exchanged with other countries.

Because of the climate, outdoor sports such as swimming, surfing, several types of football and tennis are very popular, and Australia has produced many Olympic champions. Horse racing is widely enjoyed, and betting on the horses is a consuming topic of interest among all. The Australians have a justified reputation for an energetic wit and love of fun.

Though it has vast spaces and relatively few people, Australia is highly urbanized, perhaps because most population growth and development has taken place only over the past 75 years. More than 80% of the population lives in urban centers and more than 60% are concentrated in five major state capitals.

Two cities dominate urban life. Sydney faces the southeast coast and has a population of more than 3.5 million; Melbourne (2.8 million) faces the southern Bass Strait. All of the cultural entertainment and events common to Europe and America are abundant in both. Perth, with a population of 850,000 and lying on the southwestern coast, is caressed by a gentle climate similar to that found in the Mediterranean and Caribbean resorts of the western world.

Australia's Federal Capital is Canberra, a 20th century city, the basic plan for which was conceived by Chicago architect Walter Burley Griffin shortly before World War I. Today, it is a garden city of more than 265,000 people—with over 8 million trees planted in the last half century—and it occupies the site of a former sheep station (ranch) in the foothills of the Australian Alps.

The English spoken by the people is unique, and sometimes a bit difficult for the unaccustomed ear. Neologisms (new words, idioms and phrases) are frequent; at the same time the highly educated people are inclined to use the purer "King's English." In recent years a number of fine Australian films, such as *Breaker Morant* and *Crocodile Dundee* (and now, *Crocodile Dundee II*) have attracted international attention.

Economy: Australia's economy has changed much in the last fifty years from one which relied heavily on primary production to a mature, diverse one with nearly two–thirds of production in the service sector.

World War II and post–war immigration spurred rapid expansion of secondary industry, diversification and overall economic growth. Large investments were made in mining and energy projects.

Although the agricultural and mining sectors account for a small part of the country's production, they account for 75% of total exports. Australia leads the world in wool production and is a major supplier of wheat, meat and sugar. Australia is also a leading exporter of coal and a major supplier of iron ore, gold, bauxite, and alumina.

The export base was diversified in the 1980's, with the fastest growth in manufactured products and in services. Tourism was particularly strong. The country has had strong economic and employment growth over the past twenty years. In the 1980's, the Australian economy ranked fifth and employment was second in terms of growth among the OECD countries. These figures would, however, put Australia far behind its ASEAN neighbors.

The main agenda item for the Australian economy in 1994 was deficit reduction. The goal was to reduce the red ink to one percent of GDP by the 1996–1997 fiscal year. Unfortunately, by late 1994 it was heading up toward 17 billion. The country runs on a mid–year to mid–year budget. Forecasts for 1994–1995 were very positive. The recession of the early 1990's was definitely on the run, and at the end of 1994, one national official stated that the economy was in its best shape in thirty years.

What a difference a year can make. At the end of 1995, complaints were being heard about the economy. Unemployment was high although jobs were being created at an expanding rate. The current account deficit for fiscal 1995–1996 was predicted to be about $16 billion, worrisome but considerably better than last year's $20 billion. For the same period, exports are predicted to grow by about 17% to $50 billion, while imports should be about $55 billion with 6% growth. In November two liquid natural gas (LNG) projects were announced for Western Australia. On completion an estimated nine million tons of LNG per year will be available for export which should improve the balance of trade considerably. Gross Domestic Product (GDP) will be considerably less than the 4.8% for 1994–1995. At the end of 1995, unemployment was above 8% while inflation was in the 3+% range. The government raised some eyebrows by selling off some national assets, including Quantas airlines. At the end of 1995, the economy was not in desperate shape, but it was not in good shape for a government facing an election.

The Future: Australia faces no immediate external threats. Her growing involvement with the countries of East Asia, particularly the ASEAN states of Southeast Asia can only help to improve her regional position. Growing trade with Japan China, and Vietnam will also provide a boost to the lagging economy. Increasing tensions in the ASEAN region over the South China Sea and arms build–ups may require a greater military presence by Australia in the region, especially if the United States becomes less visible in the next few years. Good relations with the United States are essential and the difficulties of 1993 have not been allowed to alter the close and long standing relationship. Australia has the resources and location to be a vital full partner with the countries of East Asia. Any immediate challenges or consequences may well be internal in origin. By mid-1996, however, they were hard to find. However, this is something the new government must learn. Any attempt to pull back from Asia too abruptly could be misunderstood by Australia's new friends.

Koala kindergarten

Brunei Darussalam

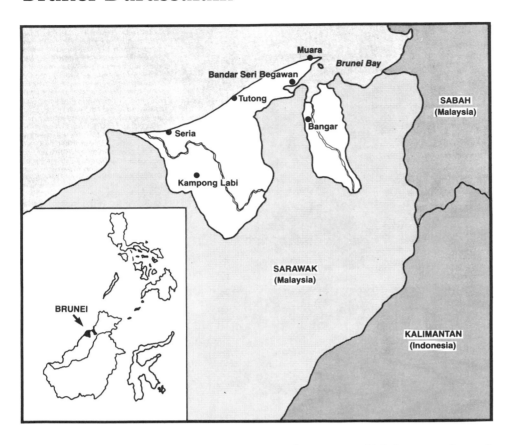

Area: 2,226 sq. mi. (5,765 sq. km.)

Population: 292,000.

Capital City: Bandar Seri Begawan (named in honor of the present Sultan's father, Pop. 121,000, estimated).

Climate: Tropical.

Neighboring Countries: The East Malaysian states of Sarawak and Sabah enclose Brunei on the large island of Borneo, also known as Kalimantan, two thirds of which is Indonesian.

National Language: Malay. English is the second language.

Other Principal Tongue: Chinese.

Ethnic Background: Malay (64%), Chinese (20%), Other (16%).

Principal Religion: Muslim (60%, official State religion); Buddhist, Christian, traditional native beliefs.

Main Exports: Crude petroleum, liquified natural gas, and wearing apparel.

Main Imports: Aircraft, electronics, other manufactured goods, and foodstuffs.

Currency: Brunei dollar.

Former Colonial Status: Previously independent, it was a British protectorate (1888–1983).

Independence Day: January 1, 1984.

Chief of State: His Majesty the Sultan and Yang Di–Pertuan of Brunei Darussalam, Sultan Hassanal Bolkiah Mu'izzaddin Waddaulah (b. 1947).

National Flag: A yellow field crossed diagonally by single white and black stripes upon which is centered a red crest.

Annual Per Capita Income: U.S. $16,000 (1993 est.).

Brunei *Darussalam* (meaning "abode of peace") is one of the most unusual nations in the world. Having two distinct parts, with Malaysia's state of Sarawak plugging a 15–mile gap between the two, it is also one the wealthiest sovereign nations *per capita* on earth.

Much of inland Brunei is dense jungle scattered with remote villages and alive with brilliantly–plumaged birds, but its gleaming capital city, Bandar Seri Begawan, on the Brunei River about nine miles from its mouth, is sleekly modern, has several international–class hotels— and no slums! The country's main port is bustling Muara.

Malays form the majority of the population, but there are also about 70,000 non–Malays, most of them Chinese involved in trade and commerce. In 1961 Brunei passed a law allowing non–citizen Chinese to become Brunei citizens if they had resided in the country for 20 of the previous 25 years and could pass a Malay language test. There are also small groups of British, Dutch, American and Australians associated with the oil and gas industry. Education is free up to a doctorate if one's scholarship takes him

that far. There are three "streams" in the educational program—Malay, English, and Arabic; students may pursue advanced studies at schools at government expense. Over 2,000 students are enrolled in foreign universities.

Brunei has many splendid beaches, and hotels provide excellent service and delectable foods, often combinations of rice, meat and vegetables. The country's cattle are raised on a ranch in northern Australia, which as it turns out, is larger than Brunei! The cattle are flown into the country and slaughtered according to Muslim customs. Television is common in most households.

History: From the 14th to the 16th century, Brunei was the cornerstone of a powerful Muslim empire which encompassed most of northern Borneo and the Philippines. However, the advance of the Dutch and the British, internal corruption, and warfare took their toll as the 17th century dawned. Brunei's rule was confined to an area today formed by Sarawak and part of Sabah. Towards the middle of the century, in 1841, in a rather desperate move to secure military help against marauding South China Sea pirates, the Sultan ceded to the English adventurer Sir James Brooke the entire region of Sarawak. Brooke styled himself *Rajah* ("prince" or "king") of the area and was succeeded by his nephew and the latter's son until 1946. By 1847 the British secured from the Sultan the island of Labuan off the northwest coast of Borneo, which they speculated could become an imporant naval base, although the plan never came to realization.

There were further concessions and further treaties. In 1865 the United States government under President Lincoln's administration, concluded a treaty with the Sultan. The *American Trading Company of Borneo* was created and granted vast land holdings, but this venture was soon thought worthless and was abandoned. Sixteen years later the British set up the *North Borneo Company*, which acquired the assets of the U.S. firm and pushed further land concessions from the Sultan who had little power to refuse the mighty British Empire. Brunei was thus reduced to its present size.

With a fragile economy and no way to defend itself against the many European powers which were continuing to colonize the entire area, Brunei chose British protection in 1888 and, later in 1906, permitted a British commissioner to take up residence in the country; the Sultan was required to take his advice in all matters involving defense and foreign affairs, but not the Islamic faith and Malay customs.

During the next few years the country's economy began to grow, first with the cultivation of rubber. Then the economic picture drastically changed as vast oil reserves and natural gas were discovered in the 1920's in the western part of the nation followed by offshore deposits in the 1960's. Brunei was on the road to enormous wealth.

There was a rebellion in 1962 led by a pro–Indonesian leftist. A state of emergency was imposed which banned all political parties and allowed the government to detain people without trial, a condition which generally remains in force today.

When the Federation of Malaysia was established in 1963, to be composed of Malaya, Sabah, Sarawak and Singapore as a bulwark both against Indonesian dictator Sukarno's territorial ambitions and a possible communist takeover in Singapore, the Sultan of Brunei was urged to join. The still–vital father of the present ruler rejected the plan, fearing for the erosion of his political position and determined that Brunei's oil and gas revenues would be reserved for the benefit of native Bruneians.

Brunei Darussalam regained its independence after almost one century on January 1, 1984. Political figures from around the world attended the colorful ceremonies which turned out over 30,000 spectators. A member of the British Commonwealth, Brunei has since joined the UN and the Association of Southeast Asian Nations (ASEAN) among others. At the Sultan's request, the Gurkha army units from Nepal stationed in Brunei while it was under British protection have stayed on to aid the Royal Brunei Armed Forces. The government continues to pay for

His Majesty The Sultan of Brunei, Bolkiah Mu'izzaddin Waddaulah

their maintenance, but they are still under British command.

The Sultan heads the government and is responsible for the day–to–day administration of the country. Other key government posts are held by members of his immediate family. The Sultan, born in 1946, has, as Muslim custom allows, two wives; he has three sons and six daughters. Educated in Brunei and Malaysia, the Sultan then enrolled as an officer cadet at the Royal Military Academy at Sandhurst, England.

He was crowned the 29th ruler by his father in 1968 upon the latter's abdication. He has no bodyguards—rare among heads of state—and he moves among his people with ease, frequently making helicopter tours of outlying villages. Widely traveled and an avid sportsman, he is one the the most accessible leaders in the world.

Politics and Government: Brunei is a democratic Islamic Malay monarchy according to its constitution. The constitution dates to 1959. Parts were suspended under the state of emergency declared in 1962. Additional modifications have occured since independence in 1984. There is no suffrage. Freedom of speech is limited. The country's legal system functions under Islamic law. There is a Supreme Court.

Sultan Hassanal Bolkiah, chief of government and head of state, rules the country with the help of the Council of Cabinet Ministers, most of whom are family members. The unicameral legislature, *Majlis Masyuarat Megeri*, has been an appointed body since 1970.

In February 1995, Haji Abdul Latif Chuchu was elected president of the *Brunei Solidarity National Party*, the country's only legal political party. Haji Latif and other party officials then called for

The Omar Ali Saifuddien Mosque

A marketplace in Bandar Seri Begawan

democratic elections in a meeting with the Sultan. He has since been banned from all political activity. The party does not appear to have much of a following and most citizens seem content with the Sultan's rule. In 1990, the Sultan introduced a new ideology, *MIB*, to reinforce the monarchy.

The Sultan's father, who still had considerable power, died in September 1986. His son then reorganized the cabinet and began to play a more active political role.

In 1992, Sultan Hassanal Bolkiah celebrated his 25th anniversary of accession to the throne. The country, a Sultanate, is ruled by the Sultan and his immediate family. There are no political parties in Brunei. However, there is no visible opposition to the Sultan's rule. An emerging ideology designed to reinforce the monarchy involves the MIB concept. MIB stands for Melayu, Islam, and Beraja (Malay, Islam, monarchy). MIB was brought into the secondary schools in 1992. Christian and Chinese mission schools may also be subject to some exposure to Malay and Islam in the classroom. Some observers are concerned for the multi–ethnic future of the country. Undoubtedly the country's leadership sees MIB as a mechanism for strengthening its continued leadership role. Yet, forcing Islam and the Malay language on non–Malays could bring about the very opposite of the desired results: political instability. At present there appears to be no inclination on the part of the country's leadership to move toward any democratization.

Defense: While tiny in size, Brunei has a modern and capable defense force. Internal and external security are under the control of the Royal Brunei Armed Forces (RBAF), the Royal Brunei Police, the Gurkha Reserve Unite, and the British

Army Gurkha Battalion. Recent defense expenditures have been around 10% of the national budget. The RBAF has about 4,000 personnel and includes several hundred women who were recruited beginning in 1981. The armed forces used British officers on assignment from the British army or hired by contract. These officers were to be phased out in the early 90's. The air force and navy are small but well equipped. Joint military exercises have been held with Malaysia, Thailand and Singapore. The latter trains its troops in Brunei's jungles. An option for Brunei would be to join the Five Power Defense Agreement (Singapore, Malaysia, New Zealand, Australia and Britain). About 1,000 British Gurkhas rotate between the country and Hong Kong. What will happen after 1997 is unclear.

The Gurkha Reserve Unit of some 900 men is directly under the control of the Sultan and is composed of retired British army personnel. The Royal Brunei Police Force of approximately 2,000 is the fourth component of national defense.

Negotiations over a Memorandum of Understanding (MOU) with the United States on national defense matters were initiated in early 1993, and were still in progress at year's end. Brunei could enhance its security substantially with such an agreement. The United States could be interested in using the country as a staging point for air surveillance in the region.

Foreign Relations: Brunei foreign policy stresses the security of the nation. A true mini–state, the country must rely to a considerable extent on the goodwill of its neighbors. The fact that it is surrounded by its two Muslim brother states, Malaysia and Indonesia, is advantageous. Brunei joined the Association of Southeast Asian Nations (ASEAN) just after independence in 1984. Membership has

helped the country establish close diplomatic and military ties with the other ASEAN states. Singapore is a particularly good example.

In 1995, Brunei was the venue for several important ASEAN meetings. On July 29, the 28th ASEAN Ministerial Meeting (AMM) opened in Bandar Seri Begawan, the Bruneian capital. The Sultan of Brunei, Haji Hassanal Bolkiah, called on the ASEAN member states to push up regional trade liberalization by three years to the year 2000. The Sultan demonstrated that Brunei is not timid about approaching delicate regional matters matters.

One day after the AMM meeting, the ASEAN Regional Forum (ARF) opened. This is the second time for this group to meet. Last year's inaugural meeting was held in Bangkok. The ARF is a consultative body which focuses on Asia–Pacific security matters. ARF was initiated by the ASEAN states. Brunei was given high marks for its role in the second ARF which ended with a statement by Bruneian Foreign Minister Mohamed Bolkiah: he politely but clearly raised the concern over China's aggressive moves in the South China Sea. The annual ASEAN Postministerial Conference (PMC) followed the AMM and the ARF. This meeting allows ASEAN member states to meet with their "dialogue" partners to discuss a wide variety of topics having to do with economic cooperation. As a result of such meetings, Brunei is highly regarded for its diplomatic skills.

Brunei became the first Muslim state in the region to recognize Israel. Earlier in the year, it established ties with the Palestine Liberation Organization and opened an embassy in Iran. In August, President Fidel Ramos visited Brunei. A rift over the possible involvement of Philippine entertainers with Brunian royalty was apparently patched up. A more important topic of discussion concerned the establishment of an East ASEAN Growth Area, comprised of Brunei, southern Philippines, East Malaysia and part of Indonesia. Brunei has offered significant investments to get the project off the ground.

Brunei will be the host for the second ASEAN regional forum security conference.

Culture: The country is ruled by the royal family. The royal line goes back some twenty–nine generations farther than any of the other twenty–eight monarchies in existence today. Brunei Malays are similar to the Malays of Malaysia and Indonesia. All are followers of Islam, have a preference for living in coastal areas and speak the Malay language. They differ significantly from other ethnic groups in Brunei. Traditionally Brunei Malays were fisherman, traders and craftsmen.

Today's generation is seeking more "modern" means of employment. About ten percent of the Brunei Malays claim royal blood, having been descended from one of the Sultans. Many of the Malays live in Kampong Ayer, the Malay community consisting of about thirty–five villages. Marriages were once arranged by the village headman and the family. Now, however, more modern methods prevail. Under Muslim law, a man is permitted to have up to four wives. This is rare in Brunei. Men dominate the society, being the wage earners and have the advantage of Muslim inheritance law. Women, on the other hand control the family and as such are very influential.

The Kedazans are the second most populous indigenous group. They are similar to Malays in their practice of religion, language and appearance. The greatest difference is that they have tended to be rice farmers. They do not have the same status in society as the Malays. Other smaller indigenous groups include the Bisayas, who are pagans; the Penans, nomads of the jungle; the Muruts, who once populated the military for the Sultan; and the Ibans, whose numbers are increasing compared to the other smaller groups and who are know for the past head hunting activities. The Chinese are far more important than their numbers would suggest. They dominate the Sultan's commercial sector. They also provide the managerial and technical talent for the country. The older generation follows Taoist–Buddhist traditions. Less than ten percent of the Chinese in the country have been granted citizenship. While they have lived in the country long enough, they have difficulty passing the Malay language requirement. Some would argue that the Chinese are made to feel unwelcome in Brunei.

Economy: Oil and gas provide Brunei with more than 90% of its export earnings; it is the third largest oil producer in Southeast Asia after Indonesia and Malaysia. The Seria oil field was discovered in 1929 and by the 1950's it was producing 115,000 barrels a day. Offshore production began in 1964 and there are today over 200 rigs operated by Brunei Shell Petroleum Company, jointly owned by the government and Shell. Production in 1995 was about 60 million barrels, less than in previous years, since Brunei wants to conserve this source of income for the future. Most oil is exported to Japan—almost half, and the rest goes to other nations, the United States receiving about 10%. Brunei uses only about 3% of its production for domestic use—almost every urban family owns at least one (more often, *two*) cars. There is no income tax, state pensions are generous and government loans are available at 1% interest per year.

Brunei is also the world's fourth largest supplier of liquid natural gas, a venture owned by the government, Royal Dutch Shell Group and Japan's Mitsubishi Corporation. Five million tons are exported annually to Japan alone. The petroleum sector still accounts for around 50% of Brunei's gross domestic product (GDP). This figure was over 80% in the 1980's.

Another growing source of revenue is foreign investment which is now producing almost as much money as the petroleum sector ($2.5 billion according to one estimate). Oil production has been slowed over the years to stretch out the revenue stream. Given enough time, Brunei's estimated $36 billion in overseas investments (as of 1993) could become the major source of revenue for the mini–state.

In 1992, the government announced its Sixth National Development Plan for the 1991–95 period. The largest chunk of the B$5.5 billion plan is devoted to social services—education, health, housing, and religious affairs. The main focus of the plan is to steer the economy away from dependence on oil and natural gas.

However, this attempt to diversify the economy has been less than a smashing success. It is made especially difficult because the government employs more than half of the labor force. A new joint–venture garment manufacturer was forced to import Philippine and Thai workers because locals were either too few in number or not interested. Brunei is not subject to quotas on garment exports. Thus, an opportunity to expand is at hand.

The government has frozen civil service pay in an attempt to make state employment less attractive. However, in a country where health care and education are free, and where subsidized loans are readily available, there is little pressure to change. There may be some ambivalence on the part of national leaders concerning economic change. An influx of foreigners and new ventures will surely disturb the confortable and traditional environment of this Islamic mini–state. Nevertheless, in June 1995, Brunei applied for membership in the World Bank and the IMF. It is unlikely that Brunei needs to borrow funds. The government does appear to be looking for assistance in broadening the economy.

While Brunei faces a long term structural problem with the economy, it has the time and resources sufficient to see it through.

The Future: With a per capita Gross Domestic Product (GDP) of $16,000 per year, the country faces no serious economic problems. The discovery of new oil deposits insures that the country will be pumping petroleum for many decades to come. Self–sufficiency in food is a worthy but not essential goal. The country's wealth has spawned growing environmental problems. Local waterways are being clogged with styrofoam, old refrigerators, and even cars. This is a serious problem that can only get worse until the government takes action.

Although Brunei has good relations with its neighbors, long term defense requirements need attention. Brunei probably should join the Five Power Agreement to strengthen its international security. Finally, domestic tensions could rise if MIB is forced too aggressively. Like Malaysia, Brunei is a multiethnic society which can only survive with a good bit of tolerance and acceptance of diversity. For the forseeable future democratic reform is not likely. If it does occur, it will originate in the royal palace and not from the streets of Bandar Seri Begawan.

An early morning traveler swings through the towering trees in Bardar Seri Begawan
Courtesy: Sarah Cassell

19

၁၉၇၅-ခု၊ တပို့တွဲလဆုတ် ၁၄ ရက်၊ ကြာသပတေးနေ့ (၁-၃-၇၅) (၃၀/၆၄)

ပြည်သူ့ ဥပဒေ အကျိုးဆောင်အဖွဲ့ အဖွဲ့ဝင် မန်အောင်မြို့နှင့် ရမ်းဗြဲမြို့များတွင် ဆွေးနွေး

ဒေသပါတီကော်မတီ အတွင်းရေးမှူး စပါးပိုင်များလေ့လာ

တောင်သူ လယ်သမားနေ့ စုပေ ၆င်းရှ် ဂုဏ်ပြုကြိုဆို

★ဓာတ်ပုံ—၇ ကော်ဖန်နံ့ဖြန်

ပါတီစည်းရုံးရေး ကော်မတီနှင့် ပါတီစိတ်ညှိနှိုင်း

မြန်မာ့ ကျောက်မျက်ရတနာ ပြပွဲ ကျပ်ငွေသန်း၄၀ ကျော်ဖိုး ရောင်းချခဲ့ရ

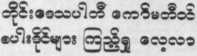

တိုင်းဒေသပါတီ ကော်မတီဝင် စပါးပိုင်များ ကြည့်ရှု လေ့လာ

မိုးလယ်မိုးနောင်းသီးနှံ စိုက်ပျိုး ရေးပြ ပွဲ ဖွင့်

★ဓာတ်ပုံ—၇ ကော်ဖန်နံ့ဖြန်

ပါတီတွင်း သဘောတရားရေးရာ ဆွေးနွေးပွဲ ဖွင့်

မိုးထစ်ချုန်းဖွယ်

A Burmese newspaper

The Union of Burma (Myanmar) (The latter is the name of the country in Burmese.)

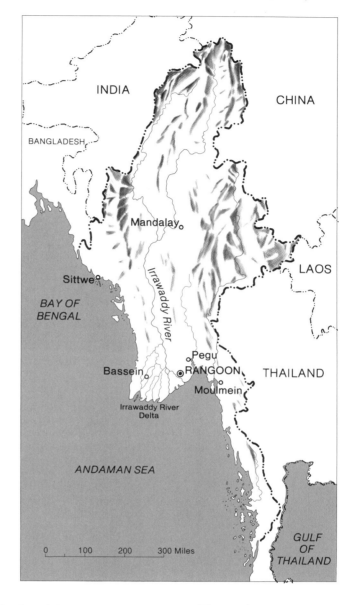

Area: 261,700 sq. mi. (676,600 sq. km., almost as large as Texas).

Population: 45 million (estimated).

Capital City: Rangoon (Yangon, Pop. 3.5 million, estimated).

Climate: Tropical, with torrential rains during the summer monsoon (June–November) in the coastal areas.

Neighboring Countries: China (North and East); India, Bangladesh (West); Laos (East); Thailand (East and South).

Official Language: Burmese.

Other Principal Tongues: English, Chinese, Karen, Shan.

Ethnic Background: Oriental Mongoloid mixtures, including Burman (72%) in the central valley area, Karen (7% in the Pegu Yoma and Karen States), Shan (6% in the Shan Plateau and Chindwin Valley), Chin and Kachin (5%) in the western mountain and extreme north, Wa (2%), a very primitive group along the Chinese border; Chinese, Indian, Bengali and other (8%).

Principal Religion: Buddhism.

Main Exports: (to Singapore, China, Thailand, India and Hong Kong) Beans, teak, rice, hardwood.

Main Imports: (from Japan, China, Thailand, Singapore, Malaysia) Machinery, transportation equipment, chemicals, food products.

Currency: Kyat.

Former Colonial Status: British dependency (1886–1947)

Independence Day: January 4, 1948.

Chief of State: General Than Shwe, Chairman, State Law and Order Restoration Council (since April 1992).

Secretary, SLORC: Kin Nyunt.

National Flag: A red field with a blue union in the upper left–hand corner containing a large white gear (representing workers) superimposed with a sheaf of rice (representing peasants) surrounded by 14 small white stars symbolizing the states and divisions of the country.

Annual Per Capita Income: U.S. $930 (1994 estimate).

The long western coastline of Burma faces the tropical waters of the Bay of Bengal in the North and the Andaman Sea in the peninsular southern regions. The northern part of the country is actually a moist and hot basin—it is separated from India and Bangladesh by high, forested ridges and lower valleys, and from China, Laos and Thailand by the mountains and by the Shan Plateau, which combine to form a crescent enclosing Burma.

The mountains of the plateau region are not particularly high when compared to those in other countries of southern Asia; they reach a maximum height of about 9,000 feet. The Irrawaddy River originates in the mountainous region of the north, turbulently descending to the lowlands where it is transformed into a sluggish, muddy stream of water. It is along this river and also along the Sittang River that the largest cities of Burma are located, including Rangoon and Mandalay.

The northern mountains are inhabited thinly by people who are mostly non–Burman; they live principally in the thick forests where teak and other valuable trees grow. Many are primitive and non–Buddhist—rumors of head–hunting in this area have persisted for centuries.

The great majority of the people live in the crowded central valley where great quantities of rice are raised each year, much of which is exported. The comparatively cool and dry season, which starts in November, ends in about mid–February when the wind changes from the north and begins to blow from the Bay of Bengal. The air becomes hotter during April and May, and periodic storms appear on the horizon.

In June the full force of the southwest monsoon rains inundate the coastline. It is in this region that an average of 200

Rush hour in Rangoon with Longgyi-clad men clinging to bus entrance
AP/World Wide Photos

inches of rain fall each year, but the further inland regions receive less rain as their distance from the coast increases. The rains abate in late October; the wind again comes from the North, providing a cooler and drier relief from the oppressive moisture of the preceding months.

History: In the early centuries of the Christian era, the fertile coastal region of Burma was inhabited by the Mons, who had cultural characteristics quite similar to those of India. In about 1000 A.D. they became converted to *Hinayana* Buddhism which had come from India by way of Ceylon (Sri Lanka); they in turn transmitted this sect to other people living in the region, including the Burmans.

The adjective "Burmese" is used by Americans to describe all of the people living within the country; "Burman" is used to designate the largest ethnic group; the British usage is exactly the opposite. Burmans are closely related in terms of language and appearance to the Tibetans, and seem to have moved southwest into Burma from the remote regions of eastern Tibet beginning about 800 A.D. Although they have the characteristic oriental flat nose, they usually do not have the eyelid fold of their Chinese neighbors; the color of their skin varies from deep brown to extremely light in color.

The Burmans emerged as the most powerful force in the country by the mid–11th century under King Anawrata, who established a national capital in the cen-

tral city of Pagan, from which most of the country was subdued. The Shan (Thai) people, who lived in the northeastern part of Burma, disliked Burman rule, and in the late 13th century requested the protection of the Mongol empire which ruled China. The emperor Khubilai Khan sent a large force of cavalrymen who invaded Burma, totally destroying the Burman kingdom.

The Mongols did not remain for any great length of time; when they left the Shan established a number of states which were under Burman influence, but which governed the nation. From about 1300 to the mid–18th century, Burma's history is one of repeated destructive civil wars among the Burmans, Mons and Shans. No one emerged victorious; these wars served only to limit the development of Burma.

European merchants and explorers appeared along the coast after 1500; although the Dutch had trade bases for a brief period, there was no early colonization of Burma. In 1753 a new Burman kingdom emerged, rapidly reuniting the several small states into which Burma had been split by civil war. This warlike kingdom raided Thailand, fended off two invasions by the Manchu dynasty of China and in the early 19th century invaded Assam to the west.

The British East India Company, which was in control of Assam at that time, sent British troops to push the Burmans out of the area in the First Burmese War (1824).

The British took over the Arakan and Tenasserim coasts and advanced up the Irrawaddy River. Faced with defeat, the Burmans surrendered those coasts and permitted the British to maintain a minister at the Burman capital of Ava. However, they treated the British with contempt and interfered with colonial commerce, which led to the Second Burmese War of 1852. Trade relations were eventually established in a commercial treaty in 1862 giving the British the right to trade throughout Burma.

Thibaw became king in 1878, and rapidly alienated the British by again interfering with their trade and establishing relations with the French. This resulted in the Third Burmese War (1885–1886) which ended Burman rule. The country was governed as a province of British India until 1937 when it became a Crown Colony.

The emphasis during the British colonial period was on profitable trade and not on the welfare of the various ethnic groups in Burma. In depriving the Burmans of control, the British aroused the hate of this largest group; the minority Karen, Shan, Chin and Kachin people looked to the British for protection from the Burmans, and thus were less antagonistic towards their colonial rulers. The British also undermined the influence of the Buddhist monasteries and imported large numbers of Indians to perform skilled and semi–skilled tasks rather than training the Burmans for these jobs. Thousands of Chinese also entered to engage in trade. These foreign minorities caused anti–Indian and anti–Chinese riots in 1931. The anti–foreign Burmans resisted adoption of European skills and cultural patterns more successfully than the people in almost all of the other British colonies.

There was considerable economic growth during the colonial period. Burma became the chief rice exporter of Southeast Asia; the lower Irrawaddy valley was cleared of its dense forests and brought under cultivation. Burmese labor was used for the cultivation of the huge crops.

The British granted a degree of self–government to Burma in 1937 which included an elected legislature and a cabinet. The lack of experience in government on the part of the Burmans created a basic instability in the government; there was little support among the people for the elected members and officials.

When the Japanese invaded Burma in 1942, they were welcomed by the people, including many Buddhist monks. Chief Minister Ba Maw of the colonial government accepted leadership in a puppet government established by the Japanese in 1943. Even though the people had welcomed their conquerors, the Japanese quickly set up a very oppressive administration designed to exploit Burma's capacity to produce rice. Active resistance soon formed around the *Anti–Fascist People's Freedom League (AFPFL)*, a political movement composed of left–wing nationalists and some communists, leading a guerrilla army under the Burman popular hero Aung San. The Allied forces, in an effort to establish a supply route to southwest China, in order to support the war against the Japanese in that country, slowly fought their way through Burma in 1944–45. The country was eventually liberated by mid–1945.

The British tried to establish a government along prewar colonial lines, but friction erupted immediately with the *AFPFL* led by Aung San. The British, controlled by the *Labor Party* government of Prime Minister Attlee, was anti–colonial and nearly bankrupt; it was in the process of giving up its control over India and Pakistan. It agreed in 1947 to give Burma its independence; the *AFPFL* chose then to leave the British Commonwealth entirely.

Aung San was assassinated in 1947 at the instigation of U Saw. (In the Burmese language, "U" is a title, not a name.) U Nu, an attractive and fervently Buddhist member of the *AFPFL*, took control of the government. Burmese communists threatened the government of Burma in the years following 1948—in 1949 the government controlled little of the nation outside Rangoon. The lack of cooperation among the insurgents enabled the Burmese army under Ne Win to reduce the rebellion to a much lower level by 1951, although it was not eliminated.

China, Burma's largest neighbor, fortunately was not involved in the civil strife. The Burmese, although independent, were not experienced in operating an effective government; the *AFPFL* split and became a coalition of parties with a high degree of inefficiency, corruption and factionalism. The leftist–socialist group was led by U Nu; the more conservative wing was led by Ba Swe. The split between the two factions resulted in the forced resignation of U Nu in the fall of 1958; Burma was then ruled by the military commanded by Ne Win until February 1960. Little progress was made toward solving the political problems of the country, or toward getting the sluggish economy moving during this period of military rule.

Elections were permitted in 1960 which resulted in U Nu's faction being returned to office, but in 1962 adverse political and economic conditions again caused the military to intervene. This time, Ne Win abolished the existing political parties, imprisoned a number of political leaders, including the highly popular U Nu, and established a military dictatorship under the *Union Revolutionary Council* which he led. He dramatically announced that he would make Burma a completely socialist—although not a communist—state.

The revolts had continued, particularly in rural areas during the post–independence years. Ne Win was unsuccessful in negotiating an end to these revolts in 1963 and then launched military operations and jailed a number of communist leaders. Relations with China, which formerly were polite and sometimes even cordial, deteriorated in the spring of 1967, principally because of the effects of Mao's "Great Cultural Revolution" on ethnic Chinese living in Burma, who are regarded with some distrust by the Burmese.

However, by 1968 it became increasingly evident that the Burmese had acquired greater confidence in their ability to withstand the displeasure of China. Contributing to this awareness were the good harvest, the reported killing of a communist leader, Than Tun, and a tendency of some of the tribal insurgents to draw closer to the government because of pressures from the Burmese communists and the regime of Mao Zedong and his supporters in China.

Ne Win invited some of the former political leaders in early 1969 to advise him on Burma's political future. They urged a return to elected government instead of military rule. When Ne Win refused, U Nu went into exile and announced that he would try to lead a political movement for the overthrow of Ne Win; however, he gave up the plan and returned to Burma in July 1980. Ne Win launched a process of making Burma a one–party state, controlled by the *Burma Socialist Program Party*, a leftist movement with some communist elements, headed by himself. The military government of Burma was repressive and unpopular; the army proved unskilled and ineffective in managing the economy.

A new constitution was adopted by referendum at the beginning of 1974. Burma was renamed the *Socialist Republic of the*

Lord Louis Mountbatten, supreme allied commander in Southeast Asia (1943–46), later *Earl Mountbatten of Burma,* **talks with British troops near Mandalay in April 1945**

Union of Burma. Real power was exercised by a 29 man Council of State, chaired by President Ne Win. However, the government remained repressive, unpopular and inept.

Inflation, shortages of rice, and floods contributed to political unrest in 1974. In December, the funeral of U Thant, former Secretary General of the United Nations, provided the occasion for Buddhist and student organized riots which were quickly suppressed by the military. Ne Win survived an attempted *coup* in 1976. In May 1983, the President purged his security chief and other officials for offenses including drug smuggling.

The resulting confusion probably made it easier for North Korean agents to plant a bomb in a public monument which killed 17 visiting South Korean officials and journalists on October 9th. High Burmese officials were narrowly spared from this terrorist attempt. Infuriated, Ne Win again shook up security services and broke diplomatic relation with North Korea.

The army improved its position against insurgency somewhat in 1985 as China reduced its support for the communists in the Wa and Shan states and as a number of Karen insurgents were driven across the border into Thailand. On the other hand, the so–called Shan United Army, which in addition to defending the interests of the Shan tribes in Burma and Thailand involved in the opium trade, transferred its operation from Thailand to Burma in 1982.

The *National Democratic Front,* a coalition of ethnic insurgent groups, attempted to engage the government in talks on the key issues of ending military rule, restoration of parliamentary government and autonomy for ethnic minorities.

In August 1987, Ne Win made an unprecedented public admission that he and his government had made some mistakes. These included authoritarian policies that led to demonstrations which in turn caused the closing of all educational institutions at the secondary and higher levels.

In March 1988, a long series of massive demonstrations against the ruling regime by students, monks, and urban residents seemed to promise a democratic or liberal revolution like those in the Philippines and South Korea. The army proved too strong and determined, however, to permit such an outcome. Another problem was that although Ne Win resigned in July as chairman of the ruling *Burma Socialist Program Party,* he stayed in the Rangoon area and continued to give orders to the army from behind the scenes.

At the end of July, Ne Win was succeeded by a close associate and tough former general, Sein Lwin, who also became president of the Union of Burma. He proclaimed martial law in Rangoon and tried to control the demonstrations by military force but failed; he resigned on August 12. His successor in both posts was a relatively moderate civilian, Maung Maung, who pledged multi–party elections in which none of the current leaders would run for office. There was great popular joy at this, but also widespread demand for an immediate interim government; former Prime Minister U Nu proclaimed such a government, composed largely of opposition leaders, on September 9.

To end the growing confusion, Defense Minister Saw Maung seized power on September 18 and assumed both the chairmanship of the ruling party (now renamed the *National Unity Party,* a less ideological label) and the presidency of the state. Protest demonstrations were dealt with by many arrests and much shooting on the part of the army, which succeeded in clearing the streets of the major cities. Press censorship was reimposed. On the other hand, the new regime tried to cope with the country's perennial economic stagnation by promising limited privatization of the heavily socialized economy. Multi–party elections were still promised for 1990.

Several foreign governments, including that of the U.S., protested the military coup and suspended economic aid to Burma. The opposition, calling itself the *National League for Democracy,* discarded U Nu and accepted as its leader Aung Gyi, a retired general. A more popular figure, however, was Aung San Suu Kyi, the daughter of national hero Aung San (assassinated in 1947); she benefited not only from his name and memory but from the atmosphere surrounding the funeral of her mother on January 2, 1989, which amounted to a peaceful demonstration against military rule.

In preparation for the supposedly free election scheduled for May 27, 1990, the military leadership disqualified the most prominent opposition figure, Aung San Suu Kyi, from running (January 1989) and placed her under house arrest in July of that year, together with other leading members of the opposition. One of the control techniques used by the military was the forced migration of about half a million people from the cities to the countryside, where they experienced serious hardships.

The opposition parties won 80% of the vote for the National Assembly in May 1990 elections. The army refused to surrender power, however, and intensified its campaign of repression. In December, Aung San Suu Kyi's party and the Karen guerrillas proclaimed a coalition government in opposition to the army–dominated one.

In spite of brutal repression by the military, unrest continued to grow, both in the cities and in the rural areas. The government closed the universities in December 1991. The army, strengthened by purchases of more than $1 billion in arms from China, launched a series of offensives in ethnic minority areas. One result was a stream of refugees out of the country, including Muslims fleeing to Bangladesh.

In 1994 and early 1995, the State Law and Order Restoration Council (SLORC) neutralized much of the opposition by signing individual ceasefire agreements with rebel groups. Their support was thus denied to anti–government democratic forces in urban areas. Supporters of democracy had to go underground. In January 1995, government forces captured Manerplaw, the legendary Karen rebel base located on the Thai border. This was made easier by the death of Saw Maw Reh, President of the Karen rebel state, in March 1994. In April 1995, the Karen National Union (KNU) sent a letter to the head of SLORC seeking peace.

Government and Politics: After independence from the British at the end of 1947, the Burmese political system which emerged was nominally a parliamentary democracy under the leadership of Prime Minister U Nu. However, the multi–ethnic nature of the state, the lack of experience with the Western–style government and the inability to confront important political, social and economic problems, led to the entry of the military into government in both 1958 and again in 1962. Since then the country is best characterized as a military dictatorship. The dominant political figure has been General Ne Win, who in 1993 still commanded great loyalty. He ruled from 1962 through 1987 through the country's only political party, the Burmese Socialist Program Party (BSPP). This was, however, only a front for military rule. The period from 1988 to the present, as described in the previous section, was one of crisis, in which the military sought a way to maintain control and regain legitimacy.

The political culture of the country is both hierarchical and paternalistic and thus is a contradiction to the ideas of democracy, i.e. human rights, equality, individual rights and representative institutions. Effective control of the government now rests with the military junta officially known as the State Law and Order Restoration Council (SLORC), created in 1988. Effective power within SLORC rests with its chairman, General Than Shwe, who also serves as Prime Minister.

The People's Assembly (Pyitha Hluttaw) was never convened after the May 27, 1990 elections because of the victory of the democratic forces. The judicial branch is subject to the power of SLORC. The major political event of 1995 was the July 10 release of Aung San Suu Kyi, the most famous opposition figure in the country who had been under house arrest since 1989. In all likelihood, there are several reasons why the release occurred. First, by early 1995, SLORC had consolidated its power. It probably has little to fear from its opponents. Second, ASEAN's "constructive engagement" policy spearheaded by Indonesia and Thailand may have encouraged SLORC. Third, SLORC was also facing tougher sanctions from the United States. Finally, SLORC recognizes that it needs trade and investment from abroad if it is to survive. Because political activity is restricted in the country, Aung San Suu Kyi is, in effect, still prohibited from fulfilling her role as a major opposition figure.

After the release, National League for Democracy (NLD) MP's who fled the country when the 1990 election results were not upheld, met in Sweden to decide the opposition's course of action. One result was that they recognized the National Coalition Government of the Union of Burma, which should have taken power as a result of the 1990 elections.

SLORC, for its part, created the Union Solidarity Development Association (USDA) as a front organization. The USDA has set up branches throughout the country in an effort to channel support to SLORC. USDA appears to be modeled after Indonesia's GOLKAR, a political party which supports the role of the military in Indonesian society. USDA

officials visited Indonesia in the middle of the year. The Burmese military apparently is more than a little interested in the Indonesian style of military rule, something the Indonesians are not too comfortable with.

Defense: Much of Burma's defense policy is internally directed against the various ethnic groups which seek either total independence or some degree of autonomy. SLORC continued its efforts to put an end to ethnic insurgency in 1995 and early 1996. On January 14, 1996, SLORC further improved its hold on the country when Khun Sa, the number one opium and heroin producer in the Golden Triangle, surrendered his 10,000 man Mong Tai army to Burmese officials. The "triangle" refers to the area where the borders of Burma, Thailand and Laos meet.

In return for the surrender, Khun Sa has apparently been assured that he will not be extradited to the United States, where a grand jury would like to talk with him. Amnesty from Rangoon and the right to maintain control over part of the Shan state with a downsized army may have also been part of the deal. Of course, business as usual will continue. Such a deal will make it hard if not impossible for U.S.–Burmese relations to improve.

On June 29, 1995, the Burmese government signed an agreement with the New Mon State Party (NMSP). The military agreement gave Mon rebels control over

20 designated areas in their home state in return for a ceasefire. Rangoon also initiated new military action against remnants of the Karen National Union which had signed an agreement with the government after the fall of Manerplaw in the spring. A new offensive was also launched against the Karen National Progressive Party. These actions are a clear indication of Rangoon's determination to put an end to rebel activities in the country. Success, however, is not assured.

In July, the military situation along the Thai–Burmese border was tense. Rangoon accused Thailand of providing sanctuary and help to the Karen rebels, SLORC was also angry about a March attack by Khun Sa's army on Tachilek, a Burmese border town. The attackers allegedly used Thai territory to their advantage. Burmese military forces also conducted raids against refugee camps across the Thai border. General Chawalit Yongchaiyut, Deputy Prime Minister and Minister of Defense for Thailand visited Rangoon in early September at the invitation of the Burmese Deputy Prime Minister, Vice Admiral Maung Maung Khin to smooth things over.

The People's Republic of China is also important to the Burmese defense equation. Since 1993, Burma has reportedly received some $1.2 billion in military equipment from China.

In late 1994, an agreement was signed for another $400 million in equipment. There is also the recognition that with

The pavilion of the Shwe Dagon pagoda, Rangoon

Young monks contemplate lottery tickets, Rangoon. Photo by Jon Markham Morrow

military equipment comes technical assistance and a limited presence.

Both India and Indonesia as well as the other ASEAN states are concerned about Chinese access to three strategic islands (Ramree, Coco, and St. Matthew's), off the Burmese coast. St. Matthew's island is less than 200 miles north of Malaysia. China may well have an irreversible foothold in Burma.

Foreign Policy: As Burma emerges from its self–imposed isolation, it faces a complicated international environment. It has neighbors with which it must maintain acceptable relationships: China, India and the ASEAN states (Thailand and Singapore are the most important within ASEAN). Chinese penetration of the country is already significant through military assistance described above and because of significant immigration and trade from the provinces north of Burma. India cannot accept an unchecked Chinese presence in Burma and especially on its offshore territories. In 1994, India attempted to warm relations with SLORC and back off on its pro–democracy position. In fact, the Indian hard line against SLORC may have in part led to Rangoon turning more toward China.

Relations with Thailand continue to be acceptable but uneasy because of cross–border activities, including illegal logging on the part of the Thais, and assistance to

groups opposing SLORC. In July 1994, Thailand invited the Burmese foreign minister, Ohn Gyaw, to be an official guest at the first ASEAN Regional Forum which focused on Asian security problems. An important benefit of Rangoon's presence was that the Clinton Administration apparently re–evaluated its hard line approach toward SLORC. In November, Thomas Hubbard, Deputy Assistant Secretary of State for East Asia and the Pacific, visited Rangoon. He is the highest ranking U.S. official to visit the country since the coup in 1988.

Another significant issue for Burma in 1994 was the repatriation of several hundred thousand Rohingya Muslim refugees who fled to Bangladesh in 1991–1992. This issue almost brought the two countries to conflict. Rangoon has stated that repatriation should be completed in 1996.

In 1995, Burma continued to move cautiously toward re–association with the countries of Southeast Asia. Rangoon's Foreign Minister, Ohn Gyaw was an invited guest at the mid–year Association of Southeast Asian Nations Ministerial Meeting in Brunei, Burma's "instrument of accession" to the ASEAN Treaty of Amity and Cooperation was presented. Burma is seeking "observer status" in ASEAN. If all goes well, full membership could be achieved in several years. ASEAN is keen on bringing Burma into the organization as a means of providing

Rangoon with other alternatives to China which has established strong ties with the country over the last decade.

The United States, on the other hand, can afford to be driven more by principle and its commitment to encouraging democracy in Asia. In September, Madeleine Albright, United States Ambassador to the United Nations, visited Rangoon and delivered the message that there would be no significant change in U.S. policy toward Burma until SLORC changed the way it treats the Burmese people. Washington would do well to take ASEAN's concerns more seriously.

Culture: *Hinayana* Buddhism pervades almost every aspect of Burmese culture. Monks are numerous and influential; most Burmese males spend at least part of their lives in monasteries. The countless temples and shrines have been constructed with great care and with precious materials which combine to create structures of exquisite beauty; the best known of these is the huge and ornate Shwe Dagon in Rangoon. A large and beautiful complex of temples at Pagan, near Mandalay, was seriously damaged by an earthquake in 1975. Although the Buddhists teach the normal traditions of Buddhism, there is still among the people a widespread belief in animism, especially with respect to the existence and activities of "nats" which are spirits within objects.

The monasteries dominated education under the old monarchy and still are a major source of learning in Burma. Women have enjoyed a high degree of freedom and social equality; they can inherit property, keep their native names after marriage and have equal rights in contracting marriage and suing for divorce. They have, however, had little input at the national level. Aung San Suu Kyi is truly an exception, not the norm.

While Burmese constitute the largest ethnic group in the country, other groups such as the Karens, Shans, and Kachins are important. Their demands have tended to be for autonomous states within a federated Burma as opposed to total independence.

Economy: In 1995, the government continued to work toward the transformation of its centrally planned socialist style economy into a market economy. In March 1994 the government announced that it would do away with the old 45 and 90 kyat notes in favor of more conventional denominations; 20, 50, 100 and 500 kyat notes. While the Burmese, who have been accustomed to thinking in nines, may find the change difficult, Western businessmen and investors, whom the government is now courting, will feel much more at home. In an effort to stimulate the inflow of foreign currency and to improve the hotel and tourism ($565 million). Seventeen hotels were under construction in Rangoon at the end of 1994. The government has dubbed 1996 as "visit Myanmar year."

The GDP has increased by about 5.2% since 1992. A figure of about 5% may have been attained for the 1994–1995 fiscal year. Foreign investment grew to over $2.6 billion by mid–1995. A major gas pipeline project accounted for a good proportion of this investment. Foreign banks are now allowed to operate in the country and, foreign businesses can in theory repatriate profits. Thanks to British colonialism, a workable legal system including patent and copyright law is in place.

Nevertheless, the bottom line is that Burma remains a very poor country and faces a number of significant challenges in the economic sector. These problems include a significant foreign debt, a continuing trade deficit, high inflation, an unrealistic exchange rate, a very poor infrastructure, a failed educational system, and the prospect of no immediate assistance from the international community as a result of SLORC's anti–democratic behavior. And several American companies, including Eddie Bauer, Liz Claiborne and Levi Strauss have discontinued operations because of the country's international reputation. Investment from the ASEAN states, such as Singapore, cannot rectify the situation though they may help. For the time being, tourism is the only game in town.

The Future: Burma's move toward ASEAN in 1995 is encouraging. Washington is too concerned with principles which play well at home, and too little aware of the precarious relationship that SLORC has entered into with China. No one cares about SLORC's future. However, Southeast Asia needs an independent and economically stable Burma. Democracy is only a distant hope at this time.

A major shake–up in the Burmese military, which replaced many of the hard–liners in 1995, is also encouraging. A more pragmatic and hopefully less ruthless generation of leaders may be easier to work with and more open to slow change. A more optimistic view of Burma's future is at this time unrealistic.

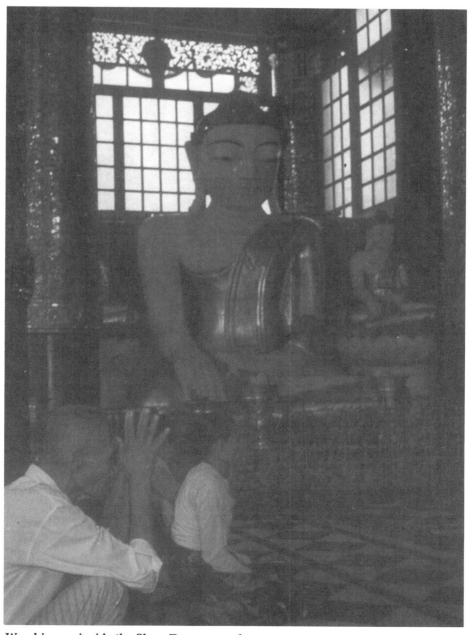

Worshippers inside the Shwe Dagon pagoda   Photo by Jon Markham Morrow

27

The State of Cambodia

The temple of Angkor Wat built by Khmer warrior kings a thousand years ago

Area: 68,898 sq. mi. (181,300 sq. km.; slightly larger than Missouri).

Population: 9 million (1993 est.).

Capital City: Phnom Penh (Pop. 450,000, estimated).

Climate: Tropically hot with a rainy monsoon season during the summer from May to October.

Neighboring Countries: Thailand (North and West); Laos (Northeast); Vietnam (East).

Official Language: Khmer (Cambodian).

Other Principal Tongues: French, Chinese, Vietnamese.

Ethnic Background: Cambodian (Khmer, about 80%) Vietnamese (semi–permanent or permanent, about 12%), Chinese (5%), other, including primitives, (about 2%).

Principal Religion: Buddhism (Hinayana sect, but religious observances are not permitted.)

Main Exports: (to China) natural rubber, rice, pepper, wood; export trade is almost nonexistent.

Main Imports: (from China, North Korea, Vietnam and Russia) international food aid and some economic development aid from the Soviet bloc.

Currency: Riel.

Former Colonial Status: French protectorate (1863–1949); Associated State within the French Union (1949–1955).

Independence Date: September 25, 1955.

Head of State: Norodom Sihanouk, King (Sept. 24, 1993).

Heads of Government: Prince Norodom Ranariddh and Hun Sen, First and Second Prime Ministers.

National Flag: A plain red field upon which is centered in gold the ancient temple Angkor Wat.

Per Capita Income: US$130 (estimated).

Cambodia has a rather short coastline which runs about 150 miles along the warm waters of the Gulf of Siam. The land stretches from this coast in a wide plain, which is traversed in the eastern part by the broad waters of the lower Mekong River. The western part of the plain is dominated by a large lake known as Tonle Sap, twenty miles wide and one hundred miles long—a body of fresh water that produces a heavy annual harvest of fish needed by the Cambodians, who do not eat meat because of Buddhist beliefs.

The borders with Laos and southern Vietnam run through thickly forested foothills that rise to highlands at the demarcation lines. The greater part of the northern border with Thailand consists of a steep series of cliffs; the part of Thailand closest to Cambodia is a plateau which is situated about 1,500 feet above the plain. The western border with Thailand and most of Cambodia's coastline is occupied by the Cardamom, Kirimom and Elephant Mountains, which rise to heights of 5,500 feet.

Much of the central plain, which is the largest by far and is economically the area of prime importance in Cambodia, is regularly flooded by the mighty Mekong River in an uncontrolled fashion—there are no elaborate dikes to contain the waters such are are found along the Red River in northern Vietnam. The rains which begin in May are the first cause of flooding; melting snows in Tibet and China in July add to the volume of water, which is also joined by monsoon waters from Thailand and Laos. By mid–September the flood water may cover as much as 8,000 square miles of land. These are not violent waters—they deposit a fine silt which enriches the land and they also bring huge quantities of fish to the Tonle Sap lake, permitting annual harvests of up to 15 tons per square mile of water surface.

The waters recede in October and the winter season begins in November, bringing slightly cooler and much drier weather except in the western and southern mountains, where there is sporadic rainfall.

History: The Khmer people, from whom the modern Cambodians (Kampucheans) are descended, first organized themselves under a state usually known by its Chinese name of Funan, which emerged about 500 A.D. in southern Cambodia. This was apparently a result of trade with, and immigration from, India to Cambodia via the Kra Isthmus which is now the southern part of Thailand. In the early 10th century a powerful state known as the Khmer Empire arose, with its capital at Angkor, north of Tonle Sap, where huge and complex palaces were painstakingly constructed during the course of several centuries and are a major tourist attraction during periods when there is no civil or military strife.

The people were converted after 1000 A.D. to the southern school of Buddhism which originated on the island of Sri Lanka and is referred to as *Hinayana* Buddhism. At its height in about 1200, the Khmer Empire controlled much of what is now Vietnam, Thailand, Laos and Burma. For a number of reasons, including the over–extension of its resources and attacks by the Thai from the North, the empire declined a century later and was ultimately destroyed by the Thai about the end of the 15th century. For the

next three and one–half centuries, Cambodia was sandwiched between the Annamese of Central Vietnam and the Thai to the north and west, and was almost continuously dominated by one or the other, or both.

French interest in Cambodia was stimulated in the late 1850's by British advances in Burma. Both powers thought of Southeast Asia principally as a stepping stone to the supposedly vast treasures and markets of southwest China. Although it established a protectorate over Cambodia in 1863, France did not dethrone the reigning family; the area was increasingly drawn into the Indochinese colony created at the end of the century in an attempt to rival the much larger British Indian Empire. The French prevented the Thais from moving against Cambodia and protected it also from its other traditional overlord, the Vietnamese, who had also become part of the French Indochinese empire.

This protection was welcomed by the Cambodians, and as a result, there was not the violently anti–French attitude that existed in neighboring Vietnam. As in other parts of South Asia, the existence of a stable colonial administration attracted a sizable number of Chinese immigrants, who quickly emerged in a virtually dominant position in profitable ventures as commercial middlemen.

Japan quickly overran Cambodia in 1941, and as a token of appreciation, two of the Cambodian border provinces were awarded to Thailand, by then the official ally of the Japanese. Although

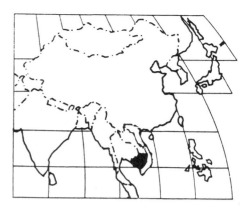

they were returned after World War II, the Cambodians have a lingering suspicion that the Thai still covet them.

Politics in Cambodia were dominated after the return of the French in 1946 by a single popular and unpredictable man who ruled until 1970: Prince Norodom Sihanouk. He had been made king by the French in 1941, but became impatient with the conservative traditions of the monarchy and interested in the liberal political movements within the country; he abdicated in 1955. Freed of the burdensome ceremonial duties and able to play a free role in politics, he became premier and quickly took advantage of the French defeat in Vietnam (see Vietnam) to declare the independence of Cambodia.

Sihanouk abolished the monarchy in 1960 and became the titular as well as the actual chief of state. Nationalistic, but not anti–French, he had an immense popu-

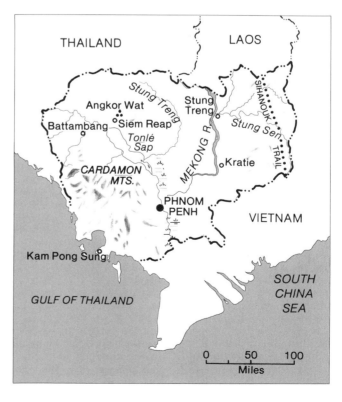

29

Days of the monarchy: young King Norodom Sihanouk, 1946

larity with the people of the nation. He skillfully used this popularity to cope with what he regarded as major domestic problems—the traditional aristocracy, the partly westernized intellectuals, the businessmen, the small communist movement and a segment of right–wing opponents who he believed were supported by Thailand. His efforts were almost uniformly successful at first. He founded and continued to lead the *Sangkum*, or the *Popular Socialist Movement*, which was the only significant political party. He did, however, allow his Premier, General Lon Nol, to exercise some power.

But for the popularity of Sihanouk at home, Cambodia would never have been able to deal with the external pressures with which it was faced. In order to keep open the largest number of possible alternatives, Sihanouk remained "neutral" in the international "cold war" and aloof in the hot war in Asia. He engaged in active and skillful diplomacy which often puzzled the most astute foreign ministries. His view after independence was to the effect that Cambodia was surrounded by potentially hostile forces and neighbors, with the exception of Laos.

To counter–balance the threat of North Vietnam, he established close relations with the People's Republic of China beginning in 1956—the government of Mao Zedong (Tse–tung) was not anxious to see Ho Chi Minh's Vietnam dominate Cambodia, and apparently restrained its southern ally sufficiently to satisfy Sihanouk.

Sihanouk hoped that he could rely on the senior allies of Thailand and South Vietnam to restrain any ambitions of the communists toward Cambodia, but also had doubts about the sincerity and effectiveness of U.S. support of those countries. For this reason, and also because the U.S. and South Vietnam resented the fact that Cambodia served as a sanctuary for and an area through which North Vietnam supplied the communist forces in southern Indochina, relations between Sihanouk and the U.S. were strained after the early 1960's. Complaints by the U.S. increased sharply in late 1967 as the fighting in

South Vietnam became more intense; there were some hints that the United States would claim a right to pursue the communist *Viet Cong* into the eastern provinces of Cambodia. Prince Sihanouk announced he was willing to discuss the possibility of pursuit of the Viet Cong with a U.S. emissary, but when the diplomat arrived back in the U.S., he was denounced by the Prince, who proclaimed that the only item on the agenda was the "territorial integrity of Cambodia." The whole situation was made more complicated by Cambodia's claims to areas in South Vietnam, which were used at the bargaining table repeatedly when dealing with the U.S.; he refused to grant the U.S. any concessions unless it recognized the validity of Cambodian claims. When the U.S. agreed in 1969 to recognize Cambodia's existing frontiers, diplomatic relations, severed four years earlier, were restored.

The ever–changing and shrewd diplomacy of Sihanouk impressed the U.S., its allies, Britain, France, China and the Soviet Union to the extent that its Asian neighbors did not constitute a direct threat to the survival of Cambodia. There was a significant increase in communist–led revolts in the provinces bordering Thailand and Laos in the latter part of 1968, as well as the number of *Viet Cong* illegally present within Cambodia. The displeasure of anti–communist Cambodians grew so great that in 1970, while Sihanouk was out of the country, major anti–Hanoi demonstrations broke out in Phnom Penh. General Lon Nol and Prince Sirik Matak proclaimed the ouster of Sihanouk and a new government un der their leadership. The communist problem, however, was not the only issue—there had been disputes over Sihanouk's socialist economic policies.

North Vietnamese and Cambodian communist forces promptly began to expand their military activities in various parts of the country; at the end of April 1970, American and South Vietnamese forces entered to clean out the "sanctuary" areas along the border from which the communists had been conducting raids into South Vietnam. A secondary objective was to give some support to the new Cambodian government.

American ground forces were withdrawn in mid–1970 and South Vietnamese soldiers left soon afterward. The country suffered severely as a result of this military campaign.

Although in poor health and under heavy military pressure from communist forces, Lon Nol remained in power until 1975. He dissolved the National Assembly in late 1971 and began to rule by decree. He then proclaimed himself President, reshuffling his cabinet drastically and excluding Sirik Matak from it.

During the following years, public confidence in the government eroded badly and the communists (with North Vietnamese support) made major military gains. The American military role included continuous bombing in support of Lon Nol's army, but with no advisors in the field and no ground forces. The bombing was halted in mid–1973 because of U.S. Congressional action.

The communist rebels, often called the *Khmer Rouge,* and at the time supported by North Vietnam, claimed to be loyal to a government headed by Sihanouk and based in China, but in reality they had their own local leadership. Communist military efforts came close to isolating Phnom Penh by early 1975. Undermined by his own shortcomings, political bickering, uncertainty as to continuing American support and communist military gains, Lon Nol's government evaporated. The rebels refused to negotiate with it, leaving it no alternative but to surrender amid ominous proclamations of a collection of "blood debts" from the leadership. The final collapse came in early May 1975, when Phnom Penh fell to the communists. The United States confined its active role in this situation to the rescue of an American merchant ship seized by Cambodian communists and the transport of several thousand refugees to safety.

The policies of the new regime, which was pro-Chinese and soon became anti-Vietnamese, reflected the guerrilla mentality of its leaders and personnel. The major cities, including Phnom Penh, were forcibly evacuated to a considerable extent, allegedly on account of food shortages. There were executions of supporters of the former regime and widespread atrocities, mainly against persons of middle class background.

Sihanouk returned from China in 1975; most of his entourage, however, chose to go from China to France the following month. Cambodia was actually run not by Sihanouk, but by a shadowy leadership of the Cambodian Communist Party known as the *Angka* ("organization"), of which Pol Pot was Secretary General. An election held in 1976 filled 250 seats in the *People's Representative Assembly.* All 515 candidates were picked by the *Angka.* Sihanouk resigned, together with the rest of the government. He was placed under house arrest. An entire communist government was announced, with Pol Pot in actual control.

Then began in 1976 one of the horror stories of the 20th century in "Democratic Kampuchea." Once a happy, rather carefree society, Cambodians found themselves brutalized by one of the harshest governments known, and a veil of secrecy shrouded the nation. The formerly beautiful capital of Phnom Penh with 1.3 million was left with 90,000. Boarded-over store fronts and virtually deserted

streets told the story. The new regime wanted to stifle religion, wipe out any education system conflicting with the hopes of the "new order," and stamp out family ties.

Families were driven from the cities to labor from dawn to dusk in the fields. First priority was the destruction of the *intelligentsia* and *middle class.* Reports indicate that more than 3.4 million Cambodians were killed. The method of execution even saved the cost of a bullet: a skull–penetrating blow to the rear of the head by a pick axe used on a kneeling person. Silent, massive piles of bones throughout the country attest to this grisly activity. Others simply starved to death.

The new regime had immediate friction with all of its neighbors, the most serious with Vietnam, which erupted into continuing border warfare from early until late 1978 when a massive assault was launched on Cambodia. By early January 1979, Pol Pot had fled to western Cambodia, and a new pro–Vietnamese government known as the *People's Republic of Kampuchea* had been set up in Phnom Penh. Pol Pot's forces continued to fight a guerrilla war. This was one of the main reasons why China staged a brief invasion across the Vietnamese border in early 1979 with the announced purpose of "teaching Vietnam a lesson."

For a decade after 1979 there was fighting in western Cambodia between Vietnamese troops and Pol Pot's forces, as well as tension between Vietnam and Thailand over the Cambodian refugees grouped near the border. A coalition under Sihanouk, including what was left of Pol Pot's regime, emerged in opposition to the Vietnamese–dominated government in Phnom Penh. This group retains Cambodia's seat in the UN. The membership of ASEAN tried to negotiate a settlement of the Cambodia conflict and a Vietnamese withdrawal.

The unpopular Pol Pot "retired" as commander of the forces of the Khmer Rouge, the strongest faction in the anti–Vietnamese coalition. Son Sann, the head of another faction, survived a challenge by some of his colleagues in December 1985.

The Phnom Penh government, which was very repressive, continued to be dominated by the Vietnamese. The estimated 160,000 Vietnamese troops in Cambodia appeared to be concentrating on the resistance forces within Cambodia rather than putting pressure on the Thai border, as they had been doing earlier.

In March 1986, the anti-Vietnamese coalition, with the approval of China and ASEAN, softened its position somewhat by agreeing to negotiate with the pro-Vietnamese government in Phnom Penh. By the end of the year, it appeared that Hanoi, probably under Soviet pressure,

was modifying its objection to the inclusion of the Khmer Rouge in any such talks.

Except for helping to keep the anti–Vietnamese coalition in possession of the Cambodian seat in the United Nations, ASEAN has tended to become less and less relevant to the conflict and its potential resolution. The initiative passed in 1987 to Sihanouk, who, under the sponsorship of Indonesia, held some inconclusive talks with the pro–Vietnamese regime but was frustrated by lack of support from his partners in the coalition. Accordingly, he resigned as head of the group in January 1988.

In May 1988, Hanoi announced that it would withdraw 50,000 of its 120,000-odd troops then in Cambodia by the end of the year, with the others to follow by first March and then September 1990. The reasons for this major policy shift included the dismal state of the Vietnamese economy, the small chances of aid from abroad while the Cambodian occupation continued, and Soviet pressure or at least persuasion; it is probably not a coincidence that only the month before Moscow had formally agreed to remove its troops from Afghanistan by February 15, 1989. Hanoi also tried to improve its relationship with the U.S. by agreeing to let more refugees out of Cambodia and to try harder to account for MIA's (Americans missing in action during the Vietnam war).

The prospect of Vietnamese withdrawal naturally accelerated the pace of political and diplomatic activity relating to Cambodia, both within and outside the country. The main problem was that the Vietnamese evacuation might lead to a second seizure of power by the Khmer Rouge, who had been heavily armed by China and were apparently still as bloodthirsty as they had shown themselves to be fifteen years earlier. They intended to dominate the four-party coalition government (the parties to the resistance coalition loyal to Sihanouk, which include the Khmer Rouge, plus the pro–Vietnamese regime in Phnom Penh, headed by party chief Heng Samrin and Premier Hun Sen) that everyone agreed in principle should be created to end the conflict. Prince Sihanouk, the titular head of the resistance coalition and the most likely leader of the future government, was torn between his fear of his ferocious Khmer Rouge "allies" and his detestation of the regime installed by the invading Vietnamese. He tried negotiating with Hun Sen, but without much success; on the whole, he managed as best he could having been more or less stuck with the Khmer Rouge.

As the Vietnamese began to withdraw from western Cambodia, Khmer Rouge troops followed them from bases near the border with Thailand. They herded Cam-

Jakarta, Indonesia, July 1988: Another fruitless meeting with (l. to r.) *Khmer Peoples National Liberation Front* leader Son Sann, Cambodian Prime Minister Hun Sen, and Prince Norodom Sihanouk
AP/Wide World Photo

bodian refugees back into Cambodia from camps in Thailand, to provide themselves with a labor force and a population they could claim to rule. They stockpiled arms in various places and attacked other forces, including those of their "allies." At times the Vietnamese relaxed their evacuation, turned back, and fought the Khmer Rouge.

Under these conditions, it was hard to see how the Khmer Rouge could be prevented from dominating Cambodia after the Vietnamese left. There were many efforts to do exactly that, however. In mid–1988 China agreed to cut off its arms transfers to the Khmer Rouge when the Vietnamese finished withdrawing and conceded in principle that the Khmer Rouge could not be allowed to dominate the future Cambodian government. In late July, an informal meeting ("cocktail party") of the four Cambodian parties was held in Indonesia, the first of a series to be convened under the auspices of ASEAN; the results were inconclusive, mainly on account of the extreme hostility between the Khmer Rouge and the Hun Sen group. In August, the Khmer Rouge tried to improve its image by agreeing that the future unified Cambodian army should be under international supervision, while continuing to insist that the existing pro–Vietnamese government in Phnom Penh be dissolved. At the end of August, a series of Sino–Soviet talks in which Cambodia was the main single topic were convened. The Chinese supported the Khmer Rouge position and wanted the future international (UN) peacekeeping force to be armed; the Soviet side favored an unarmed force

and the formation of the future coalition government around the existing Phnom Penh regime as its core. In the fall the UN General Assembly passed a resolution opposing a return to power by the Khmer Rouge alone; China voted for it. In November, Philippine Foreign Minister Raul Manglapus visited Hanoi. Indian Prime Minister Rajiv Gandhi's visit to China in December 1988 marked the beginning of an effort to put India forward as the mediator in Cambodia; the idea seemed to be acceptable to ASEAN and Vietnam.

Early 1989 saw a further flurry of diplomatic activity relating to Cambodia. In January, the Thai Foreign Minister visited Hanoi, and Hun Sen went to Thailand; Sino–Vietnamese talks, principally on Cambodia, were held in Beijing. February saw a visit by Chinese Premier Li Peng to Thailand and a meeting in Beijing of the three parties to the resistance coalition. U.S. authorities said it might support a government headed by Sihanouk and even provide armaments toward that end, provided it did not include the Khmer Rouge, now backed by about 40,000 heavily armed guerrillas.

Hanoi announced in April 1989 that it would withdraw the remainder of its troops from Cambodia by September 1990, but in reality they were out a year earlier than that. This withdrawal, as well as major negotiations held from time to time, had the effect of escalating the fighting in Cambodia. The two sides, the Khmer Rouge and its non–communist allies (who tended to become increasingly dependent on it for arms as only a limited supply reached them from other sources, including the United States), and the

pro–Vietnamese regime in Phnom Penh, tried to improve their strategic positions prior to a possible future cease–fire. Several thousand Vietnamese troops returned to Cambodia covertly in late October 1989 to help the Phnom Penh regime defend cities in western Cambodia which were threatened by the Khmer Rouge.

Both sides tried to improve their images at home and abroad. In mid–1990 Phnom Penh, for example, dropped the name *Kampuchea* in favor of the former Cambodia. The Khmer Rouge announced, not for the first time, the "retirement" of its notoriously murderous leader, Pol Pot.

Phnom Penh's objection to the inclusion of the Khmer Rouge in a coalition government tended to freeze various negotiations and conferences. By 1990, however, pressure from the Soviet Union, and probably Vietnam as well, had compelled Premier Hun Sen of the Phnom Penh regime to Khmer Rouge participation.

The Australian government proposed in late 1989 an enhanced role of the UN in a prospective settlement for Cambodia. The contemplated election would involve a contest among all four of the parties on an equal footing. This was done in spite of the fact that the UN officially recognized three of them (the anti–Vietnamese coalition) as the legitimate government of Cambodia, even though the Phnom Penh regime had been claiming that status itself. This complex formula, however, failed to win a level of acceptance at a conference held at Jakarta in February 1990. Agreement (and even the usual "joint communique") was impossible.

In March the five permanent members of the UN Security Council began trying to get the parties to accept an increased UN role along the lines of the Australian proposal.

In mid–1990 the United States withdrew recognition from the anti–Vietnamese coalition and began to negotiate with Hanoi in the hope of moving the "peace process" along. The situation continued to be seriously complicated by Chinese arms shipments to the Khmer Rouge, via Thailand.

In October 1991, nineteen nations (including the four Cambodian factions, signing as one nation) signed a treaty in Paris providing that, under United Nations supervision, and with the presence of a UN peace–keeping force, a ceasefire would go into effect and elections would be held when feasible. Meanwhile, the four Cambodian factions would participate in a Supreme National Council, under Prince Sihanouk.

The following month, the three coalition parties began to return to Phnom Penh. Sihanouk promptly aligned himself with Hun Sen, announced that he favored trying the Khmer Rouge leaders, and tried to keep the Khmer Rouge out of the coalition government. For its part, the Khmer Rouge claimed to support the Paris settlement but, alleging that there were still some Vietnamese troops in Cambodia, it continued fighting in the hinterland against the Hun Sen forces.

On October 23, 1991, the Paris International Conference on Cambodia adopted an agreement on a Comprehensive Political Settlement of the Cambodia Conflict, which created the United Nations Transitional Authority in Cambodia (UNTAC) with a force of 16,000 military and 6,000 civilians to begin arriving in Cambodia in early 1992. UNTAC's function was to disarm the Cambodian warring factions and create a political climate where free elections could take place.

Politics and Government: UNTAC took control of the government in Phnom Penh. There were four factions competing for power: the *Khmer Rouge Party of Democratic Kampuchea (PDK)*, the current government party; the *People's Party of Cambodia (PPC)*; *FUNCINPEC*, Prince Norodom Sihanouk's party and the *KPNLF, Khmer People's National Liberation Front,* led by Son Sann, former Cambodian Prime Minister.

Leading up to the election, the government was in the hands of a twelve–member Supreme National Council (SNC) with six members from the old Hun Sen government and two each from the three other parties. SNC was to be under the guidance of Prince Sihanouk. UN officials were placed inside the State of Cambodia (SOC) ministries of Defense, Foreign Affairs, Public Security, Information, and Finance to determine impartiality. UNTAC was also to guarantee the civil rights of all Cambodians during the transition period.

The Khmer Rouge did not cooperate with the UN through the latter part of 1992 and early 1993. They would not allow UNTAC to disarm their troops. Therefore, UNTAC suspended further disarming of the other three forces so as not to create a further imbalance. By May 1993, there had been many incidents of PDK forces firing on UNTAC people.

Election results were announced on June 2. *The Royalist Party, FUNCINPEC,* or the United National Front for an Independent, Neutral, Peaceful, and Cooperative Cambodia had gained the largest share of the vote. This meant that former Prince Sihanouk would return to power after almost two decades. *FUNCINPEC* received 46% of the vote while the *PPC,* representing the Phnom Penh government, received 38%. This outcome was what UN and other political observers had hoped for. The results required a coalition government. Had *FUNCINPEC* won the majority the *PPC* would almost

certainly have rejected the results. What emerged was a new parliamentary style government, complete with a national legislature. The new Cambodian government is, however, a bit unorthodox. In order to split political power between *FUNCINPEC* and the *PPC* the government has two Prime Ministers. Prince Norodom Ranariddh holds the position of 1st Prime Minister. He is a son of Norodom Sihanouk, sworn in as the constitutional monarch in September 1993. The 2nd Prime Minister is Hun Sen; the cabinet also features dual ministers representing both parties.

After the election, the half brother of Prince Ranariddh, Prince Norodom Chakrapong led a secessionist movement which briefly claimed to have control over seven Eastern provinces. The central government prevailed. UNTAC's mission in Cambodia ended on September 24; about 500 UN troops remained in Cambodia as 1994 began.

In 1994, the FUNCINPEC–PPC coalition survived a move in May to turn power over to the King to form a provisional government as part of a peace settlement with the Khmer Rouge, and a July 2 coup attempt, and set about creating a working government. The fact that the two factions were able to work under the dual–government arrangement was in itself an accomplishment. There is little doubt however that the Hun Sen led faction, the PPC, holds most of the power.

The Khmer Rouge and what to do about it was the major issue which faced the government. In February and March government forces captured Khmer Rouge headquarters in Anlong Veng and Pailin in Battambang province near the Thai border. In both cases, however, the government was routed by the Khmer Rouge. The engagements illustrated the problems of the Cambodian armed forces. They are ill–equipped, poorly trained, top heavy with officers many of whom are corrupt, and, as the two defeats revealed, lacking in good strategy and tactics. One American official commented to this writer that when the government captured Pailin, they had no idea what to do with it. The military setbacks led to renewed calls for peace negotiations.

In May 1994, the King called for peace talks with the Khmer Rouge. There was also a move to have Sihanouk form a

H.R.H. Samdech Krom Preah Norodom Ranariddh

Their Majesties the King and Queen of Cambodia

provisional government. In June, while in Beijing, he announced that he would be willing to return to be the head of government as well as head of state and that he would form a government of reconciliation which would include the Khmer Rouge. The Hun Sen faction opposed the plan and Sihanouk withdrew his offer on June 18. On July 10, the Khmer Rouge announced the formation of their own government, the Provisional Government of National Union and National Salvation of Cambodia. In January 1995, the King was back in the country in Battambang province with a new initiative for peace.

The July 2 attempted *coup* in Phnom Penh was of greater significance for the future of the country than the problem of the Khmer Rouge. The failed *coup* revealed deep divisions within the government and outside participation. One leader of the coup was Prince Norodom Chakrapong, former deputy prime minister, son of King Sihanouk and brother to first prime minister Norodom Ranariddh. The coup also involved high ranking officials from Hun Sen's PPC and 19 Thai nationals, some of whom were military and security officials. While the *coup* failed, it indicates how fragile the fabric of government is. It may also indicate that outside forces have an intense interest in who is in charge in Phnom Penh.

The coalition government survived 1995. However, progress toward democracy was non–existent. In fact, those in power have little or no use for democracy in spite of what Western observers might like to read into the political landscape. During the first half of the year, several newspapers were closed down for printing stories too critical of the government. The Minister of Finance, Sam Rainsy, was booted from the National Assembly and left the country temporarily.

In November Prince Norodom Sirivudh, half brother to King Norodom Sihanouk, was arrested for allegedly planning to kill co–prime minister, Hun Sen. Princess Christine Alfson–Norodom, wife of Sirivudh, received a death threat in early 1996 and was warned not to attend the trial at which her husband was sentenced in absentia to 10 years in prison. Many believe the Prince was framed in an attempt to silence his criticism of the government.

Also in early 1996, Sam Rainsy returned to Cambodia to lead the *Khmer Nation Party (KNP)*. It was under a ban by the government and the party headquarters was raided by military police.

Radio announcer, Ek Mongkol, who was very outspoken, opposing Vietnamese border incursions in recent months, was shot. These events made worse an already tense situation between the governing coalition parties. There also was internal strife within the third and smallest coalition member, the *Buddhist Liberal Democratic Party (BLDP)*, a successor to the *KPNLF*, now headed by Son Sann.

Another point of contention was the reestablishment of January 7 as a national holiday, anniversary of the day the Vietnamese invaded the country in 1979. *FUNCINPEC* members were dismayed that their prime minister, Prince Norodom Ranariddh, did not take a stronger stand against Hun Sen and the *PPC*. With elections approaching in 1998, observers fear that the situation will continue to deteriorate.

In January 1996, the government mounted a major operation against Khmer Rouge bases along the Thai border. It is unlikely that this effort will be any more successful than previous attempts.

Foreign Relations: Throughout its history, Cambodia has been in the unfortunate position of being caught between contending forces beyond its borders. In the precolonial era both Thai and Vietnamese empires occupied parts of Cambodia. The country was also caught between the United States and the Vietnamese during the Vietnam war. The North Vietnamese used overland routes through Cambodia to transport war materials to the south to carry out the war against the South Vietnamese and their U.S. allies. And, the U.S. used the North Vietnamese supply lines through Cambodia for target practice. Prince Sihanouk, could neither prevent the North Vietnamese from using his territory, nor satisfy the United States that his policies were not pro North Vietnamese. During the Vietnamese occupation which was backed by the Soviet Union, Cambodia was a pawn between the Vietnamese and their ally on the one hand, the Chinese, who backed the Khmer Rouge, and the United States which recognized the Khmer Rouge for a time as the legitimate authority over the country. With a new government in place the country's leaders must sort out with both the Thais and Vietnamese possible territorial boundary alterations which may have taken place in recent years. Maritime boundaries in the gulf of Thailand may also cause difficulties in Phnom Penh's foreign relations. International drug trafficking through Cambodia is also a serious and growing problem.

Relations with Bangkok showed some positive signs in 1994, although allegations continued that Bangkok was still aiding the Khmer Rouge. The Phnom Penh government was given access to Khmer Rouge assets in Thailand and there was increased cooperation along the Thai–Cambodian border. In August 1994, high ranking Thai national security and foreign policy officials indicated to the author that it was not official policy to aid the Khmer Rouge. It should be recognized, however, that Thailand has legitimate national security concerns over the future of Cambodia and therefore Bangkok is likely to press its interests with those in power in Phnom Penh.

The most important event for Cambodian foreign relations in 1995, was the securing of "observer status" with the Association of Southeast Asian Nations (ASEAN) in midyear. Malaysia and Singapore, both ASEAN members, are important investors in Cambodia. It can be expected that ASEAN will do what it can to help Cambodia prepare for eventual full membership in the seven–member organization. This will greatly benefit Cambodia.

Problems continued with Hanoi over the fate of a group of several hundred Vietnamese on the Cambodian side of the border. Vietnam wanted the people repatriated. However, Phnom Penh did not wish to appear "soft on Vietnam" in the eyes of the Khmer Rouge. Relations with Thailand improved with the signing of several border security agreements. Bangkok also appeared to be controlling cross–border activities of the Khmer Rouge.

The president of Laos, Nouhak Phoumsavan, visited Cambodia and invited King Sihanouk to visit Vientiane at the end of the year. The two countries are cooperating on the development of transport and telecommunications along the Mekong River.

Culture: The art and culture of the Khmer Empire, based largely on its Indian, Hindu and Sri Lankan Buddhist origins, were an elaborate and comparatively highly developed combination to which distinctly local elements were added during the centuries which have passed. The surviving specimens of the Empire are mainly of stone and bronze which display highly stylistic and ornate techniques. The modern Cambodians, prior to devastating conflict and the years of Pol Pot, were conscious and proud of the fact that they are heirs of the once–mighty Khmer Empire. The culture and livelihood of the peasants have remained relatively unchanged until recently; the French made no major effort to modernize them.

A unique mixture of Buddhism and Hinduism has persisted until the past few years; the Buddhism of the *Hinayana* sect, which spread from the island of Sri Lanka (Ceylon), predominated in religious life. The Khmer (Cambodian) language was spoken prior to the arrival of Indian influence and is now written in a script derived from India. Among the few remaining educated, French is still spoken.

Economy: A major challenge for the new government is to establish a national economy. Two decades of conflict and revolution have destroyed much of the country's infrastructure. The presence of UNTAC caused distortion in the economy. In 1993, prices for housing went out of control. Some government offi-

cials actually sold state property. The local currency, the riel, lost almost 50% of its value against the U.S. dollar. The price of rice more than quadrupled. At one point UNTAC imported rice to feed the poor.

Cambodia continues to have severe problems with deforestation although raw log exports were banned in 1992. Both Thai and Japanese entrepreneurs were still operating in 1993. Additional contracts were signed in 1995, in spite of the ban.

Cambodia's national budget was approximately $330 million for 1995. About half of the country's operating budget comes from foreign aid. And, as might be expected, the military commands about 20% of the entire budget.

The country continued to receive substantial amounts of aid and loans from individual donor countries, the International Monetary Fund (IMF), World Bank, and the Asian Development Bank (ADB) in spite of the deteriorating political conditions. One bright spot for the Cambodian economy in 1995 was the jump in foreign investment to about $2.5 billion which included several major hotel chains. Other growing enterprises in-

cluded smuggling and money laundering which will not be internationally tolerated indefinitely.

The Future: Cambodia's economy is being kept afloat by foreign donors who apparently believe that throwing cash at Phnom Penh is acceptable as long as the government bows to private enterprise. However, the government is in danger of coming apart at the seams even though the Khmer Rouge is in retreat and is losing support. Cambodia is rapidly earning a reputation as Asia's newest "narco–state." In early 1996, Washington placed Cambodia on its "watch list" of trafficker states. Ambassador Charles Twining has charged that the country's richest businessman is a major drug trafficker who also happens to be underwriting the government.

The odds for a peaceful transition to a democratic government are nil. The government, *in its present form*, will be lucky if it lasts until the 1998 national elections. In fact, Cambodia will be lucky if elections are held at all. Whoever holds power in 1998, will be in no mood to listen to the will of the people.

A young Buddhist monk

The People's Republic of China

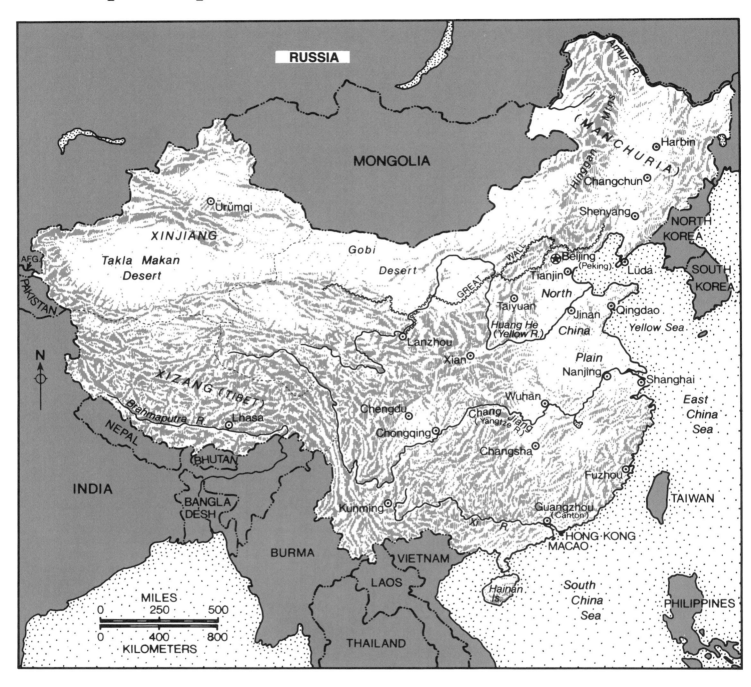

Area: Approximately 3.7 million square miles, including Inner Mongolia and Tibet, as large as the 50 United States plus another Alaska.

Population: 1.17 billion (estimated).

Capital City: Beijing (Peking), Pop. 9.9 million, estimated. Pronounced Bay–jing.

Climate: Dry, cold with bitter winters in the mountainous West and North, temperate in the East, subtropical with rainy monsoons in the South.

Neighboring Countries: Russia (North-west, North, Northeast); Mongolian People's Republic (North); Korea (Northeast); Taiwan (Southeast); Vietnam, Laos, Burma, India, Nepal (South); Pakistan and Afghanistan (Southwest).

Official Language: Chinese (Mandarin, the dialect of the majority, spoken in Central and Northern China).

Other Principal Tongues: South and West Chinese dialects, including Cantonese, Hakka, Fukienese and Wu, and the Tibetan language. Tribesmen of re-mote Xinjiang, Inner Mongolia and Manchuria have their own languages and dialects.

Ethnic Background: Chinese, sometimes referred to as *Han* (about 95%). Relatively small minorities of Mongol, Turkic, Tibetan, Thai and of other ancestry live in the remote regions of the interior.

Principal Religions: Confucianism, Taoism, Buddhism, Islam and Christianity, all of which have been severely discriminated against by the communist

The Republic of China (Taiwan)

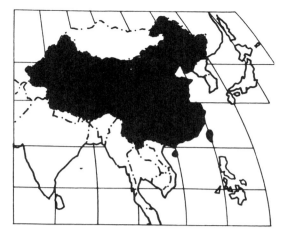

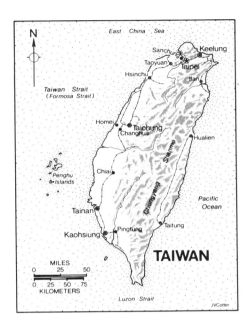

Political Status

The Government of the People's Republic of China (in Beijing, on the mainland) and the Government of the Republic of China (in Taipei, on Taiwan) agree that Taiwan is part of China; the basic disagreement is over which of the two is the legitimate government of the whole of China. Most foreign governments, including the United States (since 1979) recognize the PRC, without necessarily endorsing its claim to Taiwan. The United States regards Taiwan as part of China but not as part of the PRC; in other words, it leaves it to the two rival governments to decide, eventually and jointly by peaceful means, on the permanent relationship between Taiwan and the mainland, and to help ensure that the outcome is peaceful, it sends arms to Taiwan. Only a few foreign governments, including the Republic of Korea (South Korea) and Saudi Arabia, formally recognize the ROC on Taiwan. No government has diplomatic relations with both the PRC and the ROC because neither of them will tolerate "cross–recognition." Beijing has repeatedly offered Taiwan "autonomy" as part of the PRC, but no one on Taiwan has shown any observable interest in this proposal.

---

government and now have much less importance in public life than prior to 1949.

Main Exports: (to Hong Kong, Japan, U.S., West Germany, Australia) manufactured goods, agricultural products, oil and minerals. Mineral resources have only been partially explored, but are known to be substantial.

Main Imports: (from Japan, U.S., Hong Kong) grain, chemical fertilizer, steel, machinery, equipment.

Currency: *Renminbi* (people's currency) expressed in units called Yuan.

Former Colonial Status: None

National Day: October 1, anniversary of the founding of the *People's Republic* in 1949.

Chief of State: Jiang Zemin, President (since March 1993).

Head of Goverment: Li Peng, Premier (since April 1988). Pronounced Lee Pung.

General Secretary, Communist Party: Jiang Zemin (since June 1989).

Dominant Political Figure: Deng Xiaoping. Pronounced Dung She–*ow*–ping.

National Flag: Red, with one large and four small five–pointed stars at upper left.

Per Capita Income: U.S. $400.

Taiwan

Area: 13,885 square miles.

Population: 20.5 million (estimated).

Capital City: Taipei (Pop. 2.8 million, estimated).

Climate: Subtropical and humid in the lowlands, with an eleven–month growing season; in the higher elevations of the central mountains the temperatures are cooler.

Neighboring Countries: The Republic of China has been on the island of Taiwan, sometimes called Formosa, located 100 miles from the southeast China mainland, since 1949. It is about 300 miles north of the Philippine island of Luzon.

Official Language: Chinese (Mandarin, which is spoken in Central and North China).

Other Principal Tongues: Amoy, a Chinese dialect, is spoken by the majority of the population, known as Taiwanese, or Formosans. Tribal aborigines in the mountains speak a number of tongues related to Malay.

Ethnic Background: Chinese, sometimes referred to as *Han.* The highlands are occupied by a small group of Malayo–

Polynesian ancestry who resemble the people of Indonesia.

Principal Religions: Confucianism, Taoism, Buddhism. These three, which migrated with the earliest Chinese from the mainland, have not been and are not clearly defined, but tend to blend together.

Main Exports: (to the U.S., Japan, Hong Kong); textiles, clothing, electrical and electronic equipment, processed foods.

Main Imports: (from U.S., Japan, Kuwait); industrial equipment, automobiles, oil.

Currency: New Taiwan Dollar.

Former Colonial Status: Taiwan was a Japanese dependency from 1895 to 1945.

National Day: October 10, anniversary of the Chinese Revolution of 1911.

Chief of State: Lee Teng–hui, President (1988); pronounced Lee Dung Hwei.

National Flag: A red field with a blue rectangle in the upper left containing a 12–pointed white star.

Per Capita Income: U.S. $10,200.

Note: At the beginning of 1979, China (not Taiwan) officially adopted an already existing system, known as *pinyin*, for spelling Chinese words and names in the Latin alphabet. For example, in this book, you will find the capital of the People's Republic of China referred to as Peking (most frequently used by the news media), or the new form, Beijing. Both are correct.

Occupying a land area larger than that of the 50 United States, China stretches for a distance of 3,400 miles from its northeastern region adjacent to remote Soviet Siberia to the mountainous regions of Tibet bordering on Nepal and India. In terms of temperature, altitude and roughness of terrain, fertility of the soil and rainfall, there are two basically distinct regions. The invisible line which divides the two starts in the distant north at the Amur River and runs southward through the crest of the Great Khingan Mountains. It follows the contours of the Huang He, or Yellow River, turning northwest and then west to accommodate that part of the river that arches toward Mongolia. Turning again southward, it searches out the upper part of the river, passing through the region around Lanzhou and Chengdu and finally becomes obscure in the hilly southern area of Kumming near the Vietnamese border.

To the south and east of this demarcation "line" lies China proper; to the north and west the area is referred to as "outer" China. The land is relatively fertile south and east of this "line," and in the eastern region of Central "inner" China there are few hills which break the monotony of the level land. In the south, the land is also fertile, but is more hilly.

In the West, on the left hand side of the rough demarcation line, the land is a combination of closely crowded mountains with rough surfaces possessing little greenery even in the warmer regions of the lower altitudes. The towering peaks are occasionally interrupted by expanses of flat territory which is also desolate and dry, being surrounded by a natural barrier that withstands the invasion of rain clouds. The mountains in the North on the edge of the "line" give way to the Gobi Desert, filled with shifting earth, ugly rock formations and harsh extremes in temperature, all of which combine to exclude more than occasional visits of man and beast. The mountains envelop this desert which extends from Manchuria into southern Mongolia.

These areas of outer China are largely unmapped by Western standards. The thinly scattered people of Tibet, Xinjiang and Manchuria have traditionally relied on herds of animals as their principal resource, although great treasures of mineral wealth probably lie buried below

From the surging waters of the Huang He (Yellow) River . . .

AP/World Wide Photos

38

. . . to the parched wastes of the Gobi Desert

AP/World Wide Photos

the surface of the earth. A short growing season provides the small amount of greenery available. The air is dry in both summer and winter, blowing out of Asiatic Russia (Siberia). The great distance the wind has traveled prior to its arrival in China has taken almost all moisture from the air. The absence of bodies of water in the endless expanses also make the dry winds cold—bitterly so, almost beyond belief, in the winter.

In the spring enough warmth arrives to melt the snow in the lower altitudes of the mountains. This is sufficient to support limited agriculture at the lower edges of the mountains bordering the Gobi Desert of western Manchuria and Mongolia in the area between the mountains and the Taklamakan Desert in Xinjiang and the valleys of Tibet, but only during the brief summer season.

To the south and east of the "line" the land changes into temperate farmland; it is relatively flat and somewhat drier in parts of northern China, notably in the North China Plain. The hillier and more mountainous areas found in southern China have more moisture and warmer temperatures, producing thick growths of forest on the land not under cultivation. The three main rivers, the Huang He (Yellow), the Yangzi and the Xijiang (West River) have their origins deep within the remote territory west of the mountains, but flow through the more level eastern regions in a sluggish manner. Refreshed by the cool water of melting snow, they are quickly swelled in the spring by rains brought by the southeastern monsoon, and overflow their banks, spreading rich silt over the surrounding land. Flood control has been considerably improved in recent years, however. They also are a traditional source of communi-

cation and transportation in the region, but this value is being replaced by railroads.

The lower valley of the Huang He is temperate and is the area in which the modern Chinese civilization was born. The river itself is unpredictable. It left its old course south of the Shandong peninsula in which it had flowed for more than 800 years, and assumed its present course north of the peninsula in 1853, a shift of more than 500 miles. The immense quantities of silt it carries in its waters gave it the name "Yellow River" and also have built up a river bed over the years which is higher than the surrounding land. When it enters flood stage, the results have been catastrophic.

The growing season increases in the central and eastern region of China which is drained by the Yangzi (Yangtse) River; it becomes almost continuous throughout the year in the southeastern area through which the Xijiang (Sikiang) River flows. If the rainfall in these regions was uniform from year to year, both would produce great quantities of food to feed the millions of Chinese. The variations in rain, however, cause periodic loss of crops by either drought or flood. During a prolonged drought, even the violent summer rains are not of much help, since they run quickly into the rivers and flow into the sea rather than watering the land, which then dries out, unless there is further, preferably steady, rainfall.

The island of Taiwan, also known as Formosa, has an elongated oval shape and its entire length is dominated by a chain of mountains rising with regularity to heights of 6,000 to 11,000 feet. These peaks lie close to the eastern side of the island and drop steeply at the coastline into the warm waters of the Pacific. The

western slopes descend gently to a fertile plain that occupies almost one–half of the island's surface. The climate varies from tropical to temperate, depending upon altitude. As is true on the Chinese mainland 100 miles across the Taiwan Strait, the summer winds bring abundant rain which supports intense agriculture. The smaller rivers do not cause the catastrophic floods of the three mighty rivers of continental China, so that bountiful harvests of a variety of produce, principally rice, are regularly gathered.

History: The origins of Chinese civilization are buried in the impenetrable mists of the Paleolithic and post–Paleolithic periods. Knowledge of these beginnings is inadequate since it is derived from the discovery of scattered tools and skeletal remains of the people who lived in China from the period of about 8000 B.C. to about 4000 B.C. It is probable that between 5000 and 3000 B.C. a small number of people of basically Mongol ancestry (members of the "yellow race") migrated from remote eastern Siberia into what is now northern China, where they mingled with people already in the area.

This combination experienced cultural changes and advances in the primitive tools they used to provide shelter and food which came from central Asia as the result of sporadic contacts with what is now considered the Middle East. These developments included such things as the idea that spoken language could be portrayed in a manner "heard" by the eye—in writing—as well as the techniques of making bronze, from which useful tools and art objects could be cast to kill and cultivate food as well as to satisfy the need for beauty. This combi-

The 1,400 mile long Great Wall of China

nation of people and ideas produced the earliest known ancestors of the modern Chinese between about 2000 and 1500 B.C.—a society which had become recognizably Chinese in language, appearance and culture.

By the period 1500–1000 B.C., the Chinese had begun to develop into a highly complex pattern. Advanced and very artistic techniques of casting bronze developed. The system of *ideographic* writing was refined and became the method of communicating and recording of ideas; it did not and it does not now have an alphabet, but consists of a collection of thousands of symbols, each of which represents a word. For many hundreds of years this system of writing was known only to scribes and intellectuals and has only recently become more widely known. The language is now undergoing fundamental, officially sponsored, changes in mainland China to permit the use of modern mechanisms such as the typewriter and, more important, computers.

The Early Dynasties

During this early period, the Chinese were ruled by kings of the Shang dynasty.

The Shang rulers were replaced by the Zhou (Chou) dynasty, which governed briefly from about 1100 to 800 B.C., when their power rapidly diminished. North China then disintegrated into a number of feudal states led by "princes" who occupied their time, and that of their subjects, in a variety of wars against each other. The use of iron tools in agriculture during this period produced a high yield from the earth, which, together with irrigation and (after 1,000 A.D.) the widespread cultivation of rice, permitted a correspondingly high rate of population growth. As the people pressed outward, they came into greater conflict with non–Chinese people who inhabited central China around the Yangzi River.

The stronger rulers subdued the weaker and smaller states, and the number of feudal princedoms became less, gradually falling under the control of two major states: Chin in the west central and northwestern part of China and Chu in the central Yangzi valley. By 221 B.C. the Chin ruler, who led a highly organized and militarily strong state, conquered his rivals, including the Chu, and established control over all of north and central China as well as part of the southern regions.

In the 5th and 4th centuries B.C. China

enjoyed a classical age comparable to that of Greece during the same period. Literature and the arts flourished, and the desire for knowledge and social order led to the creation and formalization of the two religions which originated in China: Confucianism and Taoism, a mystical and contemplative system of belief (see Historical Background). Both of these became a source of satisfaction for the learned Chinese as well as providing the element of legitimacy and the security arising out of obedience by the uneducated peasant majority

The Chin dynasty unified the empire in more ways than military conquest; the Great Wall of China was constructed laboriously over a period of years to ward off the periodic raids by the nomadic Mongol warriors from the North; roads and other public works were built and the system of writing and weights were standardized. Actually the rule of the Chin was extremely oppressive and produced much discontent among the Chinese people, and it was soon overthrown by a new dynasty that took the name *Han*.

These rulers governed for almost 400 years before and after the beginning of the Christian era. The people of China today are sometimes referred to as *Han* to differentiate them from the minorities that live in the outer part of what is modern China. In spite of a brief collapse at the halfway point of their reign, the Han succeeded in making China into an empire of power, wealth and cultural brilliance comparable to the other great civilization of the same period, the Roman Empire. Its boundaries were pushed well into central Asia, where local leaders were awed by the brilliance of Chinese advances in learning and military prowess. Even if not directly supervised by the Chinese, rulers of the outlying states of Asia were often willing to acknowledge themselves tributary and vassal states of the mighty empire.

When the Han dynasty collapsed, the following four centuries were marked by frequent nomadic invasions from the North which resulted in a series of states in northern China ruled by non–Chinese. A Chinese, or *Han* state did survive in the South, however, under a series of weak dynasties. *Mahayana* Buddhism, sometimes referred to as northern Buddhism (see Historical Background) spread quickly following its arrival from northern India by way of Central Asia at the beginning of the Christian era.

The Middle Dynasties

China was reunited by the Sui and Tang dynasties after 581, and under an energetic succession of emperors it once more extended the area of its power far into Central Asia. For the first time in world history, a written examination was developed for civil servants, appointment of whom on the basis of ability, rather than family ties, had begun under the Han dynasty. The emperors of the Tang dynasty were Confucian, and the hierarchy of officials and local gentry shared their belief; the believers in Buddhism were occasionally persecuted because of their religion, leading to a decline in its influence.

There was a short period of disunity following the decline and fall of the Tang dynasty in the 10th century A.D. The brilliant cultural advances of the ensuing three–century period centered chiefly on the art of painting and the discipline of philosophy. Under the influence of Buddhist theology, official Confucianism was modified by about 1200 into Neo–Confucianism, which concerned itself more with abstract philosophy than had the original form of this belief. The country was ruled by emperors of the Song (Sung) dynasty and was continually threatened by a succession of powerful non–Chinese states that emerged along the northern border; the end of this era came with defeat by the most powerful northern force, the Mongols, who were able to succeed in their conquest only after a long and bitter campaign. The

Song had withstood the Mongols longer than any of the other civilizations of the world into which the conquerors intruded, but ultimately became a part of a vast empire stretching from the Pacific to what is now the Middle East.

The Mongols ruled China for a century, taking the name Yuan dynasty. Already disliked by the Chinese in a number of ways, the Mongols had but slight respect for Confucianism and the civil service examinations and systems, factors which led to even greater opposition by the Chinese, particularly the upper classes. The rulers were actually religiously tolerant, and permitted small communities of Franciscan missionaries to introduce Christianity into several parts of coastal China.

Both the Mongols and Christianity were expelled from China in 1368 in a great upheaval with strong anti–foreign tendencies. The new dynasty which came to power, the Ming (1368–1644), at first ruled firmly and energetically, creating a powerful empire, but a period of decline began about 1500. Japanese pirates began to increase their activities along the coast. Internal weakness became an increasing problem which was transformed into an even greater liability by the rise in power of the Manchu rulers to the north. In 1644, a combination of domestic rebellion and Manchu might was sufficient to overthrow the Ming dynasty; within a few decades, the Manchus had subdued all of China.

The Manchus

The new rulers took the name Qing (Ching) dynasty, but are more commonly referred to in the West as the Manchus. Although Chinese culture was by this time largely static to a degree that made basic changes all but impossible, under the Manchus the country was once again united and became rapidly powerful. In an effort to consolidate their positions, the Manchus ruled through existing Chinese institutions, including the very formal civil service with its Confucian orientation; for this reason, and others, they became accepted rapidly by their Chinese subjects. After an initial period of wise and successful rule, the Manchus indulged themselves in a period of energetic, but arbitrary and costly warfare in the late 18th century which undermined the power of the dynasty and ultimately caused the beginning of its decline.

Europeans, principally British, started to seek Chinese silk and tea in the 18th century, but had little to offer in return at first that interested the Chinese and consequently their efforts presented few problems to the Manchus. In the late 18th and early 19th centuries, two developments occurred which led to dramatic changes in China's relations with the

Silk tapestry   B. R. Graham

western powers. The British discovered that opium, grown in their possessions in India, could be sold at a handsome profit in China; at the same time, Britain underwent its Industrial Revolution, making it possible to manufacture cheap cotton textiles and other goods in much greater quantities than before. The Manchus made an unsuccessful effort to prevent the importation of opium—the failure of their effort was caused by widespread smuggling when legal means of marketing the narcotic were closed.

The Industrial Revolution, particularly in Britain, not only created economic wealth, but also furnished a base for a greater military power. Determined to promote the sale of huge quantities of textiles and other products, and also to "legalize" the sale of opium in China, the British fought a series of small wars with the Manchus beginning with the Opium War of 1839–42. Additional goals were to exempt foreigners from the cruel criminal laws of China, abhorred by European Christians, and to open de-

41

pendable diplomatic relations. The British achieved their purposes. The other major powers, including the United States, also profited from the efforts of Great Britain, by means of the "most favored nation" clause in their commercial agreements with China. Under this principle of international trade, all nations were granted the same advantages which China had accorded to the "most favored nation," Britain. At the insistence of various Christian mission organizations from a number of countries, the Manchus were forced to permit the re–entry of Christian teachings into China.

The "Diplomacy of Imperialism"

Under a series of treaties which are termed "unequal treaties" by the Chinese and were signed under pressure in the last half of the 19th century, China lost a large part of its sovereignty. Its best ports were carved into foreign "concessions" which were administered by foreign consulates and were places where non–Chinese could live and carry on business with a minimum of interference from Chinese officials. At the end of the century, near the close of this period, since termed one of "diplomacy of imperialism," much of China was carved up into foreign "spheres of influence" by virtue of some further "unequal treaties" forced upon the Manchus. In each of these, a particular western power (with the exception of the United States) was granted sweeping and exclusive economic rights in its area, coupled with a great degree of political influence.

Russian domination was established in Manchuria, but the fertile southern portion of that region went to the Japanese in 1905 after their victory in the Russo–Japanese War. The Germans established themselves in the province of Shandong (Shantung); the British became the major power in the Yangzi valley region; the Japanese controlled Fujian (Fukien) Province and the French asserted their dominance over Southwest China. Outside what had been China, the states which had paid tribute to the Manchu emperors also became colonies or spheres of influence of Britain, France, Russia and Japan. Russian influence became paramount in Outer Mongolia, now known as the Mongolian People's Republic, and penetrated into Xinjiang (Sinkiang) in the 1930's. The British became a powerful influence in Tibet and remained so until 1947.

These losses of territory and authority were dramatic demonstrations of China's basic backwardness and weakness by the standards of western powers and were an insult to the sense of national pride of the Chinese. The economy of the coastal regions, traditionally more wealthy than the interior areas, was almost totally dominated by foreign trade and investment, the introduction of manufactured goods and new industrial techniques coupled with economic organization along European lines. The awkward process of modernization was thus started, but brought China the pains that usually accompany this process. Missionaries and Chinese who studied western culture and ideas spread them widely, undermining the basic confidence of a growing number of people in the truth and wisdom of many aspects of traditional Chinese culture. Most important, the values of Confucianism were substantially weakened. These developments created somewhat of a cultural vacuum, into which a variety of foreign influences flowed.

Millions of Chinese rose in a devastating revolt against the Manchus in the mid–19th century under the leadership of a religious figure in Guangxi Province who incorporated some Protestant Christian elements in his teachings and founded the short–lived Taiping Kingdom. This rebellion was quelled largely due to the loyalty to the Manchus of able Chinese officials devoted to the traditions of Confucianism. The revolt ultimately resulted in reforms and some modernization by the reigning dynasty.

Following the death of the Emperor in 1861, his widow, referred to as the Empress Dowager, was co–regent during the reign of her son and wielded considerable influence during that period. He died without heirs, and the throne passed to her nephew, but this remarkable woman, Cixi (Tsu–hsi) wielded actual power until her death. Ruthless, able and extremely conservative, she embodied the traditions cherished by the Manchu court officials who clung to the security of the past. She was able to imprison her nephew–Emperor when threatened by his attempt in 1898 to modernize the government and the country.

At the popular level, there were several anti–foreign and anti–Christian outbreaks of violence in the years following 1870. Both sentiments joined to provide discontent resulting in the 1900 Boxer Rebellion, which was encouraged by influential members of the Manchu court. A joint military expedition, in which the U.S. took part, was sent in by the western powers and soon crushed the Boxer Rebellion. American troops actually entered Beijing on August 14, 1900, a fact which still lurks in the mind of many Chinese. The Empress Dowager, shaken by defeat, granted her reluctant assent to certain innovations in the imperial government, but her life, and the effective authority of the Manchu Dynasty, ended in 1908.

During the last part of the 19th century, as the power of the Manchus continued to decline, there came into the political life of China a slowly growing number of people who knew something of the political ideas of the West. Although they did not attain high official status, they became aware of the need for China to adopt western political and technical ideas in order to preserve the identity of China as a state in the world, and in order to perpetuate those elements of the Chinese culture that could be salvaged. These early reformers were not unified; their disunity prevented them from achieving any real influence on the Manchu court until it was too late. Because of their inability to obtain positions of leadership within the official government, reform leadership passed to the more radical elements in this group.

Sun Yat–Sen

The most important of the radicals was Sun Yat–sen, who dedicated himself to the overthrow of the Manchus and to the modernization of China along semi–western lines. Although he was able to attract a relatively large following, Sun was not really a major intellect and was almost totally lacking in political skills. When the Empress Dowager died in 1908, the Manchu court installed the "last emperor," a two–year–old boy. He reigned until 1912 through regents appointed by the court; he was later to become "Emperor" of Manchukuo (Manchuria) as a Japanese puppet. When revolution unseated the Manchu court in 1912, Sun Yat–sen became Provisional President of the new Republic of China. His rule was brief—he resigned in a few months in favor of a former Manchu official. In the following years he devoted himself to the forming of a new political party, the *Kuomintang (National People's Party)* and drawing up plans and a political theory for the modernization of China.

The *Kuomintang* broke with the new government in 1913, but the party was easily defeated because it had almost no real power. Although the current dictator tried to proclaim himself emperor of a new dynasty, he died in 1916 without achieving his ambition.

Disintegration

Following his death, China literally disintegrated into a score of petty states run by individual military governors, usually referred to as "warlords." They had little governing ability and their rule was almost uniformly oppressive. The legal government of China in Peking continued to be recognized diplomatically by the foreign powers. In reality this "government" was an ever–shifting combination of one or more warlords,

大清國當今慈禧端佑康頤昭豫莊誠壽恭欽獻崇熙聖母皇太后

The Empress Dowager Cixi

sometimes under the influence of one or more foreign nations, possessed of no power beyond the personal power of its leader or leaders. Communications were extremely poor and there was a thin scattering of modern arms in the outlying regions, making it almost impossible to achieve any genuine national unity. Sun Yat–sen set up headquarters in southern Guangdong Province and tried in various ways, without success, to overthrow the shadow government at Peking and to unite the country under the *Kuomintang.*

In addition to the trend toward economic modernization in the cities and coastal regions during the 1920's, there was a marked growth of nationalism among the Chinese, who sought an end to foreign influence in their country and an identity in the world community. The government was in the hands of a group under Japanese influence in 1919 to the extent that it was willing to sign the Treaty of Versailles, turning over what had been German territory and interests in China to Japan, rather than recognize Chinese authority. An outburst of patriotism, led by students, which became known as the May Fourth Movement, prevented the actual signing of the treaty. The people of China, particularly the youth, desired the end of foreign influence and internal disunity and came to believe that these goals could only be achieved through a major political and social revolution. Some chose the *Kuomintang,* and a smaller number joined an infant communist movement.

The *Chinese Communist Party* was founded in 1921 by young, leftist, nationalist Chinese, some whom were students. The movement quickly came under the control of the Third International, more familiarly known as the *Comintern* led by Russia under its energetic revolutionary leader, Lenin. The picture became even more complicated when the *Comintern* decided to enter into an alliance with Sun Yat–sen's *Kuomintang* and ordered the local Chinese communists to do the same. This unstable union was produced by a common, overwhelming desire to expel western and Japanese influence from China and to eliminate the power of the warlords.

To accomplish these aims, the *Comintern* reorganized and greatly strengthened the *Kuomintang* through money and military aid, but it also hoped that communists could gradually acquire control over it by infiltrating top positions, and by putting pressure on the party through communist–dominated labor and peasant unions. The plan made considerable progress at first while the party was led by the politically inexperienced Sun Yat–sen, but after his death in 1925 he was succeeded by General Chiang Kai–shek, who became alarmed at the threat

of Soviet domination of China and the more immediate threat of an ill–defined "social revolution." He determined to head off these threats by military force, which he began to do in 1926 and 1927, by breaking with the *Comintern,* the Chinese communists and the left wing of his own party.

He was able to seize Peking, the nominal capital of China, in 1928, and then proclaimed the new Republic of China at Nanking under the control of the *Kuomintang.* Actually his regime controlled only the eastern provinces of China and was faced with tremendous problems: a large army that had to be fed and clothed, floods, famine, political apathy and backwardness and continual pressure from the Japanese. They seized Manchuria in 1931–32; the territory was renamed *Manchukuo* and the "last emperor" of the Manchu Dynasty, Manchu pretender to the throne, youthful Henry Pu–Yi, took the throne as Emperor. This interesting character had been tutored in the western classics after the ouster of the Manchus by a Britisher, who suggested that he take an English name. He was proclaimed emperor in 1934; Japan began an intensive program of industrialization of Manchukuo.

The communists had certainly lost a battle, but were not defeated. Areas of communist control began to emerge in Central and South China by 1930. Chiang Kai–shek, beset with all of these problems, made probably the poorest choice of remedies: increasingly conservative and oppressive measures that ultimately lost him the support of increasing num-

bers of educated Chinese. It is possible, on the other hand, that he would not have been overthrown by the communists but for the actions of the Japanese.

In the enclaves controlled by the communists, a leader gradually emerged in the late 1920's and early 1930's: Mao Zedong (Mao Tse–tung). The pathway to success was difficult—in 1934 the communists were forced by overwhelming *Kuomintang* military pressures to evacuate their base areas in Central and South China. After a long dramatic trek (the Long March), they took refuge in the more remote and desolate regions of Northwest China.

Japanese forces invaded eastern China in 1937; the weakened condition of the communist movement in China prompted the Soviet dictator Stalin to urge the communists to enter into another alliance with the *Kuomintang* in order to resist the invaders. Mao probably saw an opportunity not only to resist the Japanese, but to overthrow the *Kuomintang* after it had been weakened by the enemy, and made the agreement which Stalin and Chinese opinion were demanding. The expansion of the communists from that time forth was actually at the expense not only of the Japanese, but also of the *Kuomintang,* referred to at that time as *Nationalists.* The Japanese conquered the prosperous coastal regions of China, depriving the *Kuomintang* of its major economic and political bases. Driven into the hills and mountains of southwest China, it became even more conservative and subject to corruption than before.

The newly installed *Orchid Emperor of Manchukuo* **reviews Japanese troops at Dairen in 1934**

Japanese troops entering Shanghai, 1937

Inflation and weariness sapped the strength of the *Kuomintang*, enabling the Japanese to inflict some further heavy defeats on it as late in World War II as 1944. In the areas which they controlled, the Japanese were unable to prevent the communists, more skilled in the art of guerrilla warfare than the Nationalists, from infiltrating and setting up base areas within territory that was supposed to be Japanese. Partly in retaliation for this resistance, the Japanese committed terrible atrocities against the Chinese people in the occupied areas, driving many into sympathy with the communists and thus assisting them to seize political control on an anti–Japanese, more than an anti–*Kuomintang*, platform.

Increasing numbers of Japanese soldiers were withdrawn from China starting in 1943 because of the defeats that were being suffered in the Pacific war. This permitted the communists to expand rapidly, so that by the end of the war they controlled nineteen base areas, some of which were quite large, in various parts of China, principally in the North and Northwest.

The elimination of Japanese troops from China at the end of the war brought about a frantic flurry of political and military activity by both the *Kuomintang* and the communists. The U.S. was the major political power in the Pacific area at this time, and it attempted to bring about some sort of settlement between the two so that there could be an end to civil strife. The talks, conducted under the encouragement of U.S. General George C. Marshall, special envoy of President Truman, completely broke down in 1946 because neither side had any real desire for an agreement, but preferred a trial of armed strength.

Nationalist–Communist Conflict

The *Kuomintang* was plagued by the basic inability of Chiang and his colleagues to deal with China's very serious problems: inflation, corruption and loss of political unity. The military leadership employed very poor tactics against the communists, so that the *Kuomintang* lost almost all the major battles at the same time the "home" front was deteriorating to the point of collapse. By the end of 1949 the *Kuomintang* was driven to the island of Taiwan. The Chinese communists under Mao then controlled all of mainland China except for Tibet. They proclaimed the People's Republic of China and changed the name of their capital to Peking from Peiping, as it had been called by the Nationalists.

Communist troops invaded Tibet in 1950–51; although there was some initial resistance, the "roof of the world" was brought under Chinese control; the Dalai Lama, spiritual leader of the Buddhists, who also was vested with rather wide governing powers, soon was a figurehead. He fled Tibet in 1959 after some unsuccessful uprisings against the Chinese in the eastern part of the region; the people continue to be deprived of a leader to whom they traditionally ascribe divine powers and character.

The "People's Liberation Army" brought the new regime to power, and it remained important as a defense against possible enemies, both internal and external. The *Chinese Communist Party* was the real instrument behind Mao and his regime; its members held and now hold all important public offices and it is the only political force since the Manchus that has demonstrated itself able to hold China together. Mao Zedong played an apparently overpowering role, and with his colleagues' consent, he made himself into a father–figure dictator whom all Chinese, especially the youth, were taught to worship to a degree that would have created envy in the hearts of previous emperors.

Mao, Party and Army

The combination of Mao, party and army held together quite successfully until about 1965 and achieved a number of results which were impressive, considering the backwardness of the country and the handicaps imposed by the adoption of the highly centralized Soviet system of economic planning and administration. The people doubtless regarded the regime as the only hope of escape from the long nightmare of civil and foreign war, general chaos and abject poverty, and therefore gave it overwhelming support. The communists restored the defunct economy and launched an impressive program of heavy industrialization with Soviet technical assistance and equipment. The small plots of farmland were collectivized into larger acreages patterned after the farms of the Soviet Union, not only to promote progress toward "socialism" but to give the government greater control over the people and boost output of rural areas. In short, China progressed from rampant disorganization toward a centralized, autocratic and rationally (with some exceptions) administered state. Traditional Chinese culture and society were forcefully changed in directions desired by the communists, with

His Holiness The Dalai Lama of Tibet

widespread, fundamental and seemingly impossible effects.

In foreign relations, the Chinese regime initially established a close alliance with the Soviet Union, then led by the dictatorial and aging Stalin; it also entered into diplomatic relations with all communist countries and with a number of neutral and western nations. The United States, which had become protector of the nationalists on Taiwan, refused to recognize Mao's government, which in

turn had shown little interest in diplomatic relations with the U.S. With only slight success, the Chinese communists initially tried to promote revolutions elsewhere in Asia, but retreated from this policy somewhat in the mid–1950's in order to be in a better position to cultivate the friendship of the neutral Asian nations.

The Korean War

When combined nominally U.N. (principally U.S. and South Korean) forces threatened a rout of the North Koreans in October 1950, the Chinese, with the support of the Soviets, committed massive numbers of "volunteers" to come to the aid of the besieged North Koreans. Nevertheless, American–South Korean successes continued until General MacArthur was relieved by President Truman after he threatened a second invasion of North Korea and perhaps an attack on China. This indicated to the Chinese hierarchy that the U.S. was dangerous if directly challenged, and more important, that the Soviet leadership was not willing to risk its own destruction on China's behalf in the event of an all–out Chinese–United States clash.

Russia's aged Stalin died in 1953 and within four months an armistice was signed in a small Korean village in July 1953. Chinese forces withdrew from the peninsula in 1958; U.S. forces remained in South Korea.

Mao Zedong (Mao Tse-tung) in 1945

Chiang Kai-shek as President of the Republic of China (on the island of Taiwan) in 1950

New Directions

In the mid–1950's policy differences and political tensions began to appear between the aging Mao and some of his colleagues who were more pragmatic than he. Clinging to the ideals of his revolutionary youth, Mao seemed to believe that a sort of continuous revolutionary process throughout China, conducted largely by the young people who had been indoctrinated in his "thought" and taught that to revere him, was absolutely necessary for progress. Some of his colleagues much preferred a more conventional and bureaucratic approach to political control and nation building rather than the more radical strategy of their leader.

In 1956, largely to strengthen his own political position, Mao launched a series of major policy changes in both the domestic and foreign areas, culminating in a huge movement called the "Great Leap Forward" in 1958. This resulted in herding the peasants by propaganda and other pressures into "people's communes," where they were worked to the point of near exhaustion. Crude and inefficient "backyard furnaces" were promoted to boost steel production, but actually were almost totally useless, since the small quantity of metal they produced was inferior and economically worthless. All of these programs were failures, and they seriously strained China's relations with the Soviet Union, then the only source of economic and military aid, to the point where the Soviet leader Khrushchev cut off all aid in 1960. Actually a clash between Mao and Nikita Khrushchev was probably inevitable—the former regarded the younger Khrushchev as an upstart and at the same time, Khrushchev, blessed with an overabundance of ego, considered Mao a fanatic and adventurer.

After 1958, growing Chinese political pressures on the Soviet Union, calculated to prove the correctness of Mao's brand of communism and the error of the Soviet "deviation," soon produced serious and fundamental tensions not only between the Soviets and the Chinese, but within the entire communist world. In the summer of 1958, Mao engaged in another unsuccessful gesture—the shelling of the islands of Quemoy and Matsu, controlled by the Nationalists, close to mainland China in the Taiwan strait. Whatever his original intentions had been, nothing more than an artillery and airpower duel occurred, notwithstanding the alarm of other nations because of the possibility of a Chinese–U.S. confrontation.

The result, after economic setbacks and failure to succeed in doing serious damage to the Nationalist–held offshore islands or to Taiwan, was that instead of being stronger, Mao was somewhat weaker. On the other hand, he was able to persuade his colleagues to rally around an anti–Soviet policy. The Soviet Union was accused of being as great if not a greater political enemy than the United States. The task of struggling against the supposed imperialistic designs of the U.S. was in effect assigned to other revolutionary movements in Asia, Africa and Latin America.

The revolutionary zeal of the Chinese, and their tendency to urge radical and nationalistic movements to greater tasks than were possible, with endless quantities of advice and of Mao's "thoughts," coupled with quantities of arms, did not produce the desired results. A number of moderate nationalist and socialist leaders of Asia and Africa became rapidly aware of the not yet serious threat, and took steps to expel Chinese agents. There were especially serious setbacks in Indonesia and in sub–Sahara Africa, which had seemed promising in the years 1963–1965.

After the fall in 1964 of Khrushchev, who had handled the revolutionary impatience of the Chinese rather clumsily, his more practical successors offered China a limited agreement, which was spurned by Mao. With this refusal, Mao worsened his relations with some of his critics at home and abroad, who wanted a less antagonistic attitude toward Russia and toward the United States, particularly in view of the possibility, however, remote, of a major war with the United States.

By the last half of 1965, the aging Mao, impatient and convinced that the time was at hand to silence, refute and overthrow his critics within the party and outside of China if possible, and also to put his stamp indelibly on the Chinese revolution for the indefinite future, manufactured a second great campaign: the "Great Proletarian Cultural Revolution." His first obstacle, the reluctant municipal boss of Peking, Peng Zhen, was overthrown by a combination of political pressures and military threats by mid–1966. Mao then proceeded to rely on the revolutionary young people, organized into "Red Guards" and enjoying the support of the army under the command of Mao's companion and emerging heir, Defense Minister Lin Biao. The Red Guards attacked and terrorized Mao's real and imaginary opponents in the universities, in the party structure and anywhere else they were thought to be found. In some cases, persons were declared to be anti–Mao whether or not they were, in order to provide a continuing series of targets at which the "Great Proletarian Cultural Revolution" could focus and fire.

However, early in 1967, it was necessary for Mao to urge the army to intervene in order to prevent chaos and yet to keep the Cultural Revolution moving. The army quickly discovered that these two tasks were incompatible and increasingly began to emphasize the restoration of order in place of the disorder created by the unruly Red Guards. In 1967, Mao was brought, willingly or unwillingly, to endorse a turn towards a more conservative line. After that time, the impact of the Cultural Revolution on everyday life lessened. During 1968 the army acquired more and more local power, and with Peking's consent, it forcibly suppressed the Red Guard movement.

The Vietnam War

China actively supported North Vietnam during the war in Vietnam (approximately 1965–1975), but in ways designed not to involve itself directly in hostilities with the United States. China sent some arms (mainly infantry weapons) to North Vietnam, cooperated to a degree in trans-shipping Soviet weapons by rail to it and sent railway engineer units to help keep the main Vietnamese railway lines open under American bombardment. After the American withdrawal from the war in 1973, China stepped up its flow of arms to Hanoi and in this way contributed significantly to the fall of South Vietnam in the spring of 1975.

By that time, however, Hanoi had already begun to show signs of abandoning its neutrality in the Sino–Soviet dispute, and was "tilting" toward Moscow. By 1977 it was involved in a border war with Cambodia, where the pro–Chinese rather than the pro–Vietnamese wing of the Khmer Rouge (the Cambodian communist movement) had come to power in 1975. When China began in 1978 to put pressure on Vietnam in support of Cambodia, Hanoi expelled several hundred thousand "boat people," many of them of Chinese ancestry, and moved still closer to Moscow. At the end of 1978, it invaded Cambodia and installed a puppet government in Phnom Penh. Accordingly, China invaded Vietnam briefly in February–March 1979 with the announced purpose of teaching Hanoi a lesson.

The lesson did not take, and Sino–Vietnamese relations have remained tense since that time. There is a military confrontation in the vicinity of the common border, as well as naval rivalry in the South China Sea. China (and the Soviets) pressured Vietnam into withdrawing from Cambodia. At the same time, it urged that Vietnamese ties with the Soviet Union be lessened. This, together with increasing Soviet economic stress since about 1985 and slowly improving Sino–Soviet relations, have led to a lessening of tensions between China and Vietnam.

A military crisis along the Sino–Soviet

border in early 1969 led rapidly to some remarkable shifts in Chinese policy. A moderate coalition within China, led by Premier Zhou Enlai (Chou En–lai) and some of the military (possibly with the reluctant cooperation of a by then semi–senile Mao) tried to restore a greater degree of domestic stability and more workable foreign relations. Zhou felt it advisable, after several months of Soviet threats, to enter into negotiations on the mutual border dispute and related matters, downgrading disputes concerning communist theory. By the end of 1970, it appeared that the negotiations had resulted in a deadlock, mainly because of Soviet unwillingness to reduce military pressures in the absence of a political agreement.

Defense Minister Lin Biao and some other top military leaders were purged in 1971, apparently at the initiative of Premier Zhou Enlai, who wanted to decrease the political influence of the armed forces and eliminate an arch opponent of better relations with the United States. The next year, Nationalist China was expelled from the United Nations and the People's Republic of China became the official representative of China at that organization.

An upsurge of political ferment reflected radical dissatisfaction with Zhou's policies starting in 1973. In spite of this, Zhou, a highly skilled and educated person, remained in power (or a power to be reckoned with) until his death, counterbalancing the influence of the waning Mao, who grew increasingly weak and inactive, but was still perceived as supporting, or at least protecting, the radicals. The moderates launched a campaign in early–1974 in the interest of stability to curb the power of the radicals. Zhou Enlai was effectively in charge, even though he retired to a hospital in mid–1974; he probably sought to conserve his energies, survive Mao and ensure that an early demise on his own part did not give radicals an opening to resume their initiatives.

Government and Leadership Changes

A new state (not party) constitution abolished the post of Chairman of the Republic (chief of state) in January 1975; it made a few other changes, none of them basic. It was adopted by the National People's Congress (China's version of a parliament) which met for the first time in ten years. This was one of several signs that political conditions were returning to normal after the swirl of the Cultural Revolution.

The death of Zhou Enlai in January 1976 deprived the world of one of its most astute statesmen and placed the future of the moderates in Peking in jeopardy. Vice Premier Deng Xiaoping, Zhou's main assistant since 1973, had badly antagonized the radicals and did not remain in office long; he was forced out in April 1976, presumably with Mao's approval. The new premier announced at that time, however, was not a radical, but a compromise choice, Hua Guofeng, whose record suggests a closer affinity with the moderates than the radicals. A major earthquake in July 1976 tightened the political ties between Hua and the army, which handled most of the relief work.

Frail and senile, Mao died in September 1976; his death removed the main shield of the leading radicals, including his widow, Jiang Qing (Chiang Ching); they were purged by Hua a month later. The so–called "gang of four" was accused of fomenting disturbances and riots in various provinces during 1976; even after their purge, propaganda against them continued unabated. Deng Xiaoping was "rehabilitated" and became the most powerful man in the country. The apparent trend toward stabilization of the new regime was indicated by the successful holding of a Party Congress in 1977 and a National People's Congress in 1978; both have been more or less annual events since then.

Shift to the West

Because of concern over the Soviet military buildup along the Chinese–Soviet border, China exhibited increased interest in improving its relations with the United States in the hope of having a diplomatic counter–weight. To the surprise of Americans, China extended an invitation to an American ping pong team to visit in 1971. This was quickly followed by a visit by Dr. Henry Kissinger in July 1971 and one by President Nixon in 1972. In its propaganda, however, China in some matters continued to be critical of U.S. policy, especially in East Asia. Further visits by American officials, including President Ford, occurred during the subsequent years.

Peking became seriously concerned over what it considered the inadequacy of United States efforts to cope with the Soviet Union's expansionism, both in East Asia and on a worldwide basis. On the other hand, Peking was pleased when it succeeded in reaching an agreement with the United States to "normalize" their relations in late 1978. At the same time, the United States terminated its formal diplomatic relations and its defense treaty with the *Republic of China* on Taiwan. Other important ties, however, remained intact and the U.S. continued to sell arms to Taiwan.

Deng's Period of Reform

During the 1980s Deng Xiaoping brought about significant changes, both in the leadership of the *Communist Party* and in the policies it subscribed to. First, he forced the retirement of Premier Hua Guofeng, replacing him with Zhao Ziyang. Hua lost the chairmanship of the *Communist Party* the following year to another Deng protege, Hu Yuobang. He then successfully went forward with the trial of the "gang of four," thus neutralizing radical opposition, some of which was within the army.

The purge of radicals continued in both the party and the bureaucracy during the

Mao Zedong in 1966

AP/World Wide Photos

48

early 1980s. In 1985, 64 members of the Central Committee "resigned" under pressure from Deng. Zhao Ziyang was named General Secretary of the party in 1987, replacing Hu Yuobang. He in turn was replaced by Jiang Zemin in 1989.

Deng was the driving force behind significant agricultural reform during the decade, which led to partial de–collectivization. In 1984, control over industry was eased, giving local managers more authority. Prices were set at the local instead of the national level (at least in theory), and food and housing subsidies were reduced for urban dwellers. In 1985, the economy grew by 15%. Unfortunately, inflation and corruption also exploded. Attempts by more conservative forces to reign in the freer economic environment were not successful. Deng also took a more "open" approach toward the outside world. Relations with the U.S. improved after the issue of American arms sales to Taiwan was aired in 1982. A cautious move to improve relations with the Soviet Union was also undertaken.

In October 1987, the Thirteenth Party Congress signed off on a policy of moderate political and economic reform. Deng held on to most of his authority. But in 1988, probably as a reaction to rapid uncontrolled growth in the south, a two year suspension of further price reforms was enacted.

The death of Hu Yaobang in April 1989, once considered the likely successor to Deng, ignited student aspirations. By early May they had turned out by the hundreds of thousands in the larger cities, particularly Beijing, waving banners with statements unheard of in China: "Down with Corruption! . . . Long Live Democracy!" . . . "Press Freedom!" . . . "Down With Rule By Men, Long Live The Rule Of Law!" A shaken Zhao Ziyang mingled with the student demonstrators and made some vague concessions, but he appeared to have been placed under house arrest by Deng and hard–line Premier Li Peng. There apparently were conflicting opinions among the leadership on just how to deal with the protesters, and for a few days the soldiers, about 200,000 strong, kept largely on the outskirts of the capital.

Suddenly on June 4, 1989, tens of thousands of well–armed troops smashed their way through Beijing to the heart of the city, Tiananmen Square. The tanks crushed many in their path; estimates of those killed and wounded were in the thousands. There were reports of soldiers firing indiscriminately into the crowds, invading hospitals to yank out life–support systems of the wounded, attacking doctors and engaging in other violent acts too brutal to mention. The hard–liners had won, at least for the time being.

Chinese students outside the country reacted with grief and horror; they may

President Nixon contemplates the Great Wall, 1972   AP/World Wide Photos

well be among the future leaders of China. The massacre in Beijing was followed by a massive nationwide campaign of political repression involving many arrests. This evoked outrage abroad and some limited, largely temporary, sanctions on the part of China's major trading partners, which had little effect on the hardliners dominant in Beijing. By mid–1990, President Bush was speaking of restoring trade relations.

Parallel with this political crackdown, Deng Xiaoping's economic reform program went into reverse. Central control over the economy was strengthened, prices were more closely controlled and there was even talk of the "voluntary" re-collectivization of agriculture. The "open" policy toward the outside world remained in effect, and foreign investment continued to flow in, from the United States as well as from other sources.

In 1990, Beijing tried to improve its international image by taking a moderate public position on the Cambodian and Kuwait crises. It undid much of this, however, by taking advantage of the distraction created by the war in the Persian Gulf to try to sentence a number of political prisoners accused of involvement in the 1989 demonstrations.

Although opposition continued to be sternly repressed in the name of stability, China in the early 1990s experienced one change with important political possibilities. The provinces were gaining in autonomy and authority at the expense of the center. This was especially true of the comparatively prosperous and dynamic provinces along the coast. The hardline mentality of the leadership came out clearly in August 1991, when the media

indicated support for the unsuccessful anti-Gorbachëv coup in Moscow. Political discontent in China was prevented from assuming serious proportions partly by the state of the economy, which was doing well in the private and cooperative sectors although poorly in the state sector.

In early 1992, Deng Xiaoping and his supporters prevailed over conservatives to institute economic reform. The private sector received encouragement and the free market concept was legitimized in the Constitution in 1993.

Politics and Government: Communism is in decline in China. Economic reforms continue to pick up speed, leading the country further away from its Maoist past. Power at the center, in Beijing, continues to slip away. As the economies of the provinces, particularly those in the South, continue to grow, so does their political power and independence. Beijing is dependent on the provinces for revenue.

The central government in China is also suffering from an aging leadership. At 90, Deng Xiaoping is nearing the end of his political career. Yet, there is no legitimized procedure for the succession of new leaders. Much depends on personal alliances and the support of others with access to the levers of power. Western democracies rely on constitutionally sanctioned procedures for leadership change. China will very soon once more rely on the usual struggle and intrigue which has pervaded the political life of the country for much of its history. In the past, the revolutionary ideology of the political elites was a mitigating factor to the chaos of the succession struggle. Today, as bureaucrats replace ideologues, the system will benefit from more skilled leadership but suffer from one which may be less united in purpose. Modern, complex nation–states cannot operate successfully without regularized procedures to govern leadership change. China's time may be running out. China could be heading for a very unstable future where power becomes decentralized to the point that the central government is incapable of providing political order. After Deng, there are no more great revolutionary leaders around whom the country can rally. Furthermore, the PLA (People's Liberation Army) has itself bought into the economic boom of the country. The military, like the civilian population is benefitting from economic progress. There may be no overriding commitment to the central government which is strong enough to force the PLA to intervene in any future civilian leadership struggle.

During 1994 China watchers continued to wait for the end of the reign of Deng Xiaoping. In early 1995, everyone was still waiting. But it was very likely that the real leadership change had already taken place. There is little reason to believe that President Jiang Zemin, and Premier Li Peng will be challenged when Deng passes. Of the four vice premiers, Zhu Rongji, who also heads the Bank of China and is a central figure in economic reform, has the upper hand. This could change if the economy spins into chaos. As for who will replace Deng, the answer may well be no one.

In 1994, it did seem that those responsible for policy were reluctant to make many decisions of real import. China's new leaders were still not sure about their permanence. The prospect of having Deng Xiaoping look over one's shoulder remained daunting.

There were important changes at or near the top which may effect the future direction of the country. In September, at the fourth plenum of the Fourteenth Central Committee, Huang Ju became a member of the Politburo, the highest major decision body in the Communist party. He is now the fourth member of the Politburo from Shanghai. The others are Jiang Zemin, Zhu Rongji, and Wu Bangguo. The four have either served as mayor or party secretary for Shanghai. In addition, several other Politburo members have their roots in Shanghai. This suggests that at a minimum the interests of the region will not be overlooked. In 1995, existing domestic problems worsened. And, in March 1996, the leaders in Beijing demonstrated their incompetence in foreign affairs as well, with the ill–conceived, thuggish attempt to keep Taiwanese voters from participation in the island's first democratic election for the post of president.

The specter of Deng Xiaoping, pervasive corruption, and an increasingly irrelevant ideology continued to act as a brake on reform. It was clear that this situation would remain unchanged as long as Deng was alive, even though he no longer played an active role in politics.

A major actor in the inevitable power struggle is the People's Liberation Army (PLA), which continued to benefit from preferred treatment when it came to the 1995 budget. And, the military's stake in the future of the country by way of massive involvement in the industrial sector, remained in tact. Jiang Zemin appeared to strengthen his position on the Central Military Commission.

Another possible player in China's power calculus is the National People's Congress. In 1995, it successfully opposed changes in the education system and banking reform sponsored by party leaders, as well as the appointment of Jiang Chunying as vice premier. The body also became the locus for increasing popular expressions of opposition to government policy. A number of petitions were received prior to the June 4 anniversary of the massacre at Tiananmen Square, calling for political reform.

The authorities responded with a crackdown on dissidents. For example, Chen Zeming, a participant in the 1989 protests, was rearrested after having been released from a 13 year sentence in 1994. American citizen Harry Wu was also arrested while trying to sneak into the country. Wu was responsible for revealing previous human rights abuses in China. The incident further frayed relations with Washington. In March 1996, a human rights group issued yet another report, this time focusing on the plight of orphans in China who, the report charged, were being deliberately starved in state institutions. Many Americans who have adopted Chinese orphans came forward to report their positive experiences with the Chinese.

In an attempt to gain international legitimacy, China hosted the UN sponsored Fourth World Conference on Women, and a parallel conference of non–governmen-

May 21, 1989: A *People's Liberation Army* convoy is engulfed by demonstrators in Tiananmen Square, Beijing.   AP Wide World Photo

On the way to school, Beijing

tal organizations (NGO's). The advertised facilities were not ready. The NGO meeting was moved and delegates were prevented by various means from attending. Americans received perhaps their most vivid picture of these events via National Public Radio which aired daily reports from China, revealing the failure and ineptness of Beijing's attempts at stage managing the gatherings.

In sum, the political behavior of China's leaders did little to improve their domestic record or international reputation.

Foreign Relations: China has entered an assertive period in its foreign relations. There can be no question that the PRC's economic success has created conditions where the country's leaders feel it possible and appropriate for China to assume a higher profile internationally. Beijing has also committed substantial resources to rebuild the national defense. It is unclear as yet as to how the increased capabilities of the PRC will be employed. Southeast Asian leaders profess not to be worried about Chinese intentions. But, then, what else could they say?

In 1994, a significant part of China's foreign policy centered on resolving issues with the United States. During the first part of the year, Clinton Administration policy was still geared toward exacting concessions in the area of human rights from China before economic relations could progress, this included hold-

ing up most favored nations (MFN) status for China.

In May, however, Washington realized that little headway was being made and the policy was changed to one of comprehensive engagement, which in many ways resembled the constructive engagement of the Bush Administration. This policy delinked China's human rights policy from other issues. Soon afterward, Commerce Secretary Ron Brown flew into Beijing with a plane load of American businessmen. When they left, they took with them over $6 billion in contracts. In October, Washington ended the ban on hi–tech exports to China, which responded with an agreement not to sell ground to ground missiles to other countries.

A major sticking point in China–U.S. relations was the former's desire to be admitted to the GATT and to be a founding member of the new World Trade Organization (WTO). Beijing was especially galled at the idea that Taiwan might wind up in the WTO ahead of the mainland. It was not able to meet the conditions set by the developed countries so that at the end of the year Beijing was still out in the cold. By March 1995, however, the U.S. and China had signed two agreements, the first providing for the protection of copyrights in China, and the second which further opened up the China market for American business. These agreements came only after U.S. Trade Representa-

tive Mickey Kantor threatened Beijing with a 100% tariff increase on over a billion dollars of Chinese exports to the United States.

As a result, the United States agreed to work for China's admission to the WTO as a founding member. China may have also helped the U.S. with the ongoing North Korean problem. Certainly, Beijing helped itself by making diplomatic channels available.

China continued to apply pressure to any country which did anything to make the government of Taiwan more legitimate in the eyes of the international community. The Japanese uninvited President Lee of Taiwan from an Asian games meeting in response to pressure from Beijing but did invite a lesser official. In May 1995, the Chinese Minister of Defense postponed a visit to the states because President Lee was granted a visa to attend his college reunion at Cornell University.

It appears that the Clinton Administration, under pressure from the Republican majority in the Congress, underestimated Beijing's reaction, which was to take Lee's visit as part of an orchestrated move toward Taiwanese independence. In late 1994, the Administration had altered its policy to allow for contact with Taiwanese officials at the Cabinet level. Thus, Lee's visit was viewed as another step toward the abandonment of Washington's "one China policy."

51

Throughout the year, other events, even internal ones, such as the arrest of Harry Wu in June, served to exacerbate the situation. In the international arena, China's occupation of Mischief Reef in the South China Sea (see "Defense" below) sent a wake–up call throughout Southeast Asia, though Washington initially ignored the matter. China's sale of nuclear technology to Pakistan and its own nuclear tests in May and August were protested globally. Japan even cut aid to China in response to the May test.

In June, the Chinese Ambassador in Washington was recalled to Beijing for consultation, and the American Ambassador, Stapleton Roy, left Beijing before his replacement arrived. The renewal of China's Most Favored Nations status by the U.S. Congress prevented any further deterioration in relations at least temporarily. By September both countries had their ambassadors back at their posts, and Mrs. Clinton's harsh words for China at the World Conference on Women passed with little uproar. U.S. and Chinese officials had met in July at the ASEAN Regional Forum in Brunei and raised the possibility of a Jiang–Clinton meeting in the U.S. later in the year. Unfortunately, misunderstanding and a disagreement over the location and level of the meeting nullified much of the goodwill that could have been achieved.

In March 1996, U.S.–China relations were at an all–time low. As Taiwan's first presidential election was about to take place, Chinese naval forces initiated military maneuvers off the coast of the Republic. Washington responded by sending two carriers into the waters off Taiwan. The election took place with a smashing victory for President Lee. China had not succeeded with its scare tactics. While Washington and Beijing both publicly stated that conflict was not eminent, it remained for them to withdraw from a needless confrontation. Relations were further poisoned by China's refusal to rule out additional shipments of nuclear technology to Pakistan. Chinese officials do not deny that specialized magnets used in the uranium enrichment process were sold to Pakistan. The Clinton Administration was seeking any assurance from Beijing so as to avoid the imposition of economic sanctions which could include cutting off all Export–Import Bank financing for American businessmens' deals with China.

Relations with Taiwan have also been severely damaged. In the early part of 1995, President Jiang himself was participating in cross–straits affairs. Even Lee's June visit to the United States was initially condemned. However, when Prime Minister Lien Chan followed the president's lead and took a "private trip" to Europe, Beijing went ballistic, conducting

missile tests off the coast of Taiwan in July and August and cancelling further talks. As the March 1996 election drew near Beijing kept up the threatening rhetoric. In the end, it was all for naught.

China's occupation of Mischief Reef also galvanized the ASEAN states of Southeast Asia. The issue was a major topic for discussion at the second ASEAN Regional Forum held in Brunei in July. Beijing made moves to smooth relations with the Philippines, which claims Mischief Reef, and agreed at the Forum to negotiate the issue of the South China Sea on a multilateral versus a bilateral basis, and in accord with international law.

Defense: The military is enjoying the fruits of economic expansion. One estimate is that about one fifth of all domestically produced consumer goods in China are produced in factories owned by the military. The army apparently keeps the profits. The army also handles foreign military sales. And, because of their support of the government during the demonstrations of 1989, the defense budget has steadily increased. The Party may be attempting to hedge its bets by insuring the loyalty of the defense establishment.

As a result of this new found wealth, China may have purchased as much as $2 billion in military hardware from Russia in 1992. China was also able to buy computer equipment from the U.S. China was beginning to worry her neighbors who were concerned about the possibility of military expansionism. Of particular concern was the Chinese claim to the South China Sea and especially the Spratley Islands. While an agreement with Vietnam was reached in the fall to put aside the claims in favor of cooperation in developing under–sea oil deposits, military officials in the region are continuing their own plans for upgrading naval and air capabilities. (Portions of the South China Sea are claimed by China, Taiwan, Vietnam, the Philippines, Malaysia and Brunei. Indonesia has hosted several meetings in an attempt to achieve a settlement). In 1993, Chinese technicians were at work in Burma, assisting with the upgrading of that country's military facilities.

In early 1995, China landed personnel on Mischief Reef, a small speck of land in the Spratley islands about 110 miles off the Philippine coast. Philippine patrol boats responded by blowing up Chinese markers in the area. Sixty–two Chinese fisherman were also detained by Manila. Then, in May, a Philippine vessel carrying an international group of journalists was blocked from approaching Mischief Reef. These events led up to the ASEAN Regional Forum (see above) and an apparent modification in China's position.

Economy: For 1995, all the numbers looked good. Foreign investment was up to $37 billion from $33 billion in 1994. But negotiations for future investments were down significantly which should mean a slowdown for 1996. Inflation was under 15% for the year, down from 22% in 1994. The target for 1996 is 12%. However, the government used "grain coupons" in at least nine provinces as subsidies to stem inflation. These subsidies conceal the real inflation rate.

On the bright side, exports rose 23% to $148 billion for the year, against a 14% increase in imports to $132 billion. Gross Domestic Product increased by 10.2% compared to 11.8% for 1994. For 1996, the target is 8%.

This rosy picture masks a fundamental and significant problem facing the Chinese leadership: The cost and inefficiency of state owned enterprises (SOEs). Of the approximate 100,000 SOEs, only about 50% are profitable. The total cost of propping them up may be as high as $50 billion. About 100 million workers or about 70% of the country's industrial workforce is employed in the state sector. With unemployment already high and underemployment at perhaps 20% in the state sector, only token layoffs were politically possible in 1995. According to one estimate, to make the state sector profitable, massive closings and a reduction in the workforce of at least 30% would be required. However, this would spell disaster for the government. On the other hand, the continued drain on the national economy will eventually produce a crisis of major proportions. The best that Beijing could do was to encourage partnerships between profitable and nonprofitable enterprises. A few enterprises did take a more radical approach. For the very brave, there are currently four SOEs on the New York Stock Exchange.

President Lee Teng-hui

Solitary Beauty Peak (Du Xiu Feng) in Guilin, one of hundreds of such peaks along a 50–mile stretch of the Li Jiang River valley of southern China. Many of these limestone formations have caves with intricate Buddhist carvings   Photo by Miller B. Spangler

Another serious and related challenge to the economy and the political leadership in 1995 was the growing migrant worker population. Neither the state nor the party could control this mass of people. The private sector is not growing fast enough to meet the demand for jobs. And, as economic growth slows as it must to insure stability and stem inflation, the situation will worsen. Urban areas are feeling the influx of poor, less educated, rural Chinese, and are reacting negatively. There is little that Beijing can do. Things will apparently have to get worse before the party bites the bullet on support for state owned enterprises. And, it most assuredly will.

The lack of planning continued to plague the economy in 1995 although there were signs of positive change. In Guangdong province, while GDP grew by an average 18% per year between 1981 and 1994, the quality of life had declined. Pollution had become so bad that a thermal–power plant project was banned in May. Several automobile manufacturers were told to go elsewhere in China. Universities have been forbidden to expand.

Paper plants were told to either install pollution control equipment or shut down. And a land set–aside program has been established in an attempt to restore rice self–sufficiency for the province.

There were also indications in 1995, that Beijing was taking a hard look at the country's four special economic zones. A case in point is the city of Shenzhen, located in Guangdong province. The city of three million didn't exist in 1980. Look for a move to restrict the privileges of the special zones as an attempt to force more rapid development in the interior of the country. Spreading uncontrollable capitalist growth may be one of the few options that Beijing has left.

In spite of President Lee's successful personal diplomacy, by the end of 1995, Taipei still was no closer to membership in the United Nations. Taiwan had to be content to be represented at the November Asia–Pacific Economic Cooperation meeting in Osaka by a private citizen. The president was not permitted to attend. Finally, a bid to host the Asian Games in 2002 was squashed by Beijing.

THE REPUBLIC OF CHINA
(Taiwan)

Politics and Government: Politics in the Republic of China constitutes one of the more clear and encouraging cases of how democratization can take place over time alongside a modern, rapidly developing economy. Even critics of the Kuomintang, the Nationalist Party which has dominated the political system since the break with the mainland, would have to acknowledge that substantial progress has been made.

By 1991, most of the holdovers from the National Assembly elected on the mainland in 1948 had retired. Discussion of politically sensitive issues such as whether Taiwan should be independent of the People's Republic was permitted at first grudgingly by the *Kuomintang*. A viable political opposition in the form of the Democratic Progressive Party emerged and free, relatively clean, elections have become part of the political landscape.

In the December 1991, elections, the *Kuomintang (KMT)* won 71% of the votes and 79% of the seats in the National

Assembly. The *DPP* won 24% of the vote. One year later, in another round of National Assembly elections, the *KMT* won 53.2% of the vote and 96 of 161 seats against the *DPP's* 31.3% of the vote and 50 seats.

In 1993 neither the *DPP* nor the *KMT* did as well as they had hoped. The first did not attain any gains in local elections, and the *KMT* Premier Hau Pei–tsun resigned. The new Premier was Lien Chan, a supporter of President Lee Teng–hui. Disaffected *KMT* members then bolted from the party to form the *Chinese New Party*, making for the possibility of a three party system. Much of the contention among the parties centered on the independence vs unification issue. The *New Party* was more representative of the old line *KMT* which claimed the right to rule over one China. President Lee's *KMT* took a centrist approach while the *DPP* was openly supportive of an independent Taiwan. At the end of 1994, Taiwan still had a two party system. The *KMT* lost the mayoral race in Taipei to the *DPP* but held on to the governor's post. The *Chinese New Party* was not able to establish itself nationally.

The year also witnessed further evolution of the political system when steps were taken to strengthen the position of the President. Constitutional amendments provided for the direct election of the president and also granted the president the authority to appoint and dismiss high government officials without the consent of the prime minister. The *KMT* dominated legislature also strengthened presidential power over three important agencies. By the end of the year, the position of president was far more than ceremonial.

On March 23, 1996, Taiwan held its first ever presidential election. The incumbent president, Lee Teng–hui, was elected with 54% of the vote. The voters apparently rallied around their serving president who had skillfully raised Taiwan's diplomatic profile in 1994 and 1995 by meeting with several ASEAN heads of state, and visiting the United States in June of last year. To make matters worse, Peng Ming–min, the *Democratic Progressive Party* candidate, came in second with 21% of the vote. Peng is an open supporter of Taiwan independence. This means that three/fourths of the voters on Taiwan were in no mood to bend toward Beijing. Most analysts saw the results as a total humiliation for Beijing. President Lee was expected to initiate moves to repair the rift in cross–straits relations. China was expected to do the same.

Foreign Relations: A fundamental goal of Taiwan's foreign policy is to gain international recognition. This in turn is seen as essential to the island's survival as an independent state, which more and more seems to be the emerging favored option. As Taiwan draws closer to mainland China because of huge investments flowing in that direction, leaders know that they will need a counter balancing force capable of preventing the country from being swallowed up. There is no question that Taiwan is an independent entity in economic terms. The question of political independence has not yet been settled. China, for its part, adhered to the "one country, two systems" idea. But Taiwan, with its NIC (Newly Industrialized Country) size economy was already viewed as an independent actor by much of the global community.

In January 1994, the prime minister visited Singapore and Malaysia. President Lee then visited the Philippines, Indonesia and Thailand. The Thai prime minister, under pressure from Beijing, did not meet with the president. The meeting in Indonesia was unofficial. Only President Ramos of the Philippines met the Taiwan head of state. Another major disappointment was that the president was not able to attend the second APEC meeting in Indonesia in November. The APEC nations' deference to Beijing does not change the fact that Taiwan is a major economic player in Asia. Finally, Taiwan was unable to make any real progress on gaining admission to the United Nations. Everyone thinks China is just too big to ignore. A minor upgrade in U.S.–Taiwan relations did occur when the Clinton Administration agreed to a name change for the North American Coordination Council in Washington. More important, officials from the American Institute in Taipei were allowed to meet with Taiwanese officials.

In 1995, President Lee continued to work to raise Taiwan's international profile by visiting Jordan and the UAE. However, the biggest foreign relations coup

A mother and child framed in a decorative wall-window in Hangzhou

Courtesy: Jon Markham Morrow

54

The Challenge of Population

China accounts for 21.3% of the world's population. In April 1993, the government announced that it had lowered the birth rate to levels comparable to the West. How did they do it? China proclaimed a "one family, one child" policy in 1979. In 1992 some 6.5 million people were sterilized. The figure was 10 million in 1991. Forced abortions may have accounted for a large decline in 1983–1984.

According to 1992 surveys, the government claimed that the birth rate had fallen to 18.24 per 1000 from 21 per 1000 in 1990. The 1993 figures suggested that the fertility rate was below the 2.2 level needed to maintain the population. Birth rates in Shanghai, Beijing and northeast China were reported to be as low or lower than the rate in many West European states. However, the great success was apparently short lived.

The government recently admitted that the population program was failing. Officials now estimate that the population has already passed the 1.2 billion mark, five years ahead of earlier projections. The problem seems to be in the rural areas where the party no longer has the coercive power it once did. The figures from large urban areas were simply a deception. Apparently, China's population continues to grow. Some population experts have concluded that if China is unable to control population growth, global food supplies will be under severe pressure within several decades.

occured on June 7, when President Lee left for the United States for a speaking engagement at Cornell University. It was made possible when the Clinton Administration gave in to pressure from the Congress where support for Taiwan was very strong. The Taipei government had accomplished a breakthrough in the country's international relations. However, critics could rightly argue that the cost for Taiwan and for Washington was high and unanticipated. For the remainder of the year, Taiwan's relations with Beijing deteriorated. Cross–straits talks were suspended and in early 1996, Chinese military exercises were conducted just off the coast of Taiwan, as a warning to those who might support pro–independence candidates in the March 1996 presidential election. In spite of President Lee's efforts, unemployment remained at 8%. (Most countries would consider this as full employment) Although still doing very well, Taiwan may be moving into a situation where it is the victim of its own success. As the economy matures and wages rise, it is harder to maintain competitiveness with the "younger," booming economies of Asia. The country was also rocked by significant financial scandals during the year. In addition, slumping real estate prices, a sagging auto market, and a business downturn resulting from tensions with Beijing all combined for a less than spectacular 1995.

Economy: In 1994, the economy repeated the performance of the previous year with growth at about 6.2%. Per capita GDP was $10,200. The government predicted a trade surplus of $8 billion. Economists worried about a possible slowdown—rising wages, costs of land and increasing concern for the environment are all important factors.

Like so many rapidly developing countries, there is a problem with infrastructure. Because domestic investment was not all that strong, the government held up many projects needed to modernize the country. While the outflow of investment funds signaled opportunities for Taiwanese businessmen to reap substantial profits, some of these funds could have been used at home to directly benefit the domestic economy. Hundreds of construction projects outlined in the Six Year Plan were curtailed, including a high speed rail system. Taipei's mass rapid transit system (MRTS) also ran into serious trouble which will result in delays and loss of funds.

For 1995, GDP advanced 6.4%, slightly below expectations. Unemployment for the year was the highest since 1987, at 10%. Finally, note must be taken of China's continuing struggle with population growth. Even with the decline in the birth rate, the population of China will increase by about 12 million in 1996. With continued economic growth, consumption will also increase. As reported in this volume two years ago, China will single–handedly be responsible for the elimination of grain surpluses on the international market, which could lead to a substantial increase in cost for everyone.

Culture: The fundamental and lasting institutions of family life and farming completely dominated Chinese culture for thousands of years; this was certainly true throughout most of Asia, but these two foundations were developed to a higher level within China. Agriculture combined the careful cultivation of cereal grains, skillful efforts to control water by the construction of levees and irrigation ditches, and the return of all available fertilizer, including human waste, to the soil. This permitted high nutritional content of the harvests, which in turn permitted a rapid rate of population growth. The family was the basic social unit—above it stood the village, governed usually by the heads of the leading families; contact with central government officials was avoided by the elders with varying degrees of success.

Traditional upper class culture was also based on the family and on the group of related families which together formed a clan. Ancestor worship, involving sacrifices to dead forebears, who were not considered to be actually divine, began among the upper classes and spread to the lower classes. The wealthy avoided manual labor and regarded literacy and education—especially in the Confucian tradition—ownership of land and public service as the highest social goals and symbols of status. This upper crust, dominating education, government service and land ownership, was not so exclusive that the lower classes were entirely excluded from it. Unlike India, China never had a caste system as part of its culture, but in reality, it was highly unusual for a

Open air market, Shanghai

A family planning billboard on a modern boulevard in Chengdu

person of peasant origin to acquire enough education, wealth or influence to move to the top of the social scale.

The scholarly elite, as this upper class may be called, developed an almost unbelievably complex writing system derived from the priests of the Shang era. Learning this was a major undertaking, and over the centuries it became the medium of almost ever type of literary effort, except for the epic poem, which never emerged in China. Other varieties of verse, as well as history, plays, novels, essays, encyclopedias and other writings were produced in enormous abundance. The poetic works of Mao Zedong, composed with skill, are a modern counterpart of these ancient scholarly and literary efforts. About 900 A.D. a form of printing was developed: a character or page was carved in reverse on a block of wood, which was then used as a stamp. It has been estimated by some that under this system, up to the time of the 18th century, more literature was printed in Chinese than in all of the other languages of the world combined.

In spite of tendencies toward conservatism and anti–foreignism, traditional Chinese culture was probably the richest, and certainly the longest lived and most continuous of the great civilizations,

ancient and modern, of the world. It was relatively free from the religious bigotry and intolerance that was evident in much of western history. In contrast to the principles of decaying despotism of France under the Bourbon kings, China's traditional philosophy and culture greatly impressed well–educated Jesuit missionaries who came to China in the 17th century. Through their writings, the French writer and philosopher Voltaire communicated some of the Chinese ideals to the educated of Europe.

The decline of the traditional Chinese political system in the late 19th and early 20th centuries also brought a decline in the vitality and self–confidence of most of the traditional Chinese cultural values. Education was increasingly altered to conform to western ideals; literature began to be written in the vernacular, or conversational language, rather than in the old, difficult and formal literary language. During the 1920's, the ideals of Marxism gained ground among intellectuals, but not always in the form of communist doctrine.

At the level of the uneducated, the solidarity of the family was greatly weakened by the beginning of economic progress toward industrialization, which created jobs for women, drawing them away from

their families to the factories in the cities. The Japanese invasion in 1937 and the ensuing chaos uprooted millions of people and heavily contributed to the further breakdown of the traditional social and cultural order. The communists have exploited this fluid and unstable situation to press ahead toward their own goals of a new culture and a new society, to be achieved, to a large extent, by overhauling the educational system. This has produced a new generation of Chinese heavily indoctrinated in the desired ideals and cast in a completely new mold.

The fundamental purpose of all of this is to break down the traditional ties of family and religion, as well as other values that have interfered with the purposes of the regime. The ultimate desire is that every Chinese be willing, and indeed eager, to do what the state wants of him, to encourage others to do the same, to report on them if they do not and in general to exist in order to contribute to the oft–changing programs and goals of the leadership.

Progress toward these goals has been faster in the cities, where indoctrination and control are easier than in the countryside. Less progress has been evident among the peasants. The Beijing dialect of Mandarin (Northern Chinese) is being taught in all schools, several hundred of the most complex written characters have been simplified and the regime has shown at least a passing interest in the development and replacement of the cumbersome character–writing system with an alphabetical process. The official adoption of *pinyin* spelling of proper names in 1979 was a possible indication of a future planned move in this direction. Literacy is now much more widespread than before the advent of the communists, but the ability to read, as well as the school system, are both basically used to indoctrinate and propagandize the people along the lines indicated above, rather than to encourage creative and independent thought, especially independent political thought.

The adoption of alphabetical spelling to replace the character system poses a greater problem than might be imagined by an English–speaking person. The meaning of Chinese words *as spoken* varies with the tone level of speech and with inflection—change of tone in the middle of a syllable.

The regime in the past has permitted the people almost no contact with the outside world, with the exception of closely guarded diplomatic missions. This policy has eased considerably since about 1984, particularly in higher education available elsewhere and considered valuable by the government.

The traditional conservatism is being ignored by the educated youth of China. Some 40,000 students are now enrolled in the United States, many in high–level graduate programs. When they complete their education, a substantial number, disenchanted with the regimentation typical during past years in their homeland, don't want to return. The Chinese are apprehensive about a "brain–drain" such as occurred in Taiwan a decade ago, and increasing restrictions on foreign travel and education have been the result.

With a burgeoning population of more than *one billion* people, China has been pursuing an energetic program to reduce population growth to zero or below. Stringent regulations have been promulgated which include stiff taxation, forced abortions and criminal penalties upon couples who exceed the established limit of one child. Local officials have often forced pregnant women to abort. The program has been relatively successful according to the government, but this is impossible to verify. This program is very controversial both inside and outside China. Since 1984, the regime has made it easier for couples to get permission to have a second child, if the first is a girl, for example.

On Taiwan, the basic cultural pattern is that of the modern intellectual classes of China of the first half of the 20th century.

To this has been added a large degree of foreign education and adoption of western customs, as a logical result of American influence. The inner circle of the Nationalist regime is still conservative and is now elderly, but an able, younger generation, much of it educated in the U.S., is gradually taking over.

The Future—China & Taiwan: China's economic progress is not matched anywhere else in Asia. However, it's population growth rate has not been lowered. The economy remains beyond the ability of Beijing to control. While there have been changes at the top, China's new leaders are not yet willing or able to take the decisive steps necessary to bring basic direction to the nation. Some historians see a similarity between the unsettled conditions of today and the chaos at the end of previous dynasties. A few see the positive side, believing that China is on the verge of greatness.

Diplomats and businessmen argue that the United States and indeed the rest of the world cannot afford a crisis leading to disintegration in China. It should be remembered, however, that similar statements were made about the old Soviet Union. And, if the world was able to endure the breakup of the "evil empire," it can probably survive chaos in China. This

may not be a desired outcome, but it cannot be discounted.

Assuming that China's leaders are able to achieve a firmer degree of control and adopt suitable reforms, there will still be reason for concern. The present world cannot accommodate a developed, industrialized China which consumes huge amounts of the world's resources. Thus, all of China's futures have inherent dangers. There is no more than an even chance that the outcome will be ideal. Furthermore, there is very little that the rest of the world can do. American businessmen have already exposed their corporations to considerable risk by rushing to China. Their optimism is admirable. Their judgment is another matter.

Taiwan: Taiwan needs to continue on its quest for international legitimacy. Its economy is sound and its politics is evolving in the right direction. If it can protect itself against shock waves coming from the mainland, its future can be bright. Those who still support unification with the mainland will continue to experience a decline in their political fortunes. The ties of the new generation are not that strong and the success of a relatively small, reasonably well run political system cannot be denied.

The Great Wall of China, still one of the world's major tourist attractions

The Republic of Indonesia

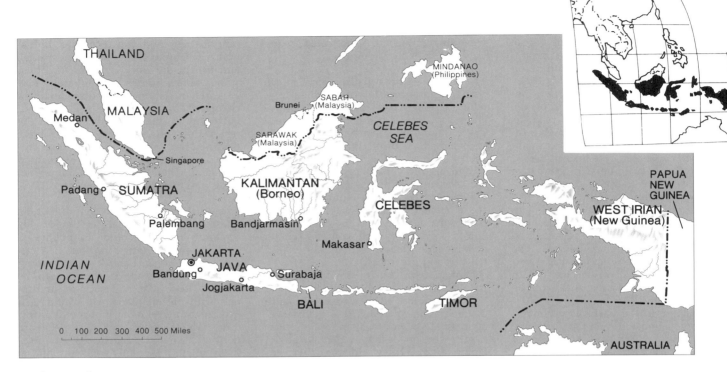

Indonesia

Area: 741,040 sq. mi. (1,906,240 sq. km., covering an expanse equal to the width of the U.S. coast–to–coast.)

Population: 190 million (estimated).

Capital City: Jakarta (Pop. 7.2 million, estimated).

Climate: Tropical, with a monsoon season from November to March.

Neighboring Countries: Malaysia and the Philippine Republic (North); Australia (South); Papua New Guinea (East).

Official Language: Bahasa Indonesia (a formal version of the Malay language).

Other Principal Tongues: Malay, Common Malay (a dialect), and about 250 other Malayo–Polynesian languages and dialects, also such as Sundanese and Madurese, Japanese, Dutch, Chinese.

Ethnic Background: Malayo–Polynesian (a mixture of Polynesian, Mongolian, Indian and Caucasian many centuries old, about 95%; Chinese (about 3%); other (including European, about 2%).

Principal Religion: Overwhelmingly Islam, with small groups of Christians, Hindus and Buddhists.

Main Exports: (to Japan, Federal Republic of Germany and other European nations); Petroleum, liquefied natural gas, carpets, fruits, nuts and coffee.

Main Imports: (From U.S.) aircraft and equipment, cotton textile fibers, engines, civil engineering equipment, pulp and waste paper.

Currency: Rupiah.

Former Colonial Status: Dutch Colony from about 1625 to 1949.

Independence Day: December 27, 1949. (August 17th, the anniversary of the 1945 date when revolutionaries proclaimed the Republic of Indonesia.)

Chief of State: President Soeharto (since 1967).

Vice President: Tri Sutrisno.

National Flag: Two horizontal bands; the top is maroon and the bottom is white.

Per Capita Income: U.S. $670.

Stretched along the Equator between Australia and the Asian mainland for a horizontal distance of about 3,000 miles, Indonesia consists of about 3,000 individual islands. The largest are Sumatra and Java; Kalimantan occupies the southern portion of the island of Borneo, and West Irian is the western portion of the island of New Guinea. About one–fourth of the land is covered with inland waters.

If Indonesia did not have a great variation in elevation, its climate would be uniformly oppressive because of its equatorial location. The heat and humidity of the coastal areas give way to more moderate temperatures as the altitude rises to breathtaking heights. Although West Irian is predominantly low and swampy, as is Kalimantan, there are mountains that are snow–covered throughout the year on New Guinea.

This is an area of volcanic peaks—some dormant and some active—which have enriched the soil greatly during their centuries of destructively explosive activity. Krakatoa, located on a tiny island between Java and Sumatra, exploded with such force in 1883 that it produced a tidal wave which was felt around the world and which inundated parts of nearby seacoasts. In other areas of the world, torrential rainfall such as occurs during the monsoon season is the enemy that washes valuable topsoil to the sea, expos-

President Soeharto

58

ing infertile land to the sun. In Java, the downpours are welcome—they wash away old soil and expose even richer volcanic ash and dirt which is fertile almost beyond belief.

The wildlife of Indonesia is more interesting and varied than almost any other country of the world. The Komodo dragon, ten feet long and a remnant of prehistoric times, inhabits the island of Komodo east of Java. The Javanese rhinoceros makes increasingly rare appearances in the *Udjung Kulon* ("western tip") preserve on the end of Java, where successive governments have tried to maintain the natural setting of plants and animals. The gibbon, most agile among the primates, swings overhead in the tall trees that provide thick shade for the banteng, a native ox with white legs that resembles an ordinary dairy cow. Although crowded by a multitude of species adapted to its character, this area, as well as most of the interior of the Indonesian islands, is extremely inhospitable to modern man.

History: Fossils and other prehistoric remnants of human skeletons indicate that Indonesia was the scene of one of the earliest areas of the world to be inhabited by man. The present population of the area acquired its somewhat uniform appearance about the second millenium before the Christian era, a time when there was gradual intermarriage and mixture between native Polynesians and people from the Asian mainland. This combination, relatively stable since that time, is now referred to as Malayo–Polynesian.

The arrival of Indian cultural, religious and commercial influences about the beginning of the Christian era greatly influenced the people. Hinduism and Buddhism, mingled with the ancient animist background of the Indonesians, produced an extremely complex, varied and unique culture, especially on Java and nearby Bali. The advances brought by the Indians and the availability of good harbors in the Malacca and Sunda Straits were the basis for the rise of two powerful commercial and naval empires at the beginning of the 9th century, A.D. *Srivijaya* was based on the island of Sumatra; *Sailendra* arose on neighboring Java. The empires thrived on a lively trade centered on the production of spices treasured throughout the rest of the world, though available only here.

The Indians brought Islam to the islands at the beginning of the 11th century, but it did not have much influence at first. The development of the Indonesian empires was briefly disrupted in the 13th century by a naval expedition sent by the power Mongol emperor of China, Khubilai Khan. Shortly afterward, a new empire, known as *Majapahit*, became dominant, and seized control of the valuable spice trade. Islam had been spread-

ing slowly, and by the end of the 16th century, the vast majority of the people had become Moslems.

The lure of profits in the spice trade brought the Europeans to the East Indies, or Dutch East Indies as the islands were later called. Rumors of untold wealth had sifted into medieval Europe—they furnished a basis for investment in exploration, the purpose of which was to earn large sums of money as well as to discover unknown lands. The spices were, and now are, grown principally in the Moluccas (Spice Islands) and on Java.

There was a keen interest in the area on the part of Portugal and Great Britain, but the Dutch were ultimately successful in dominating Indonesia, controlling the area through a commercial organization, the Dutch East India Company. The *Majapahit* empire had weakened greatly, leaving the island of Java a relatively easy conquest—this was the island quickly identified as the most strategic and fertile, producing coffee, indigo and some spices. The local leaders who came to power after the empire were either militarily defeated or scared into surrender by the Dutch, who compelled them to deliver produce to the Company.

The colonial period was much the same as in other parts of the colonized world: relatively uneventful and centered around the process of extracting wealth from the colony. The Napoleonic Wars in Europe resulted in a brief period of British occupation of Java from 1811 to 1816. When the Dutch returned they tried at first to continue a pattern of free economic activity established by the British, but the tribute system was restored from 1830 to 1870 to supplement revenues lost by the Netherlands when Belgium and its industrialized wealth broke away from the Dutch Crown.

In the last part of the 19th century there was a return to free economic development based on private investment, principally from Dutch sources. This period also witnessed a large influx of Chinese, who quickly acquired a place in the economy second only to the Europeans. Indonesian nationalism began to crystallize at the start of the 20th century, but was directed against the Chinese as much as against the Dutch. The colonial government adopted the "Ethical Policy," under which strenuous efforts were made to promote the welfare of the Indonesians through public works and health measures in 1900. However, education and preparation for self–government were badly neglected, resulting in a rapid growth of both nationalism and communism in the 1920–1940 period in spite of increasingly harsh police measures by the Dutch.

Indonesia was a prime target for the Japanese offensive in Southeast Asia in 1942 due to its great natural wealth.

Weakly defended by a government in exile which had been driven from its European homeland by the Germans, the islands rapidly fell. The Indonesians had some pro–Japanese feeling based on their dislike of the Dutch and Chinese during the first part of the occupation, but the brutality and greed of the Japanese quickly ended such sentiment. Native leaders, supposedly by agreement, divided into two groups—those who pretended to collaborate with the Japanese and those who went underground and launched a resistance movement. Sukarno (many Indonesians possess only a single name) was the most prominent member of the "collaborators," who hoped to persuade the Japanese to set up a united Malay state including Malaya and Indonesia under Japanese leadership in exchange for allegiance to Japan. The Japanese indicated some interest which died quickly as the fortunes of war turned against them.

Although they were foreign conquerors, the Japanese not only destroyed the prestige of the Dutch in the eyes of the Indonesians, but in addition gave the latter valuable experience in political activity and public administration. The nationalists of the islands decided to make use of this knowledge against their colonial rulers. Sukarno immediately proclaimed the independent Republic of Indonesia when the Japanese collapsed in 1945; this move had widespread support of other leaders and among the population of the outlying islands.

The Dutch, who returned later in the year, desired continued control over the people and wealth they regarded as their own, and began four year years of complex fighting between the Dutch and the Republic of Indonesia. The U.S. and most world opinion favored Indonesian independence. The situation was further complicated in 1948 when the *Indonesian Communist Party (PKI)* attempted an armed rebellion against the Republic of Indonesia led by Sukarno.

A settlement was reached at the end of 1949 that recognized the independence of Indonesia, which was supposed to be linked to the Netherlands through the Dutch Crown. West Irian, part of the island of New Guinea, was not included in the agreement; Dutch–owned industry and investment were to remain intact. The new Republic of Indonesia, based on Java, promptly abolished the federal system created by the Dutch administration and established a unitary republic which later cut all ties with the Netherlands.

The Indonesians faced independence under almost insurmountable difficulties, geographic and cultural differences, poor communication between the islands, the dominant power of the Javanese, resented in the other islands—referred to as "Outer Islands"—the political turmoil left by the years of Japanese occupation and battle against the Dutch, and the primitive state of economic and political development. In addition to these liabilities there was the leadership of Sukarno. Flamboyant, popular, unpredictable, self–indulgent, articulate, dictatorial and lovable are adjectives that have been used to describe him, depending upon the point of view of the observer. He created external problems to cover up the miserable state of the Indonesian economy, beset with rising prices and stagnation. The country became a political triangle of the *PKI* communists led by the young and energetic Aidit, the army and Sukarno. Anarchy was prevented by the popularity of Sukarno, who was able to command the support of the communists and the obedience of the army.

The promises given to leave foreign investment intact were temporary—Dutch assets were seized in 1957, some Chinese investment was nationalized in the following years and most American assets were confiscated in 1963–1964.

Supported by Soviet diplomacy and aid, Sukarno threatened West Irian with a substantial military force using Soviet weapons; under American pressure and mediation, the Dutch surrendered this western portion of New Guinea in 1962 rather than fight for it. The appetite for additional conquest was whetted, and at the same time the economically and politically miserable life of the Indonesians was ignored by Sukarno, who announced that Malaysia was the next target. This area of Southeast Asia was formed by the British when they united Malaya, Singapore and North Borneo (Sabah and Sarawak) into a single, independent nation in 1963. It soon became clear that the British were willing to fight to protect Malaysia.

The confrontation with Malaysia, launched in 1963 by Sukarno, led the *PKI*, which had achieved considerable power, to demand the arming of communist–led "workers and peasants." This demand was resisted by the army, but endorsed by China and was given an increasingly enthusiastic reception by Sukarno in 1965.

In this tense atmosphere, the dictator fell ill in mid–year. By this time, Sukarno had decided to create conditions for a leftist orientation for Indonesia by supporting the *PKI* in a *coup* against the army leadership. When the time came for its execution, however, he failed to give it public endorsement.

The *PKI* forces killed a number of army leaders quickly in the chaotic violence of the first day of October 1965, but failed to capture two powerful generals, Nasution and Soeharto. Seizing leadership, Soeharto crushed the rebellion. Resentment against the *PKI* which had been smoldering in the islands for years, particularly among the Moslems, erupted into a mas-

Presidents Sukarno and Eisenhower enter the White House, May 1956

sive slaughter that resulted in the death of thousands of communists. The *PKI* was almost annihilated and was outlawed as a political party, in spite of the efforts of Sukarno to protect it. The army stripped Sukarno of all power in March 1966; he died in 1970.

Having achieved effective control of Indonesia, Suharto and the army ended the "confrontation" with Malaysia without much publicity, and at last began to tackle Indonesia's massive economic problems. Steps were taken to rejoin the UN, from which Sukarno's government had withdrawn in 1965. An interest was shown in resuming normal economic relations with the non–communist world, including the Netherlands and the United States.

China undoubtedly knew and approved of the attempted revolution in 1965 and supplied the *PKI* with some arms; it then denounced the present regime as a gang of fascists, particularly after there was some anti–Chinese violence following the military seizure of power. The Soviet Union had more mixed feelings; it did not wish for communists to be slaughtered with the arms it had provided, but since the *PKI* had adopted the Chinese side of the dispute in international communism, the Soviets undoubtedly were gratified by the example of its failure—an example to other communist movements of the world which had sided with Peking.

After the 1965 *coup*, the appointed *Provisional People's Consultative Congress (MPRS)* was purged of pro–communist elements. In a March 1967 meeting, it proclaimed Soeharto president for five years and set the next general congressional elections for 1971.

The new government made peace with Malaysia in 1966 by disavowing Sukarno's threat to "crush" that nation. When the Dutch withdrew from Dutch New Guinea, now West Irian, in 1962, the UN promised that a popular vote would be taken to determine the will of the people. The alternatives were independence or union with Indonesia. However, Indonesian military officers present in West Irian in 1969 rigged a unanimous vote for union with Indonesia. This was possible because the vote was taken in Consultative Assemblies that had been created earlier.

After a failure of the *coup* in Indonesia and the end of the "confrontation" with Malaysia, in 1967 Indonesia joined with Malaysia, Singapore, Thailand and the Philippines to form the Association of Southeast Asian Nations (ASEAN). Brunei joined in 1984. The main original purpose of this organization was to minimize the chances of another expansionist outburst on the part of Indonesia, the largest and most powerful member of ASEAN. At first, its main visible functions were to maintain easy access for its members' raw materials to the markets of the developed countries and to cooperate to a limited extent against communist insurgency. After the Vietnamese invasion of Cambodia at the end of 1978, ASEAN, with Thailand as the "frontline" state in the lead, began to play an important role in trying to negotiate an end to the struggle on terms that would include a Vietnamese military withdrawal.

It was announced in late 1969 that general elections would be held in mid–1971 in Indonesia. The result was an overwhelming victory for the government party, the *Sekber Golkar*, a federation of about 260 trade, professional and regional groups.

Widespread discontent among the people over the lack of political freedom and social justice erupted in serious riots in early 1974; antipathy was directed against inflation, commodity shortages and mainly against the government. Other elements included dissatisfaction with the economic influence of Japan, which had grown by leaps and bounds and the mercantile activities of the local Chinese.

In the wake of the riots, President Soeharto made some personnel changes that had the effect of strengthening the position of his principal assistant, Ali Murtopo. But government corruption, food shortages, an inferior educational system, tensions between the Indonesian majority and the important Chinese minority—and other problems—continued to dog the country. In 1975, *Pertamina*, the government oil monopoly, nearly went bankrupt as a result of overborrowing and poor administration.

In Indonesia's third general election in 1977, *Golkar* won 230 out of 360 seats in the House of Representatives. The *Development Unity Party (PPP)*, a coalition of Moslem parties, won 108 seats and the *Democratic Party (PDI)* won 22 seats.

Again in 1982 *Golkar* was victorious, winning approximately 75% of the popular vote. Another body, the *People's Consultative Assembly*, elected Soeharto to another 5–year term as President both in 1978 and 1983.

The central government is dominated by Javanese, of whom Soeharto is one. It has defended the lack of political progress in recent years on the ground of economic development—whereas Sukarno used to justify the lack of progress under his rule by displays of political dynamism—but recent economic difficulties have tended to discredit this rationalization and increase the pressures for political reform. Members of Soeharto's family control profitable, but economically damaging, import and export monopolies. A large number of these were set up after 1983, when the price of oil fell; some were abolished in 1986, but the biggest ones remain. On the positive side, both the Sukarno and Soeharto governments have dramatically raised the educational level of the Indonesian people. Demanding a high degree of conformity, they have both tried to assimilate the Chinese community, which has complied to some extent; the government, however, does not want to pressure them to the point where they can no longer make an important contribution to the national economy.

Soeharto's rather heavy-handed rule has naturally aroused opposition. Against him are ranged some of the most prestigious names in the country. In addition, there are two small legal opposition parties: the *Indonesian Democratic Party* and the *United Development Party* (the latter is Moslem-based).The opposition objects to what it sees as a tendency on the part of the U.S. to support the Soeharto government. It viewed in this light President Reagan's first visit to Indonesia, which took place in April-May 1986. At the time, the Indonesian government barred two Australian journalists and expelled one American for having written critical articles about the Indonesian political system.

In preparation for a parliamentary election scheduled for April 1987, the government screened all candidates, as usual, for "security." *Golkar*, the government party, was allegedly "rejuvenating" itself through the appointment of younger people to important positions; in many cases, however, these were the children of the previous generation of leaders. Unrest continued in West Irian (taken over from the Dutch in 1962) and East Timor (obtained from Portugal in 1975).

The April 1987 elections resulted in a predictable victory for *Golkar* over the *Indonesian Democratic Party* and the (Moslem) *United Democratic Party*. It won 73% of the popular vote. There has been some liberalization of Soeharto's authoritarian political system in the last several years, partly under the impact of democratic developments in the Philippines and South Korea. One form this has taken is the revival of unofficial, as well as official, interest in the personality and career of the late President Sukarno. Soeharto's family continues to be widely criticized for corrupt business activities. In an unusual display of disagreement, the army put forward its own candidate for vice president, its new commander Sutrisno; Soeharto's candidate, Sudharmono, was elected instead.

There has been severe political repression in East Timor, where there is a large Catholic community because of the area's former status as a Portuguese colony. Pope John Paul II alluded tactfully to this situation during a visit to Indonesia, including East Timor, in October 1989, and urged respect for human rights.

In November 1991, a pro-independence demonstration in East Timor was violently suppressed by the army. The government's statement on the massacre, although promising some improvement of conditions in the area, amounted to a whitewash.

Politics and Government: Indonesia's government is headed by a strong president and is based on Pancasila democracy. This state ideology incorporates the five principles of nationalism, democracy, internationalism, social justice, and belief in one God. All political parties must accept Pancasila. The armed forces have a legitimate role in the political process through the official government party, *Golkar*. Soeharto has held the presidency since March 1967. The national parliament (DPR) consists of 500 members. The political parties including the official party, *Golkar*, contest for 400 of the seats. The other 100 are filled by the military. Indonesia can hardly be characterized as a Western style multi–party political system. Indonesia's fifth national election took place in June 1992. *Golkar* won 68% of the vote, down from 73% in 1987. The *Development Unity Party (Muslim)* captured 17.5%, and the *Indonesian Democratic Party* (a secular three–party coalition) took 15% of the vote.

On March 19, 1993, the People's Consultative Assembly elected the 71 year–old Soeharto to yet another term as president of Indonesia. The Assembly consists of 1000 members, 500 come from the House of Representatives and 500 are presidential appointees. The new vice president is Tri Sutrisno, a former presidential military aide and retired commander of the armed forces. Thus, it is likely that the military will continue in its strong role in government. There is pressure building for more democratization. As Soeharto moves through what should be his last term as president, some changes are possible.

The vice president is in an ideal position to succeed General Soeharto in the 1998 presidential election. To fill the void left by Sutrisno's elevation to Vice President, Edi Sudradjat was named Defense Minister. The position carries the rank of cabinet minister but does not put him in the line–of–command. The selection of Sutrisno by Soeharto may have resulted from pressure from the military. There has been a growing rift between Soeharto and his old colleagues, particularly General Benny Murdani. Soeharto further aggravated the relationship by appointing a civilian, Harmoko, as the chairman of the official state political party, *Golkar*.

President Soeharto also made significant changes in his cabinet, replacing nearly half of its members with young technologists.

Human rights continued to be a problem for the Soeharto government in 1994. In June in East Timor, demonstrations erupted after the Indonesian military was involved in a scuffle with locals. In July, a second incident arose when several hundred Timorese attempted to protest the apparent insulting of two Catholic nuns. The military used force to restrain the demonstrators. In another incident, a prominent activist, Nuku Soleiman, was sentenced to four years in prison for insulting the president. When the case was appealed, an additional year was tacked on to the sentence.

In 1995, the government's policy of trans–migration contributed to internal problems. The policy calls for moving people from heavily populated areas like Java and Sumatra to less populated areas such as East Timor and Irian Jaya. The inflow of perhaps 100,000 Indonesians into the mainly Catholic East Timor, a former Portuguese colony, is a case in point.

The Indonesian government currently has six battalions stationed in East Timor in an attempt to suppress *Fretilin,* the primary organization working for Timorese independence. Since September 1995, some fifty Timorese have sought asylum in various foreign embassies in Jakarta. According to a Timorese exile in the United States, thousands of people have been killed on the island by Indonesian military. In 1995, there were several incidents which resulted in the death of a number of Timorese at the hands of the Indonesian army.

Irian Jaya (West Irian) shares the island of New Guinea with the independent country of Papua New Guinea. Indonesian troops are currently stationed in Irian Jaya as well to oppose the *Free Papua Movement,* which seeks independence.

While Indonesia is much more cohesive as a country than it was even thirty years ago, separatist sentiments continue. The trans–migration policy is not making matters better. Neither is the heavy hand of President Soeharto. Even worse, unrest is not confined to minority regions, and in the last half of 1995 it had reached epidemic proportions. While Jakarta wants to blame the unrest on re–emergent radical organizations, the real problem is the unmet rising aspirations of Indonesia's rural poor.

Meanwhile, Indonesia celebrated its 50th anniversary on August 17, 1995. Soeharto used the occasion to improve the country's human rights image by freeing 81 year old former Deputy Prime Minister Subandrio, 77 year old retired air force commander Omar Dhani, and 77 year old police Brig. Soetarto, all of whom had been sentenced to death for their alleged role in a 1995 coup attempt.

As in 1994, the government kept the pressure on the media, this time by arresting three members of the *Alliance of Independent Journalists* for slandering the government through their publication *Independent.* The government has even set up an Association of Indonesian Journalists to which all reporters must belong. In a surprise, devastating to the government, Information Minister Harmoko had a State Administrative Court rule that he had acted unlawfully in closing the popular publication *Tempo* in 1994.

Meanwhile, *Golkar,* the official government party attempted to ban *Indonesian Democratic Party* chairman Megawati Sukarnoputra, the daughter of former President Sukarno, from East Java. This is an area where *Golkar* did not do well in

Balinese vendor

Photo by Jon Markham Morrow

the 1992 elections. It apparently fears growing opposition from the *PDI.*

Military promotions seemed to go to those with demonstrated loyalty to the president. Two former presidential adjutants and a bodyguard made general.

Foreign Relations: As the fourth largest country in the world, Indonesia has always considered itself to be number one among equals within the Association of Southeast Asian Nations (ASEAN), composed of Brunei, Indonesia, Malaysia, the Philippines, Singapore and Thailand. And, it is fair to say that the other ASEAN states usually have accepted the "big brother" role of Indonesia. The ASEAN headquarters is located in Jakarta. For its part, Indonesia has worked within the context of ASEAN though Jakarta has often been less enthu-

siastic about the rapid elimination of trade barriers since it is the least developed of the member states.

Indonesia prides itself on being an arbiter of disputes and a conciliator. Indonesia played an important role early on in the settlement of the dispute in Cambodia by hosting a series of informal "cocktail" parties to which the competing sides were invited. More recently, Indonesia has sponsored several seminars on the conflicting territorial claims in the South China Sea and especially the Spratley Islands. Six countries claim all or part of the sea.

Indonesia was a key player at the beginning of the non–alignment movement which traces its beginnings back to the Bandung (Indonesia) conference of 1955. In 1994, President Soeharto was serving as the group's head. Indonesia has followed a non–aligned foreign policy. Under former President Sukarno, the policy definitely leaned left. Sukarno tried to organize the New Emerging Forces which linked Indonesia to such countries as China, North Korea and Vietnam. After his fall, President Soeharto placed the country on a much more centrist path. The non–aligned nature of the policy is evidenced for example in the fact that the country does not have defense treaties with any major outside power or group of powers. This sets Indonesia apart from her ASEAN neighbors, excluding Brunei.

In November 1994, Indonesia was the host of the second Asia–Pacific Economic Cooperation meeting. The first meeting was held in Seattle, Washington, in 1993. President Soeharto met with all of the Asian leaders, excluding President Lee of Taiwan, who was not invited, and issued the "Bogor Declaration" at the conclusion of the leaders' summit. The declaration states that the developed APEC states will strive for free trade by the year 2010 and that the less developed states, including Indonesia, will reach this target by 2020.

Indonesia also replaced Pakistan in a two year non–permanent seat on the UN Security Council. This will elevate the visibility of the country worldwide.

The country's territorial waters expanded geometrically when the UN Law of the Sea Convention went into effect. Under the convention, all of the waters between the country's 3,000 islands now become Indonesian territorial waters.

In 1995, Indonesia enjoyed both successes and embarrassment in its foreign relations. Jakarta could be proud of its role in helping to secure a degree of freedom for the Burmese opposition leader, Aung Sang Suu Kyi, because of the good communications between the military regimes in Rangoon and Jakarta. The foreign minister Ali Alatas was also pleased that the Chinese publicly proclaimed their non–interest in the territory around Natuna island in the South China Sea, with its significant gas fields. Relations with Australia deteriorated to a dangerous level at mid–year when Canberra embarrassed Jakarta by raising questions about Indonesia's designated Ambassador. Canberra waited a very long time before asking questions about Lt. General Mentiri's comments about the 1991 military actions in East Timor. He apparently expressed no regret over the violence which had taken place. In December, the two countries concluded an agreement designed to bury the hatchet over past difficulties. This should ease Australian criticism of Jakarta, particularly in the area of human rights, and also improve Indonesia's regional standing.

In June, a round table dialogue on the issue of East Timor was held in Burg Schlaining, Austria. While Indonesian diplomats tried to brush off the meeting,

clearly it had elevated the topic in the international diplomatic community. If and when CNN discovers the East Timor issue, Jakarta will be in for difficult times.

Culture: Indonesia is a country of great cultural differences; this diversity is compounded by the presence of a great number of commercially active Chinese. This is a nation of islands which traditionally had mainly indirect contact with each other—a nation ruled in effect by a cultural minority located on the island of Java. Although the vast majority of Indonesians are at least nominally Muslim, this powerful belief has not united the people because it has been imposed on a basic blend of Hinduism and animism. In the Outer Islands, where religion was less formalized before the arrival of Islam, the religion of Mohammed is practiced in a much purer form than on Java and Sumatra. Bali, the island fabled in story and song in the western world, is the exception; it is an almost classic host of traditional Indian Hinduism.

Non–violence and courteous agreement are a tradition in Javanese culture. Open disagreement is avoided—differences are buried in an atmosphere of agreement, no matter how unreal. But, once it becomes apparent that differences cannot be hidden, violence becomes painfully real as it did in 1965. The Malay word *amok* has passed into English to denote the terrors of blind violence.

Arts and crafts of many varieties are highly developed in Indonesia—they combine the artistry of the Polynesian with the industrious character of the Chinese in an ever changing variety reflecting the customs of the islands.

Economy: Indonesia has a diversifying economy. Economic growth in GDP (Gross Domestic Product) has averaged about 6% annually since the 1970s. Foreign investment from 1988 through 1991 totaled $26 billion, more than twice the amount approved in the previous twenty years, aided by a less restrictive banking system. Indonesia's participation in the "growth triangle" with Singapore and Johore state in West Malaysia are proving the merits of the private sector in the development process. Corruption continues to be a severe problem, although it is not as bad as in the Philippines, the leader of the ASEAN states in this respect.

In 1995, exports grew 13%, against a 29.7% increase in imports, shrinking the trade surplus to $3.7 billion. Inflation slowed to 8.6% (the government wants a 5% rate). In order to keep inflation from taking off, banks must now keep a reserve of 5.5% of commercial deposits. One year loan rates are an astonishing 21%. All of this means that GDP growth for 1996 should fall to a little above 7%.

A basic fact about Indonesia is the high cost of doing business. A case in point occurred in January 1996 when beer brewers cut off supplies to Bali, the tourist Mecca of Indonesia, as a protest to the 400 rupiah (17 cents) levy applied to each bottle of beer by a company controlled by President Soeharto's grandson. The President intervened and the levy was rescinded. This is one of many levies which have been revoked in an effort to convince businessmen that corruption is declining.

A major problem for the economy is that Indonesia's foreign debt is not being handled correctly. This could cause the rupiah to devalue by as much as 5% against the dollar. Debt is being driven up by the fact that Japan is Indonesia's biggest lender. The rise in the value of the yen thus has artificially expanded what was already a significant debt. Government officials fear that investors will now begin to shy away from the country as a possible investment location.

Indonesia moved to reduce tariffs on over 400 capital goods items to help local producers. Also, on the positive side, foreign investment increased by 64% to $39.9 billion for the year. Domestic investment grew by 31% to $30 billion.

As a negative, the issue of East Timor should not be dismissed lightly. It could prove to be more than just an embarrassment to Jakarta.

The Future: Indonesia has come a long way since the days of Sukarno. Continued sustained growth should put Indonesia firmly into the mid–level developing nations category by the end of the century. A per capita income of $1,000 is not out of the question by decade's end. As economic progress continues, Indonesia can be expected to play an increasingly important role as the regional political leader. As the fourth largest country in the world, with almost 190 million people, such a role is not inconceivable. As the end of the Soeharto era draws closer, however, uncertainties over who will take over will have to be dealt with effectively and quickly.

Tokyo's shopping district, the Ginza, at night. *Courtesy: Japanese Embassy.*

Japan

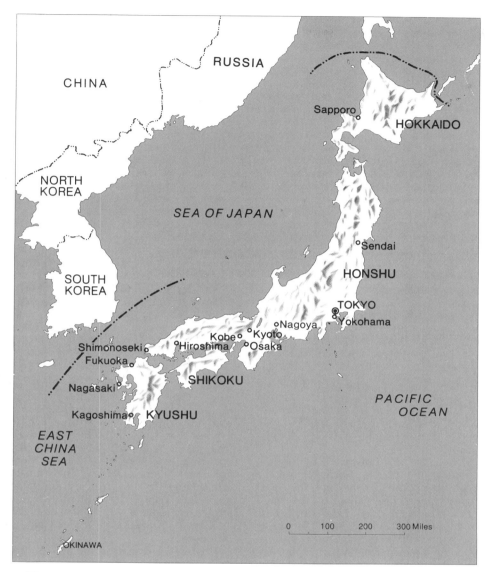

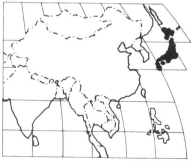

Japan

Area: 142,726 sq. mi. (370,370 sq. km.)
Population: 124,800,000 (est. 1993).
Capital City: Tokyo (Pop. 9.5 million, estimated).
Climate: Subtropically warm in the extreme South, becoming temperate in the North. The high elevations have much lower temperatures than the coastal areas. There is a rainy monsoon from June to October.
Neighboring Countries: The islands of Japan are closest to Russia (North); Korea (West); and mainland China (Southwest).
Official Language: Japanese.
Ethnic Background: Overwhelmingly Japanese, with mixed Mongol–Turkic–Caucasian origins which emerged in the pre–Christian era. There is a very small community of Ainu on Hokkaido Island who are a primitive people of Caucasian ancestry.
Principal Religion: Shinto, the official religion, is largely extinct. Buddhism is widespread and split into many old and new sects; Christianity.
Main Exports: (to U.S., nations of Southeast Asia and Western Europe) Products of heavy industry, including ships and autos, products of lighter industry, including electronic appliances and parts, cameras, and a wide range of other items, i.e. textiles, iron, steel, fish.
Main Imports: (from nations of the Middle East and Southeast Asia) Oil, raw industrial materials, foodstuffs.
Currency: Yen.
National Day: December 23 (birthday of the Emperor).
Special Holiday: April 29, called "Green Day" to honor the late Emperor's interest in the environment.
Chief of State: Emperor Akihito.
Head of Government: Ryutaro Hashimoto, Prime Minister (January 1996).
National Flag: White, with a red disk representing the rising sun in the center.
Per Capita Income: U.S. $28,200.

The island nation of Japan consists of four larger bodies of land, Hokkaido, Honshu, Shikoku and Kyushu and the smaller Ryukyu Islands south of Kyushu. The southern half of Sakhalin and the Kurile Islands to the north, which Japan possessed at the height of its World War II power, were lost to the Soviet Union at the close of the conflict.

Geographically, Japan is part of an immense hump on the earth's surface which extends from Siberia on the Asian continent through Korea and Japan southward, rising above water again in the areas of Taiwan (Formosa) and the Philippines and extending further south into the eastern portions of Indonesia and Australia. As is true in other portions of the ridge, Japan is geologically unstable and subject to frequent and sometimes violent earthquakes.

Thermal pressures from deep in the earth escape periodically through the many volcanoes which are interspersed among the mountains. Mt. Fuji, its lofty crater surrounded by a mantle of snow during the entire year, visible from the streets of Tokyo on a clear day, and one of the most beautiful sights in Asia, has not been active since 1719. All of the mountainous areas, volcanic and non–volcanic, are scenic—the taller peaks on Honshu have justly earned the name "Japanese Alps."

The mountains leave little level space; only about 15% of the total land area is level, and much of the only large plain is occupied by the huge and busy capital of Tokyo. As a result, farms are located in the hilly areas of the islands and are made level by the labors of the farmers, who have constructed elaborate terraces over long periods of time in order to win more land for their intense cultivation. Japanese farming is actually better called gardening, since the small units of land, an average of 2–1/2 to 5 acres per farm, are tilled with such energy that

"Bullet" train streaking commuters home against the majestic background of Mt. Fuji

none of the soil or available growing season is wasted. This tremendous agricultural effort produces almost enough to feed the people, most of whom live densely packed in the urban areas.

The climate of the islands is totally dominated by the seasonal winds, or monsoons. Cold winds blowing from the Asian continent invade the land beginning in September each year. All of Hokkaido and a substantial part of Honshu lie buried in snow from December to March. In the spring, the winds shift, blowing from the warm equatorial South Pacific; the growing season of Honshu and Hokkaido then commences.

The subtropical island of Kyushu remains warm all year around, permitting two or three harvests of paddy rice each year. Only one crop of dry, or field rice, grows in the much shorter summer of Hokkaido. In the last half of August and in September, the southern monsoon brings typhoons (hurricanes), laden with rainfall and often destruction from the Pacific to the shores of Japan.

Rainfall and weather are also affected by the oceanic water currents which envelope the islands. The warm southern *Juro Siwo* dominates the summer months; the arctic *Oya Siwo* descends as far south as Tokyo in the winter. Both currents bring a huge number of fish to the off–shore areas on the Pacific side, and an even larger number to the Sea of Japan. Depending almost wholly for animal protein upon this bounty from the sea, the Japanese raise only an insignificant number of livestock on the islands.

History: The earliest known inhabitants of the Japanese islands were the Ainu, a primitive people of white Caucasian ancestry who probably had come to Japan earlier than the people we now call Japanese.

Driven steadily northward by the Japanese in the period shortly before the beginning of the Christian era, they exist today in small reservations on the island of Hokkaido. The men have much more body and facial hair than the Japanese; the women have the curious custom of tatooing a moustache on their upper lip, and dress in a manner similar to the men.

The Japanese came primarily from the mainland of northeast Asia, by way of Korea, and are of the same ancestry as the Koreans. They were mainly of Mongolian stock whose ancestors had lived a nomadic existence on the continent of Central and Northeast Asia. This ethnic group became the predominant one, but there were also other elements from the South China coast and the Southwest Pacific. Japanese architecture, adapted because of the threat of earthquakes into a flimsy style of wood and paper inadequate to withstand the colder months of the winter, is similar to that of the southwest Pacific.

All of these elements gradually blended into a people possessing very similar physical characteristics, considering the large size of the present population. In the first centuries A.D., the Japanese lived mainly around the Inland Sea, a body of water almost completely enclosed by three of the four large islands. They were essentially primitive, organized into many warring clans and had no writing system with which to express their language, which is derived from mainland Asiatic dialects originally spoken in what is now Manchuria, Mongolia and Siberian Russia. The Yamato clan emerged as the strongest and most respected group; its leaders became known as emperors when Japan emerged as a more civilized state under Chinese influence.

This process began in the 5th century A.D., probably as a result of visits by Chinese merchants to Japan. The Japanese were greatly impressed by the tales told of Chinese military power, wealth, prestige and culture, especially during the Chinese T'ang dynasty (618–907 A.D.) and quickly set about importing a number of the elements of the more highly organized culture of China. One of the most important of these was Chinese character writing which the Japanese adapted to their own tongue. The intricate symbols, which represented words to the Chinese, were modified by the addition of special ones representing the actual sounds of syllables, and also to indicate the endings of words, or inflections, in order to convey different meanings. In contrast, the Chinese character writing has never expressed the sound of the spoken Chinese language.

In an attempt to imitate the T'ang dynasty, the Japanese imperial court built a capital at Nara, near the waters of the

66

Inland Sea on the island of Honshu. The creation of a central government was not possible, however, because many clans, particularly those in central and northern Japan, were strong and independent and still preoccupied with battling the Ainu people and each other. These clans did not attempt to overthrow the imperial court, however. They contented themselves with largely ignoring it on the scattered occasions when they received directives from the Nara capital.

Kyoto became the imperial capital in the late 8th century instead of Nara and became the home of a brilliant culture. Ancient legends were altered and more were created to prove the divinity and supremacy of the imperial clan and represented as truth. An arbitrary date in the 7th century B.C. was selected as the time that the sun goddess gave the blessing of creation to Japan and established the reign of her descendants on the islands. The arts flourished, particularly a highly distinctive and fine literature in the form of novels produced by ladies of the imperial court in the modified writing system adapted from the Chinese characters.

Although the more martial, semi–independent clans outside the capital admired and imitated the cultural achievements of Kyoto, they were primarily interested in their military power. The Taira, one of the two most powerful military clans, defeated the other, the Minamoto, in 1160 and then seized control of Kyoto, but without remaining in power. Shortly afterward, the Taira were in turn defeated by the Minamoto, whose leader Yoritomo was appointed as the first *Shogun*, or *Generalissimo*, of Japan by the emperor and founded the Kamakura Shogunate which remained in power for 150 years.

The imperial family was not disturbed by the powerful Shoguns; its male members often married women from other clans, notably the Fujiwara, which usually dominated the imperial court. The Shogunate quickly became the real government, rendering the emperors revered, but powerless figureheads. The Kamakura Shogunate was faced with the external threat of the powerful empire established by the Mongol emperor Khubilai Khan in China in the 13th century. Two attempted Mongol invasions were defeated by a combination of Japanese military resistance and timely, violent typhoons. The failure of these invasions added substance to the growing belief of the Japanese that they possessed a unique and superior character and were under divine protection.

The succeeding shogunate came into power through the overthrow of its predecessor and remained supreme until the middle of the 16th century. It was noted principally for its patronage of the arts.

The *Zen* school of Buddhism, stressing mysticism and contemplation, became very popular with the aristocracy and with the *samurai*, or warrior class. Fighting was truly a profession among the *samurai*—they developed a crude military science which gave the art of fighting a formality almost beyond belief, as well as being fanatical and conservative.

Japan disintegrated into a state of feudal warfare in the 16th century resembling that of the Wars of the Roses in England. Commercial interests continued, however, to promote trade and build roads. Warfare was gradually brought under control in the later part of the century by two persons—Oda Nobunaga and his brilliant general, Toyotomi Hideyoshi, who succeeded Nobunaga as dictator *(Kampaku)* when his overlord was killed by a dissident general.

In the middle of the 16th century, Portuguese ships and Jesuit missionaries began to arrive in Japan, which had not previously been touched by western discovery and exploration. The Jesuits converted a large number of people, particularly in Kyushu and its largest city of Nagasaki. Their position was enhanced by the conversion of a leading feudal lord of the island to the faith of the missionaries, which led many vassals and followers into the arms of the Church. Firearms and other western methods of violence were introduced and eagerly adopted by the Japanese.

Spanish Franciscans, who arrived in 1593, began a period of even greater efforts toward conversion of the Japanese and also confused the non–Christian rulers of the islands by periodic bickering with the Jesuits. The dictator, convinced that Christianity was nothing but a veil concealing a future European invasion,

embarked on a course of persecution of priests and their converts, who numbered as high as 250,000.

The anti–Christian, anti–European sentiments of the dictator were continued and expanded by the founder of the Tokugawa Shogunate, a lord who established himself at Edo, now Tokyo, in 1600. This level area underwent a period of phenomenal growth in the first half of the 17th century as the seat of the Shogunal government from which brutal persecutions of Christianity were directed from 1615 to 1640. In addition, the anti–western sentiment of the ruling Shoguns led to the closing of all ports in the islands to foreign ships, with the exception of ten Chinese and one Dutch ship each year, which landed at Nagasaki.

The Tokugawa governed Japan with a heavy hand. In order to control the other clans they used a number of devices, including the taking of hostages from the families of the clan heads. Their control was weakest in the Southwest, where a number of clans were accustomed to contacts with the outside world and impatient with the official ''Exclusion Policy,'' as it later came to be known.

The clans, each ruled by a powerful lord, or *daimyo*, built ornate castles beginning in the 17th century, around which towns arose. In this way, Japan acquired the most important single base for modernization, a multitude of moderate–sized towns, as distinguished from cities, which were primarily political centers. Agriculture prospered, sporadically interrupted by revolts of the peasants, who lived in abject poverty. Trade flourished, the population increased, and a merchant class emerged which quickly acquired a great deal of influence over the *daimyo* and the martial *samurai*

An Ainu elder

Courtesy: Jon Markham Morrow

by making loans to them. There was much intellectual activity, which was conservative, to the extent that it advocated that the imperial clan, which had survived over the centuries, should be restored to full power and replace the usurping shogunate. Conservative political thought included a study of Japan's Shinto religious heritage.

Sporadic attempts by western powers to "open" Japan to foreign trade were largely unsuccessful until the 1850's. Just as the mystery of Japan, and the lure of commerce, prompted Russian, British and U.S. attempts to penetrate the islands, many educated Japanese were interested in western nations and their scientific achievements—their appetite was whetted to a keen edge by the limited trade and cultural contacts with the Dutch.

The confusion among the Japanese when Commodore Perry of the United States sailed his fleet into Tokyo Bay in 1853–1854 is hard to describe. The interest in western trade and ideas was keen among some of the *samurai*, particularly in the southern region, and for this reason, they opposed the Tokugawa. The element among the clans which was anti–foreign was also against the shogunate, and saw the threat of the foreigners as an opportunity to urge that the Tokugawa accomplish an impossible task—the exclusion of the Americans and other intruders. The weakened regime, in a desperate move, asked the advice of the other clans. Commodore Perry was therefore able to get the treaty desired by the U.S., and other powers soon had their agreements. All of these were patterned after the "unequal treaties" that were being imposed on the waning Manchu dynasty of China during the same period. The opponents of the Tokugawa, especially the powerful clans of the Southwest, accused the government of weakness and continued a fanatic anti–foreign campaign. Western naval bombardments at Kagoshima in 1863 and Shimonoseki in 1864 convinced them of the folly of their demands, and they did an about–face, becoming eager advocates of learning as much as possible from the West—in order to be better equipped to resist its influence and power.

The shogunate system of government ended in 1867 after 700 years of power with the collapse of the Tokugawa regime. The powerful clans, principally those of the Southwest, "restored" the emperor and moved the imperial capital to Tokyo, the city of the Tokugawas, in 1868. The emperor actually reigned, but did not rule—he was the institution used by a few dozen young *samurai* who were determined that Japan would be modernized.

Mutsuhito, the dynamic young emperor on whom this government centered, received foreign representatives at his imperial court at the beginning of the *Meiji* period (1868–1912). (The reigns of the Japanese emperors are not described by their own names. A "period name" is used instead; thus Yoshihito ruled during the *Taisho* period from 1913–1926, and Japan was in the *Showa* period under Emperor Hirohito.)

By the end of the *Meiji* period, known commonly in the West as the *Meiji* Restoration (1868–1912), Japan had largely achieved its goal of modernization—a feat not duplicated by any other traditionalist nation in the world in such a brief period, or indeed anywhere on such a tremendous scale. The leadership set up a strong central government and governed in an almost dictatorial style that nevertheless made some concessions to Western parliamentary institutions, which were established. Economically, a small group of *zaibatsu* (large family–owned holding companies) arose which dominated the beginnings of industry in Japan in a manner reminiscent of Carnegie, Harriman and Morgan in the United States, but there was abundant room for small business. This balance between central control and local initiative, coupled with the rapid urbanization of Japan, its fairly low rate of population growth and the fact that the prople demanded so very little in personal comforts, permitted a rate of modernization unparalleled in history.

The new leaders wiped out the old clan system of authority and at the same time modernized land tenure. The landowning peasants were rather heavily taxed, however, yielding greater funds for modernization. Modern communications were established and new machinery was imported to manufacture textiles and other goods. A modern education system, geared to the production of literate and obedient subjects of the Emperor, was created.

An effective army and navy and a modern legal system also emerged within a short time, permitting the Japanese to repudiate the "unequal treaties," but the leadership avoided foreign military adventures at first. It tolerated but largely dominated the political parties which emerged in the early 1880's. It created a *Diet*, or parliament, under a constitution of 1889 that proclaimed the emperor as a virtual god, behind whom the governing oligarchy continued to rule. The period of adopting foreign institutions and techniques diminished and practically ended by 1890, when an intense nationalist, anti–foreign reaction set in, with an emphasis on ancient Japanese institutions and customs and their legendary superiority. The emperor became the object of still greater glorification, even though he possessed little more than nominal power.

Increasing agitation by the political parties against the government and the growth of military strength and prowess led Japan to pick a fight in 1894 with the decaying Manchu empire of China. The Japanese army and navy seized control of Taiwan (Formosa) and conquered Korea, which was annexed in 1910.

In its war with China, Japan fought

A Japanese custom is to greet the sunrise on New Year's Day.

Courtesy: Marilynn and Mark Swenson

largely alone, without the support of any of the major Western powers. As a result, the Japanese were forced to give up at the bargaining table much of what they had won on the battlefield. This lesson left a lasting impression on Japanese leaders. In their minds, the "Western imperialists" had their own set of rules; outsiders, like the Japanese, were not part of their "club" and were not permitted the same freedom of action as other world powers. In 1903, the Japanese concluded an alliance with Britain that lasted until the 1920's. The ensuing period saw a tremendous growth in Japanese military and political power at the expense of its neighbors, a result of its strengthened position as a member of a Western alliance.

The Japanese did not conquer territory from the Chinese alone—the Russians were competing in the same period for influence in northeast Asia; they had a "sphere of influence" in Manchuria dating from 1898. The Japanese launched a victorious land and sea campaign against the Russians in 1904 (the Russo–Japanese War) and thereby established themselves as the leading power in Asia, and in fact one of the world's major powers.

Japan did not waste the opportunity offered by the vulnerability of Germany during World War I. It quickly declared war on Germany in order to seize German holdings which had recently been established in Shandong (Shantung) Province in China, as well as several small island groups in the Pacific. At the same time, it shipped considerable quantities of munitions to the Allied Powers, including to Russia, its former enemy. But at the end of the war, and after the Bolshevik Revolution of 1917, Japan sent a large military force to occupy eastern Siberia to see if the region could be added to the growing Japanese empire. Internal and external pressures forced them from Siberia and also from Shandong in 1922, and Japan agreed to limit the size of its navy by treaty at the same time.

The post–World War I period in Japan was one of transition. The voting lists were enlarged to include the whole of the adult male population, and political parties became more influential than before. But the speed of modernization in Japan left unsolved some problems and created many others. The rural population remained isolated from urban progress, while continuing to pay for it by increased taxes, rents and difficult conditions in the countryside in the 1920's, all of which created much discontent. The cause of the peasants was championed by ambitious army officers, partly in sincerity but also for political reasons. The officers, who were largely of rural origin, found allies among some civilian nationalists. They adopted the position that rural poverty had two basic causes: poor

The late Emperor Hirohito at his coronation, 1926

government by the political parties and economic practices by the large combines. They criticized the political parties, who were more influential during the 1920's than at any previous time. The *zaibatsu*, as the economic combines were called, also came under fire for their devotion to the goal of high profits. The military and civilian nationalists also blamed injurious and "insulting" tariffs and discriminatory trade policies of some foreign nations for the adverse conditions of the peasants.

This line of argument had a broad base of appeal, and the rightists strengthened their position by taking forceful action in the form of assassinations and *coups*. The

extreme right wing did not succeed in seizing power, but it was able to force the more moderate right in the government and in the army to take control after 1936 and to adopt a somewhat more extremist outlook. All political parties were abolished in 1940.

Japan took advantage of the conflict between the nationalist forces of Chiang Kai–shek and the communist revolutionaries led by Mao Zedong in China. Increasing pressures, both diplomatic and military, were brought to bear in order to give Japan great influence in, if not direct control over, China. The Japanese army seized Manchuria in 1931–1932, soon after the local authorities had threatened

Japan's interest by accepting the authority of Chiang Kai–shek's government. Renaming the area Manchukuo, the Japanese military established Henry Pu–yi, the "last emperor" of the Manchu dynasty, as its puppet—the *Orchid Emperor*. Frequent military clashes with China led to an invasion of eastern China in 1937, in the course of which a multitude of atrocities were committed by the invading soldiers.

Merciless bombing of the mainland cities alienated the Chinese completely and enabled both Chiang and Mao to rally support for their separate struggles against the Japanese; an uneasy truce emerged between the two Chinese leaders because of the Japanese threat, but the Japanese forces remained in occupation of the major cities of eastern China.

These Japanese efforts at expansion led to increasing criticism and pressure from the outside world, including the United States. In an effort to limit the capability of the Japanese war machine, the U.S. gradually cut down shipments of oil and scrap steel (the "moral embargo").

This reduced shipment of strategic materials caused the Japanese to look for sources elsewhere, particularly to iron in the Philippines and oil in Indonesia. The German victories which took place in Europe in 1940 provided an example of the rewards of aggression. Fortunately for the rest of the world, cooperation between Nazi Germany and Japan was always very unsteady even though they and Italy formed an alliance in 1940. All three, but most of all the European "Axis" powers, had the habit of making bargains with other nations without consulting or informing their allies.

Japan decided to force the issue with the United States in late 1941 and demanded an unfreezing of its assets in the United States, which had been frozen in response to the Japanese invasion of Indochina in July 1941. Washington further refused to resume oil and scrap steel shipments, and in addition, encouraged the Dutch in Indonesia to withhold their oil unless the Japanese agreed to a political settlement in Asia, which would have involved an end to aggression and withdrawal from China. Believing that the U.S. would oppose any Japanese seizure of the resources of Southeast Asia, the Japanese decided to knock out the U.S. Pacific Fleet stationed at Pearl Harbor in Hawaii. The American Ambassador cabled from Tokyo on November 17, 1941, that it was possible the Japanese might make a sudden sneak attack, and on December 7 Japanese airplanes almost wiped out the U.S. battleship fleet in Pearl Harbor in a few short hours.

The Japanese army and navy quickly overran Southeast Asia, which was weakly defended; their military performed with maximum efficiency in this campaign. Initially, their superior might in the Pacific was close enough to cause the fear of an imminent naval–air attack on California. The Japanese army met its greatest resistance in the Philippines, where the people cooperated with the U.S. defense force led by General Douglas MacArthur, but ultimately the islands fell. Apart from unwise attempts to gain still further territories from Australia and India and in the central Pacific, the Japanese military settled down to occupy and exploit their newly won empire. The only land resistance during this period was sporadic and weak, from Chiang Kai–shek's forces, which were contained in southwest China, and from scattered communists in the northwest region of China under the command of Mao Zedong.

By their brutality the Japanese military very quickly alienated leaders of the local people who were not already anti–Japanese. Even when they proclaimed supposedly independent governments in Burma and in the Philippines in 1943, they failed to arouse any real enthusiasm, even among local nationalists. Their actual reason for these moves was that Burma and the Philippines were two areas of their empire most exposed to Allied military pressures. In the later years of the war, active resistance to the Japanese formed in most Southeast Asian lands they had conquered, and much of it had a prominent communist element.

As the war economy of the United States came into production, the Japanese suffered increasing defeats in naval and air battles with the U.S. starting in mid–1942. Australia initially served as the main base for the Allied campaign; it and New Zealand also contributed fighting units to the war. Island after island fell to American Marines and Allied Army units. U.S. aircraft and warships, principally submarines, increasingly cut the Japanese islands off from their Southeast Asian and the Southwest Pacific conquests by sinking tremendous amounts of shipping and by defeating the Japanese navy.

By 1944 General Tojo, who had led Japan to war with the U.S., was deposed as premier and disappeared from the circle of military officers who were in control. Important persons in the imperial court and the government saw that the war was lost and believed that peace should be negotiated as soon as possible in order to save the Emperor and avoid a communist revolution. The military insisted on continuing the losing battle; the Emperor might have overruled them but chose to remain silent.

On August 6, 1945, the sky above Hiroshima was lit by the fiery destructiveness of the first atomic bomb used in the history of the world. The Japanese were already hard pressed by the Allied troops, who were being reinforced by soldiers that arrived in the area after the fall of Germany earlier in the year. On August 8, the Soviet Union declared war on Japan. It had agreed to do this the preceding February in exchange for post-war control of Outer Mongolia, which had been a nominal Chinese territory prior to the war, and also for Sakhalin Island and the Kurile Islands in Northern Japan, as well as important railway and port rights in Manchuria. A second atomic bomb was dropped on Nagasaki on August 9; the next day the war and peace factions submitted the choice of war or surrender to the Emperor.

The Emperor, in an act of great moral courage, chose surrender—the final terms of capitulation were agreed to by August 14, 1945, and the formal agreement was signed aboard the U.S.S. Missouri in Tokyo Bay on September 2, 1945. The islands had been terribly battered and exhausted by the war. National morale was almost completely crushed; some army leaders and high government officials chose *harakiri*, a formal suicide which eliminated the necessity of facing their conquerors or the people they had led.

Japan's Foreign Minister Shigimitsu signs the documents of surrender aboard the *U.S.S. Missouri*, while General MacArthur broadcasts the ceremonies

THE POSTWAR OCCUPATION

The American occupation of Japan after World War II was literally an attempt to remake Japan's political, economic, and educational institutions in a way that would prevent the future reemergence of militarism. Supreme Commander of Allied Powers (SCAP) MacArthur's headquarters, which became a euphemism for the American authorities in general, rewrote the Japanese constitution, broke up the powerful *zaibatsu* business conglomerates, and completely revamped the Japanese educational system. In many respects, some of the reforms forced on Japan in the war's aftermath were more liberal than many comparable U.S. policies.

The American efforts were as much the product of ignorance, however, as they were of a concerted effort to remake Japanese society in America's image. Many American efforts were abruptly curtailed as the U.S. hastily sought to firmly anchor Japan as an anticommunist bastion in the Far East. Nevertheless Japan has been saddled with a political and educational system which doesn't quite fit. While Japan has squirmed, sometimes uncomfortably, under this yoke, the overall system has been largely maintained.

The war in Korea had a profound impact on the course of the occupation. The socialists, who naturally supported some of the liberal reforms proposed by the Americans, were now eyed with suspicion and many were purged from government positions by SCAP authorities. Japanese moderates were genuinely frightened by prospects of political unrest and the fear of communist takeover right on their Korean doorstep. Discredited conservative politicians, removed from office due to their support of Japan's war effort, were rehabilitated as anticommunist allies.

The war had a number of other effects as well. While the Japanese adhered to the constitutional prohibition against maintaining armed forces, under U.S. pressure a national armed constabulary was formed. Heavily armed, these "police" effectively replaced U.S. occupation troops, freeing them for combat on the Korean peninsula. Japan's devastated industries were slowly revived by the Korean war boom, providing supplies and equipment for the U.S. war effort. Almost overnight, the nature of the U.S. occupation and U.S.–Japanese relations had changed dramatically.

A peace treaty was signed with the United States and some other Western and Asian nations in 1951, but the communist bloc refrained from concluding formal peace accords. Under the U.S. treaty, Japan regained its independence, but lost all of its empire outside the home islands; further reparations were left to be determined between Japan and each individual country concerned. A security treaty was signed with the U.S. under which America was to maintain military bases in Japan and to administer Okinawa in the Ryukyu Islands, where it had established its largest military base in the

Mother and child.   Courtesy: Marilynn and Mark Swenson

western Pacific. This treaty was renewed in 1960, but was modified at that time by the inclusion of certain concessions to Japan; it was renewed a second time in 1970. The island was finally returned to Japanese jurisdiction on May 15, 1972.

POST-OCCUPATION POLITICS

The new constitution introduced in 1946, under the Occupation, had established a constitutional monarchy and a parliamentary system resembling those of Britain. It also provided (in the famous Article Nine) that Japan forever relinquished the right to make war and even to maintain armed forces. This article, which on the surface would appear to ban even self–defense, has been gradually loosened over the years. Japan created an armed constabulary in the early 1950's, which, after being armed with heavy weapons, aircraft, and tanks, expanded into the Japan Self Defense Force. Japan's deepening commitment to the U.S. alliance and growing global importance have today expanded the role of self–defense to include responsibility for shipping lanes out to a 1,000–mile radius from the Japanese islands; Japan's navy (Maritime Self Defense Forces) is one of the largest in Asia.

The constitution failed to mention, and in this way repudiated, any divine attributes or political power on the part of the emperor. In spite of this, or perhaps because of it, Emperor Hirohito remained a generally respected symbol of the nation. In 1986 he celebrated his 85th birthday and also the sixtieth anniversary of his accession to the throne—one of the

longest reigns in modern history. He adjusted remarkably well to the tremendous changes in Japan since World War II—essentially from a military–dominated authoritarian state to a parliamentary democracy. He was kept informed of political developments by the prime minister (premier). He was the only Japanese emperor to have traveled abroad; he visited the United States.

After one of the longest reigns in history, and after a long illness, Emperor Hirohito died on January 7, 1989. He was succeeded by his modern–minded son, Crown Prince Akihito (sometimes referred to as the Rising Son), who took the title Heisei (Achieving Peace) for his reign. This transition evoked a great deal of soul searching in Japan about the responsibility for World War II in the Pacific and about Hirohito's role in that war, as well as controversy over the same subjects in other countries. The fairest verdict seems to be that Hirohito had not favored Japanese aggression but had felt bound as a constitutional monarch (although theoretically divine) to accept the advice of his officials. At the end of the war, he certainly showed great moral courage in dealing first with his own militarists and then with the American Occupation authorities.

As in earlier periods, post–Occupation Japanese politics has been dominated by political and economic conservatives, an elite that became much more effective after the war because of being compelled to renounce its previous reactionary ideology and its tendency to war and military expansion. They have remained in power mainly because they are effective

Former Emperor Hirohito addresses the opening of the Diet.

and are much more on the wavelength of the majority of the people than the leftist opposition is.

The mainstream of the conservative political establishment centered at first, under the Occupation, on two political parties, the *Liberals* and the *Democrats;* many of their leaders were retired bureaucrats (since the bureaucracy had not been purged by the Occupation to the same extent as had the politicians). The serving bureaucracy and the large firms were and are other important components of the conservative establishment; because of the huge profits that the Japanese economy has generated, big business has tended to gain in influence at the expense of the bureaucracy and the politicians.

The *Liberals,* the more influential of the two conservative parties, collaborated wholeheartedly with the Occupation, and their leader, Shigeru Yoshida, was premier from 1946 to 1947 and again from 1948 to 1954. A strong personality and a "high posture" politician, he believed that Japan must renounce the traditional means to national power, especially military strength and its employment abroad, in favor of long–term economic growth as a safer and surer way to express Japan's formidable energies. It was not until after he left office, however, that the Japanese economy began its astonishing resurgence (see Economy).

The *Democrats* necessarily accepted the broad outlines of the Occupation but believed that its policies had gone too far too fast and needed to be modified somewhat to suit Japanese conditions. Under Yoshida's successor as premier, Ichiro

Hatoyama (1955–6), who was a *Democrat,* few such changes were made. More important, the two conservative parties merged in 1955 to form the *Liberal Democratic Party (LDP),* which has governed Japan ever since. Hatoyama established diplomatic relations with the Soviet Union in 1956, but to this day there is no Japanese–Soviet peace treaty ending World War II. The main obstacle is a strong disagreement over the status of the southern Kurile Islands, which the Japanese claim as their Northern Territories, but which the Soviets have held since 1945 together with the rest of the Kuriles.

The next premier, Nobusuke Kishi, was a "high posture" politician who got into trouble at home and abroad. He antagonized the People's Republic of China, with which Japan had no diplomatic relations at the time, but with which it was doing considerable trade, by being not only pro–U.S., but pro–Taiwan, and in 1958 Beijing cut off trade with Japan for a time, in an unsuccessful effort to drive him from office. At home, Kishi antagonized the left by ramming through the *Diet* (Japan's parliament) a bill to increase the powers of the police, which had been greatly reduced under the Occupation, and by negotiating in 1960 a revision and extension of the alliance signed with the U.S. at the end of the Occupation. The furor over the new treaty, which actually was more favorable to Japan than the original but was perceived by the left as a prop of conservative rule, was so great that a scheduled visit by President Eisenhower had to be canceled.

The effects of the war and the Occupa-

tion, rapid urbanization and the still shaky state of the economy combined to produce a great deal of social discontent during the 1950's. It found organized expression through student organizations, unions and federations of unions, such as the Teacher's Union, and opposition political parties. The largest of the latter was (and is) the *Japan Socialist Party (JSP),* formed in 1955 through the merger of a more moderate (right–wing) and more radical (left–wing) *Socialist Party;* both are Marxist, but the latter has generally favored the cutting of ties with the U.S. and the adoption of a posture of "unarmed neutrality" and friendship with the Soviet Union. There is also a smaller *Democratic Socialist Party (DSP),* which is critical of the ruling *LDP* but does not go as far as the *JSP.* The *Communist Party (JCP)* is well led and dynamic, but has been troubled by splits (between pro–Soviet and pro–Chinese factions, in particular) and hampered by the basic conservatism of the Japanese public. In addition to these, a widespread neo–Buddhist movement, the *Soka Gakkai,* developed during the 1960's a political arm, the *Komeito* ("Clean Government Party"), which nominally disaffiliated from the parent organization. An extreme leftist, violent student organization, the *Zengakuren,* which was comparable to the Chinese Red Guards during the Cultural Revolution, was crushed by the police at the beginning of the 1970's.

During the 1960's, the *LDP* appeared to be in gradual decline, and it was widely believed that it might eventually lose power to a coalition of opposition parties.

That has not happened. The *JSP*, the *JCP*, and the *Komeito* tried for a time in the 1960's to form such a coalition, but the effort foundered, mainly on the obvious intent of the *JCP* to dominate it. The opposition parties have repeatedly bumped their heads against a ceiling, expressed in terms of approximate maximum percentages of the popular vote and seats in the Diet: roughly 20% for the *JSP*, 5% for the *DSP* and 10% each for the *JCP* and the *Komeito*.

Much of the wind was taken out of the opposition's sails by the remarkable growth of the Japanese economy which began in the 1960's. Premier Hayato Ikeda (1960–4) avoided the controversial behavior of his predecessor Kishi, cultivated a "low posture" in politics and launched a program to double the gross national product by the end of the decade, a goal that was more than achieved.

His successor, Eisaku Sato (1964–1972) was more "high posture" and created considerable controversy, mainly by staying in office for the unusually long period of eight years and by being perceived, especially in Beijing, as being too pro–U.S. and too pro–Taiwan. In 1965 he announced his determination to regain jurisdiction over Okinawa, and after prolonged negotiations with the U.S., the island, as well as the rest of the Ryukyus, reverted to the Japanese in 1972. Sato cooperated with the U.S. to a degree during the first several years of

the Vietnam war, from which Japanese firms made large profits by selling supplies and equipment to the U.S. for use in the conflict, as they had during the Korean War. In 1969 he gave President Nixon, who was planning a withdrawal of American ground forces from Asia under the Nixon doctrine and was anxious not to have this lead to another war in Korea, an apparent promise that the U.S. would be allowed to use its bases in Japan for the defense of South Korea if it should be attacked again. He was unable to satisfy Nixon, however, on the issue of curbing Japanese textile exports to the U.S., and in 1971 he was punished by a series of what the Japanese called "Nixon shocks": Henry Kissinger's first, initially secret, trip to China in July (the U.S. had promised not to make changes in its China policy without prior notice to Japan), special duties on Japanese goods (especially automobiles) a month later, and in the fall pressures of various kinds that forced Japan to revalue the undervalued yen upward, from about 365 to the dollar to about 260, with a damping effect on Japanese exports. Toward the end of his tenure, Sato signed the Nuclear Nonproliferation Treaty, an act for which he was later awarded a Nobel Peace Prize. He became the object of strong denunciation by Beijing, mainly on account of his unwillingness to establish diplomatic relations with China.

Kakuei Tanaka, a farmer's son and popular politician whose formal education ended with the 10th grade, was elected president of the ruling *Liberal Democratic Party* in 1972, thus assuring him the prime ministership. He paid a successful visit to Beijing and established diplomatic relations with the People's Republic of China. But in 1973 a series of political and economic setbacks badly eroded the Tanaka government's popularity. Inflation, pollution and corruption continued to be major issues. When there was a temporary Arab oil embargo against Japan arising from the Middle East war of late 1973, dramatic results were produced in Japan, which imports 80% of its oil from the Middle East. The price of oil quadrupled. The government made some statements critical of Israel and began to woo the Arab states in other ways as well, in particular, by promising them $3 billion in aid of various kinds in return, it was hoped, for exemption from any embargo in the future.

This crisis reduced Japan's economic growth in 1974 roughly to zero and further weakened the Tanaka government. In order to recover, the ruling *Liberal Democratic Party* spent large sums of money received from business contributions in an effort to influence elections in mid–1974 for the upper house of the Diet, the House of Councillors. The party emerged with only half the seats (126 out of 252), however, and suffered a further setback—business contributions began to decline. Several leading figures resigned from the cabinet, and the feeling grew that if Tanaka stayed in office until his term expired in 1975, he would bring disaster to his party in the next elections to the lower house of the Diet, also scheduled for 1975. The Watergate affair in the United States and President Nixon's resignation in 1974 focused the attention of the Japanese public on the behavior of their own leaders.

The final blow fell in October–November 1974, when a series of press articles exposed Tanaka's personal wealth and the questionable means by which it had been obtained. He resigned in late November, only a few days after a state visit by President Ford which he had vainly hoped might save him.

Feeling that it might be facing its last chance to save itself from losing power, the *Liberal Democratic Party* dispensed with the usual jockeying for the premiership and entrusted the selection to the party's Vice President, Etsusaburo Shiina, whose surprising choice fell on the moderate Takeo Miki. The latter published a list of his personal assets (an unprecedented step in Japan) but could not persuade his colleagues to do the same.

Miki's political position was weaker than that of several other leaders of his party, including Tanaka. Miki tried with

Tokyo's expressways curve and divide as they crisscross the city.

Courtesy: Japanese Embassy

73

Seaweed, widely used in cooking, is gathered off the rocky coast.

Courtesy: Marilynn and Mark Swenson

some success to improve his image and strengthen his position by a number of initiatives. One was a trip to the United States in 1975, following which Emperor Hirohito also made a similar visit. In late 1975 he participated with five West European premiers in a conference on economic matters, the first time a Japanese premier had done this. At his insistence, a general strike of government workers was called off.

However, in early 1976 it was revealed in the United States that over the previous twenty years the Lockheed Aircraft Corporation had paid about $21 million in bribes to various Japanese officials and politicians to promote the sales of various types of military aircraft. The U.S. Central Intelligence Agency was probably already aware of these, but other agencies of the government, including the U.S. Securities and Exchange Commission, cooperated with the Japanese government's investigation of the scandal, which rocked Japan. Miki's investigation aroused the anger of some of his senior colleagues in the party, who evidently feared that they and their friends might be implicated. As a result, Miki was in danger of being forced out of office even before the general election of November–December 1976. Nevertheless, the inquiry proceeded, and resulted in, among other things, the trial and conviction of Tanaka.

Following the election, Miki resigned and an able, experienced conservative leader of the party, Takeo Fukuda, became Premier.

A new system was introduced for selecting the leader of the party, who is

also the Premier. This consisted of a direct vote by all members of the party for two candidates, with the final choice made by the party members in the Diet. When the primary was held in November, it resulted in an upset victory for Masayoshi Ohira. Fukuda resigned in his favor without waiting for the final vote in the Diet. But in May 1980, Ohira lost a vote of confidence arising from charges of corruption in office; he died on June 12th of a heart attack. He was in turn succeeded by the virtually unknown Zenko Suzuki as head of the party, which then won the June 1980 Diet elections with a surprisingly solid majority (284 seats out of 511).

Suzuki's performance was weak, and in late 1982 he was replaced by the able and energetic Yasuhiro Nakasone, who began to try to improve relations with the United States which had become frayed by economic issues and by American pressures on Japan to strengthen its military posture at a faster rate.

Nakasone was a controversial figure, partly because of his desire for a larger defense budget and partly due to his close connection with former Premier Tanaka—they are sometimes referred to collectively as Tanakasone. Nevertheless, the *Liberal Democratic Party* did well in the elections to the House of Councillors in mid–1983. In spite of its successes, the party continued to have a major black mark—Tanaka remained in the Diet (even though he had nominally resigned from it) and controlled the largest faction of the party. Worse yet, he was convicted

and sentenced to four years in prison, although he never went to jail.

The party dropped from 286 to 258 seats in the lower house in late 1983 elections, holding on to a bare majority of the 511 seats. The main opposition parties, other than the communist, made gains; Tanaka was reelected. The party had to enter into a coalition for the first time to ensure continued control in the lower house; the political marriage of convenience was with a small independent party, the *New Liberal Club*.

Without opposition, Nakasone was reelected to a second term as president of the party and, therefore, prime minister in late 1984. However, he faced some continuing, serious problems. He was still dependent on the support of the disgraced Tanaka. Further, it was only after considerable delay and great effort that he was able to push Japan's defense budget to a level above 1% of the gross national product. He did not take effective steps to reduce the huge trade and payments imbalance in Japan's favor as requested by the United States. Japanese markets have yet to be opened sufficiently toward accomplishing this objective. The prime minister also faced a rising level of political activity by opposition parties, especially the Socialists under their new, moderate leader, Masashi Ishibashi.

Prime Minister Nakasone maintained a rather high profile abroad as well as at home. He visited the United States in January 1983 and Southeast Asia the following May. President Reagan returned the visit in November.

Nakasone threw his considerable prestige and popularity in 1985 behind an appeal to Japanese business and the Japanese public to import and buy more foreign (especially American) goods, so as to reduce Japan's huge payments surplus. This appeal had little effect, except to worry the Japanese about their economic relations with the United States and the possibility of American "protectionism"; Japanese consumption patterns remain fairly rigid and there are many non–tariff and informal barriers to imports on a large scale. No basic solution to this problem for Japan's trading partners is yet in sight.

Early in 1986, Nakasone decided to call an election for the lower house of the Diet for July, to coincide with the regular election of one–half of the upper house every three years. He apparently wanted a third two–year term as President of the *Liberal Democratic Party* and as Prime Minister. The issue he selected to campaign on was the denationalization of the efficient, but unprofitable, Japanese National Railways, a very controversial move, especially on the political left. In reality he appeared to be trying to distract public attention from a potentially even more controversial issue, certain legislation, including an Official Secrets Act, that he was trying to get through the Diet so that the United States would consider the Japanese government able to maintain security on sensitive information—as it had been notoriously unable to do in the past—so that the U.S. would be willing to have it participate in the development of techniques for the Strategic Defense Initiative ("Star Wars").

In the July 1986 elections, helped by the premier's good image, the *LDP* won 309 seats in the lower house, more than ever before. Its main gains were in the cities and at the expense of the *JSP*, which dropped to 87 seats in the lower house. In an effort to make a fresh start, the *JSP* then elected a woman, Takako Doi, as its chairwoman, an unprecedented step for a major Japanese political party.

Nakasone then got a one–year extension of his premiership (until the summer or fall of 1987) and moved ahead with two of his favorite projects—a tax reform bill (modeled partly on the one in the U.S., and introducing a 5% sales tax), and the privatization, or denationalization, of the major government monopoly corporations, including the railways. He also tried to get a tougher law against espionage—which flourishes in Japan, especially on behalf of the Soviets, in view of the current light penalties—so that Japan could take part in research on the Strategic Defense Initiative ("Star Wars") jointly with the U.S. and other countries. These moves proved to arouse much opposition to Nakasone, who in any case had never been really popular with the politicians in his own party. He also damaged his prestige with some remarks he made in September 1986, to the effect that Japan's relatively homogeneous population gave it a marked advantage over the U.S.; he disparaged the abilities of Black and Hispanic Americans. Thus, in spite of the July 1986 electoral victory, Nakasone's political future suddenly seemed insecure.

Nakasone resigned in October 1987 in favor of Noboru Takeshita (pronounced Tah–*kesh*–tah), a "low profile" politician who had just taken over the leadership of former Premier Tanaka's sizable faction in the Diet. Takeshita moved quickly to try to improve relations with the United States and China, which had cooled somewhat during the late Nakasone years.

With the advent of the Takeshita government in 1987, Japanese politics began to change. An era of "revolving–door politics began." And, as mid–decade passed, there was no indication that an end to the instability was at hand. As the accompanying table illustrates, there have been seven prime ministers since October 1987, with the longest term in office being just over two years. How should this period be interpreted. Why

has it occurred and what will the final result be?

Japan's Revolving Door Politics
Prime Ministers

Noboru **Takeshita**	Oct. 1987–Apr.1989
Sosuke **Uno**	Apr. 1989–Jul. 1989
Toshiki **Kaifu**	Jul. 1989–Oct. 1991
Kiichi **Miyazawa**	Oct. 1991–Jun. 1993
Morihiro **Hosakawa**	Jul. 1993–Apr. 1994
Hata **Tsutjoma**	Apr. 1994–Jun. 1994
Tomiichi **Murayama**	Jun. 1994–Jan. 1996
Ryutaro **Hashimoto**	Jan. 1996–

It can be argued that many of the fundamentals of Japanese politics during this revolving–door period differ little from what came before. That is, factionalism, corruption, the dominance of big business and "money politics" still pervade the system.

While the Japanese political spectrum is dominated by an essentially conservative majority, factions built around a prominent and powerful individual within this ideological category are common. Thus, the *LDP* cannot be thought of as an extremely homogeneous party. As described in the next section, more recently, these factions have broken from the party to form new independent parties.

The country's electoral system also has contributed to the instability. Until the changes in the electoral law in 1994, Diet members were elected entirely from multi–member districts. The presence of factions and, more political parties guaranteed a large number of candidates. Essentially, under this system, the way to get elected in such a district was to buy enough votes to guarantee victory. Since

each voter had only one vote, there is a fixed number of votes to be divided up. It is obvious, therefore, what a significant infusion of campaign spending can do. Single member districts may decrease the number of candidates which could lessen the importance of money.

For a long time, Japan has been dominated by "money politics." Politicians have very heavy expenses, since they are expected to make presents to many of their constituents and to make outright gifts of money to their supporters. The funds for these transactions come mostly from business, in one form or another. For this reason, the political clout of the enormously wealthy business community has increased greatly in recent years. Personal connections, often deriving from attendance at the prestigious Tokyo University, also play an important role in the business–politics relationship.

At the end of 1984, a rising but "outsider" firm, the Recruit Cosmos Company, began to try to buy its way into the inner circle by making interest–free loans to some eighty politicians (from all parties except the communists) and senior bureaucrats with which to buy stock that was cheap because it had not been publicly listed. Two years later, the stock was listed, and its value appreciated rapidly, much to the benefit of the purchasers. In July 1988, one of Japan's most influential newspapers, the *Asahi Shimbun*, began to expose this transaction, which although not necessarily illegal, (since no political favors were known to have been done in return for the benefit) was certainly corrupt. Finance Minister Miyazawa, who was implicated in the scandal, resigned in December. Premier Takeshita promptly

Suburban Washington, D.C.? No, suburban *Tokyo!*　　　　　Courtesy: Alfred Magleby

reshuffled his cabinet, but some of the new ministers also soon had to resign. In February 1989, a series of arrests began to be made as a result of the Recruit Cosmos affair.

Growing public disgust with "money politics" reached new heights when it became apparent that about 160 politicians and bureaucrats, previously perceived as honest, were implicated in the Recruit scandal.

From 1987, to the advent of the Murayama government, six prime ministers were faced with a succession of scandals and an increasingly disenchanted public. In 1994, the question was has there been a fundamental change in Japanese politics?

The Political System: Japan is a constitutional monarchy, with the constitution dating to May 3, 1947. Administratively, the country is divided into 47 prefectures. The country has universal suffrage at age 20. The legal system is modeled after European civil law with some English and American influence. The Supreme Court has the power of judicial review over legislative acts.

The Japanese system of justice has its peculiarities. Trials are often preceded by a three week period of detention. Confessions prior to trial are common. Japanese trials are really a series of one and two-day hearings carried out monthly. A complicated trial with appeals can be very long. For example, the corruption trial of former Prime Minister Tanaka lasted nineteen years. Murder cases often take five to six years. Thus, even if found innocent, the accused can serve many years in prison.

The Emperor is the ceremonial head of state. The Prime Minister heads the government and has the power to appoint the cabinet.

The legislature or Diet, is bicameral, consisting of the upper House of Councillors and a lower House of Representatives. The House of Councillors has 252 seats. Elections are held every three years for one-half the seats. Representatives to the lower house serve four year terms.

Electoral Reform: The new electoral laws took effect on January 1, 1995. The reform leaves untouched the upper house of Councillors which is less significant in the legislative process. Under the new system, the lower house will consist of 500 members. Of these, 300 will be elected from single member districts. The remainder, 200, will be chosen through a system of proportional representation. The system will work in the following manner. Each voter will have two votes. One vote will be for a party in a national election which will determine seats in the Diet proportionally, depending on the percentage of votes each party receives.

His Imperial Majesty Emperor Akihito with Empress Michiko   AP/Wide World Photos

The second vote will be for a specific candidate in a single member district contest, where only one candidate will win and hence represent that district.

Parties with at least five Diet seats and which received at least 2% of the vote in the last national election will receive government funding. Candidates can receive funds from their party, may accept a corporate contribution up to $5,000, and must report contributions over $500. The original bill banned corporate contributions. The *Liberal Democrats* changed this. The reforms on campaign spending resemble those implemented in the U.S. in the 1970's. If the American experience is any example, then it may be assumed that big business will find a way to use its money. This is a separate issue from outright corruption.

What will be the impact of the new electoral system? When combined with the new funding laws, the effect will be to make it more difficult for small parties to survive. they will be hard pressed to receive funding and without that, they will not be able to compete effectively in single member district races. For the proportional seats, they will be too small to compete against the bigger parties on a national basis. We should therefore see a tendency toward a two or three party system.

Lastly, will there be a decline in corruption? Campaign spending reform and electoral reform may have some impact. However, the political culture of Japan

cannot be overcome by tinkering with the mechanics of the system. Any real change in the system will have to be evolutionary.

Recent Political Events: Japan's revolving door politics continued from June 1993 to January 1996, but with a special twist. The *Liberal Democratic Party (LDP)* which had been in power throughout the country's post World War II history, did not control the government. During this period new political parties were formed while others disappeared. And new alliances were made which had nothing to do with ideology or issues. The most absurd proof of this was the third government in this period which lasted from June 1994 to January 1996. This government was built around a *Socialist–LDP* coalition. Some observers claimed that politics in Japan was changing, that new reform forces were finally coming into their own, and that the old "money politics" would be vanquished. However, socialist Prime Minister Murayama Tomiichi proved to be a relatively weak leader. The government lacked direction. And, the *Socialist Party* lost significant support because of the accommodations it made in order to become part of the governing coalition.

In mid–January 1996, former Minister of Trade Ryutaro Hashimoto became Japan's new Prime Minister. This was the fourth change in government since the July 1993 elections, and it returned the *LDP* to power. Hashimoto, 58, is know as a sharp dresser and a man with a temper, something unusual in Japan. He is admired for his strong stand last year against American Trade Representative Mickey Kantor in discussions over automobile imports and other issues. The new Prime Minister is supportive of the U.S.–Japan security alliance even in the wake of the Okinawa rape incidents (discussed below).

Don't expect the current government to be much different or any more effective at addressing Japan's problems than its predecessors. The *LDP, Socialist, New Harbinger* three–party coalition remains intact. The only difference is that the *LDP* now holds the prime ministership. There has been no basic change in Japanese politics. And, it is entirely possible that the new government will last only up to the next national elections which could take place later this year.

The next national elections could bring about some significant change. The fact that 300 of the 500 House of Representatives seats will be elected from single member districts will almost certainly mean that the number of political parties will decline. A two or three party system might at least provide a more stable political environment. At that point, the Japanese people can begin to hope for fundamental change.

Other Changes: On January 17, 1995 a devastating earthquake rocked Honshu Island and Kobe, a city of 1.5 million people. The quake measured 7.2 on the scale. The death toll eventually climbed over 5,000, with 26,000 injured and 300,000 left homeless. Offers for assistance poured into the country which in some cases the government was very slow in accepting. As damage assessments came in, there was speculation that the financial costs of the quake would be substantial and could impact on the national economy. It is noteworthy that the Japanese showed extraordinary courage and discipline in the wake of the disaster. A similar disaster in the United States might not have been accepted so stoically.

In mid–1995 Japanese prosecutors secured the indictment of Shoko Ashara, cult leader, for masterminding the poison gas attack which killed 12 people on the Tokyo subway three months earlier. Since the incident, numerous cult officials and members have been detained; there have been scares of additional gas attacks. One observer referred to the matter as Japan's spring of terror.

One can only speculate as to the impact of the above events. But it would seem that a society which takes such great pride in being free from the social ills and misfortunes of the rest of the world must now be wondering if indeed it is after all

On June 9, 1993 Japan's attention was riveted on a solemn but joyous event. Concern for political scandals and economic troubles were set aside. For this was the day on which the son of Emperor Akihito, Prince Naruhito, was to marry American–educated career woman Masako Owada. The ancient ceremony was watched by millions of Japanese throughout the country on high definition TV (HDTV). The ceremony, which takes the better part of a day, involves several costume changes and rituals performed in different locations. The Prince's parents did not attend the ceremony but received an official report from the Prince at the end of the day informing them of the marriage. For weeks prior to the wedding, the newspapers and television carried stories about the princess to be, complete with interviews of friends she hadn't even seen in a decade or more.

It will be interesting to see if the traditional role of the royal family remains unchanged over the next decade. As Japan comes forward to assume a greater role in world affairs, the royal family could be important to the country in more than a symbolic way. Princess Masako is Harvard educated and, prior to the royal wedding, was a highly accomplished foreign service officer for her country.

so different. No one should be pleased at these misfortunes.

Chad Rowan from Hawaii studied the art of Japanese *Sumo* wrestling, a highly stylized, ritualistic and beloved sport of Japan. Learning Japanese and taking the name *Akebono*, in 1993 he vied for the championship, winning when he heaved his opponent out of the ring in less that 5 seconds. Conservatives in the Sumo hierarchy debated furiously before reluctantly awarding him the title of *Yokozuma* ("grand champion").

On January 13, 1996, the people of Japan had reason to be proud. Koichi Wakata, Japan's first full time shuttle astronaut, operated a robot arm aboard the shuttle Endeavor to retrieve a $650 million Japanese satellite from space. Further cooperation in space is planned.

Foreign and Defense Policy: In 1994, Japan continued to expand its international role, assuming more the posture of a major power. This was most evident in the country's participation in UN sponsored missions. Japan sent 260 SDF forces to Rwanda to perform a human relief operation. Air self defense forces served in Kenya in September ferrying supplies to the Rwanda operation. Japan continued to be a major aid–giving country. About two–thirds of its overseas development assistance now goes to Asian countries. ODA is now about 4% for the budget and Japan leads all countries as a donor/lender. The capstone to the re–emergence of Japan internationally will be a permanent seat on the UN Security Council. Many observers believe this goal could be achieved in 1995.

A major element of Japanese foreign policy is the relationship with the United States. Since the 1980's there have been two issues central to the U.S.–Japan relationship. They are trade and defense. During the Reagan years, Washington pressed Tokyo to increase defense spending and assume greater responsibility for its security. This issue has been effectively addressed.

The Japanese love festivals; this one is a traffic-stopper in Yokosuka.

Courtesy: Marilynn and Mark Swenson

Yokozuma **Akebono holding young boy aloft**

Trade, or rather the imbalance in trade between the two countries, has been much more difficult. Over the last decade Japan has consistently had a sizeable trade surplus with the United States. In 1994 that surplus was estimated at $60 billion. In an attempt to address this problem the U.S. Congress passed the Omnibus Trade and Competitiveness bill in 1988. The "Special 301" section of this bill provided a powerful weapon in the form of heavy tariffs on U.S. imports from countries deemed to be engaging in unfair trading practices. "Special 301" was used with limited successes by both Presidents Bush and Reagan. The Bush Administration introduced the Structural Impediments Initiative (SII) to be used with Special 301. SII talks were aimed at eliminating the fundamental economic differences between the two countries that resulted in large trade deficits. These areas included the high Japanese savings rate and low level of support for public

infrastructure, high land prices, and unfair Japanese business practices. There was little effect on the overall trade deficit. The Clinton Administration clearly has opted to seek maximum benefit from a "managed trade" approach. Prime Minister Murayama visited Washington for two days in January 1995. The visit was too short to produce any significant breakthroughs. Although experts in both countries do not believe the relationship is in danger, the trade issue is serious.

In 1994 and early 1995, the major issue was access to the Japanese market for American autos and auto parts. On May 6, 1995, talks collapsed. The Clinton Administration responded with a plan to place a 100% tariff on the major Japanese luxury cars. It will be difficult for the Japanese to meet Washington's demands. The Japanese do not accept the idea of managed trade. The Clinton Administration may be motivated as much by domestic political considerations as by the

desire to open the Japanese market. Certainly the American automobile manufacturers were happy with the Administration plan. In 1994, Japan imported $19 billion worth of American autos and auto parts.

On an even brighter note, America did enjoy the fruits of victory when Japan began importing American apples in January 1995. The Japanese rice market was opened to outside imports at the end of 1993, and in March 1994, Motorola was awarded additional frequencies in the Tokyo–Nagoya area which allowed it to compete in the mobile telephone market. Japan and the U.S. also worked closely on a solution for the North Korea issue.

By the end of 1995, there was hard evidence that the large deficit in U.S. merchandise trade with Japan was shrinking rapidly. This was because of the high value of the Japanese yen and because of an opening market in Japan as described above. In future years, Japan bashing will probably give way to China bashing as the U.S. deficit with that country explodes.

The U.S.–Japan defense alliance was tested in 1995. In September, three American servicemen were arrested for kidnapping and raping a 12 year old Okinawan girl. They were convicted and received sentences ranging from 5 to 7 years at the end of January 1996. The crime caused a flurry of protests against the American presence. And there may be a small reduction in the size of the current 47,000 man American force in Japan as well as a scaling down of the size of U.S. installations.

The sad event was put into perspective, however, in March 1996, when China threatened Taiwan with military exercises just prior to the first presidential election on the island. Japanese officials know full well that there is no alternative to a continued American presence in Asia. A Japanese court even ordered the Governor of Okinawa to renew the leases on American bases.

Japan was in the Asian spotlight in 1995, as the venue for the third Asia Pacific Economic Cooperation meeting. APEC is here to stay and Japan has a major role to play in building free trade in the Asia–Pacific region. The Clinton Administration committed a major diplomatic error when the president did not show up for the meeting. At the time, President Clinton was in the middle of a budget battle with the Republicans. The decision not to go, however, sent the wrong message. The president's April 1996 trip to Japan was the opportunity to let the Japanese know how important they are to this country. It was necessary that this message be conveyed clearly.

In spite of a minor territorial dispute with South Korea during the year, relations probably were strengthened as a result of the tri–partite U.S.–Japan–South Korea efforts to bring North Korea into the international diplomatic community.

Culture: Before the arrival of Chinese influence, Japanese culture was rather simple and primitive; it was centered around the Shinto belief in spirits existing everywhere in nature. Under Buddhist influence, Shinto acquired a monastic organization, and in the late 19th century it was made the official state religion and became the authority for the divine power of the emperor, a descendant of its sun goddess. Buddhism, however, was not eliminated—the Japanese believed in and practiced both, interwoven, with Confucianism and some Christian beliefs. Today it is acceptable for a Japanese to marry in a Shinto Temple, to venerate his dead ancestors at the Buddhist Temple and at the same time to celebrate the Christmas holidays even if in reality he has little faith in any religion. The emphasis at Christmas is actually on gathering at the family home for fun and fellowship.

The revival of Shinto by the state did not prevent the heavy influence of Western cultural patterns in Japan after the middle of the 19th century—science and technology were and are eagerly studied and adopted, with adaptations, into the Japanese pattern. The Japanese are not the mere imitators they are often believed to be; in recent years they have been making major and remarkable technological advances and scientific discoveries. The old cultural patterns are not dead in the rural areas, but they have not posed any major resistance to modernization. The increasingly urban life of the Japanese is a distinctive one. The business sections of the city are usually constructed of reinforced concrete, but the outlying buildings are simple, but attractive, wood and paper structures. The people who work in the central city during the day go to the suburbs in the evening—thus the morning and evening commuting hours are as frantic as those in the cities of the United States. Television and radio are widely enjoyed, particularly as a result of the ability of Japanese industry to provide electronic appliances and instruments at low prices while maintaining good quality. All of the fine arts are widely found in the cities, particularly Tokyo. Traditional European and Western musical works and ballet are heavily attended, as are cultural expressions which are distinctly Japanese such as the Kabuki dancers, who perform in a highly refined style esteemed throughout the world. On another level, blue-grass and country–western music *sung in Japanese* has a large following. And today, McDonald's and

Kentucky Fried Chicken are the top two restaurant chains in Japan. Underlying this shift to western food is a far more significant outcome. Rice consumption is down 50% in the last quarter century. Consumption of meat and dairy products is skyrocketing, and Japanese young adults are definitely growing taller and bigger.

Japanese art techniques were quite advanced before World War II. In the postwar period there has been a tendency to depart from the traditional representation of landscapes and historical events in detailed canvases into somewhat more modernistic modes of expression.

Many universities and colleges provide higher learning for the Japanese student population. In most of them, English is widely taught and spoken. They do not represent any specific level of education; their degrees have many different meanings in terms of achievement. Many universities are dominated by the extreme leftist student organization known as *Zengakuren*, the influence of which, however, is less that it was in the late 1960's when student activism, as in the U.S., was at a much higher level.

A curious event was noted in 1982. Japan had to apologize for certain white-washing references in school textbooks relating to the Japanese military record on the Asian mainland before and during World War II. The sections caused an uproar in both China and Korea. A similar controversy arose in 1986.

In recent years, but especially under Nakasone, national pride and nationalism have been on the upswing among the Japanese. Many of them feel that their country is "Number One" in the world and see the U.S. as having begun to decline. There is a tendency to feel superior to foreigners and to avoid contact with them, especially when they are in Japan; this applies, for example, to the rather large number (about 800,000) of Koreans in Japan, who are seriously discriminated against. Since World War II, Japan has, unlike most other industrial countries, not imported any significant number of foreign workers, although a change in this policy is now under consideration. Japan has been notably inhospitable to refugees, such as the "boat people" from Vietnam; in general, they are not admitted.

Marunouchi, Tokyo's business district   Courtesy: PANA, Japan

79

EDUCATION IN THE U.S. AND JAPAN

The growing importance of the United States and Japan to each other has led, on both sides of the Pacific, to comparisons of many aspects of the two countries, especially their economies. Another frequent subject of comparison is their respective educational systems.

On the U.S. side, the public school system below the college or university level is highly decentralized. Control rests with state and local officials and boards, including popularly elected members. The system is permissive in many ways, the most obvious being with respect to dress. Academic standards vary widely. There are often serious disciplinary problems (violence, drugs, pregnancies and others) especially in the big city schools where the student population is often ethnically diverse.

The relatively slight pressures toward conformity produce a typical situation in which the general level of achievement has markedly declined compared to other countries such as Japan. However, there are incentives and opportunities at least in the better schools for able students to do original and reasonably advanced work. Private (including parochial Catholic) schools charge tuition rather than being tax–supported, and on the average have higher standards than the public schools, although not than the best public schools.

At the college level, the situation also varies widely, to the point where few generalizations are possible beyond the observation that there are both public and private universities and colleges, with a wide qualitative gap between the best and the worst. A student usually spends the first two years completing his or her general education, and the last two (or perhaps three) specializing ("majoring") in some particular subject or field. At the graduate and pre–professional levels, there is less variation in the quality of programs offered, and American institutioons offering such programs are widely admired abroad and attract large numbers of foreign (including Japanese) students. One of the signs of the creativity that is not only permitted, but encouraged by the American system, is the high proportion of all Nobel Prizes gained by their graduates.

On the Japanese side, the situation is considerably different, in spirit and outcome as well as in form. The system is much more highly centralized. At all levels the public schools, and to some extent also the private schools, are under the control of the Ministry of Education in Tokyo. It is politically conservative and is troubled by the fact that the teachers' unions (known collectively as *Nikkyoso*, are led by leftists who share the guilt feelings of Japanese intellectuals about the past. They are particularly disturbed by the important role of prewar teachers in indocrinating their students with the nationalist ideology of that period. To counter the influence of the current generation of teachers, the Ministry introduces from time to time, at the high school level, history textbooks that the teachers and others rightly see as trying to whitewash the imperialist past.

From the kindergarten level through high schools, Japanese students and their parents are under tremendous competitive pressure, mainly because ultimate career success is assumed to require graduation from some prestigious university (ideally Tokyo University or Todai). Below the college level, students generally wear uniforms, and conformity is expected as to hairstyles, behavior and effort. Students who rebel, as some do, are usually severely dealt with, sometimes by their own classmates. The emphasis in education is heavily on memory learning—what and how—not *why*—and individuality and creativity are discouraged and even penalized. The students have to pass through an "examination hell" in order to (1) qualify for a higher level of learning which will enable them to (2) qualify for admission to a good institution at the next higher level.

Thus, the Japanese indeed employ the "track system" which was discarded a generation ago in the U.S. because it was claimed to be discriminatory against blacks, Hispanics and other minorities. The result in the U.S. is widely acknowledged to be a steep decline in scores of the Scholastic Aptitude Test.

The result in the Japanese system has been even more tragic: an unusually high suicide rate among teenagers who feel they have disgraced their parents and

Crown Prince Naruhito and Princess Masako visit a nursing home.

80

family. An elaborate system of cram schools has developed to help students over the exam hurdles. The subject–matter is an undigested mishmash of Japanese and Western thinking.

Although hard to get into, Japanese colleges are not hard to stay in. The instruction generally adds little to what the student has already learned. There is slightly more scope for originality, but not much. Professional training, except in law and medicine, tends to be received on the job rather than in graduate school. By the Nobel test, the Japanese system of higher education does not stand up well; relatively few of these prizes have been won by graduates. In fact, the system could be described as providing training up to an adequate level of competance, but little more, rather than education.

By comparison, however, U.S. employers seeking technical job applicants and even clerical help in virtually every field lack basic skills they should have learned in the first eight years of education. These include clear handwriting (not printing) mathematical methods (crucial in many cases to determine medical dosages), the metric system of measurements and, most important, abstract and factual thinking, capped by strong motivation.

Economy: World War II brought on the virtual destruction of Japan's physical plant, but not of the human qualities that had built that plant. Among the most important of these were (and are) energy, persistence, a high level of education and basic technical skills, a high rate of saving and a willingness (somewhat declining at present) to accept relatively modest living standards. Japan may not have produced many famous scientists, but it has produced many brilliant businessmen, engineers and a highly efficient labor force.

The Occupation helped the Japanese economy, at least in a negative way, by not imposing war reparations or other excessive burdens on it. The Korean War gave it a major shot in the arm (as did the Vietnam war in the next decade), in the form of official U.S. "offshore procurement" of supplies other than weapons from Japanese firms for use in connection with the war. By that time, various American specialists were beginning to advise Japanese industry how it could increase its productivity, which was then low; it was not long before Japanese efficiency began to approach the highest world levels.

As suggested above (under Economic Development, at the beginning of this book), the Japanese government, after the end of the Occupation in 1952, systematically pursued an "industrial policy" aimed at stimulating Japanese recovery on the basis of "export–led growth." Antitrust policy in Japan is much less severe than in the U.S., and this made it possible for Japanese industry to "rationalize" it-

Refrigerator inspection line.

self to a high degree in the mid–1950's. This meant that private firms agreed with one another on the general direction that future Japanese industrial development was to take. "Sunset industries," such as textiles, were to be de–emphasized, although not necessarily phased out entirely; industries using "leading edge" technologies were to be promoted: steel, automobiles, electronics, etc. This "rationalization" process had a spectacularly beneficial effect on Japan's industrial production and its export position, beginning approximately in the early 1960's. So did such domestic factors as political stability, social cohesion and a low defense budget, held by treaty to a little bit under 1% of the GNP until 1987, and such external factors as the relative openness of the vast U.S. market to Japanese and other foreign goods after the early 1960's. These elements were coupled with relatively high tariffs imposed by the Japanese government on imports and a maze of import regulations which were actually barriers, a generally stable international scene (due in large part to U.S. policy) and the conscious undervaluing (at least until 1971) of the yen, with its stimulating effect on Japanese exports.

There have been some drawbacks to this process, even from the Japanese point of view. The cost of living is kept unnecessarily high by barriers to imports, including agricultural products; the Japanese agricultural population (about 12% of the total) is guaranteed high prices and

protected from foreign competition for political reasons, so that food is very expensive. The distribution (retail) system is very inefficient; it is divided between chains of large, expensive department stores and a huge number of mom-and-pop corner stores, also expensive. Housing, public utilities and the like have been the victims of cumulative underinvestment, so that the average Japanese lives under conditions considerably less pleasant than the overall wealth of the country (with currently a GNP of well over one trillion U.S. dollars annually) would suggest. Energy costs, especially for oil (all imported) are necessarily high; Japan is developing a major nuclear power industry (also based on imported raw materials) as a partial solution.

In spite of these problems, Japan is an industrial giant, second in the world after the United States. It has proved better able than other industrial economies to cope with the rise (since the end of the 1960's) in the cost of imported oil. Its large trading companies have proved very effective in penetrating foreign markets, especially that of the U.S. They cope with import quotas, when imposed by foreign governments, through "upscaling" (keeping the number of exported units within the quotas, but improving their quality and increasing their price, while staying somewhat below the prices of competitive goods produced in the countries of destination). Having accumulated enormous currency surpluses through exports and domestic savings, Japanese firms and banks are in a position to lend and invest abroad on a massive scale; they are currently buying banks, high–tech firms, etc., in the U.S., for example. To date, the recent rise in the value of the yen, especially in relation to the dollar, has not had much of the depressing effect on Japanese exports that would normally be expected.

Japan is well in the forefront of advanced technology; its main competitor is the U.S. There is a race between them, for example, to develop the next "generation" of computers, ceramic engines, etc. Japan has produced word processors that can cope with *kanji* (the complex Chinese characters that are still used extensively in written Japanese).

The outlook for the Japanese economy is not entirely rosy. There are sizable annual government budget deficits, although nowhere near on the U.S. scale. A downturn in the global economy can hurt exports. The population is aging fairly rapidly, partly as a result of a large number of abortions, so that its overall productivity is likely to decline, or at least to grow less rapidly over the coming years. Recently there has been an increasing feeling among some Japanese, partly, but only partly, in response to foreign (especially U.S.) pressures, in favor of increased Japanese imports, more leisure, lower savings and exports and higher consumption. On the immediate horizon, limitations on exports to the U.S., which has broad support in Congress and was expressed by the recent imposition of all but prohibitive U.S. tariffs on certain Japanese items, should be a source of alarm.

Japan's regional role in Asia has been growing significantly over the past decade. Japanese investment has spurred economic growth in much of Southeast Asia and even northern Australia. Japan is quickly becoming a leading investor in Vietnam, a country that because of the former U.S. embargo, was unable to obtain U.S. investment. While countries of the region still harbor memories of Japan's World War II aggression, they also realize the benefits of development along the Japanese model, and with Japanese investment.

Japanese transport systems, particularly rail, are as modern as can be found in the world. The *Bullet* trains between Tokyo and Osaka, as known around the world, are traveling as fast as 160 miles per hour. By contrast, Metroliner service between Washington and New York runs at the same speed it did 25 years ago in spite of billions in government expenditures, including purchase of the tracks.

Premier Nakasone's efforts to "restructure" and reinvigorate the economy and reduce the trade surplus with the United States included efforts to increase consumer spending (partly on imports, and at the expense of saving and investment) as advocated in the influential Maekawa Report, and to somehow lower the ridiculously high price of Japanese land (including undertaxed "agricultural" areas in and near cities). He tolerated a rapid appreciation (strengthening) of the yen in relation to the U.S. dollar, with relatively negative effects on Japan's exports to the U.S. The privatization program has had the effect of weakening the left wing opposition parties (the *Japan Communist Party* and the *Japan Socialist Party*) together with labor unions associated with them. A new and potentially important federation of unions in the private sector, known as *Rengo,* was formed in the fall of 1987.

The current process of "restructuring" the Japanese economy, so as to adjust to the strong yen (which tends to hold down exports and push up imports), and correct certain shortcomings such as the incredibly over–inflated price of land (especially urban real estate), has made impressive progress but still has a long way to go. Japan still holds the lead in a number of high technology fields. It is deregulating and privatizing sectors of its economy that have needed such treatment. It is constructing public works and badly needed social needs, especially housing. There has been liberalization of tariffs and nontariff barriers to imports, although this has benefited South Korean firms more than it has American firms. At American request, and as an alternative to unilateral programs, Japanese money continued to be invested on a large scale in various assets in the U.S., including Treasury bonds that help finance the national debt.

On the other hand, the Japanese public has embarked on a binge of consumerism that in time may rival that of the US, with a depressing effect on savings and investment. Some basic Japanese industries are being gradually "hollowed out" by firms moving overseas in search of cheaper labor. Public amenities (parks, etc.) are still in short supply, and urban overcrowding reaches fantastic levels in many areas. The consumerism is directly related to land value inflation on the islands. Some institutions have offered 100–year mortgages, to be passed from generation to generation to pay for tremendous housing costs.

In recent years, the Japanese economy has had a very powerful impact abroad, while developing serious problems at home.

In the face of a tendency for Japanese workers to demand, at last, higher pay and shorter hours, Japanese industry has moved much of its production, usually toward the lower end of the technology spectrum, off–shore, especially to China and Southeast Asia (Thailand in particular). In addition, there has been investment at all levels in the industrial countries, notably the United States and the emerging European Community. Since 1985, Japan has become the world's biggest creditor (and the United States has become the world's biggest debtor), with the world's largest pool of foreign exchange reserves (probably well over $100 billion). Along with the United States, Japan is the world's largest provider of Overseas Development Assistance (foreign aid)—about $10 billion per year, although much of it is "tied" to Japanese goods and services and is really a form of export promotion.

On the other hand, Japan has begun to develop some of the ills of a huge "postmodern" economy. Consumer costs and real estate prices have risen to fantastic heights, resulting in considerable public dissatisfaction and a growing demand for (cheaper) foreign imports, which are screened out in many cases by existing Japanese trade barriers. Bank loans and the stick market reached greatly excessive levels, only to be chilled by a raising of the prime discount rate by the Bank of Japan beginning in 1989. The result, by early 1992, was an impressive fall in the stock market and in public confidence in Japan's economic future. The industrial growth rate began to decline. For the first time in many years, Japan's powerful and controversial keiretsu (tightly organized industrial conglomerates) appeared to be in real trouble. Faced with difficulties at home, Japanese firms began to cut back on overseas investment and lending to try to push exports up again, a move bound to bring friction with other industrial countries, notably the United States.

The Japanese economy grew at less than 1% in fiscal 1994, which ends on 31 March 1995. This came after a flat 1993. Some Japanese officials expect 2.8% growth for 1995 but this seems overly optimistic. Low consumer demand was hurting the economy. Credit remained difficult to come by as a result of a tight monetary policy. Some analysts argue that unless some changes are made soon, the country could slip into recession.

The country did roll up another huge trade surplus with the United States and had an overall surplus of about $150 billion in 1994. However the yen is so inflated as a currency that it is difficult to believe that Japan can continue to remain competitive internationally. Ten years ago the yen was about 220 to the dollar. In early 1995 it was in the 85 to 1 range. One phenomenon occurring which helps with international competitiveness but hurts at home is the pouring of capital into other East Asian countries to set up off–shore manufacturing. There is now a major outflow of capital and jobs from the country. Officially, unemployment was 3% for 1994. However, idle workers still on the payrolls of Japanese corporations are included, so the rate could be near 10%. The consensus conclusion is that in order for the Japanese economy to recover, domestic demand must rise substantially. This will be difficult however. In the late 1980's stocks and land prices soared. Prices rose. Then the bubble burst and that is where Japan is now. Prices are still falling or at least remaining flat. Assets are shrinking.

The figures for 1995 were no better. Japan was still in mild recession. Economic growth was no more than one percent taking inflation into account. The major factor which continues to prevent a recovery is the large number of bad loans on the books of Japanese banks. Too many people are stuck with real estate with collapsed values.

In November, the Daiwa Bank was ordered to close down its American operation within 90 days by the FDIC. The Bank, with the help of the Japanese Ministry of Finance had covered up the magnitude of losses in a New York branch. Changes in the political leadership at home in early 1996 did little to brighten the country's economic future.

The Future: The face of Japanese politics continued to change in 1995, but not its substance. Changes in the electoral system will have a significant impact on the House of Representatives election in 1996. This could permanently alter the political landscape by forcing a number of the small splinter parties to join forces or disappear altogether. Single member districts will not support a multi–party system in a homogeneous society.

If stability can be achieved in Japan's politics, the question remains whether the new political bosses will be able to deal with the country's problems. Don't look for this in the short run. There is little evidence of a serious political debate of fundamental issues at this time.

Japan's economic bubble has burst. The country may pull out of the current economic recession. However, internationally, Japan's day is passing. Those who intended to study Japanese language as a way of buying into the "Pacific century" had better think about Mandarin Chinese.

A steel mill.

Courtesy: Japanese Embassy

83

The Republic of Korea (South Korea)

Skyline of modern Seoul. The grounds of the Duksoo Palace, built in the 15th century and carefully preserved, are seen in the foreground, surrounded by the bustling city.

Area: 38,452 sq. mi. (98,919 sq. km., somewhat larger than Indiana).

Population: 44,600,000 (1993 est.).

Capital City: Seoul (Pop. 9 million estimated).

Climate: Temperate, with a short winter, hot and humid in the summer with a rainy monsoon from July to September.

Neighboring Countries: North Korea (North); Japan (East).

Official Language: Korean.

Other Principal Tongues: Japanese, spoken by many older Koreans; English, spoken by many of the educated Koreans.

Ethnic Background: Korean, related to Manchurian and Mongol.

Principal Religions: Buddhism, Confucianism, Christianity.

Main Exports: (to U.S. and Japan); Textiles and clothing, electrical machinery, footwear, steel, ships, fish, automobiles and electronics.

Main Imports: (from Japan and U.S.); Machinery, oil, transport equipment, chemicals, grains.

Currency: Won.

Former Colonial Status: Korea was a tributary state of the Chinese empires for certain periods until 1895; Japanese protectorate (1905–1910); Japanese Dependency (1910–1945); it was occupied by the U.S. from 1945 to 1948.

National Day: August 15, 1948 (Republic Day).

Chief of State: Kim Young Sam, President, (since February 1993).

Prime Minister: Lee Yung Duk.

National Flag: White, with a center circle divided equally by an S–curve into blue and red portions; there is a varying combination of 3 solid and 3 broken lines in each corner.

Per Capita Income: U.S. $10,000.

The predominantly mountainous peninsula of Korea is actually an extension of the mountains of southern Manchuria, from which it is separated by the Yalu and Tumen Rivers. The spine of the mountains runs from northeast to southwest, but remains close to the eastern coastline area of Korea—east Korea is rugged, containing many scenic mountain peaks. The famous Diamond Mountains (Kimgan–san) in North Korea are particularly spectacular, reaching their greatest height in the Changpai San at the northern border, where the peaks are snow–covered all year. From these immense mountains, streams gather to form the Yalu River which empties into the Yellow Sea, and the Tumen River which flows into the Sea of Japan. The steep descent of these rivers provides one of the world's best sources of hydroelectric power, with a great potential that has only begun to be developed.

The western coastal regions contain most of the peninsula's level plains, interspersed with frequent rivers—this is the agricultural belt where rice predominates, raised in wet paddies in the South, where two crops are harvested each year, and grown in the North on dry plantations, where only one crop matures at the end of the summer. Tidal variations along the west coast are extreme; there is sometimes a difference of 30 feet between low and high tide. The offshore islands, numbering about 3,500, are the remnants of the mountain chain, standing with their shoulders above water.

The long coastline and the nearness to some of the richest fishing grounds in the world have made the people, especially in the South, skilled fishermen and have led to frequent squabbles with individual Japanese and with Japanese governments, because the people of the over–crowded neighboring islands desperately need the same protein which the Koreans harvest from the sea.

The cooler climate of North Korea resembles that of Manchuria. It is better endowed with minerals, hydroelectric facilities and capacity, and the lower regions of the mountains support thick stands of timber. South Korea has a warmer climate, which supports a greater

The Democratic People's Republic of Korea (North Korea)

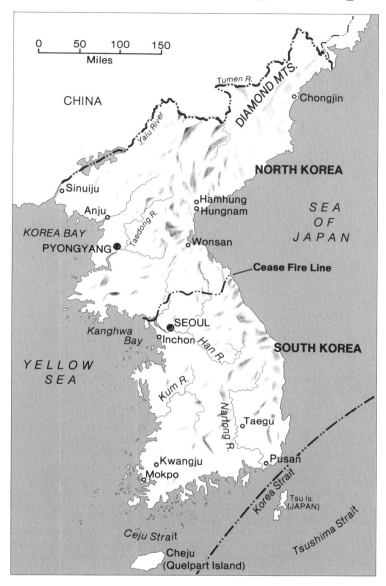

Area: 46,814 sq. mi. (121,730 sq. km., somewhat smaller than Mississippi).

Population: 22 million (estimated).

Capital City: Pyongyang (Pop. 1.2 million, estimated).

Climate: Temperate, with a longer and much colder winter than in the South; summer wet season from July to September.

Neighboring Countries: China (North); Russia (Northeast); South Korea (South).

Official Language: Korean.

Other Principal Tongues: Japanese, spoken by many older Koreans; Russian, spoken by many of the educated Koreans.

Ethnic Background: Korean, a mixture of Manchurian and Mongol.

Principal Religion: Buddhism, Confucianism. The government discourages religious activity.

Main Exports: (to U.S.S.R, China, Japan); minerals, meat products, fish.

Main Imports: (from China, U.S.S.R, Japan) petroleum, machinery, grains.

Currency: Won.

Former Colonial Status: Korea was a tributary state of the Chinese empires for most of its history up to 1895; Japanese protectorate (1905–1910); Japanese Dependency (1910–1945); from 1945 to 1948 it was under Soviet occupation; after 1948 it developed an independent communist regime allied with both the Soviet Union and with China.

National Day: September 8, 1948.

Chief of State: Kim Jong Il (not officially announced, but probable), President.

National Flag: Two blue stripes on the top and bottom separated by two thin white stripes from a broad central field of red which contains at left center a white circle with a 5–pointed red star.

Per Capita Income: US$200.

History: From their appearance and language, the Koreans appear to have similar origins to the Turkic–Manchurian–Mongol people who have inhabited northeastern Asia for more than 4,000 years and migrated to the island of Japan as well as to the Korean peninsula. By the 2nd century B.C. they began to undergo a series of waves of Chinese influence; the northern part of the country became a part of the Chinese empire.

For most of the first nine centuries of the Christian era, Korea was divided into three states: Koguyro in the North, Silla in the Southeast and Paekche in the Southwest. All of these were under strong Chinese cultural influence, including *Mahayana* (northern) Buddhism, Confucianism and the Chinese written language. There was a small area of Japanese influence along the southern coast.

agricultural production. In December, the temperatures in Pusan may be mild at the same time that frigid blasts of below–zero arctic weather envelop the remote mountains of the North. The Siberian black bear and leopard mingle with fierce wild boars, Manchurian tigers and smaller Korean tigers in the thinly populated northern region. As the warmth increases to the south, the animal life becomes more nearly tropical, dominated by herons, gulls and other birds with colorful plumage.

In August 1945, at the end of World War II, the United States and the Soviet Union agreed to divide Korea at the 38th parallel into two occupation zones, a Soviet one to the north and an American zone to the south. This line, somewhat adjusted as the result of the Korean War, has become the political boundary between two antagonistic regimes, each claiming to be the legitimate government of the entire country but in practice tolerating "cross–recognition" (i.e. of both) by other governments except for four major powers: the U.S., the U.S.S.R. (now Russia), China and Japan. North Korea (the Democratic People's Republic of Korea) is a communist state now loosely allied with Russia and China; South Korea is a non–communist republic allied with the United States.

From the 10th through the 14th centuries, the entire peninsula was united under the Buddhist *Koryo* dynasty, which although theoretically independent, was dominated and paid tribute to the nomadic Mongol empires of northeast Asia which had overrun part or all of China. In 1392 the area came under the control of the Confucian *Yi* dynasty which ruled from an imperial capital established in Seoul.

For several decades the Yi showed great creativity, wisdom and artistry, advancing in the field of astronomy and inventing an alphabet based on symbols which could be expressed by a movable metal type also devised during the period. Although ruled by a local line of rulers, Korea remained a faithful tributary of the Chinese empire; as the initial creative cultural zeal wore off in the 17th century, Chinese character writing was readopted, assisting in cultural and commercial contacts between the two nations. China provided military protection, which enabled the Koreans to withstand, but with great difficulty, a major Japanese invasion from 1592 to 1598.

The drain and exhaustion of the war rendered the prostrate Koreans an easy mark for the powerful *Manchus* from Manchuria, who after conquering the peninsula, seized China itself. There was a general decline of cultural and political activity in Korea, which became an intensely isolationist vassal of the Manchu empire in China for the next two centuries. Occasional Europeans who were shipwrecked on the rough coastline were held captive.

Shortly after the mid–1850's the major Western powers became interested in the region. China was weakened by its own efforts to resist domination by the same powers and expressed no reaction when the Japanese recognized the "independence" of Korea in 1876. Japan did not win this concession from China—it was merely taking advantage of the weakness of Korea and the Manchus. Despite its almost extreme preoccupation with anti–foreignism, the Yi rulers were compelled to sign a series of "unequal treaties" with the major powers, beginning with Japan, similar to those which had been and were being extracted from China and Japan.

Inside Korea, nationalists and modernists at the royal court and the more educated youth looked to Japan as a source of inspiration and direction. On the other hand, the elderly conservatives remained attached to the traditional Chinese empire of the Manchus. China still insisted that it was overlord in Korea. The Japanese, who had rapidly modernized their armed forces, therefore, declared war on the Manchus in 1894. With little resistance, Chinese forces were driven out of Korea, but the Japanese were not able to establish undisputed control after defeating the Manchu forces—the Russians had also started to exhibit considerable interest in the peninsula.

The short Russo–Japanese War of 1904–1905 resulted in a Japanese victory and the establishment of a protectorate over Korea, which had been the biggest issue in the conflict. With no opposition, Japan simply annexed the peninsula in 1910; Korea became the largest dependency of the growing Japanese empire.

Japanese rule was harsh and military, devoted to creating investment opportunities for Japanese capital, raising rice to feed Japan and establishing military bases for further expansion on the Asian continent. But the modern techniques of the Japanese and the advanced education which they offered created in the long run a dramatic and beneficial change from the extreme isolationism which had prevailed under the Yi emperors prior to the advent of Western powers.

Angered by open Japanese exploitation and inspired by newly learned democratic slogans used in World War I, thousands of Koreans, many of whom had been converted to Christianity, staged a massive, peaceful demonstration in favor of independence in 1919 which was brutally suppressed by the Japanese. Independence movements fled to bases outside the country or went underground; they split into a communist wing located in eastern Russia, Manchuria and northern China and a nationalist wing located mainly in eastern China. Relaxing their rule briefly because of adverse Korean and world popular opinion, the Japanese intensified their exploitation when they undertook the conquest of Manchuria and China in the 1930's. In an effort to avoid further unrest, they attempted to absorb the Koreans by forcing them to adopt Japanese names and to speak the language of their conquerors. This had no lasting effect and actually served to further embitter the Koreans against Japanese.

At the close of World War II, when Japan had all but surrendered to U.S. and British forces, the subject of the future of Korea was considered by the leaders of the "Big Three" at the Potsdam Conference in mid–1945. Russia's Stalin reaffirmed his promise that the U.S.S.R. would declare war on Japan, which it had refrained from doing prior to that time, and proposed that it would secure the Korean peninsula from the Japanese armies. It was ultimately decided that Soviet forces would occupy the northern part of Korea and accept the surrender of the Japanese troops in that region, and the U.S. forces would do the same in the southern portion. The American expectation was that the whole peninsula would come under the supervision of the then infant UN.

This decision, made half way around the world from the helpless Koreans, was to be the basis of continued conflict and friction for years, and also was to cost the loss of thousands of lives. It also ultimately was to result in an economically harmful division of the peninsula.

The U.S.S.R. declared war on Japan on August 8, 1945, two days after the first atomic bomb had burst with a terrifying holocaust on the Japanese city of Hiroshima. The Japanese accepted the Allied surrender terms on August 14, but during the few intervening days the Soviets had quickly moved into occupation of North Korea at the cost of a few light skirmishes in Manchuria. The boundary between U.S. and Soviet troops was fixed shortly afterward at the 38th parallel.

In the North, the Russians promptly installed a satellite regime run by Korean communists under the control of the Soviet occupation forces. In the South, U.S. occupation forces followed a shifting policy primarily devoted to economic recovery and to the creation of a democratic government. There were seemingly unending negotiations between the two powers in 1946–1947 on the formation of a provisional government for the entire peninsula; these broke down when it became clear that the Soviets would not settle for less than one rigged in favor of the communists, who were actually a small, predominantly northern minority. The United States laid the issue before the UN, which tried in 1948 to hold free and supervised elections in both halves of the country as a first step towards reunification.

The Russians excluded the UN mission from the North, whereupon the UN authorized elections only in the South. Syngman Rhee, a venerated nationalist figure who had been popular for decades, became the first president. The Republic of Korea was declared independent and was admitted to the UN, and the American occupation came to an end. The Russians promptly reacted by establishing the "Democratic People's Republic of Korea" in the North and withdrew their occupation forces. Soviet control and support of local communists were sufficient to maintain North Korea within the Soviet bloc with little or no Russian military presence.

After careful preparations, in mid–1950, bolstered by a heavy dose of Soviet military aid, North Korean forces invaded South Korea. Having the advantage of surprise, they were barely prevented from overrunning all of South Korea. U.S. President Truman reversed a previous decision and ordered military intervention on the side of the South Koreans; two days after the conflict began the UN condemned the aggressive acts of North

Korea and ordered military sanctions against the Soviet satellite. A combination of mass bombing of the North and a flank attack by an amphibious landing at Inchon, a coastal town near Seoul, succeeded in driving the North Koreans from the territory they had conquered.

General Douglas MacArthur commanded the UN forces. With the same energy he demonstrated in World War II against the Japanese, he insisted that the two Koreas should be reunited and invaded North Korea above the 38th parallel in October 1950. Assuming that neither the Chinese or Russians would intervene, he sent his forces rapidly toward the Yalu River, in spite of the growing concern of President Truman.

His aim of defeating the North Koreans was a miscalculation. China was not prepared to accept a threat to Manchuria and was prepared to engage in battle to obtain the prestige of a victory over the American "imperialists." In addition, both China and Russia were interested in saving the communist regime in Korea. Chinese forces, pretending to be "volunteers," crossed the Yalu River into Korea. The question remains today as to whether they merely wanted to create a buffer region to protect Manchuria or to conquer South Korea for the North Koreans. MacArthur challenged them by embarking on an offensive to clear out all North Korean and Chinese forces in North Korea; in late November, the Chinese Communists struck with great force, using the same successful guerrilla tactics they had learned in their battles with the Chinese Nationalists during the decades of their civil war.

Their effort to drive U.S. and UN forces out of North Korea succeeded, but they could not mount a successful invasion of South Korea. MacArthur advocated a wider war effort, including the bombing of Chinese Manchurian bases, but was removed by President Truman, who feared the escalation of conflict; he was replaced by General Matthew B. Ridgway.

Chinese forces tried to retake Seoul in April and May 1951, but their supply lines had become too long to support the effort. Armistice negotiations began in July 1951, but since neither side had won a clear victory, the talks dragged on for two years, while fighting continued. Each side sought to obtain a defensible position, and gradually the lines of battle hardened with heavy fortifications which would have made a major break–through by either side almost impossible. A crisis over the repatriation of prisoners also prolonged the conflict—the Chinese and Korean communists disliked, and refused to recognize, the proposition that their soldiers might choose not to return to their homelands. An armistice was reached on July 27, 1953, a few months

U.S. Marines in Korea, November 1952

after the death of Stalin had led to a reduction of Soviet support for the Chinese role in the Korean war. About 70% of the Chinese prisoners held by the UN forces refused to return to China, and they were soon released, mostly to the Nationalist Chinese on Taiwan.

American politics contributed heavily to this armistice. The popular military hero of World War II, General Dwight Eisenhower, was chosen by the Republican Party to oppose President Truman's Democratic successor. Eisenhower's promise during the campaign to *end* (not to win) the Korean War greatly influenced the American public. The settlement was a stalemate of military might— the demarcation is along about the same line as it was prior to the conflict. South Korea was saved from military conquest by the communists of North Korea and China. The biggest changes which occurred during the strife were the loss of several hundred thousand lives and an almost utter devastation of both Koreas. There was a sizable movement of refugees from north to south, both before and during the war.

Shortly after the armistice, the Soviet Union and China embarked on policies of substantial economic aid programs to North Korea. As a result, it acquired a broad industrial base and a per capita industrial production which rose to a level higher than that of China. Kim Il Sung, the political leader selected by the Soviets in 1945 to lead North Korea, soon acquired exclusive control over the local communist party at the expense of his rivals.

The Korean War and subsequent Russian–Chinese ideological disputes over what is "true communism" gave Kim a much wider degree of freedom of action within the communist sphere of the world which he readily seized. For a few years after 1960 he tended to favor the Chinese without being totally dominated by them, but after 1964 he swung back toward the Russians, then again toward the Chinese for a time, and since 1983, toward Moscow again.

In South Korea, despite massive American aid in the postwar period, the economy floundered and the elderly President Rhee grew senile, autocratic and unpopular. He resigned in 1960 and left the country in the face of rebellious student demonstrations which the army made no effort to suppress. There followed a year of political ferment and regrouping under a weak government which ended in 1961 when the army seized control of South Korea.

Efforts by North Korea to achieve reunification of the peninsula under communist auspices have failed in the postwar period. Probably in an effort to take advantage of U.S. involvement in Vietnam, Kim Il Sung began in 1965 to send terrorist teams across the 38th parallel in the hope of undermining the political stability of South Korea, but with little success. Tunnel digging under the fortifications of South Korea along the demarcation line was tried for awhile, also unsuccessfully. There was an assassination attempt on South Korean President Park Chung Hee in 1968, and the dramatic seizure of an undefended U.S. intelli-

South Korea's National Assembly in session. Housed in the nation's new building, legislators enjoy all modern technological innovations including electronic voting.

Courtesy: Embassy of Korea

gence vessel, the U.S.S. Pueblo, in waters near Wonsan after the ship had allegedly violated North Korean territorial waters. There was a widespread fear that North Korea might attempt another invasion of the South after this incident, but it did not.

After months of negotiations between the United States and North Korea at the village of Panmunjom, the same site at which the talks that ended the Korean War occurred, both sides reached agreement for the return of the crew of the *Pueblo*. This unusual accord provided for the U.S. to acknowledge in writing that the vessel had penetrated into the territorial waters of North Korea, and at the same time permitted the verbal denial of the truth of the written statement by the U.S. military representative signing the document. The vessel remained in the possession of the North Koreans.

After a period of military rule, General Park Chung Hee, the leader of the military *junta* which had seized power, nominally became a civilian and was elected president—he was reelected in 1967. Under his government, not genuinely free, but much more responsive to the needs of the people than that of North Korea, some notable gains were registered. The economy began to grow rapidly, and South Korea at American urging decided to contribute troops to

the struggle going on in Vietnam. The government was able to withstand opposition to the necessary establishment of diplomatic and commercial relations with Japan in 1965.

In spite of large–scale student demonstrations against him, President Park won a popular referendum altering the constitution in 1969; the change permitted him to run for a third term in 1971 and he was victorious in April elections. National Assembly elections held in 1972 gave 113 seats to the ruling *Democratic Republican Party* and 89 to the *New Democratic Party*.

Sentiments in favor of restriction of Korean textile imports in the U.S. and a decision to reduce United States military presence in South Korea caused great concern during 1970–1971. Increased political contacts with North Korea beginning during this period contributed to increased political ferment in South Korea and led to President Park's decision to proclaim an emergency and rule by decree. On July 4, 1972, there was an announcement by both North and South Korean governments that following a series of secret talks, an agreement had been reached to hold negotiations and to work toward eventual reunification of this divided country. As it turned out many years later, the North Koreans, although interested in the booming econ-

omy of South Korea, were not dealing with sincerity on the matter.

Citing new conditions produced by the negotiations with North Korea and the Nixon efforts to lessen cold war tensions, President Park proclaimed martial law and prohibited normal political activity in late 1972. In North Korea, the main trends of the year were the rising power of Kim Yong–ju, Kim Il Sung's younger brother, and the adoption of a new state constitution designed to make confederation and ultimate unification with South Korea more attractive to Seoul.

President Park's increasing personal power aroused considerable opposition, especially from the intellectuals, students and the powerful Christian churches. This opposition was cruelly suppressed on the ground that it gave aid and comfort to North Korea at a time when American protection of South Korea was becoming increasingly unreliable. An opposition leader, Kim Dae Jung, who had received a large minority of the popular vote for the presidency in 1971, was kidnapped in Japan by the South Korean Central Intelligence Agency in 1973 and brought home. President Park's widely beloved wife was fatally shot in mid–1974 in what was officially described as a attempt on the life of the president himself. Since the assassin had some Japanese connections, the government launched a dispute with Japan, but there were reasons to believe that this quarrel, as well as tensions in North Korea–South Korea relations which existed in 1974, were at least partly efforts by the Park government to distract attention from its domestic difficulties.

Despite his easy victory in a rigged referendum held in February 1975, it appeared that Park's heavy–handedness might cost him the crucial support of the army leadership. Although President Ford visited South Korea in late 1974, it appeared that a headstrong U.S. Congress would force budget reductions leading to a partial or even total withdrawal of American forces from South Korea. Subsequently, the Carter administration decided to withdraw all American ground forces by 1982—but changed its mind in 1979 in view of the threat from North Korea.

The fall of Indochina to communism in 1975 left South Korea the only non–communist nation on the East Asian mainland and intensified the sense of danger felt in the country. This was exploited by President Park to increase his rigid control through repressive measures. Human rights critics in the U.S. urged withdrawal of economic aid and military support. Probably for foreign propaganda purposes, North Korean military personnel killed two American officers in the Demilitarized Zone in mid–1976. After an American air and naval buildup in the area, however, Kim Il Sung issued something close to an apology.

The ruling *Democratic Republican Party* came closer to defeat in a 1978 election when it won 68 seats in the National Assembly to 61 for the opposition *New Democratic Party*; 22 seats went to independents. President Park reorganized his cabinet and released a number of political prisoners, including the *New Democratic Party's* leader, Kim Dae Jung.

Talks of reunification have occurred intermittently since 1971. Pyongyang tried to use them as a means toward a political takeover of the South. In 1975, Kim Il Sung announced two conditions under which his regime would feel justified in attacking the South: a southern attack on the North (very unlikely) or a popular revolution in the South requiring outside support. The second is also very unlikely in view of South Korea's remarkable economic progress during the 1980's. It is even more unlikely that the Soviet Union or China would support such an attack. Soviet and Chinese support was substantial in the last half of the 1970's, but has waned as those two allies deal with their own present economic problems.

For many years Kim Il Sung has been grooming his son, Kim Jong Il, now a secretary of the ruling *Korean Worker's Party*, to succeed him.

President Park was assassinated by the head of the South Korean Central Intelligence Agency in October 1979 because of his heavy handedness, particularly towards students and some of his own officials. After an interlude of confusion, the army under General Chun Doo Hwan seized power in December 1979. In mid–1980 it proclaimed martial law and crushed a revolt in a southwestern city, Kwangju.

Chun then became Acting President and began to install a new government. Martial law was lifted at the beginning of 1981 and Chun commuted the death sentence imposed on opposition leader Kim Dae Jung to life imprisonment. He launched a policy of "national reconciliation" under which thousands of people imprisoned or barred from public life were pardoned. Partly as a result of this, he was invited to Washington by President Reagan. The meeting was a great success and improved U.S.–Korean relations which had been chilly under President Carter. Although Kim Dae Jung was released at the end of 1982, he was forced to go into temporary exile in the United States.

President Chun had made a number of other foreign trips as well, with the result that his government's international image and his country's export markets have improved considerably. Seoul was chosen as the site of the 1988 Olympic Games.

In an effort to stop this upward trend and destabilize South Korea, North Korea attempted to assassinate Chun with a bomb during a visit to Rangoon, Burma, in October 1983; the bomb missed the president but killed 17 other South Korean officials and newspapermen. Alarmed, Chun tended to tighten up his essentially autocratic rule, thereby producing increasing discontent on the part of the opposition.

South Korea suffered another spectacular disaster in September 1983 when one of its airliners, which had overflown Soviet Siberian territory by mistake, was shot down by a Soviet fighter aircraft with the loss of all those aboard. International outrage was widespread. South Korea thus within the space of a few months had the image of being victimized by criminal actions of North Korea and the Soviet Union.

Chun Doo Hwan's political plans for the future were unclear. One possible successor was his brother, Chun Kyung Hwan, who was active in rural affairs. Another was former General Roh Tae Woo, who was named in February 1985 to head the ruling *Democratic Justice Party*.

In any case, Chun faced serious political problems in 1984–1985. There were mounting student demonstrations against the government, and the leading opposition politician, Kim Dae Jung, returned from the U.S. in early 1985. Although he was placed under house arrest, a new political party with which he was affiliated, the *New Korea Democratic Party*, did unexpectedly well in National Assembly elections held shortly after his return, winning 50 out of 276 seats.

Chun then reorganized his cabinet and removed the ban on political activity by 14 opposition figures; although Kim Dae Jung was theoretically included, his political role continued to be restricted in practice on the ground that he had been convicted on a criminal charge (sedition) in 1980.

In the North, Kim Jong Il appeared to be making some progress toward acceptance as his father's successor. Moscow and Beijing seemed to have acquiesced, although reluctantly. Pyongyang improved its relations with Moscow in 1984 and received some new Soviet arms, and it allowed Soviet reconnaissance aircraft to overfly its territory and Soviet naval vessels to call at some of its ports.

The events of February 1986 in the Philippines had a considerable impact on South Korea, not only because Marcos lost power but because the U.S. withdrew support from him in spite of its large strategic interest in the country. An intensified dialogue ensued between the government and the legal opposition centering on the *New Korea Democratic Party (NKDP)*. A deadlock typical of the uncompromising Korean approach to politics soon developed, however. It related to the desirable nature of a new constitution. The government and the ruling party, the *Democratic Justice Party (DJP)*, wanted a cabinet (parliamentary) system, with the real power vested in the premier who would presumably be a *DJP* member; the opposition insisted on a directly (rather than indirectly, as at that time) elected president as the effective head of the government. The opposition was hampered by disunity within the leadership of the *NKDP*.

Other elements of the opposition, including Christian clergy, lay believers and activist students, demonstrated from time to time against the government. The demonstrators, although fairly numerous, were generally outnumbered by the huge forces of police that the government deployed to cope with them. This was especially true of two demonstrations in February and March 1987, the first of which protested the death of a student from police brutality. President Chun had already fired his Home Minister and chief of national police and arrested the two officers considered responsible for this tragedy, but the police continued to behave heavyhandedly. Some of the students had been radicalized not only by official behavior, but by their own demanding routine (the "education hell," as they call it) and by contact with Marxist (not necessarily North Korean) ideas and slogans, often smuggled in from Japan.

The U.S. clearly favored compromise between the government and the opposition, and a democratization of the political system, as Secretary of State Shultz, for example, made clear during a March 1987 visit, but its influence was limited. The activist elements of the opposition tended to view the U.S. as the mainstay of the hated South Korean "establishment," which they regarded as a military and police dictatorship.

In the summer of 1987, Chun's DJP was preparing to hand over the reins of power to his designated successor, fellow former general and DJP politician Roh Tae Woo. The public outcry reached even higher levels than those of the spring. Facing potential disaster, Roh called for free elections, counting on a loyal (but minority) DJP rural political base and a divided opposition to salvage victory.

The first direct presidential elections in more than 16 years were held in South Korea in December 1987. The candidate of the ruling *DJP* was Roh Tae Woo. The two top opposition leaders, Kim Young Sam and Kim Dae Jung, were unwilling to cooperate, and the result was predictable: the winner was Roh Tae Woo with 39.9% of the vote, while the two Kims split the majority opposition vote 27.5% and 26.5%.

Amid anti-government protests, erupting into severe street rioting, Roh Tae Woo was sworn in as president in February 1988. Bitter clashes have continued periodically since then; the unrest is based on the assertion that the new president is not liberal enough, and an illogical notion that the two Koreas are prevented from uniting by U.S. interference.

North Korea continues to maintain pressure on the South; for example it started in the fall of 1986 a large dam north of the Demilitarized Zone that theoretically could eventually store enough water to flood Seoul if its waters were suddenly and completely released. The South responded by planning a counter–dam further south and offered to supply electric power to the North if the Pyongyang would halt construction of its dam.

In recent years, North Korea and the Soviet Union have drawn closer than ever before, but there has been no sign of Soviet willingness to support another attack on South Korea. China is even less favorable to the idea of another war. Pyongyang's discontent with its allies, as evidenced for example around the time of a rare visit by Kim Il Sung to Moscow in October 1986, plus internal political tensions probably centering on Kim's plan to be succeeded by his son, may have been responsible for a mysterious crisis in mid–November 1986. As a bizarre indication of this, some North Korean loudspeakers near the Demilitarized Zone announced

Former President Roh Tae Woo

that Kim Il Sung had died, which it soon became clear he had not.

In an election for the National Assembly held in April 1988, the ruling *Democratic Justice Party* won only 125 of the 299 seats. The opposition then held hearings on various abuses of power during the tenure of former President Chun Doo Hwan, and especially on the Kwangju massacre of May 1980. Chun himself refused to testify, and President Roh refused to compel him to do so, but Chun made a public apology, turned over his assets to the state, and retired to the countryside. Dissatisfied, a number of opposition politicians and radicals continued to demand that he be put on trial. Early in 1989, approximately fifty people, including two brothers of Chun's, were arrested on charges of corrupt practices under his administration.

President Roh himself had a better image than his predecessor, but the opposition in the National Assembly hoped to pass a vote of no confidence in his admin-

istration and compel his resignation. In March 1989, Roh cancelled an earlier promise to submit his administration to a popular referendum after one year in office.

Seoul's hosting of the 1988 Summer Olympic Games (September–October) went off fairly smoothly and considerably broadened South Korea's international contacts. North Korea, which had threatened to disrupt the games because it had not been allowed to co–host them, made no hostile move at the time. The games provided an excellent opportunity for Seoul to pursue its so–called *Nordpolitik*, or policy of expanding commercial and other ties with communist states including North Korea. A major triumph in this connection was diplomatic recognition by Hungary, the first communist state to establish formal ties with Seoul.

A large number, although not a majority, of South Koreans, not all of them radicals, have become strongly dissatisfied with the status of the relationship with the United States. The major issues are the American responsibility for the partition of Korea in 1945 (the alternative to which was Soviet occupation of the entire Peninsula), American support for a series of authoritarian governments in South Korea, and the alleged lack of American enthusiasm for reunification of the country. Somewhat less serious irritants are American control of the Combined Forces Command, under which South Korean forces serve; American military facilities including a golf course not far from the center of Seoul; American pressures to increase Seoul's financial support for the American forces in South Korea and to open its markets further to American products, especially agricultural commodities; the alleged tendency toward protectionism in the United States; and the nomination by President Bush of a former CIA official, Donald Gregg, as ambassador, in succesion to another former CIA official, James Lilley. A very brief visit by President Bush to Seoul at the end of February 1989, on his way home from the Hirohito funeral and a visit to China, accomplished little beyond making it clear to the South Korean side that its efforts to improve its relationship with North Korea were acceptable to the U.S.

The several years leading up to the 1993 presidential election was an important transitional period. Many did not trust the ruling *Liberal Democratic Party* or President Roh Tae Woo. It was believed that he might seek extra legal means of holding onto power. The new constitution was untested and the opposition was, for the most part, weak. There was also concern that the United States might significantly downsize its commitment to the republic. In spite of these concerns, 1993 marked the beginning of a new, more democratic era for the country.

The Political System: The Republic of Korea is composed of fifteen administrative subdivisions including nine provinces and six special cities. The current constitution became operative on February 25, 1988. The legal system is derived from both Western and Chinese sources. Suffrage is universal at age 20.

The president is the *chief of state*, while the prime minister is the *head of government*. The State Council (cabinet) is appointed by the president with the recommendation of the prime minister.

South Korea has a unicameral (single house) legislature, the *Kukhoe*. Major political parties include the: *Democratic Liberal Party (DLP)*, headed by President Kim Young–sam; the *Democratic Party (DP)*, under Yi Ki–taek; and the *United People's Party (UPP)*, Kim Tong–kil, chairman. The *DLP* was formed when the *Democratic Justice Party (DJP)*, *Reunification Democratic Party (RDJ)*, and *New Demo-*

President Kim Young Sam

cratic Republican Party (NDRP) merged in February 1990. Both the parties and their membership are fluid, with frequent name changes and membership re–alignment.

South Korea also has a number of functioning special interest groups such as the National Council of Churches, National Council of Labor Unions, and the Korean Trade Association.

Recent Political Events: On February 25, 1993, Kim Young Sam, became the country's first civilian president. His *Democratic Liberal Party* continues to be the dominant political party.

In 1993, the new president put forward three specific goals: achieve civilian control over the military and depoliticization of the military, a more caring government, and an anticorruption program.

President Kim succeeded in obtaining the agreement of all top military officials not to interfere in the political process. Charges of corruption were brought

against top military figures and several were relieved of their positions, including the army chief of staff. Army personnel who were members of the Hanahoe (One Mind) organization were removed from office. The new government also moved to dismantle the Agency for National Security Planning. A further significant move involved the release of almost 40,000 criminals and political prisoners. Helmeted riot police withdrew from the streets and the number of student demonstrations decreased. Anti–corruption measures were initiated against a number of high ranking government officials. After some thirty years of military participation in the political process, it is somewhat remarkable that the new president has had as much success as he has.

In March 1994 President Kim initiated reforms to improve the political process. In a bi–partisan move, the National Assembly passed bills dealing with campaign spending, election procedures and local government. Government subsidies

Assembly line at the Hyundai automotive company in Seoul—the *Excel*

for political parties and candidates was increased. The overall limit on campaign spending was lowered (how much a candidate could spend on his/her own campaign). Strong penalties were introduced. The legislation did not place a limit on how much a party could spend on a candidate. Overall, these changes made it easier for the opposition to compete on even footing with the ruling party. The legislation dealing with local government provided for the election of mayors to begin in June 1995. The legislature also was given increased authority over the budget and actions of the National Security Planning Agency (NSPA).

Nevertheless, the president faced significant criticism and pressure from the opposition. A primary reason had to do with policy toward North Korea. The president appeared weak in October when he accepted the United States–North Korean deal to build two nuclear reactors for Pyongyang. South Korea was not part of the negotiations. At the end of the month, the opposition put forward a motion in the National Assembly demanding the resignation of the entire cabinet including the prime minister.

Earlier in the year when Prime Minister Lee Hoi Chang asked for a role in formulating policy toward the North, he was fired and President Kim appointed Lee Yung Kuk. There was also a suggestion that the premier was sacked because he was pushing to continue with the reform movement which brought the president into power.

A series of disasters which hit the country during the year also brought criticism down on the president. In October 32 people were killed when the Songsu Bridge in Seoul collapsed. Because official appointed by the chief executive were in a supervisory capacity during the construction of the bridge, the president was held responsible by the opposition.

On December 31, President Kim was named the winner of the Martin Luther King Prize for his contribution to building democracy and human rights in South Korea.

Storm clouds swept over the political landscape in 1995 and early 1996. In October, former President Roh Tae Woo admitted to receiving over $600 million in contributions from businesses during his term in office. He also admitted that

about one/third of that money was still in his private possession. Roh's admissions came after two of his associates, one of whom managed the secret fund, revealed its existence.

It then became apparent that in return for the huge payments, large corporations such as Hyundai, Samsung, Daewoo, and Lucky Goldstar received large government contracts.

Another revelation was that Kim Dae Jung, an unsuccessful candidate for the presidency in 1992 had received over $2.5 million from Roh for his campaign. By mid–November, Roh was behind bars on corruption charges.

At approximately the same time, the Supreme Public Prosecutor's Office decided to reopen an investigation into the December 1979 coup and the 1988 Kwangju massacre. These events involved former President Chun Doo Hwan. Chun had testified about the events before the National Assembly in 1989, under an agreement signed by then President Roh and the leading opposition figures, including the current president, Kim Young Sam, which provided protection from future prosecution.

In December, apparently under intense political pressure because of allegations tied to his 1992 presidential campaign finances, President Kim publicly stated that he intended to seek a law which would allow for the punishment of those involved in the 1988 Kwangju massacre.

Thus, on January 23rd, 1996, former presidents Chun Doo Hwan and Roh Tae Woo were both charged with treason in connection with the death of some 200 pro–democracy demonstrators in Kwangju, in May 1980. Six former army generals were also indicted. The fact that two former presidents who ruled the country until 1993, could be indicted and imprisoned, must have left many Koreans in disbelief. While the Roh case points to the massive corruption of the Korean political system, the downfall of the former presidents speaks well for the emerging rule of law and democratic principles in South Korea.

Another major step toward democracy was the June 27 elections of provincial governors, mayors and heads of towns. Unfortunately, for President Kim and his *LDP*, the opposition won most of the major posts, including the post of mayor of Seoul.

In March 1996, thousands of students demonstrated in Seoul over the death of a protestor who may have beaten by police. The April 11 National Assembly elections were expected to see a further weakening of Kim and his *LDP*.

Foreign Relations: In 1995, South Korea succeeded in elevating its international status by being elected, in November, to a two year term on the United Nations Security Council. Also of great importance was the visit of President Jiang Zemin from the People's Republic of China. No head of state from the PRC has as yet to visit North Korea.

Relations with Japan were ruffled over remarks by a Japanese official about colonial rule in Korea. (Japan annexed the Korean peninsula in 1910.) Japanese Prime Minister Murayama sent an official letter of apology which appeared to smooth things over. South Korean relations with the northern cousins were rocky at best. The ingrates to the north could not even bring themselves to thank Seoul for shipping rice. They even de-

tained the crew members of the ship delivering it in August.

The issue of how and who would build the light water nuclear reactors for North Korean seemed closer to resolution. North Korea agreed to a South Korean designed reactor and to the South's role in construction. The North would, however, publicly deny the above. Throughout the year, Pyongyang did everything it could to avoid dealing directly with South Korean officials. Then, for no apparent reason, in early April 1996, North Korea announced that it no longer recognized the demilitarized zone between the North and South. Tensions soared.

Culture: Korean culture, although distinct from that of Japan, resembles it in many respects. The people have the same ethnic heritage, and have been exposed to repeated Chinese influences over many centuries. But each has retained its own individuality. The ancient pre–Chinese aspects of Korean culture, such as shamanism—the belief in occult sorcerers and worship of demons—have a Northeast and Central Asian derivation.

On this base the ingredients of Chinese

Mechanized rice harvesting in Korea. Although Korean rice yields are among the highest in the world, mechanization has become necessary as demand rises with the standard of living, and agricultural workers leave the land for jobs in industry.

culture, including Buddhism and Confucianism, were superimposed as a second layer. Since the 19th century there have been many conversions to Christianity, which today exerts a profound influence in the peninsula. Japan's influence has been tempered by its oppressive behavior in the 20th century while in control of Korea.

Since 1945, Russian influence has been dominant in the North and American ideals have had some influence in the South. It must be remembered, however, that the Koreans for centuries have been able to maintain their individual character—a highly creative and original collective personality.

Economy: For the year, the balance of trade was almost $10 billion in the red. However, exports grew by over 25% making South Korea one of only 12 countries in the world to achieve a $100 billion export level. Exports benefited from the strong Japanese yen in particular. The export market was led by automobiles, electronics and semiconductors. Overall, the economy grew by about 9% while inflation was under 5%. Per capita income was around $10,000 for 1995. Another factor contributing to this impressive growth was the general decline in labor unrest over the past decade.

The strong economy led the government to make big commitments for infrastructure development, including a new international airport, and continued subway construction.

NORTH KOREA

Political System: The Democratic People's Republic of Korea (DPRK) is one of the world's few remaining communist states. The constitution was adopted in 1948 and was revised most recently in 1992. The legal system is built on communist legal theory and German civil law. The judiciary has no authority to review acts of the legislature. Suffrage is universal for everyone 17 years of age and older. The government has both a President and a Premier. The State Administration Council (cabinet) is appointed by the Supreme People's Assembly.

The Supreme People's Assembly is the national legislature and has one house. Candidates for office are chosen by the *Korean Workers' Party (DWP)* and run unopposed. Minor parties are tolerated and hold a few seats in the People's Assembly.

On July 8, 1994, Kim Il Sung died just before he was to meet with President Kim Young Sam. Kim Jong Il and those around him continued the negotiations with the United States with skill. South Korea has been humiliated by being excluded. Both Seoul and Washington are

so afraid of the nuclear card that no one will say enough is enough. On October 21, the U.S. and North Korea reached an agreement in Geneva which provided for the building of two light–water reactors. South Korea will be the builder and may accept up to 40% of the cost. President Kim was particularly upset because while the agreement called for the immediate suspension of the North Korean nuclear program, it did not provide for inspection of the country's nuclear facilities for five years. The U.S. will also contribute funds along with other countries for the reactors. The accord also opens the way for the establishment of diplomatic relations between North Korea and the U.S., and the easing of trade restrictions against the latter. On January 20, the State Department announced the beginning of this process. At the same time, as part of the accord, the U.S. delivered 30,000 tons of heavy fuel oil to North Korea. North Korea, on the other hand, gave up virtually nothing of consequence in signing the accord.

After the accord, South Korea ended the ban on investment in the North. It was a gesture intended to give the North an opportunity to respond with a cautious but reciprocal move. The North Koreans continued to issue statements full of insults aimed at the South. Together, North Korea and the United States put President Kim Young Sam in a most difficult position. Admittedly, his earlier waffling on a policy toward the North didn't help. The two countries do trade through intermediaries.

In 1995, Kim Jong Il solidified his rule although he was not appointed to the post of party general secretary or head of state. There were no major changes in the party politburo. In October 1995, the South Korean magazine, *Chosun*, used experts to psychoanalyze a fifty–five minute tape of Kim Jong Il's conversations. In his conversations, Kim acknowledges that socialism can't feed the people and that it will be necessary to seek assistance from the West.

In August the country was hit with floods and on September 21, the government did issue a call for foreign assistance. The UN estimated the damage to be at $15 billion. However, aid did not poor in. In January 1996, the U.S., Japan, and South Korean governments were still in disagreement over an appropriate response. South Korea had been insulted instead of being thanked for a previous shipment of rice. In December, Japan agreed to sell North Korea 200,000 tons of rice. In February 1996, Washington announced its intention to donate $2 million in assistance through the UN. And, in March, a ship carrying grain to North Korea sank.

Pyongyang finally agreed to terms allowing a U.S. led consortium to build

several light water reactors in North Korea. They will not produce the by–product which can be used in the manufacture of a nuclear weapon. North Korea refused, however, to publicly acknowledge South Korea's central role in the construction and financing of the reactors.

Economy: The government of North Korea did not release a budget for 1995–1996. Massive floods and mismanagement of the economy were responsible for a disastrous year. It can be estimated that for 1995, the country was three to four million tons short on its grain supply. Even in 1993, the government launched a "let's eat two meals a day" campaign.

Per capita GNP for 1994 was put at about $900 by one South Korean estimate. The same estimate suggests a decline in trade of some 20%, to about $2.1 billion. For 1995, trade was probably below $2 billion. Between 1990 and 1994, the economy is estimated to have shrunk almost 20%.

North Korea has established a free trade zone at Rajin–Sunbong. However, investments since 1993 have been slow and are pegged at about $140 million.

Foreign Relations: North Korea is following a very unorthodox strategy in foreign relations calculated to bring it into the international community. Many observers believe that behind the negotiations over the country's nuclear program, is a desire to use the issue as a means of opening up relations with the outside world. Clearly, North Korea wants to establish relations with the big four: Russia, Japan, China and the United States. But its clumsy tactics, for example, continuing to berate Japan, accomplished very little. In November 1995 South Korea, Japan and the United States agreed to redouble their efforts to work together in approaching North Korea. This was a defeat for the North's desire to gain recognition, *while dealing South Korea out.* It seems a certainty that U.S. and Japanese relations with the North will not advance significantly until North–South interaction improves. Efforts to do *anything* to South Korea make no sense in view of the vast economic disparity of the two nations.

In April 1996, North Korea's announcement that it would no longer recognize the demilitarized zone separating it from South Korea was another unsophisticated move designed to draw Washington into closer negotiations.

The Future: South Korea withstood major political shockwave in 1995, with the arrest and conviction of two former presidents. It is amazing how fast the military has withdrawn from the political arena.

This fact, along with the success of first ever local elections speak very well for the future of democracy in the country.

Internationally, skillful diplomacy slowed North Korea's attempt to marginalize South Korea. South Korea will continue to play a key role in any strategy to establish relations with the North. Washington and Tokyo apparently agree.

North Korea is clearly in trouble. While Kim Jong Il may not be the ideal leader, he has shown an understanding of the ways of international diplomacy. The major factor preventing North Korea from joining the international community is a weird sense of "pride." It will eventually will stop insulting the South and open up a meaningful dialogue. There is little chance, however, that this will occur in the next year. Survival of the present regime to 2000 is not a sure thing.

View of the port of Pusan, South Korea

WORLD BANK photo

The Lao People's Democratic Republic

A Laotian newspaper

Area: 91,400 sq. mi. (234,804 sq. km., somewhat smaller than Oregon).

Population: 4,600,000 (est. 1993).

Capital City: Vientiane (Pop. 230,000, estimated).

Climate: Tropical, with a rainy monsoon from May–October and a dry season from November–April.

Neighboring Countries: China (North); Vietnam (East); Burma (Northwest); Thailand (West); Cambodia (South).

Official Language: Lao

Other Principal Tongue: French.

Ethnic Background: The majority of the people, living in the Mekong Valley, are the Lao, of Thai ancestry. There are a number of tribes, including the Meo, Yao, Kha and Lu, some of which are Thai, but most of which are Malay, Chinese and Vietnamese ancestry.

Principal Religion: Buddhism; animism is predominant among the tribes.

Major Exports: Electric power (to Thailand), timber and textiles.

Main Imports: (from Thailand, Russia, Japan, France, China, Vietnam); Rice, petroleum products, machinery.

Currency: Kip.

Former Colonial Status: French protectorate (1893–1949); member of the French Union (1949–1954).

National Day: December 24, 1954.

Chief of State: Nouhak Phoumsavan, President.

Head of Government: Khamtai Siphandon, Prime Minister.

National Flag: Two red stripes (top and bottom), a wide blue stripe between them upon which is centered a white circle.

Per Capita Income: U.S. $380.

Laos is a landlocked, tropical country largely covered with mountains and tropical forests interrupted by patches of low scrub vegetation in the areas where the soil is poor. From one point of view it is an extremely backward country with almost no roads, but from another point of view it is an area of the world where the natural beauty has not been greatly altered by the presence of man.

Most of the fertile land lies along the valley of the Mekong River, where it is eroded and flows as silt to the rice paddies in the Mekong Delta in southern Vietnam. The land receives ample rainfall, but the sandstone soils have little capacity to retain the moisture. In the last part of the dry season from November to May, the air becomes oppressively hot and very dry—this is the time when the tribesmen living in the mountain forests burn the trees to clear the land. This practice, coupled with natural forest fires, robs the land of much of its fertility; when the farmer ceases to cultivate the land it becomes choked with a primitive, ugly scrub vegetation.

History: The Lao people moved into northern Laos from the southwestern Chinese province of Yunnan beginning in the 11th century A.D. During the succeeding centuries they slowly expanded toward the south, founding two communities in central and southern Laos. In their efforts to settle these additional lands they came into frequent conflict with the Burmese and Thai who were also active in this part of Southeast Asia.

The French established their colonial authority over neighboring Vietnam by 1893. When there was a dispute between Thailand and Laos over demarcation of the border, the French proclaimed a protectorate over Laos in 1893, making it a dependency within the French Indochinese Empire. Because of its remoteness and lack of natural resources, the French did almost nothing to develop Laos; they did succeed in ending the payment of tribute to the kings of Thailand, however.

When the waves of Japanese soldiers inundated Southeast Asia in 1942, they supported their Thai ally in taking some border territory from Laos. A nationalist movement, known as the *Lao Issara* and directed mainly against the Japanese occupation forces, arose during World War II. When the French re–entered after the defeat of the Japanese, Thailand was forced by Britain and the U.S. to return the territory it had acquired while allied with the enemy. The *Lao Issara* promptly started anti–French activity from bases in Thailand. Preoccupied with resistance movements in Vietnam, the French granted Laos internal self–government within the French Union in 1949; this split the resistance movement. The non–communist majority took a leading role in the new government, but the communist and pro–communist minority formed itself into a party known as the *Pathet Lao*.

This communist movement opposed the new government and came increasingly under the influence of Ho Chi

President Nouhak Phoumsavan

Prime Minister Khamtai Siphandon

Minh's communist movement in Northern Vietnam. Following invasions of northern Laos by communist Vietnamese in 1953 and 1954, the *Pathet Lao* completely controlled the provinces of Phong Saly and Sam Neua on the Vietnamese border. Under the terms of an agreement reached in Geneva in 1954, it was allotted these provinces for "regrouping."

After prolonged haggling, the government, which had achieved full independence from France in late 1954, and the *Pathet Lao* agreed on political and military unification in 1957. The strong showing of the *Pathet Lao* in 1958 elections alarmed the Laotian government, and also the U.S., leading to a breakdown of the 1957 agreement. The situation became critical when the government tried in 1959 to integrate two battalions of the *Pathet Lao* forces into the army and to demobilize the remainder of the communist–oriented forces. The result was a confused, small–scale civil war in which the North Vietnamese seized the opportunity to give increasing aid in personnel and equipment to the *Pathet Lao*. The U.S. increased its assistance to the government to meet the threat.

A military *coup* replaced the rightwing government with a neutralist regime under Prince Souvanna Phouma in 1960. Diplomatic relations were promptly established with the Soviet Union; when the Prince was driven from Vientiane by right–wing forces in December 1960 he appealed for Soviet military aid. Russia promptly airlifted arms to the neutralist forces, but also sent an even larger shipment to the *Pathet Lao*, with whom Souvanna Phouma was cooperating. North Vietnam compounded the problem by sending its own forces into the mountains of eastern Laos at the beginning of 1961 in order to improve its access to South Vietnam via the "Ho Chi Minh Trail;" this was to assist in

Lane Xang Hotel, Vientiane

stepping up the revolutionary war against South Vietnam which was then in full bloom. It also increased aid to the *Pathet Lao*.

Evidently realizing that a war could not serve the aims of either side, U.S. President Kennedy and Soviet Premier Khrushchev agreed in 1961 that Laos should be neutralized. In spite of this, following intense jockeying for position, the *Pathet Lao* withdrew from the coalition government which had just been set up. The result was continuation of a highly complex and somewhat obscure, undeclared civil war. It included Thai volunteers and operations managed by the U.S. Central Intelligence Agency.

During the following years until 1971, military activity was related directly to the Ho Chi Minh Trail, vital to the North Vietnamese war effort in South Vietnam. The communists sought to keep it open, while the South Vietnamese, assisted by the U.S., sought periodically to close it, without success. As part of the accord supposedly settling the Vietnamese conflict reached in Paris, a form of agreement was reached in 1973 regarding Laos. It included many of the *Pathet Lao* demands and tended to lessen the

influence of the right wing in the central government. Fighting practically stopped and all foreign troops were to leave the country within 60 days.

A coalition government was not installed until April 1974; it then became a means whereby the *Pathet Lao* greatly strengthened its political influence. Prince Souvanna Phouma's age and ill health reduced his role, and Prince Souphanouvong, the leading *Pathet Lao* in the coalition government, assumed the chairmanship of the Political Council. He in effect made it, rather than the National Assembly, the real legislative body. Although the *Pathet Lao* military located themselves in the government areas, non–communists were not allowed to function politically in or even to enter areas held by them. North Vietnamese troops remained in the highlands after the coalition government was formed.

A heart attack suffered by Premier Souvanna Phouma in mid–1974 made things easier for the *Pathet Lao*. Following more maneuvering for position, the early months of 1975 saw demonstrations by pro–communist elements (students, etc.) in some towns, as well as

fighting in remote areas. The fall of South Vietnam and Cambodia in the spring of 1975 made a *Pathet Lao* take-over inevitable; the right–wing members of the government resigned in May. Soon there was a shift in favor of "hardline" communism—the monarchy was abolished and a new government was created with Souphanouvong as President. The ex–King was arrested in 1977.

In 1976, political "education" of the people was widespread, involving several thousand "advisors." A sizable Soviet aid program, including the building of an airfield on the Plain of Jars, was made available. Vietnamese influence was very great, and in fact, dominant. There were still Vietnamese troops on Laotian soil. Using "yellow rain" (Soviet–made natural poisons) for a time they fought Lao insurgents, some of whom are supported by China.

At a congress of the ruling *Lao People's Revolutionary Party* held in November 1986, there were some leadership changes, with a tendency toward younger and perhaps better trained men rising to the top. The party, in line with recent Russian and Vietnamese moves and clearly troubled by the bad condition of the Laotian economy, called for better relations with China, Thailand and the U.S., as one means of improving the country's general situation.

Politics and Government: Under the 1991 Constitution, the Lao People's Democratic Republic (LPDR) continues to have a Marxist–Leninist style government. Poitical power rests with the Pasason, the central organ of the *Lao People's Revolution Party (LPRP)*. The party Chairman is 69 year old Khamtai Siphandon.

The National Assembly held its first meeting in February 1993. The unicameral Assembly, with 85 members, operates under the principle of democratic centralism, which allows the leadership of the *LPRP* to control the legislative process. Nouhak Phoumsavan is the LPDR President and Khamtai Siphandon, party chairman, is the Prime Minister. The primary decision body of the Assembly is the Cabinet.

The *LPRP* also controls the electoral process. Candidates for the National Assembly are approved by the *LPRP* and in some cases picked by government departments. Assembly members also receive political training before assuming their responsibilities.

During 1993, the *LPRP* demonstrated that it had the authority to continue to rule the country. The *LPRP* continued to move the country toward a market economy and away from socialism. Like their Vietnamese neighbors, the Laotion leadership apparently wants economic reform while seeking to hold on to political power. Laos, like so many of the East Asian political systems, is moving toward an internal confrontation between the demands of an emerging developing economy and the wishes of an outmoded political leadersip.

In 1994, the *LPRP* maintained firm control—there is no real political opposition in the country. In 1990, three individuals who called for a democratic system were arrested and are still in detention.

Apparently the National Assembly has been trained to avoid politics and tend to other matters, including economic development. A second development within the government is the rise to power of military personnel, i.e., generals, who have taken over many of the cabinet portfolios and other key positions.

The top goal of the *LPRP* remains attainment of a market economy while maintaining control. The term for this is *chintanakan mai* ("new thinking"). Much of the real progress in changing the country can be traced to the Committee for Planning and Cooperation which has equal status with government ministries and consequently has become quite powerful. This committee is staffed by young, better educated technocrats who are ris-

ing to the top quickly. The Deputy Prime Minister, Khamphoui Keoboualapha heads the committee.

In 1995, the political landscape began to change with the passing of 86 year old Souphanouvong, known as the "Red Prince." Phoumi Vongvichit, a leader of the *Pathet Lao* died in 1994. Virtually all of the founding members of the *LPRP* have now either died or retired. While the party remains in firm control, Vientiane witnessed potentially important changes. For example, foreign newspapers are now available in the capital along with a new local paper *Vientiane Times*.

The Sixth Party Congress of the *LPRP* was set for April 1996. And this should be a pivotal meeting for the country and the future of the communist party. The last holdover from the old days is 80–year–old President Nouhak Phoumsavan, who was expected to retire. If this occurs, he is likely to be succeeded by the Prime Minister, Khamtai Siphandon. Who then, would become Prime Minister?

The likely choices seemed to be Khamphoui Keoboualapha, Deputy Prime Minister and Head of the State Committee for Planning and Cooperation, or Minister of Defense Lt. General Choummaly Sayasone. The former is perceived to be more oriented toward reform, while the latter was more associated with maintaining state control and going slower with reform. It is worth noting, however, that the general has presided over the expansion of the military's role in the economy of Laos. Thus, when speculating about the political future of Laos, one should not discount Burma and Indonesia as possible models. The military, more than an ideologically ill–equipped party, could be the only social organization with the skills to administer the process of economic modernization. Then too, their military cousins in Bangkok may be more than willing to help with the finer points.

Foreign Relations: LPDR foreign policy has a decided "look East" orientation.

Lane Xang Avenue in Vientiane

Lao Buddhas

The country has a long standing relationship with Vietnam. In 1977 the two countries signed the Treaty of Friendship and Cooperation. The agreement gives, among other things, the Vietnamese the authority to enter Laos whenever it is deemed necessary. Vietnamese troops withdrew from Laos in 1989. Vietnam,however, no longer dominates the concerns of the Laotion foreign ministry. In 1993, Prime Minister Khamtai Siphandon visited Vietnam. President Le Duc Anh of Vietnam returned the visit in November.

Laos is increasingly involved with its neighbor to the West, Thailand, which is already a major investor in the emerging market economy. The just opened Mitraphap bridge spans the Mekong River, and links Vientiane, the capital of Laos, to Nongkhai, Thailand. As the economic significance of this new link increases, the political influence of Bangkok will become stronger in the LPDR.

The Co–Prime Ministers of Cambodia, Prince Norodom Ranariddh and Hun Sen, also visited Laos in 1993. Vientiane supported the electoral process in Cambodia which led to the present government. Khamtai Siphandon also led a high level state delegation to the Peoples Republic of China and North Korea in December.

Relations with the United States were on good terms during the year. The two countries have worked together successfully in the areas of refugee repatriation and curbing the production of opium for export. Washington and Vientiane have also worked to resolve the status of Americans missing in action since the Vietnam war days. Initial talks were held in 1987. Today, however, reasons for cooperation are much more apparent. Victor L. Tomseth, the new U.S. ambassador, presented his credentials to the Foreign Minister of Laos in Vientiane on January 13, 1994.

During the year, President Nouhak visited Vietnam and Indonesia. High level exchanges also took place with the PRC. The Mongolian President, Punsalmaagiyn Ochirbat, visited Laos in February; and a high level delegation including the Chairman of SLORC from Burma visited in June. Laos also signed an agreement for foreign assistance with North Korea at the end of 1993. However, it seems more likely that Vientiane will be in a better position to give assistance.

In April, the United States opened the way for foreign aid to Laos. This was in return for Lao government cooperation on the POW and MIA issues.

In 1995, Lao officials continued to visit their neighbors in an attempt to broaden the base for the regime throughout the region. While Laos was not ready to become a full member of the Association for Southeast Asian Nations (ASEAN), the lines of communication were open. Laos also found itself in the position of having to struggle with the considerable flow of foreign assistance into the country. Things could be worse!

Culture: In race, religion, ancestry and other cultural aspects, the Lao are generally and accurately regarded as country cousins of the Thai. They are an extremely easygoing and lighthearted people; their country was relatively peaceful in modern times until the Vietnamese communist movement began to engage in subversion within Laos in 1953. Religious festivals, derived from very old traditions of southern Buddhism which had migrated from their origins on the island of Sri Lanka (Ceylon), are frequent and colorful, very similar to those of Thailand.

Economy: From the standpoint of economic geography, Laos falls into two clearly divided areas. In the Mekong Valley, productive agriculture centered on rice prevails. In the hills, the remote tribesmen sporadically cultivate the poor soils in a migratory fashion. Like the adjacent highlands of Burma, Thailand and China, the Laotian mountains are among the main opium producing regions of Asia. Most of this narcotic substance is smuggled out by air.

Communications are poorly developed and roads are almost nonexistent. The few that have been constructed are regularly washed out during the monsoon season.

The Lao People's Democratic Republic (LPDR) launched the New Economic Mechanism (NEM) in 1986, in an attempt to modernize the country's economy. Since 1990, reforms include the introduction of a new accounting system for production and domestic trade, assigning a permanent staff to monitor budgetary revenue, creation of central banking laws, and the integration of official and parallel exchange rates.

Foreign investment regulations were also liberalized in 1989 and again in 1994. In fact, Laos has one of the most liberal environments for foreign investment in Asia.

In 1994–1995, the country attracted significant foreign investment for the development of hydroelectric power.

The second largest sector for investment is tourism, followed by mining and manufacturing, including clothing.

One of the hydroelectric projects will be built by an Australian concern and will be the world's second highest concrete faced, rock–filled dam. The government plans to sell much of the newly generated power to Thailand which needs an expanded supply for its development needs. The two countries had not reached agreement on pricing by the end of the year.

Between 1990 and 1994, the economy averaged 6.5% growth. For 1995, the expectation was for 7%. Unfortunately, growth has been uneven with poorer production in the agricultural sector. Inflation has been high in relation to growth rates of recent years. And, in spite of impressive growth figures, Laos is still among the poorest countries in the world with a per capita income under $400.00 and a life expectancy of fifty years.

The Future: Though Laos faces many challenges, the future is bright. Relations with Thailand have improved with the signing of a Treaty of Amity and Cooperation in early 1992. Laos is also looking to the future when it can become a member of ASEAN. The government acceded to the organization's Treaty of Amity and Cooperation in July 1992. Laos is also attempting to broaden its relations by strengthening links with countries such as China and the United States. Vietnam is no longer in a position to dictate to its smaller neighbor.

Transplanting rice, Laos

101

Malaysia

The modern skyline of Kuala Lumpur

Courtesy: Embassy of Malaysia

Area: 128,775 square miles.

Population: 17.5 million (estimated).

Capital City: Kuala Lumpur (Pop. 1.2 million, estimated).

Climate: Tropically hot and humid.

Neighboring Countries: Thailand (North); Singapore (South); Indonesia (South and Southwest).

Official Languages: Malay and English.

Other Principal Tongues: Chinese, Tamil.

Ethnic Background: Malayo–Polynesian, a mixture of Polynesian, Mongol, Indian and Caucasian many centuries old (about 50%); Chinese (about 40%); Indian, primitive and other (about 10%).

Principal Religions: Islam, Buddhism, Hinduism, Christianity.

Main Exports: (to Japan, Singapore, U.S.); Natural rubber, palm oil, tin, timber, petroleum.

Main Imports: (from Japan, U.S.); Machinery and transportation equipment.

Currency: Ringgit.

Former Colonial Status: British commercial interests acquired the islands of Penang in 1786 and Malacca in 1824. The various states of Malaya entered into protectorate status from 1874–1895; they remained British colonies or protectorates until 1957 with the exception of the Japanese occupation from 1942 to 1945. Sabah was administered by the British North Borneo Company from 1881 to 1941, occupied by the Japanese from 1942 until 1945 and was a British Colony from 1946 to 1963. Sarawak was granted to Sir James Brooke by the Sultan of Brunei in 1841; it became a British protectorate in 1888; after the Japanese were expelled in 1945, Sir Charles Vyner Brooke, the ruling Raja, agreed to administration as a British Crown Colony, which lasted until 1963.

National Day: August 31st.

Chief of State: His Majesty Tuanku Ja'a-far Ibni Al–Marhum Tuanku Abdul Rahman (Yang di–Pertuan Besar of Negeri Sembilan), *Yang di-Pertuan Agong*, meaning King, or Supreme Head of Malaysia.

Head of Government: Dato' Seri Dr. Mahathir Mohamed, Prime Minister.

National Flag: Fourteen horizontal stripes of red and white with a dark blue rectangle in the upper left corner containing a yellow crescent and a 14–pointed star.

Per Capita Income: U.S. $3,400.

Located at the southern end of the Malay Peninsula, the mainland portion of Malaysia consists of a broad central belt of forested mountains. In the areas of Malaya where the mountains give way to lower altitudes, the vegetation turns into a thick green jungle situated on swampy plains, particularly in the coastal area. The climate is uniform during the year because of the closeness to the equator—hot and humid.

The Borneo states, also known as East Malaysia, contain wide coastal lowlands which have basically poor soil and are interrupted by frequent rivers. The altitude rises in the South as the border with Indonesia is approached. The division between the two occupants of the island straddles a scenic range of rugged mountains the highest of which is Mt. Kinabalu, towering majestically to a height of 13,000 feet. Few people of the western world have penetrated Borneo to view this remote area, which is inhabited by a primitive people who have advanced but little above stone age life. The people of Malaysia are quite similar to their Indonesian neighbors—a mixture of Polynesian, Mongol, Indian and Caucasian origins. There are also a large minority of Chinese who are descendants of laborers brought in by the colonial British.

History: Malaya would have been colonized sooner than it was if the Dutch had not focused their attention on the fabled riches of Indonesia. The colonial history of both nations was very similar. The absence of Dutch control permitted the

British to enter the area without opposition. In order to promote an orderly administration that would be a base for profitable trade, the British compelled the rulers of the small individual states of Malaya to accept "protection." This included the presence of a British advisor at each Malay court to insure that British goals were achieved. Four outlying, impoverished states of Siam (Thailand) in the North were added to Malaya in 1909.

The rubber tree was brought from Brazil and planted in the rich soil to grow in a climate almost ideal for the tree. Drawn by the natural resources and the stability of the area, British capital poured in, and there was a mass influx of Chinese and Indian laborers to work the rubber plantations and the tin mines. In many cases these Chinese soon entered commerce and some became extremely wealthy and influential. A fear was born among the Malays that the Chinese would become their masters—a distrust which exists to this day.

The British favored the Malays, since they were native to the area, often at the expense of the Chinese. There was some political activity by the Chinese after World War I—some favored the Nationalist government of China, others supported the communist revolutionaries. This activity was not strong enough to present a serious threat to British rule, however.

When the Japanese arrived in 1942, they treated the Chinese with much greater brutality than they did the Malays; there was some Malay sympathy for the Japanese. This resulted in an anti–Japanese guerrilla force of Chinese, most of them communists, which operated from bases deep within the thick jungles. Receiving weapons smuggled in by the British, the communist guerrillas fought their non–communist rivals as well as the Japanese.

**His Majesty
The Yang di-Pertuan Agong**

**Her Majesty
The Raja Permaisuri Agong**

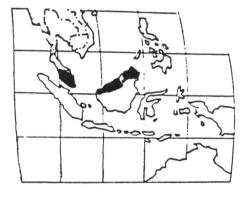

When the British returned they resumed their pro–Malay policies. This, and probably incitement by international communism, caused the guerrillas to go into revolt. They did not have much support from the Chinese community and lacked effective outside assistance. The British mounted a huge military effort which reduced the rebellion to almost nothing within a few years. Later efforts to revive the insurrection have had little success.

The British granted Malaya internal self–government in 1955, and full independence in 1957. Under the able leadership of Prime Minister Tunku Abdul Rah-

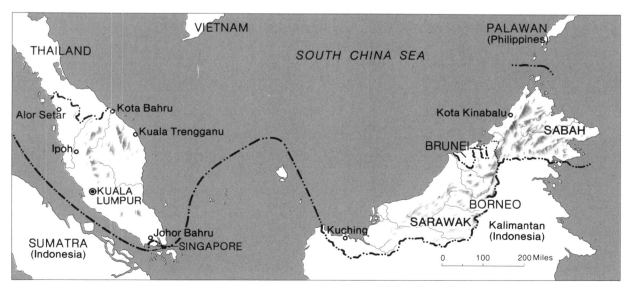

man, head of the dominant Alliance Party, (now known as the National Front) which included, and now includes a dominant Malay party, the United Malay National Organization (UMNO as well as "tame" parties purporting to represent the Chinese and Indian communities, Malaya achieved a high degree of political stability in the post–independence years. The party and the government have not succeeded in greatly lessening the basic tension between the two ethnic groups, however.

Faced with Indonesian dictator Sukarno's increased interest in dominating the region, and a marked swing to the left in Singapore politics, Rahman and the British devised a plan to unite Malaya, Singapore, Sabah and Sarawak into the Federation of Malaysia. The tiny, oil–rich Sultanate of Brunei was invited to join, but declined. After many complicated negotiations the federation came into existence in September 1963.

The communists and Sukarno in Indonesia, encouraged by their success in acquiring West Irian from the Dutch without a fight, were furious that the federation had come into being. A "confrontation" with Malaysia was started, which involved sporadic fighting in the remote parts of Borneo, and unsuccessful attempts to land Indonesian guerrillas in Malaya. The "confrontation" was quietly discontinued after General Suharto seized power from Sukarno in 1966. Some communist insurgents are still active near the border with Thailand, but pose no genuine threat.

There was continuing tension between the Chinese and Malays; Singapore, with a population overwhelmingly Chinese, resented Malay domination of the central government. Prime Minister Lee Kuan Yew of Singapore engaged in efforts to increase his party's influence and power within the federation—this led to the expulsion of Singapore from Malaysia in August 1965.

Elections for West Malaysia (Malaya) seats in the House of Representatives touched off rioting between Malays and Chinese in 1969. This led the government to proclaim a state of emergency and to suspend the constitution; parliamentary government was, however, restored in early 1971. During the 1970's, after the retirement of Abdul Rahman, Malaysia began to play a more active international role, and, particularly, to improve its relations with communist China. Malaysia's leader, Tun Abdul Razak, advocated that the Association of Southeast Asian Nations (ASEAN), of which Malaysia is an active member, seek the neutralization of Southeast Asia. (The other members are Indonesia, Thailand, the Philippines, Singapore and Brunei.)

General elections in 1974 resulted in a sweeping victory for the National Front

(the Alliance Party plus some smaller ones). The main opposition came from the Democratic Party. Strong precautions were taken to avoid the violence of 1969. Militant Islam has been and is a growing force in Malaysia, however, with the future outlook being one of continuing tension between the Malay and Chinese communities.

When Razak died in 1976, he was succeeded first by a leader forced to retire in 1981 because of ill health. There was a noticeable increase in communist terrorism in Malaysia, and in March 1977 an agreement was signed with Thailand for joint military operations against the guerrilla forces near their common border.

The Sultans of the states, and in particular the King, have been widely regarded as forces for stability. The Mahathir government now in power, however, has tried to curb their constitutional powers. In January 1984 it was successful in abolishing the Yang di–Pertuan Agong's right to veto legislation.

**The Prime Minister
Dato Seri Dr. Mahathir Mohamed**

Two political problems of fairly serious proportions appeared in 1985–86. One was leadership struggles within both the main components of the ruling coalition, the National Front: the dominant United Malay National Organization (UMNO) and the less powerful Malayan Chinese Association (MCA). The second was a rise in the activity of militant Islam, especially among the 20,000 Malaysian students in the United States and in Sabah (North Borneo), where there were violent Moslem demonstrations early in 1986 against the Christian–led state government.

In spite of a sweeping victory for the ruling National Front in an August 1986 general election (148 parliamentary seats out of 177), the party has serious problems. Its leader, Prime Minister Mahathir, is declining in popularity, and for the first time there has been a leadership

struggle within the United Malay National Organization (UMNO), the dominant party within the front. Another major party within the group, the Malayan Chinese Association (MCA), also had leadership difficulties. The ethnic minorities are somewhat restless under Malay rule. The National Front has been unsuccessful in its effort to recapture political control of Sabah from the Parti Bersatu Sabah, a local, largely Catholic party.

There were serious tensions within UMNO in 1987, reflecting a leadership struggle, a generational gap and a growing feeling that the party was strong enough to govern without the inconvenience of a coalition with other parties representing different races. Prime Minister Mahathir won a close vote for the party leadership in April and then purged some of his rivals. The relatively passive Malayan Chinese Association was troubled not only by a leadership problem, but also by a challenge from outside the National Front by the Democratic Action Party (DAP), a younger and more vigorous party.

The government cracked down on opponents of several types in October 1987, some of them UMNO members, but more of them belonging to the DAP, in a series of sudden arrests which were strongly criticized within and outside the country. In February 1988 a judge ruled UMNO an illegal organization, a bizarre holding that had the main effect of intensifying the power struggle within it. Mahathir reorganized UMNO on a legal basis and strengthened his hold on it and on the country.

Relations between the Malay and Chinese communities, although fairly tense and, like the Islamic upsurge among the Malays, the object of considerable apprehension in neighboring countries, tended to be kept within bound by a general memory of the race riots of 1969 and a desire to avoid a repetition of them.

In 1989 the Malaysian government scored two major achievements. It agreed to buy $1.7 billion worth of arms from the United Kingdom, a deal that was criticized by the Malaysian opposition as unnecessary. At the end of the year, the 40–year–long communist insurgency came to an end with the formal surrender of its leaders.

The ruling National Front won a landslide victory in an October 1990 election. Prime Minister Mahathir admires the economic dynamism of Japan and South Korea and would like to use them as models for Malaysia. He would also like to see an economic organization (the East Asian Economic Grouping) that would include the ASEAN states, China, South Korea, Taiwan, Hong Kong, and Japan, but would exclude everyone else, especially the United States; this idea has little chance of winning general acceptance.

A Hindu wedding in Kuala Lumpur

Photo by Jon Markham Morrow

Politics and Government: Malaysia, a member of the British Commonwealth, is a parliamentary democracy with a bi–cameral legislature composed of the Senate, Dewan Negara; and House of Representatives, Dewan Ra'ayat. The Dewan Negara has 58 members who serve six year terms. The Dewan Ra'ayat has 177 representatives. The parliament in Malaysia is not an effective institution for the discussion of public policy. The opposition has limited time to speak and often receives bills for consideration the same day that they are to be voted on. The Standing Order of Parliament prohibits treasonable or seditious words the interpretation of which is left up to the Speaker of the Dewan Ra'ayat who is appointed by the government (Prime Minister). Certain topics such as the special rights of Malays are not subject to discussion. Tough questioning by the opposition is rare and would not be widely reported in the media in any case since it is either owned or licensed by the government.

The country has a very unusual system for selecting the Yang di–pertuan Agong (King). The Yang di–pertuan Agong serves for five years and is selected on a rotational basis from among the hereditary rulers from nine of Malaysia's 13 states: the Sultans of Kelantan, Pahang, Johor, Kedah, Perak, Selangor, and Trengganu, the Rajah of Perlis, and the Yang di–pertuan Besar (he who has been elevated to the highest position) of Negeri Sembilan. The states of Malacca, Penang, Sarawak and Sabah have governors, Yang di–pertuan Negeri, appointed by the king. The latter two states compose East Malaysia on the island of Borneo while the former compose West Malaysia.

Elections in Malaysia have generally

been clean, unlike those in many other developing countries. The single–member district formula benefits the government as does the fact that districts are often gerrymandered to favor the Malay voter.

Malaysian politics continues to be controlled by the Malay–dominated *United Malay National Organization (UMNO)*. UMNO heads the fourteen party *Barisan Nasional (BN)* coalition which governs the country. Opposition comes primarily from the *Pan–Malaysian Islamic Party (PAS)*, the *Democratic Action Party (DAP)*, and *Semangat 46'* ("Spirit of '46 Malay Party").

PENINSULAR MALAYSIA
The nine states with hereditary rulers, and Penang and Malacca

The pivotal political event for 1993 was the November 4 election for *United Malay National Organization (UMNO)* deputy president. This post within Malaysia's dominant political party is tantamount to a guarantee for gaining the post of deputy prime minister, which eventually leads to the prime ministership. The contest involved the Minister of Finance, Anwar Ibrahim, and the current Deputy Prime Minister, Ghafar Baba. The Prime Minister, Mahathir Mohamad, seemed early on not to prefer a change of the old guard, but Anwar won a decisive victory. Ghafar Baba actually withdrew from the race and resigned from the cabinet, leaving the way open for the new *UMNO* deputy president. On December 1, the prime minister appointed Anwar as deputy prime minister.

Anwar's supporters from his pasukan wawasan (vision team) also won control of several *UMNO* party posts. However, the new team was split between Islamic and economic factions. A second splintering factor was that many votes for Anwar came from Sabah, the independent–minded East Malaysia state separated from West Malaysia by some 400 miles of South China Sea.

The coming to power of the Anwar faction can be expected to produce even more emphasis on economic development. There was some worry that it also signaled the beginning of "big money" politics in the country. The changes at and near the top probably also signal the beginning of a winding down of the Mahathir era. Clearly, Anwar and his followers have their own agenda.

In 1994, and early 1995, the *BN (National Front)* coalition strengthened its overall position and Prime Minister Mahathir demonstrated that he was not yet ready to stand aside for Anwar Ibrahim, Minister of Finance. The *BN* had barely lost an important 1994 election in the East Malaysia state of Sabah, 23 seats to 25 seats, to the *Parti Bersatu Sabah (PBS)*. However, a month later the *PBS* splintered and the *BN* wound up in control of the state. National elections and elections for all other Malaysian states excluding Sabah and Sarawak were held at the end of April 1995. The *BN* won control of all states except Kelantan, which was won by the opposition coalition of *PAS* (24 seats), and *Semangat '46* (13 seats). The *BN* won 7 seats. In Penang state, the *BN* reduced the opposition *DAP* to only one seat, down from 13. In all the *BN* won 161 of 192 parliamentary seats. The opposition in parliament is now: *DAP*, 9; *PBS*, 8; *PAS*, 7; and *Semangat '46*, 6.

In early May 1995, Prime Minister Mahathir announced his new cabinet. The supporters of Anwar Ibrahim, Minister of Finance and heir apparent to the prime ministership, were held back. The group posed a genuine threat to the multi–ethnic fabric of Malaysia.

The *BN* victory in the national elections came in spite of several problems in 1994. In August, the Chief Minister of the state of Malacca and head of the *UMNO* youth organization, Abdul Rahim Tamby Chik, was hit with sexual harassment charges. This threatened Chik's career and also cast a negative light on the UMNO youth group. *UMNO* received additional bad publicity when Chik was not prosecuted. In September a bill was introduced in parliament to disband the *Johor Military Force (JMF)* which is the private palace guard for the Sultan of Johore. It was accused of overstepping its authority in the area of local law enforcement. *UMNO* backed down in the face of opposition which was feared could hurt the party's election chances in the upcoming national elections.

The biggest challenge for the government in 1994 came from the radical Islamic group, Al–Arqam. The sect was finally banned in August. Sect leader Ashaari Muhammad was suspected of keeping an armed death squad of some 300 men in Thailand. The government became fearful when it learned that the Al–Arqam was successfully recruiting among the Malay middle class. As many as 7,000 civil servants may have joined the movement. Al–Arqam operated 257 schools and many businesses throughout the country. Total membership in Malaysia may have numbered up to 100,000.

After the 1995 elections, Prime Minister Mahathir and the *BN* sailed through the remainder of the year. However, in March 1996, an unheard of event occurred. An *UMNO* insider and former Minister of Finance, Daim Zainuddin, publicly criticized the Prime Minister in *Utrusan Malaysia*, the country's leading Malay language paper. Daim charged that debate on controversial issues within the Malay leadership was often suppressed. He went on to say that there was no debate among the Malays and that any questioning of policy, such as the commitment to rapid economic development, meant that you were anti–Malay.

In most countries criticisms of this magnitude are commonplace. Not so in Malaysia. Daim's comments could be taken as the opening round leading up to the October *UMNO* party elections. It is no secret the Anwar Ibrahim, the Deputy Prime Minister and *UMNO* Vice President, is next in line for the premiership. He has consistently indicated that he will not challenge Mahathir for the post. The question is, would Mahathir step down if factions within *UMNO* begin to break ranks. Daim's comments could be taken as just such an act.

A significant debate about the future of the Chinese parties within the *BN* governing coalition occurred in 1995. The *Malaysian Chinese Association (MCA)* and the *Gerakan* are both members of the *BN*. The leading opposition party, the *Democratic Action Party (DAP)*, is the third majority Chinese party in the country. While *UMNO* has done a good job in trying to be fair with its Chinese component parties, and with the 29% Chinese citizens of Malaysia, it has become clear in recent years that major policy decisions within the coalition are made largely without *MCA* and *Gerakan* input. In fact, both parties must rely heavily on Malay votes to defeat the opposition *DAP*.

There appears to be a growing sentiment in the Chinese Malaysian community that the *MCA* and *Gerakan* are not assertive enough within the coalition. At some point, Chinese voters could reason that their only real voice is with the opposition. Sustained economic growth for everyone has dampened such arguments. Nevertheless, defection of even a moderate number of Chinese voters from the *BN* coalition would seriously threaten the fragile multi–ethnic arrangement which the *UMNO* leadership has worked so diligently to build in Malaysian society. Prior to the 1969 riots, the *MCA* did share real power with *UMNO*. Perhaps with new leadership, *UMNO* may see some utility in returning at least partially to this governing formula.

Foreign Relations: Malaysia has been an effective actor in international politics for some time. The policy has generally been non–aligned with Mahathir occasionally using anti–Western rhetoric for effect. Malaysia recently completed a two year term as a non–permanent member of the UN Security Council. It maintains strong ties with the Islamic countries of the Middle East. It is too small in population to evolve into a regional leadership position, but continues to be a strong participant in ASEAN (Association of Southeast Asian Nations).

In 1994 the Malaysian government banned British companies from participating in any new government contracts until the press in London learned to be truthful. The Malaysian government was upset over allegations that top officials in Kuala Lumpur acted improperly with regard to the Pergau Dam project in which there were allegations, political pay off. The ban was lifted in May after the Malays were satisfied that the accusations would fade into history.

The disagreement with Indonesia over Sipadan and Ligitan islands off the coast of Sabah, East Malaysia, remained unsettled in 1994. The dispute over *Pulau Batu Putih* ("White Rock Island") with Singapore was referred to The Hague by mutual agreement. Chinese President Jiang Zemin visited Malaysia at the end of the year and reassured Kuala Lumpur that the dispute over territorial claims in the South China Sea would be settled peacefully. China, Malaysia and four other countries claim all or part of the South China Sea and the Spratley Islands. At about the same time, Chinese naval forces occupied Mischief Reef in the Spratleys just off the Philippine coast.

In June, Malaysia agreed to purchase 18 Russian MIG19's for $500 million thus becoming the first non–communist state in Southeast Asia to operate Russian military equipment. India will train Malaysian pilots and technicians as part of the deal and Russia will set up a technical service center in Malaysia. Moscow also agreed to purchase $150 million in palm oil from Malaysia. Malaysia previously agreed to purchase F18's from the United States. Analysts wonder about the wisdom of purchasing two totally different fighter aircraft for a relatively small defense force.

In general, 1995 was a good year for Malaysian foreign relations especially with respect to ASEAN dealings with neighboring states. Singapore and Malaysia came to a permanent agreement on their territorial waters boundary. They also reached agreement over Malaysian restrictions of the importation of Singaporan petro–chemicals. Relations with the Philippines and Thailand also improved somewhat. However, the dispute with Indonesia over Sipadan and Ligitan islands continued. The promising idea of a Malaysia–Indonesia–Thailand northern growth triangle was still on track (Singapore–Malaysia and Indonesia have been highly successful with the "first triangle" which encourages free trade and makes special concessions to attract foreign businesses).

Culture: Malaysia's population is very young—about 45% are under the age of 15! A high percentage of the people are literate; primary and secondary school education is provided for all, and there are a number of colleges and 5 universities. Although Islam is the State religion and Muslims enjoy certain special privileges by law, there is complete freedom of worship for other faiths.

The most intricate handiwork is produced in wood, silver and pewter, both in traditional forms and in highly modern pieces. Kuching, the capital of the East Malaysian state of Sarawak has one of the finest museums in Southeast Asia, and the nation's graceful, rhythmic dances are legendary.

Malaysians are great sports enthusiasts, and although more traditional ball game forms have dominated in the past, soccer is now the nation's most popular pastime. There is also tremendous interest in horse–racing as seen by the country's five first–rate turf clubs.

The majority of the Malay community used to live in a fairly traditional manner, principally engaged in farming and fishing, but today Malays are increasingly entering the trading, professional and other sectors of the modern economy.

Except for Singapore, Malaysia has the highest percentage of Chinese found in Southeast Asia. Divided into several linguistic groups which reflect the origins of their ancestors who migrated from China, they tend to remain apart except in economic activity—they dominate in the business community. Many educated Chinese, particularly among the younger generation, learn English and Malay. The more educated Malays usually speak English.

Among the various hereditary or conferred titles used in Malaysia are *Tuanku* (ruler), *Tun* (equivalent to the British *Lord)*, and *Tan Sri* and *Datuk* (meaning *Sir*, the former being the higher degree of the two).

Economy: Malaysia has one of the strongest and fastest growing economies in the Asia–Pacific region. Many expect Malaysia to become the "fifth tiger," joining Hong Kong, Singapore, South Korea, and Taiwan in the developed country ranks. Malaysia's current national development plan, *Vision 20/20*, calls for the country to achieve full developed status by that date. Under the former *New Economic Policy*, the government was able to substantially raise the level of Malay participation in the non–agricultural sectors of the economy. Although the precise goals were not achieved by the target date, the success of the *NEP* was such that Prime Minister Mahathir was able to announce that there was no longer a need to stress the fulfillment of targets or quotas for specific ethnic groups. Today, Malaysia has a significant and growing Malay middle and upper–middle class. There are also a significant number of very wealthy Malays, some of whom have made fortunes by having access to lucrative government contracts. The Chinese community remains very well represented in business and commerce.

The impact of sustained economic growth was very visible in 1995. Longer life, improved health care, a significant increase in the number of people owning telephones, and an expanding national highway system were all indicators of the country's economic success over the last decade.

Malaysia's third car, a van, will be produced by a Japanese–Malaysian consortium. In 1995, Malaysia's first automobile, the *Proton Saga*, sold over 25,000 units in Europe. In February, a second Malaysian–Japanese partnership agreed to produce the country's first motorcycle.

The Science, Technology and Environment Ministry reported in late 1995 that two out of three rivers in Malaysia were polluted and that those unpolluted (28%)

were deteriorating fast as a consequence of industrial waste. In March, it was estimated that 7 million fish died of the coast of Perak state from exposure to potassium cyanide. Malaysia will not have a treatment plant capable of handling toxic waste in operation until 1998. A shocking estimate is that by 2005, the rain forest in the East Malaysia state of Sabah will have no marketable timber left. Native peoples are loosing their lands to greedy state politicians, and Japanese plywood manufacturers. Malaysia's gross domestic product (GDP) grew by 9.6% in 1995 (9.2% for 1994). Per capita income was over $4,000. Inflation was moderate. Job creation outpaced the labor pool. This shortage is causing problems for the government in the immigration area. There are currently some 500,000 legal and illegal immigrants working in the country. Most are Indonesian and thus easier to absorb than peoples from other states. However, there is growing concern on this issue. There was a relatively small trade deficit of $6 billion.

Japan was the largest foreign investor. The ringgit, the national currency, finished 1995 strong against most foreign currencies.

The Future: As Malaysia continues to enjoy the benefits of rapid economic development, the old tensions generated by ethnic differences between Malays, Chinese and Indians will continue to fade. While the country was almost torn apart in 1969 by ethnically based violence, such events today would be unthinkable. The country has come too far. As part of the Malay community has moved ahead to join the Chinese and Indian communities in business and commerce, some tensions have appeared between the old Malay community and this new group. In order to maintain its dominant political position, *UMNO* will have to pay close attention to mending fences within the Malay community.

The radical *Al–Arqam* phenomenon was especially worrisome because it drew support from the entire Malay community. Even well educated middle class Malays were taken in by the sect. The ban on *Al–Arqam* was necessary and took courage on the part of the Mahathir government. It could be that the challenge of radical Islam is not over. This indeed would be a pity for a country with such potential.

Lastly, Malaysians must begin to think and talk about the country after Mahathir. The Prime Minister is talented and a shrewd political operator. If he is wise, he will begin thinking about how he wants to bring his very successful career to a positive conclusion. Malaysia continues to be a fascinating country with a very bright future.

Early morning fishing in the State of Pahang

Mongolia

Celebrating the 750th anniversary of the 13th century volume, *The Secret History of the Mongols,* **a book devoted to the Mongolian Empire and to the exploits of Chingis Khan**
Courtesy: Government of Mongolia

Area: 604,247 sq. mi. (1,564,619 sq. km., somewhat larger than Alaska).

Population: 2 million (estimated).

Capital City: Ulan Bator (Pop. 450,000, estimated).

Climate: Dry, with bitterly cold winters.

Neighboring Countries: Soviet Union (North, Northwest); China (South, East).

Official Language: Mongolian.

Other Principal Tongue: Russian.

Ethnic Background: Mongol (about 97%); Turk (about 3%).

Principal Religion: The Lamaistic sect of Buddhism; religious practice is not discouraged.

Main Exports: (to Russia): Beef, meat products, wool, minerals.

Main Imports: (from Russia): Machinery, equipment, petroleum, building materials, clothing.

Currency: Tugrik.

Former Colonial Status: Tributary of the Manchu Dynasty of China from end of the 17th century until 1912; Soviet influence since that time. Nationalist China recognized Mongolian independence in 1946, but withdrew recognition in 1952. Communist China recognized the Republic in 1949.

National Day: July 11th, in recognition of a communist revolution in 1921.

Chief of State: Punsalmaagiyn Ochirbat, President.

Prime Minister: Puntsagiyn Jasray.

National Flag: Three vertical bands of red, blue and red. The band closest to the pole has a set of traditional symbols with a five–pointed star at the top all in yellow.

Per Capita Income: US$900.

Mongolia is located in an area of extreme contrast in terms of geography. The arid rocks of the Gobi Desert in the southeast region of the country support almost no vegetation, and have a variation of temperature that splits the craggy rocks which interrupt the monotonous landscape. Proceeding northward there is a gradual change, punctuated by the presence of mountains rising to heights of more than 13,000 feet. The desert gives way to mountainous forest which ceases its thick growth in the heights where continuously present snow dominates the landscape.

Water also becomes more abundant in the North, but the rivers are uncontrolled and rough, descending in cascades over rocky beds and resembling the swirling waters of the Pacific Northwest and Alaska.

It is in this somewhat inhospitable part of the country that most of the people live in a thinly scattered existence devoted to animal husbandry. Their dwellings are constructed of felt from their animals stretched over rickety frames. Although possessing an international currency, the rural people still think that one horse, yak or ox equals seven sheep, fourteen goats or one–half of a camel.

History: Prior to the 16th century, the people who inhabited Mongolia had an aggressive, warlike character which enabled them periodically to conquer vast areas as far away as eastern Europe. This was principally due to the greatly superior horsemanship and cavalry techniques of the Mongols, acquired as a necessity due to the organization of their society which was traditionally nomadic. This pastoral existence contributed to the superior stamina of the fierce horsemen.

Several Mongolian leaders became well–known; the most famous was Chingis (Genghis) Khan; he and his successors were able to lead his men in the conquest of vast areas of eastern and southern Asia as far as Baghdad, now the capital of Iraq. However, the Mongols were eventually "conquered" by the people they had subdued. Their empire broke up in the 16th century and they were converted to Lamaist Buddhism, a pacifist religion, by contact with Tibet. At about the same time, they became dominated economically by the industrious Chinese, who possessed skills in manufacturing and trading unfamiliar to the Mongols. They soon found themselves trapped between Russia and China, two large wealthy empires, equipped with newly discovered firearms and other instruments of modern technology which rendered the skills of horsemanship and prowess in cavalry warfare obsolete.

Unable or unwilling to acquire the skills and techniques of the people they had dominated, the Mongols were reduced to the status of a tributary of the mighty Manchu Empire which had come to power in China. Russian interest in the area awakened to a greater extent in the 19th century; considerable economic and political power was gained in what was then called *Outer Mongolia* by the end of that century.

The numerous and hard–working Chinese pressed northward in the first decade of the 20th century, settling what was Inner Mongolia to the edge of the Gobi Desert, and creating a threat to the people of remote Outer Mongolia. For this reason, when the Chinese Manchu Empire collapsed in 1912, the princes and lamas of Outer Mongolia refused to recognize the claim of the Republic of China to the lands within the region.

In order to gain support for their independence, they appealed to the Russian tsar for protection. An agreement was reached in 1913 whereby China was to administer Inner Mongolia, and its legal "sovereignty" over Outer Mongolia was "recognized," but actually the region was to remain autonomous under local administration.

China took advantage of the collapse of the government of the Russian tsar in 1917 and attempted to seize absolute control of Outer Mongolia in violation of the 1913 agreement. This attempt was initially successful, but in 1921 Outer Mongolia was invaded by a force of White (anti–Bolshevik) troops from Russia. Control was then wrested from the White Russians by the Bolshevik (communist) forces, who remained until 1925.

The Russians quickly organized a communist regime, built around Mongols who were either communist or pro–communist—Mongolia became the first satellite of Soviet Russia. From the Soviet point of view, Mongolia served as a buffer against an increasingly powerful Japan, and now also serves as a buffer state, separating it from any threat posed

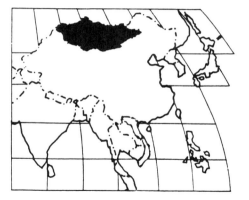

by China to the south. It also has been cited as a model of the possibilities of achievement under communism.

In the succeeding decades the communist regime brought the nomadic tribes and lamaist monasteries under increasingly centralized control. Occasional resistance was easily crushed by Soviet troops armed with modern mechanized equipment. State services, previously unknown in the region, were provided, including badly needed shelters for livestock to provide protection from the bitter winter wind and snow.

A defensive alliance between Mongolia and Russia, signed in 1936 and renewed every ten years since, was used by the Russians in 1939 to drive a force of invading Japanese from eastern Mongolia. The troops of both nations joined in 1945 to fight Japanese troops remaining in Inner Mongolia; at the same time, Stalin was able to obtain the promise of the Chinese to recognize Outer Mongolia's independence if a vote of the people showed that this was their desire. The plebiscite was held under carefully regulated conditions in October 1945, resulting in a unanimous vote for independence from China. The Nationalist Chinese subsequently recognized Mongolia's independence in 1946, but withdrew this in 1952, claiming that the Soviet Union had violated the commitments made to the Nationalist Chinese under the treaty of 1945.

The communist Chinese, with some hesitation due to their reluctance to abandon traditional claims of sovereignty over Mongolia, recognized Mongolia in 1949, and subsequently signed a boundary treaty with it in 1962. But China has occasionally shown some signs of wishing to increase its influence, using eco-

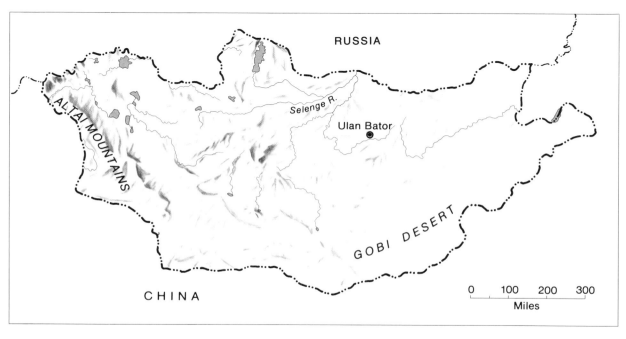

President Ochirbat's oath–taking ceremony

Courtesy: Government of Mongolia

nomic aid and other methods, and probably seeking eventual control of the region. These pressures have caused Mongolia to cling to Russia for protection—it has sided with the Soviet Union in all phases of the Sino-Soviet dispute of the past two decades. It received in return substantial economic aid, which permitted the beginning of industrialization in the country.

Mongolia sought and was granted admission to the UN in 1961, and at about the same time it started to establish diplomatic relations with a small number of "neutral" nations such as India and Indonesia. Japan recognized the Mongolian People's Republic early in 1972. Russia has, and will permit these moves so long as Russian control remains paramount in the government of the people and in the foreign relations of the nation. As there is increased contact with the outside world, the Mongols will undoubtedly become even more opposed to any form of domination or absorption by the Chinese.

The *Great People's Hural* is a single–chamber legislature of 287 members who are elected from a single–party list of candidates for a three–year term of office. It, in turn, selects nine of its members to serve on the Presidium which functions as a cabinet, conducting current matters of state. The last election was held on June 19, 1977, and was, as always, completely dominated by the *Mongolian People's Revolutionary Party.*

A decision was made in 1972 to leave vacant the Chief of State's position (Chairman of the Presidium of the Great People's Khural, also spelled *Hural)* after the death of the incumbent, Sambuu. However, the post was assumed in 1974 by Tsedenbal, the First Secretary of the ruling *Mongolian People's Revolutionary Party,* who gave up the premiership at the same time. A boundary treaty with the Soviet Union was signed in late 1976; because of tensions along the Sino–Soviet border, Soviet troops had entered Mongolia ten years earlier. In 1981, as a gesture to Mongolian nationalism, a Mongol cosmonaut was allowed to take part in a Soviet space flight. Mongolia expelled several thousand Chinese workers in 1983 for reasons that are not clear.

In August 1984, Tsedenbal, Mongolia's long–time leader, was sacked, allegedly because of age and illness, but also apparently because of his colleagues' discontent over his autocratic behavior and his subservience to the Soviet Union.

Jambyn Batmunkh succeeded him in December 1984. There was no significant change in direction—a development treaty with the Soviet Union which will continue until the turn of the century was signed in 1985.

In the fall of 1986, as part of its effort to improve relations with China, the Soviet Union began to withdraw one of the estimated five divisions it has maintained in Mongolia. Mongolia established diplomatic relations with the U.S. at the beginning of 1987; Mongolia opened its embassy in Washington in 1989, and the U.S. has rented office and residence space in Ulan Bator. In the 1960's the U.S. had tried to establish contact, but had been prevented by its relations with Taiwan, which (as the Republic of China) still claimed Mongolia. For that reason, the Soviet Union had held Mongolia from recognizing the U.S., but that attitude later changed.

The Mongolian leadership had begun to move toward political liberalization in 1985 under the influence of developments in the Soviet Union associated with the ascendancy of Mikhail Gorbachëv. By the end of 1989, the dramatic events in Eastern Europe led to the emergence of an opposition party in Mongolia, which calls itself the *Mongolian Democratic Union (MDU).* Led by Soviet–educated intellectuals, it demanded an end to the Communist monopoly of power. Surprisingly, this position won increasing acceptance from the Communist leadership, beginning with an official statement on January 22, 1990. This decision was the outcome of a debate within the Politburo during which some members urged the use of force against the demonstrators. When Batmunkh said he would agree only if all members signed the order, the idea collapsed.

In late February, Batmunkh promised free elections for April. The *MDU* tried to maximize its appeal to the voters by emphasizing nationalism, including praise for the medieval conqueror Ghengis Khan, in opposition to communism. In mid–March the entire five–man Politburo of the ruling *Mongolian People's Revolutionary Party* resigned and was replaced by reformers. Batmunkh remained as chief of state for the time being. The ruling party formally gave up its monopoly of power at that time. The new General Secretary, Gombojavyn Ochirbat, was a relatively unknown figure.

These remarkable developments are certain to arouse interest, and conceivably a degree of imitation, in other Asian countries where communism has been a significant influence. The Mongolian Parliament elected Punsalmaagiyn Ochirbat as President of the Republic.

In July 1990, the ruling party won about two–thirds of the seats in an election for the Great People's Hural. Opposition parties, however, appeared to have achieved a recognized place in Mongolian politics.

Political ferment and liberalization continued after the dramatic events of 1990. Freedom of the press brought a mushrooming of new newspapers and magazines. Freedom of religion led to a widespread resurgence of Buddhism and even to some extent of Christianity.

It established a western–style parliamentary system of government, with a unicameral legislative chamber, the Hural. The constitution provides for a popularly elected president. The president may introduce legislation before the Hural, has a veto, and may act as an ombudsman. The prime minister is the leader of the dominant party or parties in coalition which control the Hural. A Constitutional Court has the authority to review laws passed by the Hural. The name of the country was changed from the

People's Republic of Mongolia to Mongolia. The constitution also allows for private property. Pastureland continued to be under public ownership.

After the June 1992 elections, the former communist party (MPRP) controlled 71 of 76 seats in the Hural. Even the MPRP was surprised at the results. Under the new constitution, representatives are elected in single–member districts as opposed to proportional representation where more than one representative is elected from a district and where parties are awarded seats based on the percentage of votes they receive. Because the MPRP was the strongest party, it could win virtually all of the single member district contests. Since the election, the four opposition parties have merged into the Mongolian National Democratic Party (MNDP). The new Prime Minister is Puntsagiyn Jasray.

On June 6, 1993, Mongolia held its first presidential election. Candidates for the post had to be forty–five years of age and only political parties that held a seat in the parliament could select a standard bearer. The old line Mongolian People's Revolutionary Party (MPRP) nominated L. Tudev, over the incumbent President Ochirbat. The opposition Mongolian National Democratic Party (MNDP) formed a coalition with the Mongolian Social Democratic Party (MSDP) and selected President Ochirbat, who had been turned down by his own *MPRP*, to be their candidate. Punsalmaagiin Ochirbat was elected president with 58.7% of the vote. Perhaps as high as one–fourth of the MPRP supporters defected to support their old president.

The new president promised to speed privatization but also to protect those who were hurt most by the process.

In 1994, the *MPRP* continued to rule under Prime Minister Puntsagiyn Jasray, but not without challenges. Street demonstrations broke out in April. The primary issue was apparently corruption in the *MPRP* which reached as high as the prime minister. Demands that the government resign were ignored. Perhaps as a way of making peace, the *MPRP* sat down with the opposition parties in the Great Hural, the Mongolian National Democratic Party *(MNDP)*, and the Mongolian Social Democratic Party to create important reform oriented legislation. One part of the agreement between the three parties will require electoral reform to allow for a more fair representation among the parties in the Great Hural. The next election should be in 1996. The *MPRP* also agreed to the creation of an independent media, not under government control. The third area of concern addressed by the three parties was corruption which is a growing problem throughout society.

There are currently 19 parties. However, without any chance of gaining any representation most will disappear. There is the prospect that with electoral reform, the country will move toward a multi–party system.

Foreign Relations: The diplomatic year started off with a visit by President Ochirbat to Russia in May. The President was in Moscow to mark the 50th anniversary of Victory day. Official meetings were held with Boris Yeltsin, Bill Clinton and Francois Mitterrand. Later in the year officials from both countries met to discuss the terms under which Mongolia would repay its debt to Russia. The two parties disagree on the amount and the terms. One estimate puts the debt at about $15 billion. A second on–going problem, cross–border smuggling and rustling, is being addressed jointly.

Without doubt, the most prominent visitor to Mongolia in 1995 had nothing to

Ulan Bator—modest modernity comes to a proud, isolated society

111

A factory worker packs camel wool for export   Courtesy: Government of Mongolia

do with politics. People came from all corners of the country to hear him speak, and his presence signaled a rebirth of a part of the country's culture which had been suppressed under communism. The visitor was the Dalai Lama. During his 10 day visit the "God King of Tibet" conducted a mass initiation to replenish the dwindling number of Buddhist monks. One source estimated a crowd of 37,000 people or about 2% of the population. The Buddhist revival presently underway in Mongolia could well have important political implications for the country's foreign relations.

The major foreign policy initiative for 1995 was launched in August when Natsagiyn Bagabandi, chairman of the People's Great Hural (national assembly) publicly expressed Mongolia's desire to join the Asia–Pacific Economic forum. The country's leadership feels APEC membership is essential to open the door wider for foreign investment and economic cooperation.

In August, agreement was reached in Washington, D.C. for military assistance for Mongolia. Relations with China took a turn for the worse in 1995 when listening devices were discovered in the Mongolian embassy in Beijing.

The country, wisely, is attempting to reach out as far as it can. The more friends it has, the more secure it may be with its closest neighbor. Indeed, Mongolia is very concerned about China. China is so large that it can easily overwhelm Mongolia through trade and migration. The sale of timber to China was recently banned, and has delayed privatization of land for fear that the Chinese will buy it up.

Culture: The nomadic pattern of life of the Mongols, reflecting a need and desire for mobility, has slowed the growth of substantial cities until recent years. Likewise, there have been no buildings of any great size except for the monasteries within the country.

The traditional literature of the people is ancient—it first consisted mainly of epics that were sung without being written, passed down from generation to generation. In the 13th century the Mongols developed a system of alphabetical writing based on the Tibetan script which served to record the epics as well as being a tool for later literary efforts, actually of a very limited quantity.

Religion was primitive until the advent of lamaist Buddhism in the 16th century. Although the processes of industrialization and modernization intrude into the solitude of the people with increasing frequency, the Mongolians are still excellent horsemen, fond of festivals which stress the traditional skills of horsemanship—particularly racing—archery, wrestling and physical stamina. A very modest tourist industry is developing.

Economy: Because of the harsh climate and the large amount of poor land, agriculture and livestock production has been and remains the backbone of the Mongolian economy. Much of the country's industry, including wool production, clothing and leather goods is tied to the this sector. The mining of gold, coal, copper, molybdenum, tin and tungsten also figure significantly in today's economy.

The transition from communism has not been easy. The break–up of large collective farms has had a negative effect on livestock production—in 1995, livestock production (28.6 million animals) was only slightly larger than the previous record set in 1941. But the country's population is three times larger than it was in 1941.

In 1995, the country experienced a significant shortage of meat in urban areas. Chicken and pig breeding suffered from shortages of supplies and labor, as a result of de–collectivization. The production of cereal grains also fell, while the production of gold doubled.

Inefficient state–run businesses are still in operation and foreign investment has been slow to come into the country because of the uncertainty of government regulations. The national stock exchange in Ulan Bator averaged about $20,000 per day in volume. The director of the exchange, Naidansurengen Zolzhargal, a student at Harvard, is working on a cellular phone system which will allow herdsmen to trade directly with the exchange from horseback. As a result of the collapse of communism and the privatization movement, some one million Mongolians own stock. Furthermore, because the exchange is starting from scratch, it is likely that the new state–of–the–art systems will be far more advanced than exchanges in many developed countries.

Inflation fell to 53%, down from 55% in 1994. The tugrik, local currency, declined to 475 to one dollar. Mongolia's trade surplus increased from $109 million in 1994, to $123 million in 1995. The economy remains dependent on international organizations and foreign countries to the tune of approximately $200 million a year. This situation is not likely to change much in the near future.

Mongolia is currently receiving more aid per capita than any other Asian country because the outside world does not want the country to fall under Chinese influence. A group of donors headed by Japan has put up over $750 million, while the United States has pledged $10 million.

The Future: Mongolia's economic and political progress is slow. This circumstance is not likely to change significantly in the near future. Its strategy of trying to find as many international friends as it can is important. The greatest threat to the country is just across the southern border—China constitutes a significant challenge for Mongolia in the long term, as it does for much of Asia.

The pastoral life of Mongolian sheepherders

New Zealand

Cosmopolitan Wellington at dusk

Area: 103,000 sq. mi. (268,276 sq. km., the land surface somewhat smaller than Colorado).

Population: 3.4 million (1993 est.).

Capital City: Wellington (Pop. 365,000, estimated).

Climate: Temperate, with ample rainfall; subtropical conditions at the northern tip of the North Island, with colder temperatures in the South Island.

Neighboring Countries: Australia, about 1,200 miles to the northwest.

Official Language: English.

Ethnic Background: European, mostly British (about 92%), Maori (about 8%).

Principal Religion: Protestant Christianity (82%).

Main Exports: (to Australia, U.K., Japan, U.S.); Meat and dairy products, fish, wool.

Main Imports: (same trading partners); Petroleum, cars, trucks, iron and steel.

Currency: New Zealand Dollar.

Former Colonial Status: British Colony (1839–1907).

National Day: February 6 is Waitangi Day, anniversary of the signing of the Treaty of Waitangi in 1840 between the British and the Maoris.

Chief of State: Her Majesty Queen Elizabeth II, represented by Governor General Dame Catherine Tizard (since Novembver 1990).

Head of Government: The Rt. Hon. Jim Bolger, Prime Minister (since July 1990).

National Flag: A purple field with the Union Jack in the upper left corner and four 5–pointed stars in the right half of the field.

Per Capita Income: U.S. $12,500.

The remote islands of New Zealand are about 1,200 miles from their nearest neighbor, Australia, and prior to the advent of air transportation it was one of the world's most isolated nations. The North Island is the more habitable of the two, and, though smaller than the South Is-land, it has more than half the country's population.

In the North Island there are volcanic and thermal areas dominated by three volcanic peaks, Ruapehu, Ngauruhoe and Tongariro, all active and given to occasional eruptions of steam and ash. In the central plateau area there is activity caused by the thermal pressure from deep within the earth in the form of geysers, hot springs, steam vents and foul–smelling deposits of sulphur. The average annual rainfall for the whole country is about 60 inches, which allows for quick growth of rich vegetation to feed the 60 million sheep that abound in New Zealand.

The South Island is much more rugged and contains the Southern Alps which equal their European namesake in beauty and wildness. In this mountainous region the climate can sometimes be subarctic. In contrast to the abundant growth of the North Island, the grasses of the South Island are more suited to rearing Merino sheep which have a fine coat to protect them from the chilly air. Most of the sheep of the North Island are cross-breeds, designed to produce both meat and wool.

In terms of the Northern Hemisphere, New Zealand occupies a position in the Southern Hemisphere which would run from the mild climate of southern California northward to the much cooler central part of British Columbia, which has bitterly cold winters. The reversal of warm and cold zones and of summer and winter in the Southern Hemisphere make northern New Zealand the warm, subtropical area and the southern region the colder one.

History: At a time unrecorded in written history, the Maori people, vigorous and handsome Polynesians, migrated to New Zealand. Their South Pacific way of life had to change; there were no coconuts to harvest, dress had to be warmer and their overall diet had to be adjusted accordingly. Fresh water fishing in the rivers and sparkling lakes became an important new source of food.

The first European to make more than a quick visit to New Zealand was the famous British navigator, Captain James Cook, who made a landing in 1769. The growth of the whaling industry in the next decades attracted increasing British colonization and trade because of the closeness of the islands to the southwest Pacific whaling areas. Missionaries settled in 1814 and quickly began the task of converting the Maoris to Christianity.

After several thousands of Britishers had settled in New Zealand, Great Britain annexed the islands in 1839 with the signing of the Treaty of Waitangi. The Maori people resisted the colonizers. There was sporadic bitter fighting in the 1860–1870 period—the native population

which had been about 150,000 at the beginning of the century was reduced to less than 50,000 by the 1870's.

The system of individual provinces that had been in existence until 1876 was abolished, and a centralized, more efficient, administration was established. The economy provided a bare support for the colonizers and their descendants until the turn of the 20th century, when faster ships and refrigeration boosted the export of New Zealand's agricultural products, which went mainly to Great Britain. The *Liberal Party* was in control from 1890 until 1912.

New Zealand was granted dominion status within the British Commonwealth in 1907 as a result of a new vigor imparted to the country's politics and administration by energetic *Liberal* leader Richard John Seddon, Prime Minister from 1893 to 1906. For all practical purposes it was independent from that time on.

At the same time the Maori population was undergoing a gradual transformation; they adopted western dress, and among other things began to practice agriculture and animal husbandry in the manner of the Englishmen. The Maoris now number about 290,000, many of them of mixed Maori and European parentage.

As it entered World War I, New Zealand was governed by the *Reform Party*, and later by a coalition government. New Zealand fought on the allied side and took part as an independent state in the peace settlement at Versailles. It joined the League of Nations and was awarded a mandate over the islands of Western Samoa which had been captured from the Germans during the war.

Adverse economic conditions during the 1920–1940 period created an increase in labor organization and unrest. By the late 1930's, however, aided by an ambitious program of public works and social security under a succession of *Labour Party* governments, prosperity began to return. New Zealand took an active part in World War II, although it did not face the Japanese threat to the extent that Australia did. In the postwar period, New Zealand recognized the declining influence of Great Britain in Southeast Asia and the rise of U.S. power in the region; it entered into the ANZUS treaty with Australia and the U.S. to provide security against a possible revival of Japanese militarism, and later against the communist threat. It also joined the SEATO treaty with the United States, Australia, Britain, France, Thailand, Pakistan and the Philippines primarily to assure Thailand of western support against communist subversion, and generally to meet the threat posed by the growth of communism in the region.

The *National Party* dominated the political system of New Zealand, modeled

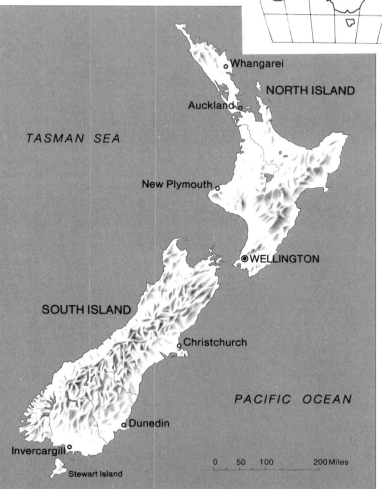

Late afternoon at Lake Hayes, South Island

after the parliamentary system of England, until 1972. The *Labour Party* came to power in that year, winning 55 seats in Parliament on a platform of more welfare benefits. This was reversed in elections held in late 1975 when the *Labour Party* was defeated because of its liberal domestic policies; the *National Party* won 55 seats. Its forceful, conservative leader, Robert Muldoon, became Prime Minister; the opposition was reduced to 32 seats and other smaller factions elected no representatives.

Because of the loss of a guaranteed market for its meat and dairy products when Britain joined the European Common Market, as well as because of its general ineptitude, the conservative Muldoon government lost support even among businessmen as New Zealand piled up an $11 billion foreign debt. Accordingly, *Labour* won by a fairly wide margin in the House of Representatives in mid–1984 (56 to 37).

The next Prime Minister, David Lange (pronounced *Lon*–jee), was much more favorable to private enterprise than are many of his *Labour* colleagues. Therefore, in order to pacify the left wing of the party, Lange announced that no nuclear–armed U.S. naval vessels would be allowed to call at New Zealand ports—he had previously been a moderate on the nuclear issue. The left in New Zealand does not feel threatened by anyone, does not want to be defended by nuclear weapons against what it regards as a nonexistent enemy, and hopes to start a trend toward worldwide nuclear disarmament. Some leaders of other countries and territories in the South and Southwest Pacific feel the same way. Since the U.S. refuses on principle to say whether or not any particular vessel is nuclear–

armed, this meant that *no* U.S. naval vessel could dock in New Zealand.

As the U.S. began to apply counter–pressures, including the withholding of some intelligence information and threats to cut back on imports from New Zealand, the ANZUS alliance (Australia, New Zealand and the U.S.) began to come under serious strain. The U.S. was afraid that New Zealand's action might be imitated by other allies such as Australia and Japan.

Finally, in June 1986, at a meeting in Manila between Prime Minister Lange and Secretary of State George Shultz, the chain broke—at least temporarily. Good naturedly, Shultz admitted to the press that, "We part company on security matters as friends, but we part." Lange was equally gracious, but stood by his government's policy of not allowing port access to U.S. ships unless it was

116

convinced that they carried no nuclear weaponry. In August the U.S. suspended its security arrangements with New Zealand under the ANZUS treaty until "adequate corrective measures" were taken.

Since the government of Prime Minister Lange was determined to bar U.S. nuclear–armed and/or nuclear–powered naval vessels from its ports, and the U.S. would "neither confirm nor deny" that any given ship was nuclear, in 1986 the U.S. declared that since the alliance could not survive without such visits, New Zealand had in effect withdrawn from ANZUS and was no longer entitled to American protection. New Zealand maintains its defense ties with Australia, which stayed in ANZUS, however. The Lange government proposed in early 1987 a buildup of New Zealand's forces that would maintain its security by being able to operate in its general vicinity, but without the mission of capability of fighting in distant areas as its troops had sometimes done in the past.

In August 1987 the *Labor Party* won an election with a 15–seat majority in the 97–member parliament, the same as before. The Lange government's program of economic liberalization and privatization, which includes lower tax rates for the upper income brackets, has aroused considerable political opposition. Unemployment has doubled. The Maoris, who have special grievances, have also become increasingly restless.

In 1989 the *Labour Party* government took a strong position against the U.S. over the issue of whether nuclear weapons were entering the country's territory aboard American naval vessels. Prime Minister Lange discussed withdrawal from the ANZUS defense treaty. The *National Party* took a more conciliatory position on the issue toward the United States. Prime Minister Lange resigned in August 1989, and Geoffrey Palmer took over the premiership. He also opposed visits by U.S. naval vessels carrying nuclear weapons. The *National Party* won the 1990 elections. Unemployment appeared to be more important than the nuclear issue.

Politics and Government: New Zealand is a member of the British Commonwealth with a parliamentary form of government. Differences with the British model include a unicameral House of Representatives with 99 seats, and a three year term for the Prime Minister. The political system is multi–party in nature with the major parties being the *National Party, Labour Party, Alliance,* and *New Zealand First.* The Queen of England is represented by a Governor General. The electoral law has been changed to a mixed–member proportional representation system for 1996. Proportional repre-

Prime Minister J. B. Bolger

sentation, which awards seats in a district based on the percentage of votes won by a party, tends to help smaller parties and encourage a multi–party system.

National elections were held on November 6, 1993. The *National Party* under the leadership of Prime Minister James Bolger, which had been in power since November 1990, was returned to office. The party won 50 seats with 35% of the vote. The *Labour Party* won 45 seats with 34.4% of the vote. *Alliance* and *New Zealand First* each won 2 seats with 18.5 and 8% of the vote respectively. The margin of victory was much closer than in 1990, due primarily to the country's weak economy.

Last year, was one of realignment among the country's political parties. The *National Party* under the leadership of Prime Minister Jim Bolger maintained control of the government in 1994, but its majority slowly eroded throughout the year. In September, Ross Meurant, undersecretary for agriculture and forestry, left the *National Party* to establish the *Right of Center Party,* which, however, did state that it would work with the *National Party.* In October, Graeme Lee, once Minister of Internal Affairs, attempted to move closer to the *Christian Heritage Party* which received 2% of the vote in the 1993 elections, but this arrangement failed. In September, Michael Laws, another *National* MP, announced that he would not seek nomination for the party at the next election but would run as an independent or with another party.

These changes were offset by the resignation of Peter Dunne of the opposition *Labour Party,* who felt the party had

moved too far leftward. Dunne intended to form a new party which would vote with the *National Party.*

Within the opposition, the *Alliance Party* had its own problems when a split developed with the *Greens.* Dissident greens left in September to form the *Green Society.* This part of the political spectrum is not insignificant and has had an effect on national policy issues.

In 1995, Prime Minister Bolger held his government together in spite of additional defections. New parties came and went. Under the new proportional representation system a party will be required to gain at least 5% of the vote in the 1996 elections in order to receive representation. Bolger's *National Party* and the opposition *Labour Party* have traded control of the government for over fifty years.

The new system certainly calls for new skills at coalition building. One possible significant change in the 1996 elections will be how the *Alliance Party* does. It won 18% of the vote in 1993 but very few seats. A similar performance in 1996 will produce a very different result. There is, therefore, a real possibility for a ruling coalition government next year.

While the shifting political landscape attracted most the most attention, there were other issues of importance in 1995. Race relations between the indigenous Maoris and the British descended New Zealanders had not been good in recent years. The problem dated back to the Treaty of Waitangi of 1840 in which Maori chiefs gave up sovereignty of their people. The Maori, which constitute about 12% of the population today, have shared little in the development of modern New Zealand. After public demonstrations in early 1995, both sides agreed to a $112 million dollar settlement involving both money and the return of Maori lands. The May 1995 deal also includes an official apology for land which was confiscated as a result of conflict in the 1860's. Most New Zealanders hoped the settlement would mark the beginning of improved relations.

Foreign Policy: In March 1995, a significant step was taken to put New Zealand–U.S. relations back on track when Prime Minister Bolger headed for Washington for a meeting with President Bill Clinton. The last meeting between heads of state of the two countries occurred in 1984, during the Reagan administration. Soon after the 1984 meeting, then Prime Minister David Lange, banned a U.S. ship from entering a New Zealand port because it was suspected of carrying nuclear weapons. Anti–nuclear legislation was then passed which in turn led to a break in military ties and an end of top level contact between the two countries. New Zealand has indicated that it is willing to undertake joint operations

Polo tournament at Cambridge, New Zealand

with the U.S. but that it is up to Washington to decide what it wishes to do. The rift between the two countries resulted in New Zealand's exclusion from the ANZUS defense pact. The commander of U.S. forces in the Pacific visited the country in April 1994. This may have provided the opening for the Prime Minister's trip to Washington.

The Bolger visit did not end the stand-off in military relations, but overall relations appear to have been mended. The Prime Minister had the opportunity to meet with the Clinton inner circle including the Vice President and Secretaries of State and Defense. Mr. Bolger also met with key Republican figures.

New Zealand was outraged at French nuclear tests in the Pacific in 1995. The government sent a ship with two members of parliament to Mururoa Atoll to observe. Military cooperation with France was suspended and the ambassador to France was briefly recalled.

The issue of establishing a common aviation market with Australia was continued from the previous year with little progress. In May, Auckland hosted the annual meeting of the Asian Development Bank. New Zealand, like Australia, is attempting to turn toward Asia with its tremendous potential as an export market. However, it was reported that the

New Zealand media does not have a permanent representative stationed in the area. The old Euro–centered world has a strong pull in Wellington.

Culture: Apart from the Maori community, life in New Zealand is predominantly British—more so than in any other nation of the British Commonwealth except for the British Isles. Isolated and relatively small, it has a reputation for being provincial and conservative, whereas British cultural values have rapidly changed since World War II. Thus, the old saying that New Zealanders are more British than the British has some validity today.

The accent of the great majority of the people is similar to that of the middle and upper class gentry of England, and in the southern highlands around Dunedin and Invercargill it is reminiscent of the Scottish speech of their forebearers.

Economy: Agriculture, livestock raising and dairying predominate in the New Zealand economy. Mining and other industries have been added in the post World War II era which will continue gradual expansion. The economy is very dependent on foreign trade and this has caused some difficulty for the unskilled

worker. The government has taken the position, however, that this is the best course for the country in the long term. The current government has undertaken significant privatization. The past four years have seen a restructuring of the economy which make it one of the least regulated in the world. Significant cuts in welfare have also been undertaken and there were significant losses in jobs. This situation, however, now appears to have improved.

The economy grew by 5.5% for the year ended June 1995, compared to 6.2% for the previous year. Growth for this year, through June 1996, should be 3%. Inflation for calendar 1995 was under 2%. Exports grew by about 4% in 1995, to $21 billion. Imports were just under $20 billion.

The average citizen received an early Christmas present on December 13, when the government announced a tax cut valued at $710 million to take effect in July 1996. This is to be followed by a $1 billion cut. The middle class tax rate of 28% will decrease and the threshold for the higher bracket will be raised from 33%. The government also intends to spend more over the next several years. It can well afford to do so. The budget went from a $1 billion deficit in 1992, to a $2.9 billion surplus in 1995, and is expected to increase to almost $6 billion by 1998. Government debt stood at $38 billion in June 1995, but is predicted to fall to $19 billion (18% of GDP) by 1999. New Zealand's small economy remains healthy if not robust.

The Future: With the continuing success of the East Asia region, New Zealand should work hard to develop existing links with its neighbors. It would be wise to emulate Australia's tilt toward East Asia for economic and political reasons.

In spite of its geographical disadvantage, New Zealand can have a bright economic future. The country faces no immediate military challenges.

Christchurch: Anglican Cathedral at night

Courtesy: New Zealand Information Service

Papua New Guinea

Mekeo tribesmen in ceremonial dress

Courtesy: Colin Freeman

Area: 178,260 sq. mi. (475,369 sq. km., somewhat larger than California).

Population: 3.9 million (estimated).

Capital City: Port Moresby (Pop. 130,000, estimated).

Climate: Tropical.

Neighboring Countries: Australia (South); Indonesia (West).

Official Language: English.

Other Principal Tongues: There are over 700 indigenous languages, and a pidgin English is spoken in much of the country.

Ethnic Background: Mostly Melanesian and Papuan, with a small minority of Australians and Europeans.

Principal Religion: Traditional tribal beliefs, with an overlay of Christianity.

Main Exports: (to Japan, Germany, Australia); Copper, gold, timber, coffee, rubber and other tropical products.

Main Imports: (from Australia, Japan, Singapore); Machinery, consumer goods.

Currency: Kina.

Former Colonial Status: Until 1975, a United Nations trusteeship administered by Australia.

National Day: September 16, 1975.

Chief of State: Her Majesty Queen Elizabeth II, represented by Governor–General Sir Wiwa Korowi.

Head of Government: Sir Julius Chan, Prime Minister.

National Flag: Divided diagonally from top left to bottom right, the top a red field upon which is centered a yellow bird of paradise, the bottom a black field showing five white stars in the Southern Cross.

Per Capita Income: US$800.

Occupying the eastern half of the large island of New Guinea, the western portion—West Irian—being part of Indonesia, the nation was formed from Papua, the southeastern quarter of the island and the Territory of New Guinea, the northeastern quarter plus the nearby Admiralty, northern Solomon and Bismarck island groups.

The terrain is covered largely with very high mountains, swamps and jungles. The climate is uniformly tropical except in the more temperate altitudes of the mountains. There is an extremely small European minority; the indigenous inhabitants belong either to the Papuan group (on New Guinea) or to the Melanesian people (on the islands).

History: Prior to the late 19th century, apart from missionaries, New Guinea attracted two main types of Europeans: explorers and investors, lured by its supposedly substantial mineral resources. Dutch influence based on Indonesia became dominant in western New Guinea. The northeastern part of the big island and the smaller islands to the east were annexed by Germany in 1884. The southeastern part of the island known as Papua was placed under British protection in the same year, during the greedy scramble for colonial possessions that was then underway worldwide. Britain soon changed its policy toward Papua to a less possessive one and later transferred the area to Australia.

The German holdings in northeastern New Guinea and the nearby islands were seized by Australia during World War I and then were awarded to it under a League of Nations mandate which after World War II became a United Nations trusteeship.

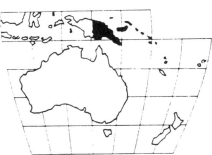

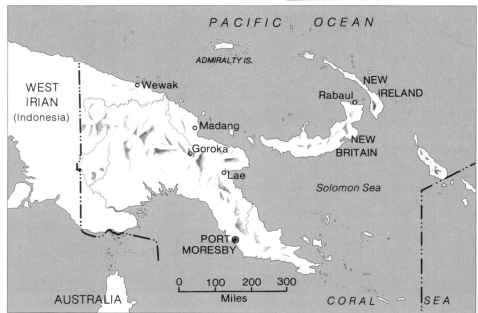

120

In reality, Australia administered the entire dependency until 1974 from Port Moresby with out regard to the legal distinction between the status of Papua, a direct Australian dependency, and New Guinea, the trusteeship.

In 1942 the Japanese conquered the islands east of New Guinea and invaded parts of the large island itself, including both of the eastern regions. Some of the bitterest fighting of the Pacific war occurred during the next two years as Australian and American forces drove the Japanese out of all but a few strongholds. Following the end of the war, Australian civil administration was restored. In response to growing UN criticism and a growing demand for self–government, an elected assembly was established in 1968.

In elections in 1972 to the House of Assembly (the parliament), the *National Coalition*, led by Michael Somare was victorious. His program, which called for full self–government in 1973, was accepted by Australia soon afterward, even though it was opposed by many of the European and indigenous inhabitants.

Politics and Government: Government in PNG for the last two decades after full independence was achieved has been all but unproductive. Endless coalitions have come and gone; votes of "no confidence" were passed with tedious regularity. The result was government control being wielded by a huge, corrupt civil service.

This disunity has led to severe financial problems, and most recently, a seven–year war on the island of Bougainville, rich in copper and desirous of independence.

Voting in 1992 was for 1600 candidates for 109 parliamentary seats; only seven won by a majority. Efforts to strengthen the central government in 1993 were controversial—any organization can be declared terrorist, with stiff fines and imprisonment for its members. A pass system for all citizens is under consideration.

When the sitting government failed, a coalition led by Sir Julius Chan was elected, 70–32, by the parliament in 1994. Wages have been frozen and the currency has been devalued. In addition to the continuing revolt on Bougainville Island, the government has been dealing with independence demands from the New Guinea Islands.

This past year was one of reassessment for the country. Many people, including national leaders feel that after twenty years of independence, the country has squandered its resources and made very little progress in improving the lives of the common people.

A major governmental reform was undertaken which resulted in the elimination of the country's 19 provincial parliaments. Non–paid local government officials along with the national parliamentary representatives formed local assemblies. They took the place of some 600 paid politicians who composed the provincial parliaments. The MP's in the new assemblies with the largest representation became Governors. They are to be the primary link between the local assemblies and the capital. The move may also have some impact on the unstable political party system, where new parties appear frequently, and where members shift from one party to another regularly.

In spite of the severe economic crisis and demands by the World Bank for reform, Prime Minister Chan was able to keep as a part of the national budget $250,000 for each of the country's 109 parliamentarians which they could spend as they pleased for their constituents. Prime Minister Chan appeared to be in firm control of the government at the end of the year.

Foreign Policy: Prime Minister Chan has altered PNG foreign policy from a "look North" (toward Asia) to a "look everywhere" approach. PNG may be especially interested in strengthening ties with the Pacific island nation–states.

In January 1995, Pope John Paul II visited PNG. This was his second visit, the first coming in 1984. While in the country his primary message was for peace and reconciliation with the Bougainville Revolutionary Army.

Culture: A small portion of the indigenous inhabitants still live at an Old Stone Age level, hunting and gathering for a living. Others, somewhat more advanced, practice a primitive subsistence agriculture. The social system is based on clans and tribes. Fighting and gruesome head–hunting among different tribes, once common, were suppressed by the Australian administration during the 1930's.

Pope John Paul II visited the highlands of Papua New Guinea, which has a sizable Catholic population, in 1984.

Economy: The economies of the two areas, Papua (in the south) and New Guinea (in the north) are basically similar, except that most of the mineral deposits (copper, gold and silver) so far discovered are located in New Guinea. The external trade of Papua New Guinea is largely with Australia, the United States and Germany.

Almost 70% of PNG's exports come from mining. The country is now the world's sixth largest producer of gold. There are also substantial oil and gas deposits. Production was disrupted at several sites throughout the country by ban-

dits and local armed gangs backed by land owners who want an increased share of the benefits from the country's resources. At the end of the year the World Bank and other international observers were concerned over how the country's budget was being handled. A new Investment Promotion Authority was initiated with the power to allow increased foreign equity in designated national industries. Giving foreign investors a greater share of ownership is a common mechanism to induce increased foreign investment.

In spite of the country's political difficulties, economic growth has been extraordinary: 9.5% in 1991, 11% in 1992, and 14.9% in 1993 and 1% in 1994. The problem is that much of the benefit of this huge increase has not been spread across the entire society.

In September, PNG hosted the annual meeting of the 16 member South Pacific Forum. The country was also represented at the third Asia Pacific Economic Cooperation meeting in Osaka. Perhaps the most significant event involved the joining of the World Trade Organization. For, it signaled that the government was attempting to liberalize and open up the national economy—something necessary if the current economic crisis is to be overcome.

In 1995, the country narrowly avoided financial collapse. In mid–year the government was forced to accept a World Bank–IMF structural adjustment package involving some $350 million. The package forces certain reforms on the government and its economic policies and included such items as: reduced restrictions on foreign investors, removal of price controls, halting tax concessions and the granting of monopolies, introduction of strategies to maintain a sustainable timber industry, and opening of the national books on debt (transparency). At the end of the year, the economy was in better shape. The government had initiated two freeway construction projects in Port Moresby and had taken other steps to put national finances in order.

The government was facing a $3 billion law suit for environmental damage from a large mining concern. If the suit is successful, others will follow. There are virtually no environmental policies in place to protect against pollution by the mining industry.

The Future: PNG's biggest problems are internal. The government must work to establish stability in the political system and to eliminate the budget deficit. The strife on Bougainville is wasteful. Intelligent use of vast resources would be of great help.

The Republic of the Philippines

Majestic Mayon volcano, the most symmetrical mountain on earth, looms mistily over Legaspi City at the southern tip of Luzon. Still active, a curlicue of smoke issues from its summit.

Area: 115,700 sq. mi. (300,440 sq. km., occupying an area somewhat smaller than New Mexico).

Population: 66 million (estimated).

Capital City: Manila (Pop. 7.5 million, estimated).

Climate: Tropically warm with rainy monsoons in the summer.

Neighboring Countries: the Philippines' closest neighbors are Nationalist China on the island of Taiwan (North) and Malaysia (Southwest).

Official Languages: Filipino (a formal version of Tagalog) and English.

Other Principal Tongues: Tagalog and tribal dialects of principally Malay origin, including Visayan, Ilocano and Bicol.

Ethnic Background: Malayo–Polynesian (about 93%) Chinese, Negritos, mixed and European (about 7%).

Principal Religion: Christianity, predominantly Roman Catholic (about 91.5%), Islam (about 2.5%), animist and other (about 7%).

Main Exports: (to the U.S. and Japan); A variety of coconut products—copra, oil and fibers, abaca,—Manila hemp used in rope making, timber—Philippine mahogany, sugar, iron ore.

Main Imports: (same trading partners plus Saudi Arabia); Industrial equipment, wheat, petroleum.

Currency: Philippine Peso.

Former Colonial Status: Spanish colony (circa 1570–1898); U.S. dependency (1898–1946); occupied by the Japanese (1941–1945).

National Day: July 4, 1946. (June 12, the anniversary of the proclamation of independence from Spain in 1898, is a national holiday).

Chief of State: Fidel Ramos, President (sworn into office June 30, 1992).

National Flag: The left edge is the base of a white equilateral triangle containing a yellow sun and three yellow stars; the rest of the flag is divided into two horizontal stripes with blue on the top, red on the bottom.

Per Capita Income: US$700.

The land which makes up the territory occupied by the Republic of the Philippines consists of a portion of a mountain chain running from northern Siberia in the Soviet Union through the China Sea to Borneo and New Guinea and the small islands of eastern Indonesia, and then southward through eastern Australia. Countless ages ago the sea invaded the lower part of these mountains—the Philippines are a small portion of the top of

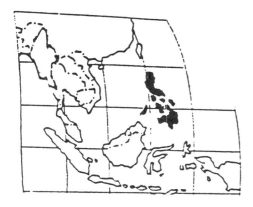

small non–Christian communities. The larger group of Filipinos of Malayo–Polynesian origin arrived in the isles from the 8th to the 15th centuries from Java and the Malay peninsula. Their migrations occurred principally during the period of the strong *Srivijaya* kingdom in the Indonesia–Malaya area and during the *Majapahit* kingdom on Java, which dominated a large area up to the beginning of the 13th century A.D.

Muslim traders and pirates arrived during the 14th century, and there was a small Chinese community. Magellan was killed in the islands in 1521 during his famous voyage around the world, but there was no serious attempt by the Spanish to establish a colony until fifty

this mountain range that has sufficient height to rise above the surface of the tropical waters of the Southwest Pacific.

This nation includes eleven larger islands with more than 1,200 square miles of land on each island: Luzon, Mindanao, Samar, Negros, Palawan, Panay, Mindoro, Leyte, Cebu, Bohol and Masbate. More than 95% of the nation's land and people are located on these islands.

The remaining 7,072 (every time they are counted the total is different) islands are desolate, jungle–infested and mostly uninhabited tiny areas of remoteness. Few have an area of more than one square mile, and about 4,631 exist as land masses in the 20th century only because it is impossible to sail across them—they are dots on navigation charts not even possessing the dignity of a name.

The temperature is consistently warm. The altitude of the terrain, most of which lies above an altitude of 1,600 feet, modifies the oppressiveness of what might otherwise be an intolerable climate. Almost all of the islands are mountainous, containing a multitude of dead and active volcanoes. The eastern slopes receive ample rainfall during all months of the year. The westward–facing parts are moistened by the southwest monsoon from May to October. All areas of the islands have periodic, often devastating, visits from typhoons of the region, which bring torrential rains.

The land is covered with vast expanses of thick jungle which grows with incredible rapidity and contains among its taller trees the timber from which Philippine mahogany is marketed to the world. The part that has been tamed by the population varies from a thick growth of poor grass which supports grazing to plantation production of coconut, rubber, pineapple and other tropical crops.

History: About two centuries before the Christian era a fairly advanced people from what is now northern Vietnam and southern mainland China migrated to the large islands of the Philippines. They practiced a system of communal agriculture based on irrigation. Many of their descendants live in the islands today as

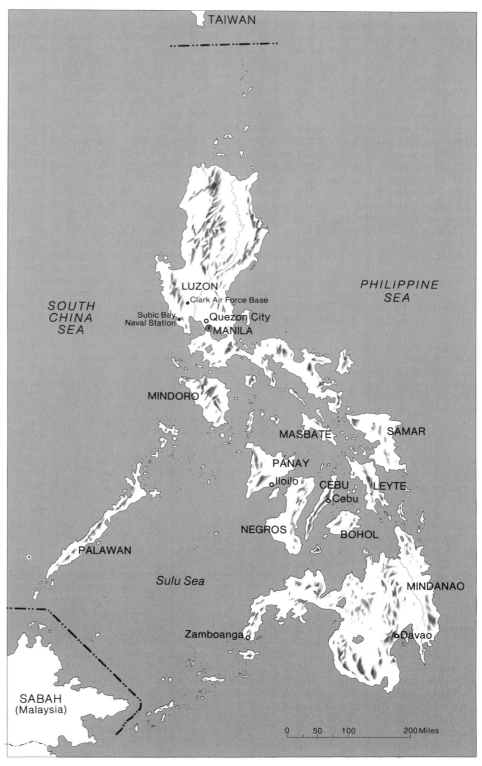

years later. The Spanish occupation forces were dispatched and controlled by the authorities in the colony of Mexico. The initial settlement was small, and had as its only contact with the European world the annual visit of the "Manila Galleon" sent to Mexico once a year.

As they had done in Central and South America, the Spanish gave large tracts of fertile land to prominent Spaniards who had almost complete authority over their domains, and exploited the native inhabitants without interference. Many of the Filipinos who were driven from their lands by the Spanish went to the more hilly and mountainous areas of the islands and developed farms based on intricate stone terracing of the steep sides to enable their crops to grow on level land. The best friends that the Filipinos had among the Spanish were the monks living in the monasteries which grew rapidly in number and in wealth based on land ownership. Many of the natives were converted to Roman Catholicism and also were provided with some educational and other social services by the religious institutions, which had a limited success in protecting them from the demands of government officials and the local Spanish land–owning aristocracy.

When Spain lost its colonies in Central and South America during the first part of the 19th century, the Philippines assumed an even more important position. Efforts to develop the economy to serve the Spanish were largely unsuccessful, as were the efforts to subdue the warlike *Moros* (Muslims) in the southern islands, who had lived there for many decades without interference. The slow growth of education, the spread of European cultural and political ideas, and unrest caused by oppressive economic polices of the Spaniards gave rise to a small group of educated Filipinos who demanded independence from Spain. Its most prominent member was the brilliant José Rizal, executed by the Spaniards in 1896, at a time when an open revolt against Spain had broken out.

Taking advantage of the preoccupation of the Spanish with the war being fought in Cuba against the United States, local leaders proclaimed an independent Republic of the Philippines early in 1898 and quickly adopted a European–type constitution. The Filipino leaders believed that the United States supported them in this independence move, and joined in a combined effort against the remaining Spanish forces in the islands. The U.S., partly out of fear that some other power, probably Germany, would seize the Philippines, forced the Spanish to cede them to the U.S. as part of the terms of the Spanish surrender in 1898.

Rebel forces led by General Emilio Aguinaldo, immediately went into armed revolt against the United States, feeling that they had been betrayed by the Americans with whom they had fought against the Spanish for six months. It took a little more than three years before guerrilla activity against U.S. forces ceased; Aguinaldo had been captured earlier in 1901.

By 1916 the United States had committed itself to a goal of eventual independence for the islands and begun the creation of internally self–governing institutions. It purchased about 400,000 acres of land from the Catholic monasteries for distribution to the people—the colonial administration also made efforts in the fields of communication, public works and education. The economic policies of the administrators were not as helpful; the emphasis was on creating areas for profitable American investment and little was done to develop the economy as a whole for the benefit of the Filipinos. A foreign trade emerged that was almost totally linked to and dependent on the U.S. market. Feudal systems of sharecropping in the rural areas, which had arisen under the Spanish as a result of land grants, continued and became an even worse problem. The local elected governments permitted by the colonial administration drifted toward control by Filipino political machines and bosses who bore a remarkable resemblance to some of their contemporaries in Latin America.

In the 1930's, Manuel Quezon, who formed and led the *Nationalist Party*, emerged as the leading politician. Political idealism was one factor that prompted the United States to adopt legislation providing for an almost fully self–governing Commonwealth to be established in 1935. The other was pressure from U.S. sugar interests for protective tariffs against Philippine sugar, which were impossible unless it was independent. The first President of the the Philippine Commonwealth was Quezon. The growing threat of the Japanese in Asia in the late 1930's lessened the desire for total independence on the part of the more radical Filipinos, who saw the need for U.S. protection.

The islands were quickly overrun by a force of well–trained Japanese soldiers who inaugurated in 1942 the same cruel type of military rule over the people that was their policy in the other areas of Southeast Asia they conquered. This resulted in a limited guerrilla movement operating clandestinely in the rural areas to sabotage the military installations of the Japanese. Quezon and his government went into exile in the United States, where he died in 1944. His successor, Sergio Osmeña, was soon able to return to the Philippines as a result of the progress of General Douglas MacArthur's forces in liberating the islands.

The economy had been devastated by the war, and it was necessary for the United States to pour in huge sums for relief and rehabilitation and to grant duty–free status to Philippine exports in the American market until 1954. Much of the aid, unfortunately, did not reach those who needed it. Osmeña died in 1946. For the next twenty years the Philippines were ruled, with one exception, by a succession of colorless, corrupt and inefficient leaders:

Manuel Roxas (pronounced *Ro*–has), 1946–1948. These years were marked by ineffective government, open corruption and black marketeering which made incoming aid of little benefit. Rural land tenancy problems remained unsolved. The armed guerrilla movement which had resisted the Japanese underwent a rapid and subtle transformation into a communist movement, usually known as the *Hukbalahap*, or "Huks," a name inherited from resistance movements dating back to Aguinaldo. In spite of these conditions, the U.S. proceeded with its plan for full independence on July 4, 1946.

Elpidio Quirino, 1948–1953. Dishonesty and scandal reached crisis proportions and the *Huks* went into open and initially successful revolt. An exceptionally able and energetic Secretary of Defense, Ramón Magsaysay, who would become the next president, enlisted American advice after his appointment in 1950; the guerrilla threat was greatly diminished. The army was transformed into an effective force forbidden to engage in its usual customs of looting and harassment. Amnesty and free land was granted to the *Huks*, who surrendered, almost totally eliminating them as a threat to stability.

Ramón Magsaysay, 1953–1957. He maintained a consistently pro–U.S. policy and took the Philippines into the Southeast Asia Collective Defensive Organization (SEATO) in 1954. In spite of his strenuous efforts the power of the small group of families who dominated agriculture, industry and trade—the descendants of the Spanish aristocratic class, continued. Magsaysay was killed in an airplane accident and was succeeded by his inept vice president.

Carlos Garcia, 1957–1961.

Diosdado Macapagal, 1961–1965. The country remained stagnant under these two leaders, the latter of whom dabbled in an active, anti–U.S. foreign policy intended to make the Philippines more popular, powerful and acceptable in the Asian community.

Ferdinand Marcos of the *Nationalist Party*, defeated Macapagal in 1965 amid a general sense of urgent need of change among the people—change toward better performance by their rulers. Marcos embarked upon a reform platform similar to that of Magsaysay, but met the same intractable obstacles as his predecessor. Corruption remained a virtual custom among minor government officials and employees for the next twenty years. The *Communist Party* (PKP) abetted by discontent among the poverty–stricken rural people, resumed its guerrilla activity against the state, although they became divided among themselves. Traditional rivalry between the *Nationalist Party* and the Liberal Party continued.

President Marcos was reelected in 1969 over a *Liberal Party* opponent by a large majority and became the first Philippine President to win a second term. *Nationalist* majorities in both houses of the Assembly were sizable. But student and labor demonstrations in Manila which occurred in 1970 were symptoms of the country's malaise; some of the dissent had an openly anti–U.S. tone. The popular discontent was diverted to the business of revising the constitution through holding a national convention. Probably for reasons of domestic politics, Marcos revived an old Philippine claim to Sabah, a part of Malaysia closest to the Republic. The predictable result was a serious crisis with Malaysia, punctuated by a barrage of bitter charges and counter–charges. The dispute fizzled out within two years and the claim was formally dropped at the end of 1987.

Serious floods and growing insurgency on the part of communist elements in Luzon created a crisis atmosphere. Marcos proclaimed martial law in 1972. In the ensuing years he had some success in improving the state of law and order except in Mindanao, where an ongoing Muslim revolt has been in progress. Of greatest importance, however, he received approval by referendum of a new constitution under which he had virtual dictatorial powers for an unlimited period. There was another such referendum in 1975.

Principal opposition to the Marcos regime came from the Catholic Church and insurgent Muslims in the southern islands. The latter received (and still receives) support from other Muslim countries, principally Libya and Sabah. Some Arab countries tried unsuccessfully in 1975 to mediate the conflict. Fearing the consequences of endangering needed oil imports, Marcos did not press the war and announced that a truce had been concluded; in reality the war continued in spite of additional negotiations in 1976 and 1977.

Martial law delegated great political power to the armed forces, which became repressive and corrupt, although providing a semblance of order.

Imelda Marcos, the attractive wife of the president, became Governor of Manila and announced ambitious plans for its redevelopment; although she set up a semblance of a power base, she remained

Mindanao's Maria Cristina Falls pounds out its dramatic message

Ferdinand and Imelda Marcos at their zenith in 1972

loyal to her husband, although her plans to succeed him became widely known.

Marcos created a *National People's Council* in 1976 to advise him on legislative matters. Elections were postponed indefinitely, however. He apparently planned to revive the political system in such a manner that he would pick the candidates from panels chosen by various public bodies. An election for an interim parliament with limited powers held in 1978 resulted in a sweeping victory for pro–Marcos candidates.

As might be expected, the militant wings of the opposition groups began to resort to terrorist bombings in 1980. In an effort to save his son, who was targeted for elimination, Marcos made a secret deal which he fulfilled only in part by lifting martial law in 1981, but the bombings continued. Insurgency, particularly Muslim and communist, became a continuing problem. Despite the lifting of martial law, there was little improvement in the political situation. The country continued to be run by an alliance led by an aging and somewhat ill Marcos, his wife, the armed forces, the ruling *New Society Party* and rich and powerful men close to the president who operated for their own benefit in an economic system known locally and informally as "crony capitalism."

Marcos had talked of forcing the U.S. out of its huge air and naval bases in the Philippines, but this was almost certainly to divert popular attention from his domestic policies as well as to get greater concessions from the United States, in-

cluding higher rents. In addition, he was determined to appear at home and abroad as entirely independent of the United States and as the leader of a truly Asian nation. Partly for this purpose, he visited and granted diplomatic recognition to the People's Republic of China in June 1975; another consideration was that he wanted, and apparently thought that he got, a pledge from Benjing not to support the small Philippine communist insurgent movement, the *New People's Army*. The Chinese urged Marcos not to squeeze the U.S. out of its bases, since Peking feared that an American military withdrawal from the region might create a vacuum that could be filled or exploited by the Soviet Union. Relations with the United States were reasonably good; President Ford visited in late 1975. Marcos established diplomatic relations with the Soviet Union in 1976. An agreement concerning lease of military bases was finally concluded with the United States in 1978 and a second in late 1983.

Opposition leader Benigno Aquino, probably encouraged by false reports that Marcos was about to undergo surgery in August 1983, decided to return to Manila from Malaysia where he had been living in exile. He was summarily gunned down at the airport upon the landing of his plane. The opposition blamed the government, and more specifically, the armed forces, for the murder. Immense demonstrations occurred in the cities against Marcos and in protest at the sham official investigation of the assassination. The confusion led to a cancellation of a visit to Manila by President Reagan scheduled for late 1983.

The opposition *United Nationalist Democratic Organization (UNIDO)* succeeded in early 1984 in getting the constitution amended by referendum so as to restore the office of vice president, the purpose being to reduce the chances that the widely–disliked Mrs. Marcos might succeed her husband to the presidency. The document permitted the election of a vice president from a different political party than that of the president.

The opposition was divided, however, on whether to take part in National Assembly elections scheduled for May 1984. Marcos' *New Society Movement* won the elections, but the opposition did well—Mrs. Marcos' candidates for seats representing metropolitan Manila were all defeated. Twelve opposition leaders announced an anti–Marcos "unity" platform in late 1984, but events in 1985–1986 showed anything but unity.

After an unnecessarily lengthy inquiry, armed forces Chief of Staff General Fabian Ver and 25 others were indicted in January 1985 for complicity in the Aquino assassination; the trial began in February and continued for months. When all the evidence was in and the jury had retired

to deliberate, the Philippine Supreme Court took the unheard of step of dismissing the charges on the ground that there was insufficient evidence. Ver had been replaced on an acting basis by the moderate and popular General Fidel Ramos.

By the fall of 1985 it became clear that the defendants in the Aquino case would be acquitted (as they were in December), and political tensions rose. Under American pressure, in early November Marcos called a presidential election for February 7, 1986. An opposition candidate, Mrs. Corazon Aquino, widow of the slain Benigno Aquino, soon attracted widespread support, especially in the cities. The communists boycotted the campaign and the elections.

Although Marcos was officially declared to have won the election, which had been monitored by large numbers of official and unofficial observers, mainly American, it soon became obvious that his supporters had been guilty of massive fraud, and Mrs. Aquino had actually won. Accordingly, the United States government switched its support from Marcos to Mrs. Aquino after mid–February. A group of army officers belonging to a military reform movement usually known by its acronym RAM then began to plan a *coup* against Marcos.

Getting wind of it, he concluded that it was the work of Defense Minister Enrile and Vice Chief of Staff Ramos and began to move against them. They and their supporters promptly came out in support of Mrs. Aquino. Jaime Cardinal Sin, Archbishop of Manila, who favored Mrs. Aquino, urged the faithful to block the streets of Manila to the passage of troops loyal to Marcos. This move was effective, and with an offer of asylum from the United States, provided he did not use force against his own people, Marcos left for Hawaii as the month ended. Mrs. Aquino was then inaugurated President.

President Aquino repealed Marcos' repressive regulations and released his political prisoners. She initiated steps to recover the enormous wealth he had stashed abroad, mainly in the United States and Switzerland. President Aquino and her middle class cabinet, faced with a pro–Marcos majority in the Assembly and the Supreme Court, then declared a "revolutionary" government in order to be better able to eliminate the legacy of Marcos' rule.

About six months after her election, President Aquino began to move against her major problems. She visited the U.S. in September, and Congress voted an extra $200 million in aid for the Philippines. She began work on an ambitious and difficult land reform program, which was badly needed. In late November she fired Defense Minister Juan Ponce Enrile, who had been seemingly threatening a military *coup* against her. At that time, Chief of Staff Fidel Ramos ensured that the armed forces remained loyal to President Aquino rather than supporting Enrile, while quietly pressing her at the same time to get rid of some other ineffective cabinet members and take a stronger line against the communists and their *New People's Army (NPA)*.

After long negotiations, the communists agreed to a 60–day truce, beginning December 10, 1986. The *PKP* used its interlude of legality to make energetic propaganda in the cities, but it ended by probably alienating more people than it impressed. Accordingly, it refused to renew the ceasefire and resumed its offensive. President Aquino countered with an offer of amnesty to any insurgent who surrendered. In January 1987 another dissident movement, the (Moslem) *Moro National Liberation Front* (based in Mindinao), signed a peace agreement with the government; it had been negotiated in Saudi Arabia.

There were some serious disorders, partly stirred up by exiled ex–President Marcos in late January, just before a referendum was to be held on a new constitution, but they were suppressed.

President Aquino's constitution got an unexpectedly high vote (about 75% of those casting ballots). It limited the president to one six-year term, created a bicameral legislature, granted the courts the power of judicial review of laws and provided that the U.S. bases must be non-nuclear and could be continued after 1991 only on the basis of a treaty approved by at least two thirds of the Philippine Senate.

President Aquino's supporters won a sweeping victory in elections for the Senate and House of Representatives held in May 1987.

But in August of the same year, in the most serious of several attempts made up to that time to overthrow President Aquino, a colorful paratrooper, Colonel Gregorio (Rambo) Honasan, led an attempted *coup* against her. It failed due to energetic action by loyal forces under Chief of Staff Ramos (made Defense Secretary in January 1988). For a time it appeared that President Aquino's position might be untenable, and in the fall her main political opponents, especially Vice President Salvador Laurel and former Defense Secretary Juan Ponce Enrile, seemed to be moving to form a coalition against her.

The president, however, staged an impressive rally. In September 1987 she curbed the influence of two important advisers, Joker Arroyo and Teodoro Locsin, who were widely regarded as leftist. Laurel resigned as Foreign Minister and was replaced by Raul Manglapus. Regrettably, President Aquino removed an able

Finance Secretary, Jaime Ongpin, who committed suicide in December. She raised military pay and met some of the other demands of the armed forces; these changes signaled a tougher, more conservative line intended to be more acceptable to the military and to the business community.

Other trends were not so favorable. Land reform was making only slow progress against entrenched rural interests. Communist insurgency continued to grow to the point where President Aquino was apparently considering proclaiming a state of emergency. Frequently brutal anti–communist vigilantes emerged in many areas.

President Aquino's candidates did well

President Fidel Ramos

in local elections held in December 1987–January 1988, albeit not overwhelmingly so.

Philippine political life continued to be riddled with corruption on the part of elected and appointed officials. There was also intense partisanship. The lower house of Congress was subservient to the popular President Aquino, whereas the Senate, whose members are elected by the national electorate rather than from local constituencies, was highly independent. Vice President Salvador Laurel evidently wanted to succeed, or even unseat, President Aquino. Former President Marcos, seriously ill in Hawaii, wanted to return to the Philippines but had not been allowed to do so. He died in September 1989.

Imelda Marcos was acquitted by a jury in New York City principally because the alleged wrongdoing, if any, took place in

the Philippines. The latest report on her is that she is interested in buying some sort of estate in a very wealthy section of Virginia.

In June 1988, Congress voted a moderate land reform program that managed to please neither the landlords nor the tenants. Social unrest and Communist insurgency continue. The latter has changed its shape somewhat in recent years in a more military direction, with numerous local victories. The New People's Army is supported by the large and influential *National Democratic Front*, which has a following not only in the cities but abroad. The government has found no real answer to the *NDF*. To cope with communist insurgency in the rural areas, it has developed a so–called triad strategy: military pressure, intelligence activity and civic action (public works, etc.). Overall, and despite continuing human rights violations by the military and by right wing vigilante groups, the counter–insurgency campaign seems to be progressing better than in earlier years. Local elections have been held, and defections from the Communist forces and captures of their leaders have increased.

There are two major issues in current relations with the U.S. One is the Multilateral Assistance Initiative'' (MAI), a program of up to $10 billion in economic aid that the U.S. is trying to organize with American, Japanese and other funding. Some of the prospective contributors are not very enthusiastic, since the Philippine government is already sitting on some $3 billion in unused aid money and has been unable to recover any significant part of the huge fortune acquired by former President Marcos, who had been indicted in the U.S. on charges of racketeering. Secondly, the U.S. bases are highly controversial in the eyes of the Philippine political elite and intellectuals, although most of the public, the non–communist Asian governments, and even China favor them. After difficult negotiations, an agreement was reached in October 1988 under which the U.S. was to give $481 million in economic aid (one third of what the Philippine side had been demanding) in 1990 and again in 1991, when the current base agreement expired. Any new agreement would have to be ratified by the Philippine Senate, and perhaps by a popular referendum. In May 1988, the Senate voted a ban on storage of nuclear weapons on the bases, but it appeared that in practice they could still be taken through in transit. No one, Philippine or American, showed any interest in a vague proposal by General Secretary Mikhail Gorbachëv that the U.S. give up its Philippine bases in exchange for a Soviet withdrawal from Camranh Bay, Vietnam.

A series of developments in late 1989 and early 1990 heightened the general impression that under President Aquino's indecisive leadership, the country was drifting or even regressing. In early December the sixth and most serious attempted military *coup* against her was quelled, but mainly because U.S. combat aircraft unprecedentedly flew over the rebel positions. Talks with the United States on the future of the bases and on economic issues began at about the same time. They promised to be long and difficult. The American side wanted continued access even after the bases passed to Philippine control. Manila wanted to get as much money as possible out of the entire transaction. Filipinos employed at the bases were concerned about their continued employment at superior wages.

Political unrest and attempted military *coups* continued to be a serious problem. As the end of President Aquino's term approached, various political figures began to jockey for succession.

One of these figures, surprisingly, was Imelda Marcos, the widow of Ferdinand **Marcos**. She returned from exile in November 1991 and got the government's permission to bury her husband in his native province, Ilocos Norte, although not in Manila as she preferred. Although facing criminal proceedings on charges of corruption, she soon began to campaign as the champion of the poor, notwithstanding her vast fortune.

The *Communist Party*, whose insurgency had not been doing well in recent years, announced in May 1991 that it would agree to a ceasefire if the government refused to extend the lease on the U.S. bases beyond September, when the agreement covering them was to expire. Early in 1992, however, after American forces actually had begun to leave the bases, the PCP intensified its military operations.

In 1991 the Philippines suffered a series of natural disasters, such as a storm that struck the central islands in November and caused unusually heavy damage (runoff and mudslides) because of heavy illegal logging in the area. The most important disaster was a massive eruption of Mt. Pinatubo, a volcano about 55 miles north of Manila and only 10 miles from U.S.–controlled Clark Air Force Base, in June, because it largely determined the outcome of the long and complex negotiations between Manila and Washington on the future of the U.S. bases in the Philippines, especialy Clark and the large naval base at Subic Bay.

Before the eruption, Manila had been demanding $825 million per year for seven years in aid, in exchange for continuation of the base agreement. Congress was unwilling to appropriate that much, and Washington had been offering $520 million per year over 10–12 years. The bases were very valuable for repair

and refueling of ships and aircraft and for training of personnel; Filipino labor was plentiful, cheap, and skilled. The U.S. side was concerned more with continued access to the bases than with control of them.

As someone said, the volcano had its own agenda, and it was clearly not the same as that of the negotiators. The eruption, apparently the most powerful anywhere in the twentieth century, not only heavily damaged the town of Angeles, near Clark, but covered the base with about a foot of ash, rendering it virtually useless; Subic and its environs also suffered some damage.

After the eruption, some haggling continued between the two sides, but the negotiations were basically over. The bases seemed much less important to U.S. strategic interests since the collapse of the Soviet Union, the main regional threat. In September, the Philippine Senate, in a nationalistic mood, voted not to ratify an agreement incorporating the U.S.'s final offer (Clark to be turned over, Subic to be kept for ten more years for $203 million per year), and American forces began to withdraw from both Clark and Subic. The units being withdrawn were to be separated into smaller packages and dispersed to Singapore, Hawaii, and Alaska. The irony was that, in the Philippine elections scheduled for May 1992, the new Senate might well have voted to keep the bases, assuming that option still existed.

Politics and Government: On paper, the Philippine political system resembles that of the United States. Prior to 1987, the Philippines was governed under the U.S. modeled 1935 constitution. The constitution provided for a bill of rights, a bicameral legislature, an independent judiciary and a president with a four year term. The 1973 Marcos constitution was approved but never put into practice because of the imposition of marshall law. This constitution provided for a parliamentary system with a prime minister.

The Aquino constitution was approved on February 2, 1987. The president is now limited to one 6 year term. Close relatives of the president cannot be appointed to public office. Both the legislature and the judiciary may review the legal reasons for the imposition of martial law. The constitution also provides for civil liberties and is basically very democratic in form.

The country has a House of Representatives and a Senate. Under the new constitution congress has the power to declare war, restrict presidential emergency powers and control the appropriation of revenue. The senate has twenty-four members with six year terms with a limit of two consecutive terms. The house can have up to 250 members elected from legislative districts apportioned by popu-

lation. Twenty percent of the seats are filled through a party–list system.

The Philippines has historically been a two party system. The *Nacionalista* and *Liberal* parties traded control of the government between 1946 and 1972. Both parties tended to serve the interests of the political elites in the country and were vehicles for elites and their personal followings. President Marcos dominated the political system through his *New Society Movement*. There was no effective political party opposition during this period. Strong opposition began to emerge around 1980 with the formation of *UNIDO* which had the backing of anti–Marcos elites. Benigno Aquino Jr. established *LABAN* ("Fight"), as a vehicle for his political ideas. The political party landscape fragmented somewhat during the Aquino years. Politics continues to be highly personalized. Support is given to individuals, not platforms, programs or ideologies.

This situation continued under President Ramos. In 1993 and 94, weak party discipline prevented the Ramos party, *Lakas–National Union of Christian Democrats (NUCD)*, and the *United Muslim Democrats of the Philippines (UMDP)* from using its large majority effectively in the House. To strengthen support for the president, especially in the Senate, *Lakas–NUCD* formed a coalition with the major opposition *LDP* party, in August 1994. The two parties had to agree on the candidates for the 12 Senate seats open in the May 1995 elections. This coalition spurred the other opposition parties, the *National People's Coalition* and the *People's Reform Party* to combine forces. The situation with regard to political parties will remain fluid and will be affected if proposed electoral reforms are passed or if a parliamentary system of government is adopted. In May 1995, the *Lakas–NUCD–LDP* coalition won 10 of the 12 Senate seats it contested, according to unofficial results.

Unfortunately, the country's form of government does not fit very well with the culture. The society is very much oriented toward "patron–client relations." Essentially, this means that political life centers on relationships that are personal and hierarchical. Political relationships are also built on the concept of "utang na loob," obligations of indebtedness. Politics is therefore dominated by personal loyalty to a hierarchical group. Patrons must provide resources to their clients to keep their loyalty. This is a major cause of corruption in the Philippines. The client in the relationship is concerned only with what the patron can deliver. Issues of national policy or rational decision making are not important.

In this type of environment, institutions like interest groups, and political parties and other organizations that could unite large segments of society are ineffective. A farmer is loyal to the elite above him in society who can provide benefits. He is not loyal to his group, farmers, which could unite in a common cause to better the groups position in society through political action. Thus, the institutions which are so effective in the United States, are of little value in the personalized political culture of the Philippines. Until the country's political culture and the governmental form are rationalized, it will be extremely hard for any leader, no matter how dedicated, to bring about real change and resolution to major problems.

Fidel V. Ramos was elected president of the Philippines in May 1992. However, as one of seven candidates, Ramos, in winning, received only 23.4% of the vote. His closest challenger, Miriam Defensor Santiago, screamed fraud and did manage to have the Supreme Court consider the charge. Ramos, in short, did not start off with a lot of support, though Mrs. Aquino backed him all the way.

Since his election, President Ramos and his government have faced several significant challenges: the need to establish law and order, opposition to the current political process by groups including the *National Democratic Front* (representing the communists), the *Muslim National Liberation Front*, the *Muslim Islamic Liberation Front*, the military officers' group *RAM–YOU* and the continuing entrenched position of the old political elite.

In 1996, these challenges were still present but somewhat diminished. In January, the government foiled a plot to assassinate Pope John Paul II during his visit to Manila. However, in April, members of the *Muslim Islamic Liberation Front (MILF)* under the leadership of Abu Sayaff attacked the town of Appall on Mindanao. Fifty–seven people were killed. In early 1996, the *MILF* was looking like a bigger threat than had been previously predicted. The year also witnessed an outbreak of bank robberies and kidnappings in Manila. On the bright side, negotiations with the *Muslim National Liberation Front (MNLF)* were progressing, and a peace agreement involving amnesty and the surrender of arms with the young military officers group, *RAM*, was concluded.

The Ramos coalition victory in the May 1995 senate elections (10 of 12 seats) should have given the president firm control of the government. However, as the year progressed, speculation mounted that President Ramos was about to move to amend the constitution to allow for a second term. The removal of the president of the Senate, Edgardo Angara, fanned the speculation. The cynicism of the electorate was high. Local

elections which returned many old line politicians did not help matters.

Uncertainty about the ability and/or insincerity of the Ramos government may have also contributed to the comeback of the year. Deposed on February 25, 1986, President Ferdinand Marcos (deceased) and wife, Imelda, underwent a comeback in Manila. Imelda, the first lady with over 1,200 pairs of shoes, was elected to the House of Representatives. Her son, ''Bong Bong'' did not win his contest for the Senate. The former first lady was convicted on graft charges in 1993 and sentenced to twenty–four years in prison. She was out on bond and fighting to overturn the conviction in 1996. Polls showed that a majority of Filipinos rated the Marcos years above Mrs. Aquino's presidency.

Many of Marcos' cronies, such as former defense minister Juan Ponce Enrile, have also been reborn politically. Senator Enrile now speaks positively about the old days. He should be glad that the current president has a higher tolerance for criticism than did Marcos.

Not everyone remembers the past so fondly. Some 10,000 individuals have filed claims against the estate of Ferdinand Marcos, estimated at between $5 and $10 billion dollars, alleging human–rights violations during his regime. The Philippine government itself is interested in recovering these funds. Fidel Ramos has done much for the Philippines. The problem is that there is still so much to do.

Foreign Policy: In 1993, Philippine foreign policy was focused on strengthening its long standing relationship with the

United States. In May Foreign Secretary Roberto Romulo stated that he favored downgrading relations with the United States, and emphasizing stronger ties with such countries as Japan, South Korea and Taiwan. The President however favored maintaining strong ties with the United States. In 1993, U.S. aid to the Philippines had dropped to about $15 million dollars. The president's two week visit to the United States in November–December was viewed in the Philippines as a success.

The Philippines is also seeking stronger ties with its ASEAN (Association of Southeast Asian Nations) neighbors. In May the Philippines participated in a nine country meeting on the territorial disputes in the South China Sea, and in September, President Ramos visited Indonesia to discuss the possibility of the East Asia Triangle, to link Mindinao in the southern Philippines, east Malaysia on the island of Borneo and Sulawesi in Indonesia.

At the end of May 1994, a chill between Manila and Jakarta developed because of a human rights conference. The conference, sponsored by the University of the Philippines, focused on East Timor, which continues to resist Indonesian rule. President Ramos disavowed the conference, barred some foreign participants from attending the meeting, and reaffirmed that the Philippines continued to recognize Indonesia's right to rule in East Timor.

President Ramos traveled to Europe and the Middle East in September and October to secure economic agreements and loans. President Clinton stopped in Manila for one day on his way to the sec-

Minutes after an earthquake in northern Luzon, a huge boulder crashed down the mountainside to block the highway
Photo by Jon Markham Morrow

ond APEC meeting in Jakarta in November.

In 1995, Manila experienced strained relations with both Singapore and China. By far, China's occupation of Mischief Reef in the South China Sea constituted the most serious problem. In early 1995, Manila discovered that one of the small islands in the Spratley chain about 150 miles off the Philippine coast had been occupied by members of the Chinese navy. Mischief Reef is in Philippine territorial waters. In May, the Philippine military officials tried to take a boatload of journalists to see the reef. A Chinese patrol boat blocked their path. The Philippine navy then detained a number of Chinese fishermen who were illegally in the country's territorial waters. At the August meeting of the ASEAN Regional Forum, ARF, the ASEAN states spoke with one voice in raising concern about the Chinese occupation. Beijing subsequently agreed to deal with the conflicting claims in the South China Sea multilaterally. Thus, Manila would have its fellow ASEAN member states as partners in negotiations over the Spratley Islands. This was far preferable than going one-on-one with the *PRC*. Nevertheless, the problem of conflicting claims, among six different countries remains a serious and difficult problem.

Relations with Singapore were ruffled in February 1995, when the latter executed Flor Contemplacion for a double murder, over the appeal of President Ramos. Many Filipinos believe Flor was framed. Manila recalled its ambassador. The real casualty of the affair was Philippine Foreign Secretary Roberto Romulo, who Ramos sacked to save his own hide. Many felt the government was being "soft on Singapore." In October, President Ramos visited the United States on the occasion of the 50th anniversary of the United Nations.

Culture: The culture and outlook of the Filipinos can best be understood through their ancestry and government. The Malay majority have the somewhat energetic and restless character of their brethren in Indonesia and Malaysia; in addition they have definitely superior learning ability. This is rooted in the Spanish rule, which lasted 350 years and provided an example of how to dominate, oppress and exploit people—traits easily absorbed and translated into a tendancy toward and tolerance of corruption. On top of these ingredients there were laid the sugary dreams of American idealism and democracy and enthusiasm for higher learning. The foregoing ingredients of instability are garnished by a Muslim minority with violent tendencies and by a traditional, rural guerrilla movement now under nominal communist control.

The contrasts in this cultural scene are dramatic. Manila, a busy, modern city, has a sophisticated cultural atmosphere which can compare with most western cities. Some of the peasants live in a poverty even more oppressive than that of their Latin American counterparts. Catholicism is predominant, but is sprinkled with many local ingredients which in the past were sufficient to shock traditional European and American Catholics. This effect has diminished, however, in the aftermath of regionalism within the Catholic Church, accompanied by a generous dose of "liberation theology."

There is a sizable Chinese community prominent in various fields, especially business. Small communities of primitive animists live on the remote islands. Although this last group is surrounded by the hostilities of untamed nature, it exists in isolation from the larger problems of the modern world.

The Filipino language, a refinement of the Tagalog spoken by the Philippine Malays, is the official language. Spanish is spoken by a dwindling number of descendants of the older aristocracy left by the Spaniards. Educated Filipinos cherish the English language as well as the esteem for formal education and academic degrees common to the United States—the economy has difficulty in absorbing all of those who have been trained to the fullest extent of their ability. For example, many Filipino medical doctors are settling in the United States.

The rural people live in innumerable villages, which although not identical are very similar in appearance. There is little variation in local customs and traditions. One of the most unique is found at a wedding celebration and feast. Elaborate preparations are made during the preceding weeks usually involving the whole village. After the ceremony, the festivities begin, highlighted by a highly stylized dance by the bride and groom. They perform intricate steps inside and outside two pairs of parallel bamboo poles, each pair at right angles with the other. The pairs of poles are opened and closed in a waltz rhythm to the strains of quaint music, alternately together and apart. The art is not to get ones' feet caught by the poles as they come together.

Economy: The Philippine Republic is fairly rich in natural resources and, with the exception of the Manila plain, is not overpopulated. The post–World War II economy has been sluggish until only recently, principally due to corruption and mismanagement in government. A sizable community of Chinese has grown over the last 70 years, engaging in intensive commerce and energetic light industry, as is common in other nations of Asia. In a manner reminiscent of Hong Kong and Singapore, they have grouped in Manila for the most part. All the Filipino political parties and machines have followed a policy of periodically blackmailing the local Chinese into paying large campaign contributions in order to avoid discriminatory legislation.

In the last few years, there has been a substantial growth in the economy, especially in agriculture, but on the whole the national income of the Republic remains

Harvesting bananas in Cebu, Philippines   World Bank photo

inadequate in relation to a rapidly rising population. Even more oppressive is the fact that much of the wealth still winds up in the hands of a small group of rich individuals and families. Corruption and inflation have been a continuing problem.

Under Marcos' *New Society*, a limited land reform program was in progress. Landlords, as part of the establishment, were well compensated by the government for what land they had lost, and this further inflated the economy. There are substantial government deficits and a very large foreign debt. Oil imports were for years more expensive than before 1973, but as of 1985–1986 were decreased in price due to the world oil glut. Philippine exports to the United States no longer enjoy special low tariff rates. On the other hand, the prices of Philippine exports have held up well.

President Marcos sold highly profitable monopolies of such commodities as coconuts and sugar to his friends, a system known to the opposition as "croney capitalism." In addition, a number of properties and businesses were taken illegally by the president's family members and supporters from Philippine businessmen who were not pro–Marcos. After President Marcos was forced from office, some individuals were able to regain lost assets. For example, the Lopez family regained control of the Manila Times.

Under President Aquino, a less stifling, but still harmful version of the "crony capitalism" that had flourished under Marcos emerged, and few of the benefits of reviving economic growth have been enjoyed by the poorer members of Philippine society.

The Philippines economy had another good year in 1995. having posted a 5.8% growth rate for the year, against 5.1% in 1994. However, the persistence of corruption, creeping inflation which galloped to 12% in September, and a rice shortage in October which required the importation of 550,000 tones, gave everyone cause for concern. The government showed a surplus but this was only because of privatization and the sell off of certain assets.

The real problem with the Philippine economy is that the expansion is not benefitting the truly poor who live in the Patayas slum in Manila, or in the provinces. Construction is booming around Manila and Makati, but job creation is still insignificant. Violent crime and kidnapping for ransom is exploding and tax evasion is a national sport. President Ramos as made progress. However, it is only the middle and upper classes who are benefitting. Toward the end of the year there was concern about the possibility of food riots resulting from high prices and shortages.

Students relax in a courtyard of Santo Tomás University in Manila. Founded in 1611, it is one of the oldest universities in the world.
Courtesy: Jon Markham Morrow

The Future: The Ramos government has a chance to bring about significant change to the country. Unlike Mrs. Aquino, the president is not from the aristocracy. He can more easily deal with those who have been involved in the systematic looting of the country. It is encouraging to note that already the Ramos administration has turned over more land to the peasants than had been done in the previous 20 years. The turn–around in the Philippine economy also bodes well for the country. If the pace can be sustained, there will be little support for the *Communist Party of the Philippines (CPP)*.

The lingering problem with the Muslim south is now heating up again. *Abu Sayyaf* is a real threat and could continue to grow. The group has received both money and weapons from radical friends in the Middle and Near East. The radical elements in the Muslim community may not be willing to settle for autonomy. Independence may be preferred.

The confrontation with China over the Spratley Islands heated up in early 1995. This is a major issue for both the Philippines and the U.S., though the latter wishes it would disappear.

President Ramos has done a good job. He will serve his country well by not pushing for constitutional changes which would allow him to run for a second term in office.

131

The Republic of Singapore

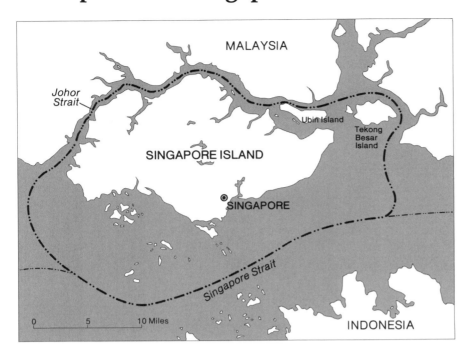

Area: 239 sq. mi. (618 sq. km., somewhat smaller than New York City).

Population: 2.8 million (mid–1993 est.).

Capital City: Singapore (Pop. 2.45 million, estimated).

Climate: Tropically hot and humid.

Neighboring Countries: Malaysia (North); Indonesia (South).

Official Languages: Chinese (Mandarin dialect), Malay, Tamil, English.

Ethnic Background: Chinese (about 77%); Malayo–Polynesian (about 15%); Indian (about 6%); other (about 2%).

Principal Religions: Buddhism, Hinduism, Islam, Christianity.

Main Exports: (to Malaysia, U.S., Japan); Rubber, petroleum, tin, manufactured goods.

Main Imports: (from Japan, U.S., Malaysia); Manufactured goods, petroleum.

Currency: Singapore Dollar.

Former Colonial Status: Possession of the British East India Company (1819–1867), British Crown Colony (1867–1958), occupied by the Japanese (1941–1945), internally self–governing (1958–1963).

National Day: August 9, 1965 (Independence Day).

Chief of State: Ong Teng Cheong, President (took office September 1993).

Head of Government: Goh Chok Tong, Prime Minister (1990).

Dominant Political Figure: Lee Kuan Yew, Senior Minister.

National Flag: Divided horizontally, with a white crescent moon and five white stars on a red field at the top and a white bottom.

Per Capita Income: U.S. $20,000.

The small island of Singapore is separated from Johor State at the southern tip of West Malaysia by a narrow strait of water; road and railway bridges provide access to the mainland. Although tropical, the island is highly urbanized. The city occupies the more agreeable part of the island on the southeast coast. Its harbor is naturally a good one, and it lies at the crossroads of Southeast Asia at one end of the Straits of Malacca. This is the best and shortest passage between the Indian Ocean and the South China Sea, and Singapore has been an important naval base and commercial port for 175 years. The busy city has an appearance of modern progress which helps to disguise its basically oriental character without entirely smothering the attractive aspects of Asian culture and tradition.

History: Prior to the arrival of Europeans, Singapore was a small part of the Malay world, inhabited by people of Polynesian, Mongol, Indian and Caucasian mixed ancestry that blended smoothly into the civilizations of Malaya and Indonesia. The Dutch virtually ignored Singapore when they arrived in the 17th century because of their preoccupation with the then superior harbors at Malacca and Penang on the western coast of the Malay Peninsula.

Sir Thomas Stamford Raffles of the British East India Company occupied the island in 1819 after realizing the commercial possibilities of the harbor. It was made a Crown Colony in 1867. In spite of Dutch competition based on neighboring Java and Sumatra, the colony began to achieve the size of a major commercial port. The opening of the Suez Canal in 1869 attracted even heavier traffic from Europe to the Straits of Malacca. At the same time, the rubber and tin resources of Malaya were being developed and needed facilities to reach the world.

This commercial development also re-

Prime Minister Goh Chok Tong

Hon. Lee Kuan Yew

Downtown Singapore

sulted in the migration of many Chinese to the island; they quickly became the majority ethnic group as numbers of workers hired to process rubber and tin were brought from China. Singapore became the principal British stronghold in the region from which they participated in the colonial rivalry underway in Southeast Asia in the late 19th and early 20th centuries. A large British naval base was constructed in the 1920's, equipped with coastal defenses intended to protect it from attack by sea.

Three days after the attack on Pearl Harbor in 1941, Japanese torpedo planes sank the *Prince of Wales* and the *Repulse,* two mammoth British warships which had been dispatched to Singapore. An invasion of Malaya was promptly undertaken by a large Japanese army highly trained in jungle warfare. Malaya fell to the invaders within four weeks and the siege of Singapore began. The British held out for two weeks before the Japanese finally captured Singapore and 60,000 prisoners on February 15, 1942, in one of the worst military defeats ever suffered by Great Britain.

As elsewhere in Southeast Asia, the Japanese mistreated those they had conquered, particularly those of Chinese origin. This behavior was ineffective; the Japanese were ultimately isolated from

Singapore and other holdings in Southeast Asia by United States sea and air action. The British peacefully returned to the island when Japan collapsed in 1945.

The British decided to keep Singapore separate from Malaya, as had been done before the war, to avoid upsetting the rather slim Malay majority on the mainland. Britain retained its bases, but decreased their size as it embarked on a withdrawal from colonies east of the Suez Canal after 1967. It maintained control over Singapore's external relations, but permitted increasing degrees of internal self–government. The government nurtured by the British was faced with serious civil strife in the mid–1950's which was promoted by labor unions and student organizations, both communist controlled, but it was able to maintain order.

After a new constitution had been adopted, the leftist *People's Action Party*, which had some communist members, came to power in an electoral landslide in 1959. The new Prime Minister, Lee Kuan Yew, was able and energetic; he quickly placed his communist supporters and allies in positions of little power and influence. Sensing British and Malayan concern over his election, he made strenuous efforts to create goodwill with them. A widespread and ambitious program of socialistic economic development and social welfare programs was instituted which caused the communists to redouble their efforts to seize control of the government—they feared a possible increase in popularity of the *People's Action Party*.

In local elections held in 1961, the communist–dominated *Barisan Sosialis Party* gained several major victories over the candidates of the *People's Action Party*. This was a major source of concern to Britain and Malaya. Prime Minister Tunku Abdul Rahman of Malaya immediately proposed that Malaya, Singapore and the Borneo territories of Sabah and Sarawak be joined into the Federation of Malaysia. His purpose was twofold: to protect the stability and progress of the entire region and to control the leftist trend in Singapore; his plan was vigorously supported by the British. Had Singapore become a communist state, Malaya would have suffered a serious economic blow, since the island processed and shipped the bulk of the rubber and tin which produced most of Malaya's foreign exchange, as well as posing a political threat. In spite of opposition by the *Barisan Sosialis Party* and by the *Malayan Communist Party*, and in spite of threats of war issued by Indonesia's President Sukarno coupled with opposition from China, the Federation of Malaysia came into existence in 1963. Sukarno immediately declared that Indonesia was in a state of "confrontation" (a sort of undeclared, irregular war) with Malaysia, severing all trade relations. Singapore suffered somewhat from this step, since Indonesia had been one of its most important trading partners, but Indonesia suffered equally, if not more. The economic needs of both gave rise to a widespread smuggling operation which helped to offset the effect of the official boycott.

The union of Singapore with the Federation of Malaysia came to an end in 1965. The Federation may have solved the immediate problems of a communist takeover, but it did not solve the basic antagonism between the Malays and Chinese; this was the greatest internal problem within Malaysia. The Malay–dominated government of the Federation preferred to deal at arms–length with the Chinese–controlled regime on the island rather than add more Chinese to the Federation's population. Lee Kuan Yew energetically tried to extend the activities of the *People's Action Party* to mainland Malaya and to exert greater influence in financial matters. Although the separation of Singapore from the Federation of Malaysia was described as a matter of mutual consent, in reality Singapore was confronted with a demand to withdraw— it had no choice but to do so.

The constitutional framework provides for a single–chamber legislature over which a Speaker presides. In elections held in 1963, the *People's Action Party* elected 39 representatives to 23 from the *Barisan Sosialis Party*. Prime Minister Lee Kuan Yew dominated the political scene in Singapore to the extent that the members of the opposition party angrily stalked out of the Parliament in 1966. Since that time, a few leading members have been held in detention and, in reality, the party has gone underground. The *People's Action Party* won all 58 seats in Parliament in elections in 1968, all 65 seats in 1972 and all 69 in 1976. A new leftist opposition party formed in April 1971 and was successful in electing *one* member in 1981; in 1984 it doubled its holding to two. Lee Kuan Yew began to bring fresh blood into the upper ranks of the *People's Action Party* and the government—including his son, Lee Hsien Loong.

The government was troubled by a series of financial scandals, by concern over ethnic tensions in neighboring Malaysia, by a hostile reaction in Malaysia to a visit to Singapore by Israeli President Chaim Herzog in November 1986 and by some repercussions of its own intolerance of opposition. In 1986, the debates in parliament began to be televised. This gave wide publicity to the speeches of one of the only two opposition members, an articulate ethnic Indian, J.B. Jeyaretnam, who in September was expelled from the body for having allegedly defamed the impartiality of Singapore's judiciary, which in fact is open to question.

The government, which maintains a form of censorship, has tried to punish foreign publications which contain articles it does not like, not by banning them, but by restricting their sale in Singapore below the level of profitability.

Prime Minister Lee, distressed by the materialistic outlook of Singapore's "yuppies," tried to revive Confucianism. Officially it is stated that this is a suitable ideology for Singapore's predominantly Chinese population. He also urged young Chinese professional women, many of whom are well paid, to marry men of the same type. This is a form of eugenics which one wit dubbed "designer genes", calculated to improve inherited qualities. But it has not worked well; many of the working women prefer to stay single and the men tend to want less educated and more submissive wives.

Increasing ethnic tensions between the large Chinese majority and the Malay and Indian minorities, as well as between the ruling *People's Action Party (PAP)* and the opposition, coupled with boredom among the educated population, have continued to be problems. Prime Minister Lee apparently intended at one time to become president with increased powers. The government wants to alter the electoral system so as to reduce the chances of an increase in the opposition contingent in the parliament. In May–June 1987, 22 oppositionists, many of them Catholic, were arrested on the charge of organizing a Marxist conspiracy to subvert the state. There was a loud outcry and nine were released in September. The opposition then became somewhat quieter. Eight of the nine were rearrested in the spring of 1988, after they had repudiated their confessions.

Prime Minister Lee saw Singapore as fragile because of its ethnic diversity and vulnerable because of its small size as compared with its neighbors. Accordingly, he and his colleagues have done whatever they considered necessary for domestic and external security in the face of these threats. The armed forces are large for the size of the country and are impressively modern. The Internal Security Act, inherited from the British, is used by the political police, known as the Internal Security Department, to control dissent, the press, etc. Activities of foreign media in Singapore are also carefully regulated. Electoral districts were gerrymandered prior to the parliamentary election of September 1988, which gave the ruling *People's Action Party* 80 of the 81 seats, in spite of spirited campaigns by numerous opposition politicians. One political opponent of the *PAP* was arrested in 1988 on charges of contacts with a U.S. diplomat, who was expelled for talks with him and other opposition figures; the U.S. expelled a Singaporean diplomat in retaliation.

Lee Kuan Yew, in office since 1959, retired as Prime Minister in November 1990 in favor of his hand–picked successor, Deputy Prime Minister Goh Chok Tong, and was accorded the special title of "Senior Minister."

Politics and Government: Singapore is a parliamentary democracy, similar to the British model. The unicameral legislature is composed of 81 seats. Elections must be held every five years if not sooner. In 1993, Singapore switched to an elected president. The office was revamped to increase the power of the president particularly in the area of government fiscal matters. The new president also has veto power over key positions in the bureaucracy and also has the power to address abuses in matters of internal security, religious extremism and corruption. The prime minister is the head of government and dominant political figure.

The political system has been dominated by the *People's Action Party* since independence. Opposition parties have gained an increasing percentage of the vote but, because of the single member district electoral system these gains have not been reflected in the total number of seats won. Elections have been fair, although the dominant party has been accused of using the law to make it difficult for an opposition to function. The press is free to print news but does not criticize the government editorially.

The Goh Chok Tong government (since 1990) has followed the path of the previous government under Prime Minister Lee Kuan Yew. The overriding commitment is to economic prosperity. To this end, the government is willing to do whatever is necessary to provide a safe, stable political environment. As a result of the government's almost puritanical attitude, Singapore is one of the safest and cleanest places in the world. Economic prosperity, however, has not been sufficient to keep the country's best and brightest at home. Significant numbers of highly educated young citizens have left the country in search of greater political freedom. While some have returned, the fact that prosperity alone is not sufficient should give the government cause to ponder how much authoritarianism is appropriate for a modern, well educated society.

In late 1993 Ong Teng Cheong assumed the revamped and enhanced position of president after receiving 58.7% of the vote in the August 29 election. The election was important because it made it clear that the "old guard" of the *People's Action Party* (PAP) still had a firm hand on the affairs of state. Both the president–elect and his opponent, Accountant General Chua Kim Yeow, were establishment candidates. Ong was a former deputy prime minister and PAP member. Two other individuals, J. B. Jeyaretnum and Tan Soo Phuan, both *Workers Party* members, had their candidacies rejected by the Presidential Election Committee. Jeyaretnum was an outspoken opposition politician who was at odds with Lee Kuan Yew for many years.

Just as the opposition was gaining credibility with the public it fell on hard times. The *Singapore Democratic Party's* founder, Chiam See Tong, was ousted by the Central Executive Committee of the party. The party won three of four opposition seats in the 1991 national elections. However, with Chiam's resignation the party was split at the end of the year.

In 1994, the Goh Chok Tong government continued to take a hard line stance against anyone who criticized the government of Singapore or its policies. It also took steps to defend the "Asian values" which are supposedly what distinguishes Singapore from the West,

Rush hour in Singapore

World Bank photo

135

A young boy in Singapore

and responsible for the success of the Asian economies. In line with the latter, the government moved to encourage the learning of Mandarin Chinese and took steps to strengthen the family. Medical benefits were denied to families of female civil servants so as to preserve "patriarchy." Adult children are now legally responsible for their parents well-being, and single mothers have been denied the right to buy subsidized housing.

In November, Christopher Lingle, an American academic teaching at the National University of Singapore (NUS), and four *International Herald Tribune* employees, were charged with criminal defamation for writing and printing an article in that influential daily newspaper, which referred to intolerant Asian regimes and questioned the independence of their judiciaries. Lingle resigned his position. In December, a government letter was published in the *Straits Times* responding to a number of letters questioning the restrictive policy on freedom of speech. Freer expression was to be expanded pragmatically. The public was reassured that over the next two decades

the society would become more open. The question is can the people of Singapore wait that long? Earlier, in May, the government administered four lashes of the cane to Michael Fay, an 18–year–old who admitted to charges of spray–painting 40 cars and pelting them with eggs. Fay later denied his guilt. The U.S. Trade Representative, playing to the American media, suggested that Singapore should not be allowed to be the venue for the first World Trade Organization meeting in 1995. Singapore officials pointedly compared conditions in their country with those in New York City. Most Americans thought that caning was not a bad idea.

In spite of "Asian values," juvenile crime in Singapore has increased 27% over the last two years. Divorce rates are also up. Finally, the government of Singapore did not win a vote of confidence when it proposed raising the salaries of government ministers into the stratosphere. The justification was that it has become impossible to recruit the best and the brightest into government service. The current salary for the prime minister is $780,000.

At the beginning of July 1995, Prime Minister Goh Chok Tong announced his intention to begin a search for the next generation of leaders. Many senior ministers were expected to leave their posts over the next several years. On January 20, 1996, former Prime Minister, Lee Kuan Yew, 72, underwent heart surgery to open a clogged artery. In March, a second operation was necessary. When Senior Minister Lee finally retires from politics, his departure from the political arena will almost certainly usher in a period of debate about the future course of the island mini–state. National elections, which should be held this year, could be especially interesting if Singaporeans sense an enhanced opportunity for change.

The Lingle case was settled in July 1995, when the *Tribune*, which printed the Lingle letter, was ordered to pay Singapore's three top leaders a total of $950,000. But the decision did not dampen the criticism. In October, Francis Seow, a Singapore lawyer, spoke at Williams College in Massachusetts and accused the Singapore judiciary of bending over backwards to please the government and Lee Kuan Yew. The *Singapore Democratic Party* supported his remarks. Mr. Lee tried to censure the party in the national parliament.

Foreign and Defense Policy: Singapore, as an independent mini–state, cannot hope to survive without friends. For years the government accepted the analogy of the poison shrimp which might be swallowed up but at great risk. In recent years, however, the strategy has been to make the country so valuable to the region that no one would wish its booming economy destroyed because of the repercussions which would be felt throughout the area. This strategy has succeeded. Singapore is one of the world's busiest ports and is the center of economic activity in Southeast Asia. Singapore intends to keep its value high by always being the best.

In 1994, Singapore continued to champion free trade and greater economic cooperation throughout the ASEAN region. In October Singapore was the venue for the third Europe–East Asia summit the focus of which was to find ways to increase trade and investment between the two continents.

Singapore was also the site for the Five Power Defense Arrangement (FPDA) meeting in September. Members Singapore, Malaysia, Australia, New Zealand, and Great Britain, agreed to measures to improve defense capabilities for the FPDA. Singapore also hosted the FPDA annual naval exercise, "Star Fish."

In March and April 1995 relations with the Philippines were strained over the hanging of a Philippine citizen, Flor Contemplacion, for the murder of another Filipino. The two countries disagreed over the facts surrounding the case. President Ramos and Prime Minister Goh agreed that bi–lateral relations should not be damaged. Ramos in particular was under some pressure to defend the national honor. He requested that the Singapore ambassador be recalled from Manila. Singapore, in the interest of good relations, agreed. By July, relations were normalized.

Singapore also came to an agreement with Malaysia on their international sea boundary. A flap over a Malaysian tariff on Singapore petro–chemicals was also put to rest. In early 1996, Singapore was working with the government of Brunei on a possible major modernization plan for the latter's defense forces.

Culture: Singapore's culture is centered around the industry of a bustling port and upon the fact that this is a city of largely Chinese descent in the middle of Southeast Asia. The colonial British had provided a thin veneer during the time they were dominant which has rapidly diminished to the point of being a fading memory. The island has acquired a genuinely cosmopolitan atmosphere imported from the four corners of the earth because of its status as a major international port which lies at the crossroads of Asia.

Economy: Singapore is heavily dependent on foreign trade and investment which it is doing its best to promote. There has been considerable industrial development, heavy as well as light, in recent years. Overcrowded, Singapore nevertheless has extensive welfare and public housing programs, and in fact has one of the higher living standards in Asia.

Since the mid–1980s the economy has been growing at a rate of about 8% a year. In 1988, because of its high level of development and its various contributions to the U.S.'s trade imbalance, and much to its annoyance, Singapore lost its preferential tariff status under the U.S.'s Generalized System of Preferences (GSP).

In 1994, the Singapore economy again grew by 10%. Wages increased by over 9% while inflation was 3.6%. It has the 16th highest annual per capita GDP in the world at $20,000. Singapore is the fastest growing middle–income country in the world.

Economic growth surpassed 9% for 1995. Per capita income was over $22,000—Singapore was second in competitiveness to the United States. However, success can bring problems. A strong currency could weaken exports. The island currently has a glut of empty retail spaces and suffers from very high rents. Wages are high and rising because labor is chronically short. Prices are rising. Singapore is a beautiful country. But, do your shopping in Kuala Lumpur.

The Future: Singapore's own government, or rather the mentality of its officials, may be the only problem on the horizon facing the country. The success of Singapore has less to do with distinct values than it does with manageable size and an optimum location. Educated youth already find the tradeoff between economic prosperity and restricted political and social freedom difficult. This will only become intensified over time. Singapore does indeed have many things which America has lost. However, a lighter touch at the helm of the ship of state will not destroy these advantages but may insure their survival.

Look for the political leadership to blink if Mr. Lee decides to leave the political arena in 1996 or 1997, and look for the emergence of a stronger political opposition.

Traffic system at rush hours to reduce congestion

World Bank Photo

The Kingdom of Thailand (before 1935 known as Siam)

Bustling traffic in Chiang Mai

Area: 198,455 sq. mi. (514,820 sq. mi., more than twice the size of Oregon).

Population: Pop. 55 million (estimated).

Capital City: Bangkok (Pop. 5 million, estimated).

Climate: Tropically hot with a wet monsoon season (May–October), dry and increasingly hot (November–April).

Neighboring Countries: Malaysia (South); Burma (Northeast); Laos (Northwest); Cambodia (West).

Official Language: Thai.

Other Principal Tongues: Thai (about 75%); Chinese (about 14%); other (about 11%).

Ethnic Background: Thai (about 75%); Chinese (about 14%); Malay (about 4%); inland tribal groups (about 2%); Cambodian refugees (about 2%); other (about 3%).

Principal Religions: Buddhism, Islam.

Main Exports: (to Japan, U.S., Singapore); Rice, sugar, corn, rubber, tin, timber.

Main Imports: (from Japan, U.S., Saudi Arabia); Machinery and transport equipment, petroleum, chemicals, fertilizer.

Currency: Baht.

Former Political Status: Siam avoided becoming a European colony by modernization in the 19th–20th centuries; it was a nominal ally of Japan during World War II.

National Day: December 10th (Constitution Day).

Chief of State: His Majesty King Bhumibol Adulyadej (b. 1927).

Head of Government: Banharn Silpa–Archa, Prime Minister (since July 1995).

National Flag: Five horizontal stripes from top to bottom; red, white, blue (wider than the others), white and red.

Per Capita Income: U.S. $1,440.

The broad central plain of Thailand, through which flows the Chao Phraya River, is the most fertile and productive area of the country and contains the principal cities, including Bangkok. Viewed from the foothills which are found on the western edge of the plain, the land resembles an almost endless window with countless "panes of glass" when the precisely divided rice paddies are flooded with water.

The North and Northwest are more mountainous, and are covered with jungles containing timber and mineral resources. Valuable teak wood is still brought from the jungle on the tusks of the Asian elephant. The northeast region is dominated by the arid Korat Plateau. Ample rainfall occurs in the plateau, but it is not absorbed by the sandstone soil— it quickly collects into streams and rivers and runs to the sea instead of enriching

138

the land. More people live here than can be supported by the limited agriculture that is possible.

The southern region consists of the narrow Kra Isthmus which is hot and oppressively humid, and the coastal belt, where quantities of rubber are produced by Thailand's Malay minority.

History: People of Thai origin, both civilized and primitive, today not only inhabit Thailand but also live in the adjacent regions of all of Thailand's neighbors with the exception of Malaysia. The original home of these people was in southwest China, where they were ruled by a highly organized kingdom in the 7th century A.D. The pressure of the Chinese and later the Mongols caused a migration of the Thais southward; they founded a state in what is now northern Thailand.

During the following centuries of slow expansion they were able to crush the Khmer Empire in neighboring Cambodia. In the 16th century, Siam, as it was then

called, was conquered by the Burmese. Apart from sporadic contact by French merchants, the Europeans did not enter the area during the centuries of exploration and colonization.

There was another Burmese invasion in 1767, but shortly thereafter Burma was invaded by the *Manchu* empire of China, enabling the Siamese to expel their conquerors. The present reigning dynasty came to power in 1782 and moved the capital city to the more secure location of Bangkok; Siam again emerged quickly as a strong state. This new dynasty soon came into conflict with Vietnam, ruled by the Annamese monarchs of Hue, over control of Laos and Cambodia.

Early in the 19th century, Siam began to have more extensive contacts, commercial and otherwise, with France and with the United States. The British gradually established control over Burma and the French asserted their power over Vietnam. Laos and Cambodia had been tributary states of Siam, but the French

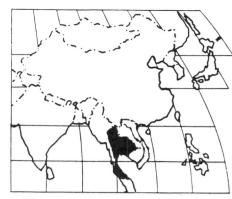

were ultimately able to combine them with Vietnam in their colony of Indochina. Thus, Siam was surrounded by the British on the West, the French on the east and the *Manchu* empire of China on the north.

Siam avoided becoming a European colony by strengthening itself through an increasing degree of modernization, actively pursued by its kings in the last half of the 19th century. Phra Maha Chulalongkorn, King from 1868 to 1910, gained fame not only by abolishing Siam's feudal system, modernizing the government and army and introducing such conveniences as the telegraph and railroad; he paid an extended visit to the European capitals. He was the son of the monarch described in the book *Anna and the King of Siam* and in the musical play *The King and I.*

Following a crisis promoted by the French, it was ultimately agreed by Britain and France that Laos would become French, but Siam would remain independent. There were some later treaties in 1904–1907 which adjusted the borders with Laos and Cambodia; under these, regions were traded back and forth between France and Siam. In order to keep other colonial powers out of Siam, France and Britain established "spheres of influence"—the French east of the Chao Phraya River and the British west of the river. As a result of its somewhat limited, but significant modernization program, and the fact that it escaped being a colony of a European power, Thailand today lacks the sense of inferiority and resentment toward the industrialized nations that many people feel in the countries of former colonial Asia.

After World War I there was a period of extravagant spending by the royal government, which was followed by a world-wide economic depression. This created tensions and discontent within Thailand and gave rise to intense political activity. The result was a bloodless overthrow of the monarchy in 1932 by a combination of civilian politicians and military leaders. The two groups cooperated in the adoption of a constitution which limited the power of the king and established a parliamentary form of government. The first

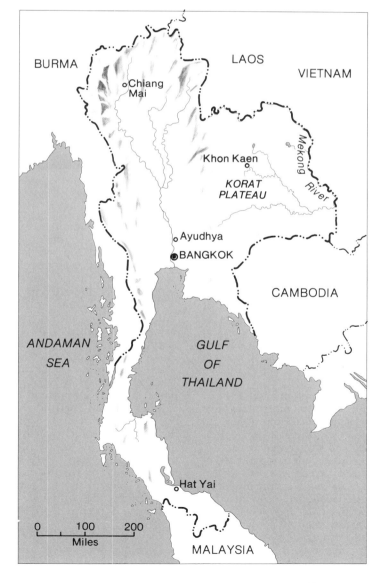

The Grand Palace, Bangkok

Prime Minister was a brilliant lawyer named Pridi Panomyong.

The king, dissatisfied with this system, abdicated in 1935, and was succeeded by his ten–year–old nephew and a regency council. This and other unsettling conditions, including the increased power of Japan in Asia, led to the overthrow of Pridi by Marshal Pibul Songgram. In theory the country continued to be governed by a coalition consisting of the Prime Minister, the military and Luang Pradit, the foreign minister. As the military acquired increasing political power, they displayed their nationalism by such means as legislation aimed at curbing the role of the Chinese commercial community and changing the nation's name from Siam to Thailand, meaning "Land of the Free."

Three weeks after the bombing of Pearl Harbor by the Japanese, Thailand signed a treaty of alliance with Japan; war was declared on the United States and Great Britain on January 25, 1942. With the support of Japanese troops, Thailand compelled the French to cede some bor-

der territories in Laos and Cambodia. The four southern states of Thailand, which had been given to the British in Malaya at the turn of the century, were returned by the Japanese after they had seized the British colony of Burma.

As the Pacific war began to turn against Japan, the adaptable Thais began to change sides. An anti–Japanese guerrilla movement arose, and American military intelligence officers were able to operate almost openly in Bangkok during the last months of the war.

Pibul resigned as premier in 1944 in favor of Pridi, who was more acceptable to the increasingly victorious Allies. At the end of the war, Britain took the position that Thailand was an enemy country and compelled payment of reparations in the form of rice, which was sent to Malaya. The U.S., taking the more moderate position that Thailand had been forced to cooperate with Japan, was able to persuade the British to adopt a similar policy. Thailand was forced to surrender the territories it had gained during the war, however.

Thailand was admitted to the UN in 1946 and established diplomatic relations with Nationalist China—a step that it had avoided in order to be freer to deal with its citizens of Chinese birth and ancestry without external interference.

The king died from a gunshot wound at the hands of an assassin in 1946; Pridi, accused of having played a part in the slaying, was deposed and later fled to China and then to Paris, where he lived as a political exile until his death in 1983. The army, still led by Pibul, again seized power. Initially it appeared uncertain as to what position Thailand would take in the Korean war, but when it took part on the UN side, it soon began to receive U.S. military aid. This further strengthened the political position of the army in domestic affairs, making the fairly frequent *coups* in Bangkok more difficult, but usually bloodier. Nevertheless, changes of government occurred without massive violence.

The war in Vietnam and French Indochina had definite effects on Thailand. Communist China began to set up orga-

140

nizations on Chinese soil designed apparently for subversion of Thailand in 1953, causing alarm within the Thai government. An appeal to the UN was unsuccessful because of a Soviet veto.

Nehru, the pacifist and neutralist leader of India, had advised other nations of Southeast Asia to adopt a policy of friendly gestures toward the communist countries. Burma had accepted this position, but Thailand decided instead to ally itself with the United States. SEATO, supposedly similar to the NATO alliance in Europe, was specifically intended to protect Thailand from attack or subversive pressure from communist China or North Vietnam.

Pibul began to permit freer discussion of political issues which resulted in some disorder and actually began to encourage a growth of neutralism. He was overthrown in 1958 by Marshal Sarit, who kept Thailand firmly in an anti–communist posture. The country had an orderly, stable and not too oppressive government. As was true in so many nations, the military leader was able to accumulate a vast private fortune through corruption.

Communist gains in Laos between 1960 and 1962 created some uneasiness in Thailand, which was dispelled when the U.S. pledged direct assistance in the event SEATO failed to act—a French veto had become a distinct possibility after the withdrawal of French forces from Indochina.

Less effective military leadership continued after 1963 under subsequent leaders. Reliance was placed upon the ability of the popular royal family to maintain the unity of the Thai people, as well as on an increased degree of official respect shown for Buddhism and its various organizations. However, communist–inspired unrest in the poverty–stricken northeast region became more serious. Although the government treated this as a genuine threat, perhaps partly to obtain additional American aid, it has been difficult to assess the exact extent of the problem. It was directed from both communist China and Vietnam—the Chinese appeared to have greater influence, however. But insurgency in the region declined after 1968; at the same time it became more serious among the Meo tribesmen in the North.

After the U.S. assumed the burden of the Vietnam war, starting in 1965, Thailand permitted the Americans to use air bases within the country from which to attack North Vietnam and the Viet Cong; later the bases began to be used for B–52 bombers capable of carrying atomic and hydrogen bombs, which were not used. In addition, Thailand sent a limited number of troops to fight in Vietnam and Laos; it participated in the struggle in a number of other ways. The communist reaction was predictable—as Thailand in-

creased its assistance to the U.S. and South Vietnam, the communists stepped up their subversive pressure and guerrilla activities within the country. An increased U.S. military buildup in Thailand was paralleled by a greater flow of U.S. aid to the Thai armed forces. After 1973, however, the signing of an armistice for South Vietnam led to the withdrawal of the U.S. Air Force presence from Thailand in 1976 at Thai insistence.

After the National Assembly was dissolved in 1968, there was no representative body in Thailand. After a long delay, a constitution was drafted by a Constituent Assembly and promulgated by the King in mid–1968. Elections in 1969 gave the *United Thai People's Party*, the government party, a total of 75 seats, the *Democratic Party* 57 seats, five small parties a total of 15 seats and independents 72. The Senate was appointed by the government. But, proclaiming an emergency because of domestic criticism of the government and the uncertainty of developments in Southeast Asia, the military suspended the parliament and reshuffled the cabinet. In 1972 a new constitution was proclaimed under which 299 members of a National Assembly were all

appointed by "the government." The "government" (i.e. the Army) was toppled in late 1973 by student demonstrations that had the support of the King and at least part of the Army itself. A civilian government was ushered in, committed to greater freedom and reform.

Recent History: An Evolving Form of Governance

Phase one of the evolution process lasted from 1932 to 1973. The first significant step toward democracy occurred in 1932, with the establishment of a constitution providing for a parliamentary form of government. This constitution did not have the support of the King nor apparently the military. The government of Prime Minister Pridi Panomyong was shortlived and was followed by a succession of military dominated regimes: Marshal Pibul Songgram, 1935–1958; Marshal Sarit Thanarat, 1958–1963; Marshal Thanom Kittikachorn, 1963–1971. After two years of martial law a student–led uprising overthrew the government.

There are undoubtedly numerous explanations as to why the transition to democracy went so poorly. Socio–cultural

Geese raised on a poultry farm south of Bangkok

141

The Royal Family of Thailand

explanations should not be dismissed. However, the most obvious explanation is that while civilian–led institutions were not yet ready for the burden of modern government, the military was. The active role of the military in the political development process is common in the history of many emerging third–world states. In many of these states, the military was often and sometimes the only modern organization with institutionalized mechanisms for administration, planning and leading. Civilian institutions such as political parties often lagged far behind.

The role of the military in Thailand was also affected by the geo–political reality in which the country found itself from the 1930's on. Conflicts which threatened the country and/or involved Thai military participation, e.g. World War II, the Korean war, the Vietnam war, and domestic insurgency, strengthened the institution's role within Thailand. Events such as these accelerated the development of the military. Civilian alternatives for governance may have existed but they did not have the organizational capacity, nor the public support necessary to propel them into power.

Phase two began in 1973. The virtual monopoly of political power formerly enjoyed by the army gave way to an informal power sharing arrangement between the army and civilian politicians and officials. Army leadership has divided between those willing to work with civilians and those who are not. Rule has shifted between civilian and military–dominated governments, with and without ex–generals in the premiership, and outright military rule. Corruption has been commonplace. One cannot detect any significant change in the most recent events. However, as described in the next section, a "window of opportunity" may now exist for movement.

The civilian government of Chatichai Choonhavan was brought down because of corruption charges by the military in a 1991 coup. Rule shifted to the military dominated *National Peacekeeping Council*. In March 1992, a three party coalition favored by the Council won control of the government with 53% of the seats in the lower house of parliament. The *NPC* appointed all 270 members of the upper house with most having military backgrounds or connections.

When agreement could not be achieved on a new prime minister, the leader of the "junta," General Suchinda Kraprayoon, a key figure in the coup, stepped into the post. Public demonstrations against Suchinda led to severe repression by the Thai military. The level of violence against the civilian population was unparalleled in the constitutional period (since 1932). The King stepped in to calm the crisis. On May 20, Suchinda appeared on national television kneeling before King Bhumibol. He was ordered to settle the crisis peacefully. After a short period of "caretaker" government, new elections were held on September 13, 1992. Chuan Leekpai was chosen as prime minister. The constitution now required that the prime minister be chosen from the lower house of parliament. The government was ruled by a five party coalition. This made it difficult to proceed with the legislative agenda which centered on constitutional reform.

The Political System: Thailand is classified as a constitutional monarchy. The current constitution dates to December 1991; amendments were passed in January 1995. Some of the bigger changes include the following: the voting age for national elections is lowered to 18 years, parliament was enlarged by 20 MP's to maintain a ratio of 1:150,000 for representatives, and the number of senators will be reduced from three–fourths to two–thirds the size of the lower house. The judicial branch is headed by the Supreme Court (*Sarndika*).

The prime minister functions with a cabinet, the Council of Ministers. The House of Representatives (*Rathasatha*) is elected. The Senate (*Vuthisatha*) in the past was chosen through the executive. In practice, this meant that the military either chose or passed on the Senate. The present Senate was chosen by the *National Peacekeeping Council* described before. If civilian rule continues uninterrupted, a new Senate will be chosen in 1996, possibly without military input.

As noted above, Thailand has struggled to evolve a modern workable political system since 1932. The first four decades of the constitutional period were dominated largely by the military. Civilian led governments have become more prevalent since the early 1970s.

The Thai political system has also suffered from a lack of a legitimate means for dealing with the succession of power. This explains the large number of coups which have occurred. The military has not been willing to leave policy decisions to the civilian sector. To some extent their concerns have been justified. Thai politics has been and continues to be highly personalized with a significant amount of corruption. Unfortunately, the military has often exhibited these same qualities. Even the most recent elections have produced charges of massive vote buying. Leaders of political movements have also "bought" high ranking figures from other

parties. Parties are often short–lived and are not consistently identified with a specific ideology. Thus, the political arena is very fluid and unstable. This is not the kind of environment in which a strong democratic form of government is likely to take hold.

The response of the Thai people to the events and tragedy of May 1992 described previously may indicate significant change for the Thai political system. Even before May 1992, the middle class was becoming weary of the military in politics. After that, it would not have been possible for the military to shoulder the responsibility of governing. In sum, for the near term, there exists a window of opportunity for civilian government to prove its worth in Thailand.

In order for civilian government to work, several things must take place. First, corruption must be curtailed. As Thailand's educated middle class grows, this segment of society, like elements of the military, will no longer accept the old way of doing things. The political parties and the elites who run them must find another way to advance their agendas if they are to survive. Secondly, national politics must be expanded beyond Bangkok to all parts of the country. Mass

political participation is essential to a well–run political system. Should the civilian politicians be unable to rise to the occasion, the military will, sooner or later, find a reason to intervene once more. However, this type of solution of national problems only prevents rationalization of the political process which, in the end, must occur if Thailand is to evolve into a modern state, capable of addressing the needs of a rapidly changing society.

In May 1995, Prime Minister Chuan Leekpai was forced to dissolve parliament when the Palang Dharma party pulled out of the ruling five party coalition. Elections took place on July 2. The Prime Minister's coalition lost. However, he now holds the record for the longest serving elected prime minister.

The election was an example of classic Thai politics in which enormous sums of money were spent to buy votes especially in rural areas of the country. Major issues centered on a land–reform scandal in which an MP's husband received choice land in southern Thailand as part of the reform, the government's inability to move quickly in the area of mass transit, and unbelievable traffic problems in Bangkok.

An informally dressed King Bhumibol speaks with villagers in northern Thailand

143

Houses in the vicinity of Bangkok

Largely because of the frustration of the urban electorate, rural voters elected the Chart Thai party's Banharn Silpa–Archa as prime minister. The Banharn government was built around a seven party coalition led by his party, Chart Thai, and the Palang Dharma which defected from Chuan's coalition prior to the election. The coalition won 169 seats in the House of Representatives. The opposition, consisting of the Democrat Party (DP), Chart Pattana, Solidarity and Seritham, holds 161 seats.

The new government came under fire almost immediately for a kickback scheme involving the Prime Minister's party and a Swedish submarine manufacturer, and for protecting a minister involved in vote–buying. However, even the opposition was in no hurry to try and oust the new government. There seemed to be a recognition that for the sake of stability and the future of democracy, the government should survive. No one wanted to create a situation which might encourage the military to re–enter politics, something high–ranking military officials told this writer was not likely.

But in late August a military radio broadcast criticizing the government for its inability to manage the economy raised concerns in Bangkok and abroad. A disagreement over military promotions

between the Minister of Defense and the Army Commanding General, Wimol Wongwanich, worsened civil–military relations. To make things worse, on August 31, the King criticized the government for the traffic chaos in Bangkok. Others feel that the only way to prevent military intervention is to take drastic action. One such group is the "Democratic Power for Political Reform."

The Banharn government was still in power in mid–1996. However, with a cabinet short on talented technocrats, and with several ministers having questionable backgrounds, the prime minister does not have a strong hand to play. What is more, the prospects for additional political/constitutional reform seem to have disappeared. Chavalit Yougchaiyudh, the Minister of Defense, may be the one member of the government whose star has risen. He successfully handled the disagreement with the military over promotions. The end result is that the top five positions in the military are now held by individuals from different cliques. "Class 5" graduates had been in charge previously. This dispersion of power may make it more difficult for the military to re–enter the political arena, should it decide to do so.

As for the fate of the Banharn government, it can only be hoped that when it

falls, it will be replaced by a civilian alternative.

Foreign Policy: Thailand's foreign relations are driven by its geographic location and pragmatism. It has a fascinating history of keeping enemies at bay through diplomatic and other means which generally have not involved the direct use of force. The country's location means that Bangkok in some ways pays more attention to Burma and the Indo–China states, Laos, Cambodia and Vietnam, than to its long–standing ASEAN partners. China too is important. Thai officials profess not to be worried about China's growing military might. However, there is concern over the potential for large Chinese migration into the country and possible impact from a flood of cheap products from the north which could undercut sectors of the Thai economy. These concerns are long term and unpublicized but they are real.

Nevertheless, rather than shut China out, Thailand wants to see relations between the two countries expand. Because of its well integrated overseas Chinese community which dominates the business sector, Thai officials and businessmen feel they have an advantage over other Southeast Asian states in opening up new economic links with China, and that they can even provide a link for the other ASEAN states to the "middle kingdom." In 1995, the huge explosion in the study of Mandarin was welcomed in Bangkok.

The defeat of the Karen rebels in Burma in January 1995, sent thousands of refugees across the Thai border and altered relations between the two countries. The Burmese believed the Thais were aiding the Karens. Bangkok was upset because of Burmese military raids on refugee camps inside Thai territory. In March, Burmese officials closed a major border crossing at Mae Sod which resulted in a significant economic loss for businesses on the Thai side of the line. In August, Thai fisherman killed six Burmese fisherman off the southern coast of Thailand. This resulted in another border closing. A visit to Rangoon by the Thai Defense minister in September may have eased tensions. However, additional fence mending needs to take place. Relations with Cambodia continued to be less than ideal in 1995.

High ranking Thai officials, civilian and military, deny that the country's current policy is to aid the Khmer Rouge. It is quite likely that individual civilians and military officers have been involved in aiding the Khmer Rouge for monetary reward. Whether one accepts Bangkok's position or not, it should be understood that Thailand has legitimate security concerns regarding its eastern border. Bangkok does not believe that the dual government arrangement in Phnom Penh can last indefinitely. And, the stronger of Cambodia's two prime ministers, Hun Sen, is probably not a favorite in Bangkok. Hun Sen was the head of the government during the Vietnamese occupation.

It is also quite clear from conversations with officials in Bangkok that the government does not view the Khmer Rouge with the same contempt as many countries do. This may be a matter of pragmatism rather than conviction.

In March, Cambodian military killed two Thai para–military personnel in Thailand. This issue was diffused when the Cambodian Foreign Minister, Ung Uot visited Bangkok. This was followed up in May 1995, with the first Thai–Cambodian Joint (border) Commission meeting in Phnom Penh. Cambodia also imposed a ban on logging in May causing several Thai operations to pull out. (The Thais have long since cut down the last tree of any size in their own country.) Other Thai concerns left Cambodia for business reasons.

In May, Thai and Vietnamese navy patrols exchanged gunfire in a territory off the Thai coast but also claimed by the Vietnamese. Thai fishing boats and crews were taken by the Vietnamese. It is worth noting that Burma and Malaysia have also seized Thai fishing boats. The Thai–Vietnamese event was played down owing to the fact that Vietnam was in the process of moving toward "observer" status in ASEAN, the Association of Southeast Asian Nations, of which Thailand is a founding member. Thailand and Vietnam have been in negotiations over their disputed exclusive economic zones (EEZ). As resources become more scarce in the sea, expect such incidents to increase.

For 1995, Thailand's foreign relations produced both success and difficulty. The move toward China holds promise for the future. The goal of turning Indo–China and Burma into economic markets will require more attention.

Culture: Shortly after their arrival in Southeast Asia the Thai were converted to the southern school of Buddhism, which came from the island of Sri Lanka. The numerous colorful festivals and the participating monks almost completely dominate the traditions of the people. Thai architecture is unique and is as extremely colorful and elaborate as the clothing, dancing and sports typical in the Chao Phraya River Valley. Although the Thai are generally fun–loving and light–hearted, they are also quite capable of violence—their boxing matches, for example, are usually quite bloody and brutal affairs. The customs and traditions of the larger cities and Bangkok have been modified somewhat by increased contacts with western nations, particularly with U.S. personnel. A Thai once remarked, "The Americans are good for our economy but bad for our culture." This undoubtedly is true from the point of view of the people who cherish their individuality and distinctive culture.

Economy: In recent years the Thai economy has been among the fastest growing in the East Asia region. If the economy continues to grow at its present rate, the country could well become the "fifth Tiger" joining Taiwan, Hong Kong, Singapore and South Korea. The country does face some serious problems with its natural resources and the environment. Because so much of the country's timber has been cut, erosion is rampant. The quality of the soil is being negatively effected, and flooding is common. And, in the first half of the 1990's, it appeared that the infrastructure of the country was unable to keep pace with the rapidly growing economy.

While the environment remains a critical problem and will be for decades to come, there is now visible evidence of government efforts. One can now see miles of newly planted trees along major highways. Most impressive is the government policy with regard to industrial development. New factories are being located outside the Bangkok area in industrial parks. Each is required to have its own waste water treatment plant. The water coming out of these plants today is far cleaner than the water taken in for use by the industries. There are over 100 such parks and more are being developed. In addition to the environmental impact, there should also be an equally important impact on the distribution of income throughout the country as better paying jobs move out of the capital to different regions of the country. Sixty percent of the labor force is still in agriculture, while the sector only produces 12% of the national GDP. The need for new opportunities is evident.

Infrastructure development is moving ahead. Parts of the Bangkok expressway are now open, and it is now possible to get from one part of the city to another without planning an all day excursion.

Inflation rose 5.8% in 1995 compared to 5% in 1994. Gross Domestic Product grew by 8.6%. One major problem is that Thais are spending too much and saving too little. The savings rate of 34% of GDP looks very good but is sustained by corporations and the government. The savings rate for individuals for 1995 was 7.3% of GDP, compared with 15% back in 1989. The average citizen has gone on a buying spree which is running up imports, increasing them by 28.4% to $675 billion in 1995. The merchandise deficit for 1995 was approximately $13.4 billion. The current account continues to look

Sculptured topiary elephants on the grounds of the Royal Summer Palace.

Courtesy: Marilynn and Mark Swenson

Carving teak furniture, one of Chiang Mai's cottage industries.

Courtesy: Marilynn and Mark Swenson

good but only because of foreign investment in the Thai stock market.

The good news is that Thailand continues to rack up impressive growth figures. Don't expect the bubble to burst in 1996.

The Future: A basic question which Thailand must decide is what is to be the role of the Thai military in the future of the country. Military interference in Thai politics has become progressively more heavy–handed. Thailand's beloved king stepped in 1992 to calm the waters, but the fabric of Thai society was damaged. While the economy propels the country toward NIC status (Newly Industrialized Country) the gap between the rich and the poor, urban and rural, is growing even though it should be closing. Many people are getting rich while others are working hard for almost nothing.

In early 1994 an ominous cloud appeared on the horizon. A report by an international organization revealed that Thailand now has the fastest growing AIDS population in all of Asia. In spite of a very successful birth control program a number of years ago, there has been little public education about AIDS. Figures for young women especially in northern Thailand are very high. In Bangkok, perhaps 50% of the prostitute community is infected. To make matters worse, a new more powerful strain of AIDS was discovered in Thailand in 1995.

Thailand still is a land of great potential. The Banharn government will probably be short lived. If 1996 passes without military intervention, real progress will have been achieved toward the creation of a stable democracy. Right now, the odds are about 60/40 in favor of continued civilian rule and improving.

Boats on the Chao Phya River

The Socialist Republic of Vietnam

Secondary school students being instructed in computer techniques.

Vietnam

Area: 128,190 sq. mi. (329,707 sq. km., about 1/3 smaller than California).

Population: 71,8000,000 (1993 est.).

Capital City: Hanoi (Pop. 2.5 million, estimated).

Climate: Subtropical, with cooler weather in the higher elevations. The Mekong Delta area is hot and humid.

Neighboring Countries: China (North); Laos and Cambodia (West).

Official Language: Vietnamese.

Other Principal Tongues: French, Chinese.

Ethnic Background: Vietnamese (about 85%); Thai, Cambodian, Lao, Chinese tribesmen (about 15%).

Principal Religions: Buddhism, Taoism, Confucianism, subdivided into many sects; Roman Catholic Christianity is a strong element in the South; animism, Islam and Protestant Christianity.

Main Exports: (to Japan, Hong Kong, Malaysia, Thailand, Singapore, and Indonesia, principally); Agricultural products, coal, minerals and oil.

Main Imports: (Japan, Hong Kong, Indonesia, and Singapore); steel products, railroad equipment, chemicals, medicines.

Currency: Dong.

Former Colonial Status: French dependency (1883–1954); occupied by the Japanese (1942–1945); in revolt (1945–1954); civil war (1954–1973).

National Day: July 21, 1954. The government recognizes September 2, 1945 when independence from the French was declared and the *Democratic Republic of Vietnam* was proclaimed.

Chief of State: Le Duc Anh, President (since October 1992). Pronounced Lay Duke An.

Head of Government: Vo Van Kiet, Prime Minister (Since August 1991). Pronounced Voh Van Key-yet.

Chairman, Communist Party: This post has been vacant since the death of Ho Chi Minh in 1969.

General Secretary, Communist Party: Do Muoi. Pronounced Doe Moy.

National Flag: A red field with a five pointed yellow star in the center.

Per Capita Income: US$215.

The map of Vietnam is shaped like a dumbbell. The northern "bell" is an area formerly known as Tonkin—it is quite mountainous, with peaks as high as 10,315 feet close to the southern Chinese border. The mountains gradually diminish in height as they approach the plains and river deltas closest to the Gulf of Tonkin.

The Red River originates in the lofty plateaus of the Chinese province of Yunnan, some 8,000 feet above sea level, and forms the border with China for a distance of about thirty miles. When it enters northern Vietnam it is 260 feet above sea level, descending through a narrow gorge until it widens; after being joined with the River Claire it meanders 93 miles to the sea, flowing in a shifting, irregular course that is 140 miles of curving and twisting water.

The two principal cities of northern Vietnam, Hanoi and Haiphong, are situated on the river and flooded by its waters during the wet season each year—waters which are colored red by the silt washing to the sea from the highlands. It is in this river delta region that the food of northern Vietnam is produced by peasants laboring in the fields with limited tools used by their forebears.

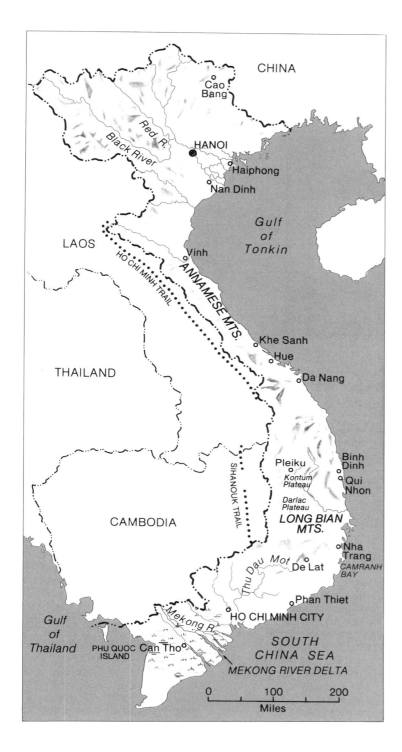

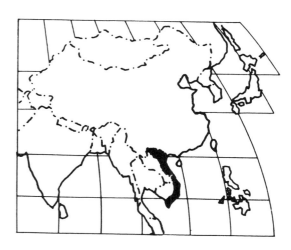

even further upriver during the wet months each year.

Intensive agriculture, dominated by rice production, has enabled the people living in the Mekong River Delta to produce large surpluses of food in the past and now. Traditionally, two harvests of wet paddy rice are possible each year—a feat possible in very few places of the world. In contrast, only dry field rice can be grown in parts of northern Vietnam.

History: From their physical appearance, the Vietnamese appear to have a common ancestry with the Malays, Indonesians and Polynesians of southern Asia, but there is a definite Mongolian element also present. They began to move southward from central and southern China in the last centuries B.C., entering what is now Vietnam shortly before the Christian era. Conquered by the powerful Han dynasty of China about 100 B.C., they remained a part of the Chinese empire for the next millennium.

It was natural that during these many centuries the Vietnamese adopted much of the Chinese political system and cultural patterns, but they actually feel a combination of respect, dislike and fear toward the Chinese. Through history, the Vietnamese have tried to simultaneously be "better Chinese than the Chinese" while trying to define Vietnam in terms of what is *not* China.

After the collapse of the T'ang dynasty in China in the early 10th century, the Vietnamese broke away from direct Chinese control. They avoided further conflict with China by acknowledging themselves to be a tributary state until conquered by the French in the late 19th century.

In the late 15th century, the Vietnamese conquered lands to the south occupied by the Chams, who spoke a language similar to that of Indonesia and had adopted many of India's cultural patterns, including Hinduism and Buddhism. By the 18th century they began to colonize the Mekong River Delta after

The "bar" of the dumbbell is a thin, coastal plain, closely confined on the west by the Annam *Cordillera*, a north–south range of mountains forming a natural barrier between Vietnam and Laos to the west. This coastal belt is narrow and somewhat inhospitable. Its lands are not enriched by the silt of any large river, and the typhoons of the South China Sea frequently do much damage.

The lower "bell" starts with an area of central highland plateaus which are heavily forested and inhabited by a somewhat backward people who till the lim-

ited available land after clearing it by burning. These highlands gradually give way to the Mekong Delta, where Ho Chi Minh City (formerly Saigon) is located.

The Mekong River starts in remote Tibet where snows gradually melt in the thin, icy air, gathering into small streams. Before reaching Vietnam, the waters travel almost 3,000 miles through some of the most rugged country in the world. The river is yellow and sluggish by the time it enters the country—the tides of the sea are felt as far back as Phnom Penh in Cambodia during the dry season, and

Town on the Mekong River

seizing the kingdom of Funan, also basically an Indian type of state.

French interest in Indochina, the name given to the eastern portion of mainland Southeast Asia, began in the 18th century. Initially taking the form of commercial and missionary contacts, the French effort did not become serious until the mid–19th century. Forces of Napoleon III conquered Vietnam in a series of military campaigns, beginning in the South and working slowly northward. The proclamation of a protectorate over the Annamese (Vietnamese) state in 1883 was followed by a short war with the Chinese to force the Manchu emperors of China to recognize the end of the tributary status of Annam.

The French divided their newly won possession into three segments: Tonkin in the North, Annam in the narrow middle belt and highland plateaus of the South and the colony of Cochin China in the Mekong Delta. These three areas were ruled by a governor general who also presided over Cambodia and Laos after 1887.

Actual administration of the colonies was by the French during the colonial period, although an imperial court was permitted to exist in Annam. The significant benefits brought to the area by the French included a narrow gauge railroad from Hanoi to Kunming in China which follows the banks of the Red River, and by which it was possible for the French to extract mineral wealth from the North. In addition, intensive cultivation methods which produced large quantities of valuable rubber were introduced.

During the early colonial period the French encouraged the migration of people from Tonkin in the North to the delta

of Cochin China; immigrant Chinese were also permitted in the southern colony.

Less attention was paid to preparing the people for independence than to the promotion of French culture among the Vietnamese. As a result, an upper class of Vietnamese emerged that was fluent in French, at home in French culture, and in some cases Roman Catholic, but usually bitterly resentful of French political domination.

Shortly after World War I, a nationalist group, composed of people supported by the French–speaking upper class emerged, competing with a communist movement in the north which was led by a dedicated patriot and communist who took the name Ho Chi Minh in 1943. Both of these movements attempted armed uprisings against the French in 1930 which were brutally suppressed. The communists survived by going underground, and Ho strengthened his position by betraying some of his nationalist rivals to the French police.

The Japanese took French Indochina by default after the Germans installed the puppet French *Vichy* government in 1940. Japan demanded the right to land forces in the area, which was granted by the French without delay; within three months the Japanese controlled all of northern Vietnam. In July 1941 they occupied the South as well.

In 1943 Ho Chi Minh was able to gain the support of Nationalist Chinese generals in southern China for what was supposed to be an anti–Japanese guerrilla movement. It turned out to be actually anti–French, through whom the Japanese nominally administered the country, and also was anti–Nationalist Vietnamese. It

had been formed by Ho in 1941 and was called the *Viet Minh.*

In 1945 Japanese ousted the local French authorities whom they correctly suspected of being in contact with General de Gaulle and the Allies. The Japanese authority was short–lived—surrender came within six months. At the Potsdam conference in 1945, the Allied powers decided to divide Vietnam at the 16th parallel into two zones for the purpose of disarming and evacuating the Japanese. The southern region was to be occupied by the British and the North was to be occupied by the Nationalist Chinese. If this had not been done before the Japanese troops had gone home, it is probable that Ho Chi Minh would have seized control of all of Vietnam in 1945.

Ho hastily proclaimed the Democratic Republic of Vietnam at Hanoi on September 2, 1945—the same day that the surrender of the Japanese was signed on the U.S. Battleship *Missouri* in Tokyo Bay. Shortly thereafter the forces of the Chinese Nationalists moved into the northern region.

Ho expanded his power in the rural rural areas of the North, eliminating Vietnamese Nationalist rivals and managing to co–exist uneasily with the Chinese occupation forces which gave every indication of intending to remain in Vietnam. The British suppressed activity by the Viet Minh in the southern part of the country, and quickly returned the area to the French. Seeking a withdrawal of the Chinese in the North, Ho and the French put pressure on them. The outbreak of civil war in China, in addition to this pressure, brought about a Chinese withdrawal in early 1946.

Ho permitted the French to re–enter

northern Vietnam, promising to keep the Democratic Republic of Vietnam within the French Union, so long as its autonomy was respected and providing it was allowed to control all of Vietnam. He certainly wanted French economic aid, but the chief reason for this attitude was very probably Stalin's desires at the time. The Russians wanted a French communist victory at the polls in France, and did not wish to alienate French voters by supporting a communist revolt in Vietnam.

COMMUNIST INSURGENCY IN NORTH VIETNAM

The French colonial regime refused to allow Viet Minh control of Cochin China, and some of its most important officials showed considerable bad faith in dealing with Ho. By the end of 1946, fighting erupted between the French and the Viet Minh, who retreated to the mountains above Hanoi to conduct a war of guerrilla activity and harassment.

In an effort to find some figure through whom they could indirectly govern Vietnam, the French selected Bao Dai, the hereditary Emperor of Annam and a descendant of the royal family which had ruled from a massive palace at Hue. He abdicated when Ho Chi Minh proclaimed independence, and he actually was fully in favor of the end of colonial rule. He accepted the French offer in 1946, but only after a series of complicated agreements were reached; he became Provisional President and later permanent chief of state of a government organized by the French to maintain their power in Indochina.

Although there were later negotiations, the war continued, with neither side winning, until 1949, when it became

clear that a communist victory in China was close at hand. Fearful that Ho would receive massive support from the communist Chinese regime, the French hastily granted independence to Laos, Cambodia and Vietnam, and appealed to the United States for aid and support, which was given to a limited extent.

The French insisted on retaining a high degree of control in military matters. On the other side, the Viet Minh received diplomatic recognition from communist China in early 1950, and, with Chinese military aid, cleared French troops from the border areas of northern Vietnam later in that year. What had been an internal, colonial struggle became the major theater of the Cold War in Asia, a fact which led to increased involvement of the United States and of the Chinese communists.

By the spring of 1953, the French prospects in Vietnam were bleak—the approaching end of the Korean war would enable greater Chinese effort in Vietnam. In desperation, the French granted further political, economic and military concessions to the non–communist Vietnamese state and substantially increased their own military efforts. Their purpose was not to defeat the Viet Minh, since such a goal was not possible, but rather to obtain an honorable political settlement which would be better than total defeat. The U.S., the Soviet Union, Britain and France decided that a conference would be held at Geneva, Switzerland, to deal with the questions of Indochina and Korea in the spring of 1954.

DIENBIENPHU

The French had fortified a position at Dienbienphu in northwest Vietnam in

response to a Viet Minh thrust into neighboring Laos. The Viet Minh stealthily surrounded the French with artillery and mortars supplied by the Chinese and laid siege to Dienbienphu. They quickly destroyed the air strip to prevent reinforcements and supplies from being sent in, and the French were finally defeated in one of the most heroic, but humiliating, efforts of the century. The tiny base fell on May 7, 1954, the day before the matter of Indochina was to come before the Geneva conference. The French were skeptical and the British were opposed to a U.S. proposal for a joint military effort at Dienbienphu made a month earlier.

There is no time in recent history when the fate of a small country depended to such a great extent on world politics as was true of the fate of Vietnam, to be decided at Geneva. The French wanted to get out of Indochina on any reasonable basis. The Soviet Union did not want to press France to the extent that it would join the European Defense Community, a proposed multi–country army including West Germany to oppose the threat of Soviet forces in Eastern Europe. Russia desired even less a direct clash with the U.S., which had only recently completed a massive series of hydrogen bomb tests in the Pacific. Communist China also wished to avoid conflict with the U.S. and did not want Ho Chi Minh to achieve too much power.

"THE GENEVA SETTLEMENT"

Ho Chi Minh's delegation to the conference arrived with a demand that the three nations of Indochina be treated in such a manner that would have produced a communist victory not only in Vietnam, but also in Cambodia and Laos. But the

Ho Chi Minh leaves the French Foreign Ministry, July 1946

Ho Chi Minh

Chinese delegation shortly thereafter conceded that a final settlement would treat the three countries separately. Ultimately, the final settlement contained some minor concessions to the communist movement in Laos, but none in Cambodia.

Vietnam was divided at the 17th parallel, considerably further north than had been demanded by Ho Chi Minh. Elections were scheduled for mid–1956, to be held in both regions. Military details of withdrawal, etc., were left to the French and Vietnamese. This was a defeat for Ho, who desired immediate elections before a non–communist government could solidify itself in the South; he was sure of victory in the North, since he was credited with expelling the disliked French. Similar sentiments were prevalent in the South, but would probably die out in time, according to his reasoning.

In order to exclude American military forces from Indochina, the settlement enjoined *any* foreign power from maintaining forces in Vietnam. A general political agreement was included in the final version in which many things were left subject to interpretation. Mainly for reasons of domestic politics, coupled with doubts about communist good faith, the U.S. declined to sign the agreement. The Chinese, although angered by this refusal, agreed to accept an informal American promise not to "disturb" the agreement by force. The settlement was "adopted" without actually being signed by the representative of any nation in July 1954.

Ho Chi Minh's regime promptly took over North Vietnam from the French and began to build a strong and effective regime with large amounts of economic and military aid from the Soviet Union and China. Exhibiting revolutionary zeal, Ho embarked on an extremely brutal pro-

gram which cost him much of his popularity, although he retained the support of his followers. The program provoked a peasant revolt in Nghe An, the southernmost province, which had to be suppressed by government troops in 1956. This caused Ho to moderate his programs in order to regain his popular support.

Nearly everyone at the Geneva conference had expected South Vietnam to collapse, or to quickly go communist via the ballot box. Bao Dai had no real authority and was almost totally under the influence of corrupt military leaders. In mid–1954 he appointed Ngo Dinh Diem, an energetic northern Catholic who had strong nationalist convictions, to be Prime Minister; the emperor resumed his more luxurious life in France and was later deposed by Diem in 1956. Bao Dai had dismissed Premier Diem in October 1955 after the premier had gained backing which called for the ouster of the chief of state. But Diem refused to resign. A referendum that month gave an overwhelming vote for Diem and against Bao Dai. In October 1956 Diem proclaimed a republic and assumed the office of president. From the time of his appointment, Diem enjoyed the support of some prominent officials in the U.S.

He quickly received the support of the several hundred thousand Catholic refugees who flooded into the South in 1954, and managed to keep South Vietnam from going communist in spite of almost impossible difficulties. He gained the allegiance of the traditionally corrupt army, defeated the dissidents of the two main hostile religious sects and was able to suppress a gang of rural bandits; ultimately he adopted a new constitution in 1956.

INITIAL U.S. INVOLVEMENT

He became the first president and actually had dictatorial powers—the constitution had been approved by a referendum which had obviously been rigged by Diem. He installed his favorites, often unpopular, in local office. The United States, impressed by his ability to put together a workable regime with apparent authority over the country, extended him massive military and economic aid and supported him in a refusal to hold 1956 elections as required by the Geneva agreement.

North Vietnam was furious and called for international action against Diem, but this received no support from the Soviets or the Chinese. Hoping that Diem's regime would literally collapse from its own weight of dishonesty and corruption, Ho discouraged communist guerrillas who had remained within South Vietnam after the Geneva division of the country. But in 1957, calling themselves *Viet Cong*, the rebels undertook a terrorist campaign to

force village support of their communist movement.

Diem and his conservatives responded as might be expected—a virtual police state was set up to smother all opposition, non–communist and communist. He was able to withstand a military revolt in 1960 and tried to promote the regime's power in rural areas by use of anti–Viet Cong measures.

This crackdown against the Viet Cong by Diem was successful enough to push them to adopt new, more militant tactics. Initial government success turned into a virtual loss of control of much of the countryside as Viet Cong strength swelled and its military activities increased.

There was no major direct support of the Viet Cong by North Vietnam until 1959 due to reluctance of the Soviets and Chinese to provoke another crisis in the region. Because of serious economic difficulties in 1960, China sharply reduced its aid to North Vietnam, which at the same time began to give substantial and active support to the Viet Cong. In response, the United States, during the first months of the Kennedy administration, increased its aid to the Diem government, raising the number of American military advisers to the South Vietnamese army. The Chinese, in return for Vietnamese support in their ideological disputes with the Soviet Union, greatly increased their support of Ho's effort to bolster the Viet Cong.

The Diem government further alienated public opinion in South Vietnam in response to growing communist pressures, resulting in a considerable degree of support for the Viet Cong. Diem infuriated the Buddhist community in the spring of 1963, alienating all of this influential segment of the public by his harsh measures. Buddhist demonstrators were joined by student demonstrations—government violence against both groups antagonized many army officers, including some who had close ties with the Buddhists and students. The U.S. government was embarrassed and disgusted with Diem by this time. An army *coup* deposed him in late 1963, resulting in his violent death, as well as that of his brother Nhu, accompanied by chaotic and popular rejoicing. Unstable military government ensued for about two years. Power was supposedly centered in Saigon, but local military leaders in the provinces were all but independent of the central government. The U.S., entering an election campaign in 1964, didn't want to disturb the shaky *status quo*. This was interrupted in August when North Vietnamese torpedo boats threatened a U.S. destroyer in the Tonkin Gulf. President Johnson manufactured a crisis out of the event and secured a vague resolution from Congress authorizing him to take military action in response; a single air strike against North Vietnam naval installations was made in retaliation. Recent disclosure of secret documents indicated that the U.S. had been planning a stepped-up campaign of "covert" operations against North Vietnam in 1964, but the resolution made open operations possible.

Because of their opposition to Diem's harsh rule, a great many non-communists had supported the Viet Cong and its political arm, the *National Liberation Front*. When he was deposed, this ended. Feeling the need of greater support, and believing it more possible that military action would succeed after the downfall of Diem, the Viet Cong embarked on wider military efforts. They were joined by regular units of the North Vietnamese army for the first time at the end of 1964.

There was a rapid increase in the area under communist control, particularly in the central highlands of South Vietnam. The Russians, sensing an imminent victory, sent their premier to Hanoi in early 1965 to give assurances of Russian participation (and, hopefully, influence), particularly in the form of defensive weapons against American air attacks on the North. At the same time, the Viet Cong launched a series of assaults on U.S. military installations in the South.

MASSIVE U.S. COMMITMENT

The result was U.S. air attacks on North Vietnam in early 1965 while Soviet Premier Kosygin was still in Hanoi. This was followed by large U.S. Marine and Army combat units being sent by mid-1965. South Vietnam was saved from the Viet Cong—temporarily.

Ideological differences had led to a rift in Soviet–Chinese relations in previous years; this now included disputes about what role each nation should play in aiding Ho Chi Minh's forces. The Maoist leadership resented the superior economic ability of the Russians to buy influence in Hanoi, and limited its assistance to the maintenance of the Chinese–North Vietnamese rail line and the shipment of infantry weapons after 1965. Although there was an agreement to ship amounts of Soviet equipment through China to North Vietnam in 1965, the trains were often delayed and harassed by "Red Guards" active in Mao's Great Cultural Revolution then in progress in China.

A dashing young Air Force general, Nguyen Cao Ky, emerged as a leading figure in the military establishment of South Vietnam in mid-1965; he became premier and retained that position for two years. This provided a welcome respite from the seemingly continuous change of rulers in the country. It became increasingly clear during his rule that the armed forces exercised almost all political power—a fact that continued to arouse Buddhist opposition, but no other person or group in South Vietnam was capable of exercising effective power.

The cost to the U.S. rose to more than $30 billion a year, placing a serious strain on the American economy and on its political system. Reasonable men found it possible to differ on the question of whether the price of the fighting, both human and economic, was too great, not only to the United States, but to both Vietnams. Some political progress took place in South Vietnam; a constitution was enacted and elections were held in 1967 for a new National Assembly. Military intrigue reduced General Ky to the candidacy for vice president; General Nguyen Van Thieu, a Catholic, was the leading candidate for president. (*Nguyen*, pronounced in one syllable "Nwen," is a very common Vietnamese name.) In spite of a heavy vote in favor of an anti-military "peace" candidate, the Thieu–Ky team won.

The new government had a broader base, but the habit of jailing political opponents persisted. The military situation, bolstered by a half million U.S. troops, improved, but the South Vietnamese army usually could not hold its own against North Vietnam and Viet Cong units. The government gained control of half the land area by the end of 1967, but in many cases this control was shaky.

As 1968 began, both sides found themselves heavily and totally involved in a conflict that was costly and had little hope for settlement. Too many pressures prevented movement toward peace. The U.S. was distracted by 1968 elections and the Soviets dared not appear to be less revolutionary than the Chinese. On *Tet*, the Lunar New Year holiday traditional to

Black smoke covers areas of Saigon during the Tet offensive

153

the Vietnamese, the communists started an unexpected all–out offensive. They invaded most of the provincial capitals, parts of Saigon and held a portion of the ancient imperial capital, Hue, for several days. U.S. encampments and installations were attacked, causing tremendous losses of materiel and manpower. Monsoon rains prevented effective defensive air strikes. In the end, however, the spectacular drive was unsuccessful. It drove the South Vietnamese and U.S. back into the larger cities and fortified positions. It raised substantial questions as to the extent of support of both the Thieu government and that of the Viet Cong. The actual goal of generating a popular uprising was a dismal failure.

A somewhat desperate U.S. President Lyndon Johnson suspended bombing of North Vietnam (except the southern provinces) in 1968 and proposed talks between the combatants, which got underway in Paris. All bombing of North Vietnam was discontinued by Johnson

in November. Knowing of the impossibility of his reelection as president because of a war which had become a nightmare, Johnson had withdrawn as a candidate in 1968 prior to the Democratic Convention. At the negotiations, the status of the Viet Cong and seating arrangements at the conference table resulted in endless haggling and utterly no progress. Richard M. Nixon was elected President of the U.S. with a somewhat obscure promise of a "secret plan" to end the war.

The conflict ground on even after seating arrangements were ironed out at the conference. No real progress was made until mid–1971. U.S. troop withdrawal started in 1969, and this move seemed to increase the chances for a political outcome of the struggle favorable to the communists. In mid–1969 they proclaimed a "provisional government" for the South and the Saigon government of President Thieu turned to what it considered the most reliable elements for

support: the armed forces and the Catholics. The economy, spurred by land reform in the South, improved. The tremendous strain of continuing the battle was showing in the North, complicated by political debates before and after the death of the elderly Ho Chi Minh in September 1969.

President Thieu was reelected (unopposed) in late 1971 in a contest his opponents charged was rigged; they dropped out of the race in protest. Although he made an attempt to build an effective government party, disruption came when the northern provinces of South Vietnam were struck by a massive North Vietnam invasion in March 1972. President Nixon, facing a reelection contest, responded by ordering the mining of Haiphong Harbor. This precipitated an international "crisis" which quickly subsided. The military stalemate was acutely embarrassing to President Nixon as the fall elections approached. He ordered a resumption of heavy bombing of the

South Vietnamese President Nguyen Van Thieu decorates soldiers

154

north, particularly Hanoi, to persuade the communists to settle.

After intense December 1972 bombing, the North Vietnamese verbally agreed to end the conflict in early 1973; the formal agreement was signed on March 2, 1973. The U.S. had already given up its insistence on a North Vietnamese withdrawal from South Vietnam and continued its own withdrawal. In exchange, it got its prisoners back, although some insist to this day that many were held against their will in violation of the promise. In recent years it is apparent that the communists withheld remains of U.S. combatants (who may have been alive at the end of the conflict) and have tried to use them at least to induce increased contacts with the U.S. Hanoi accepted a political arrangement that did not guarantee overthrow of the Thieu government as had been previously demanded.

Neither North nor South Vietnam had any genuine interest in abiding by the political provisions of the January 1973 agreement, which called in principle for a vaguely defined coalition government and general elections. To strengthen its hand, Hanoi, with the help of continuing, in fact increased, military aid from from the Soviet Union and China, began to create a "third Vietnam" under the nominal control of the Viet Cong in the highlands of South Vietnam. This activity, much of which was in flagrant violation of the agreement, included road building, troop buildups, the stockpiling of weapons and other measures. Deprived of American air support by Congressional prohibitions and unwilling to commit its own air force against communist–held areas in the highlands, South Vietnam made no genuine military effort to contain the foe.

In the Saigon–controlled areas, which included nearly all the population until March 1975, the Thieu government continued its basically repressive policies. Although Thieu fired a number of corrupt military and civilian officials, including some who had been close to him, in 1973–1974, there was no basic change in the style of the regime. Thieu seemed to have learned almost nothing from the experiences of Ngo Dinh Diem and Chiang Kai–shek. Anti–Thieu protest movements arose in 1974 among both the Buddhists, who stressed liberalization and peace, and the Roman Catholics, who emphasized opposition to corruption. Concessions were promised to both by Thieu in late 1974, but little actually happened. In reality, five major opposition newspapers were closed down in early 1975, leaving only one in operation.

During 1974, North Vietnam emphasized the development of its economy through aid from other communist countries, principally the Soviet Union and China. The military strength of Hanoi was built up as was that of the Vietcong in the highlands of South Vietnam. A strategy of "accelerated erosion" began through nibbling at Saigon's military positions in both the highlands and in the Mekong Delta. This approach was obviously inadequate to achieve Hanoi's two principal objectives: imposition of the political provisions of the January 1973 agreement and/or the downfall of Thieu. One reason for this cautious approach was probably the attitude of the Soviet Union and China, which did not want their "detente" with the United States to be endangered by a major resurgence of fighting in Vietnam.

The North Vietnamese capture of two provincial capitals in early 1975 in the central highlands and, even closer, about 80 miles north of Saigon, was the beginning of the end. Shocked by the loss of these towns and unquestionably worried by the refusal of the U.S. Congress to vote further large–scale military aid, President Thieu simply abandoned the three provinces of Kontom, Pleiku and Darlac in March. The retreat quickly turned into a rout as communist forces, taking advantage of the dry season and the government withdrawals, moved forward. By the end of March the two important coastal cities of Hue and Danang had fallen to the communists. Saigon fell at the end of April in a morass of confusion and the people with close contacts with the Thieu administration desperately fleeing in overcrowded boats and planes. The long war in Vietnam was over, although the two halves of the country remained temporarily separate entities.

The behavior of the leadership during 1975 in South Vietnam demonstrated clearly that their concern was mainly for their personal safety rather than for the future of Vietnam. Thieu issued military orders which were disastrous, changing daily and leading nowhere. He was more worried about army loyalty to him and called one commando unit back to Saigon to protect him from any attempted *coup*. Many field officers deserted to seek safety for themselves and their families, leaving their men leaderless.

Ultimately, several hundred thousand refugees fled, most ultimately to the U.S. Thieu went to Taiwan and other prominent officials moved to Hawaii. Almost all the leadership was able to depart with substantial wealth, in contrast to most of the refugees who had little more than the clothes they wore.

After its "liberation" from the Thieu regime, South Vietnam was run by men sent from Hanoi, the chief of whom was Pham Hung, who, although a southerner, was a member of the top leadership of the *Vietnam Workers Party*—the communist party. Imposition of communist controls on the South proceeded fairly slowly, and without the bloodbath that had been widely predicted. One reason was the difficult and chaotic conditions facing the new regime; another, probably, was concern for international opinion. Nevertheless there were some executions and a great deal of forced political "reindoctrination," sometimes under prison–like conditions. Former employees of the Thieu regime often found it difficult to find jobs and even food. There was some armed resistance in early 1976, mainly in the central highlands. The new regime planned to reduce the population of Saigon, renamed Ho Chi Minh City, by one–third in 1976 through forced resettlement in the countryside.

The leadership of north and south announced in late 1975 there would be elections in 1976 for a single National Assembly for the entire country. They were held on schedule in the communist manner—there were no opposition candidates. In spite of its slightly larger population, the South was allotted 243 seats, and as a token concession the voters were allowed to choose from among 281 candidates; in the North there were 249 candidates for 249 seats. The new Assembly met and adopted a new constitution; unification of the country was officially proclaimed.

The ruling party held its Fourth Congress in late 1976, at which it renamed itself the *Vietnam Communist* (rather than *Workers*) *Party*. The domination of the North over the South was clear.

Soviet aid to and influence on the new regime were substantial, although not overwhelming. It was widely assumed that Moscow would use the huge naval base at Camranh Bay built by the U.S., which later proved to be a valid prediction. Chinese influence was considerably less than that of the Soviets.

Hanoi claimed that President Nixon had promised it $3.25 billion in reconstruction aid and tried to bargain against as much of this as possible by making repeated promises to cooperate in accounting for American personnel missing in action. The U.S. declined to negotiate since not much cooperation was actually forthcoming and Hanoi was widely disliked.

Vietnam showed some interest in allowing American oil companies to prospect offshore, but no arrangement along these lines could be concluded as long as the United States maintained its embargo on trade. Relations with the ASEAN states (Thailand, Malaysia, Singapore, Indonesia, the Philippines and Brunei) have been cool. The reason was the immense stockpile of American military equipment (some $5 billion worth) added to Vietnam's existing stockpile of Soviet

Harvesting salt in the Central Plain.

equipment, coupled with the maintenance of a huge army and the Vietnamese invasion of Cambodia. This led to not unreasonable fears that aggression, either direct or indirect, was intended against regional nations. Thousands of refugees, many of Chinese origin, started to flee Vietnam in 1978, some voluntarily and some under pressure. Those who survived became a serious problem for the neighboring countries they were fortunate enough to reach. During the ensuing period, Vietnam brutally expelled another one million people, most of them of Chinese origin, claiming they were security risks. They became refugees ("boat people") and a major international problem.

In 1977 Vietnam developed a border conflict with Cambodia which was then controlled by the murderous Pol Pot regime, a client state of China, with which Vietnam's relations were rapidly deteriorating. Vietnam launched a full–scale invasion of Cambodia in late 1978, and after a brief period of fighting, only guerrilla resistance, located along the Thailand border, remained. The new leadership was pro–Vietnamese. In retaliation for this strike against its ally, China began to pour troops over the Vietnamese border in early 1979, occupying a portion of its northern territory with heavy fighting. These troops were shortly withdrawn when China felt that it had taught Vietnam "a lesson." Immediately after the conflict, Hanoi, which had signed a treaty of friendship with Moscow in late

1978, allowed the Soviet Union to establish air and naval bases on Vietnamese territory at Danang and Camranh Bay.

There was a brief crisis in mid–1980 when Vietnam sent troops across the Thai border in order to wipe out remaining Cambodian anti–Vietnam resistance. Such resistance remains, however (see Cambodia) with obvious Chinese support. Further, since 1984 China has periodically been attacking northern regions of Vietnam and, ominously, in 1986, threatened to teach Vietnam "a second lesson." The Chinese are determined that Vietnamese forces withdraw from Cambodia and have said that relations between the two countries would remain frigid until this happens.

The Vietnamese economy has been under serious strain due to the rigid policies of the leadership, which have only recently started to relax. The army is a tremendous burden, having been increased to 1.2 million men. There is some anti–communist activity in the highlands. Exodus of refugee "boat people" has continued. Their lot has been extremely perilous because of piracy and defective vessels which have sunk. If they do reach Hong Kong or Taiwan, they are usually returned to Vietnam. Further, there has been reluctance on the part of merchant and military vessels to pick up these people, since few nations have been willing to receive them. Only recently there was announced an international accord for resettlement of these unfortunate people. About 10,000 remain

in "re–education" camps—prisoners who either had supported the U.S.–backed government or more recent anti–government detainees. Interestingly, the regime has more recently complained of "anti–Vietnamese" activities of exiles in the U.S. and elsewhere with connections to opposition elements within Vietnam.

In 1986–1987, Vietnam underwent something of a political crisis. The aging, largely North Vietnamese, leadership and its inflexible policies had created an economic disaster and were resented by the people (especially in the South) and apparently also by the army high command; they were also criticized privately by the Soviet Union, the major source of economic aid. A change for the better became at least a possibility with the death in July 1986 of Le Duan, the longtime General Secretary of the Communist Party of Vietnam (formerly the Vietnam Workers Party). He was succeeded by Truong Chinh, also elderly but more flexible and with a reputation for being pro-Chinese. His new position was apparently coveted by Le Duc Tho, another senior party figure, but rivalry of this kind, although common in other communist parties, is contrary to the tradition of the Vietnamese movement.

Accordingly, at a Party Congress (the Sixth) held in December 1986, Truong Chinh, Le Duc Tho and Pham Van Dong "resigned" from the Politburo, although all continued to be "advisers." Chinh retained the presidency of the state and Dong the premiership of the government. A new General Secretary of the party, Nguyen Van Linh, a Southerner and an economic reformer although also elderly, was elected. In February 1987 there were major personnel changes in the government, although Chinh and Dong remained in place; the newcomers were mostly southerners with some economic expertise. The effects of these changes will obviously take time to become clear.

Vietnam's relations with its patron, the Soviet Union, remained edgy. The Soviets retained major naval and air bases at and near Camranh Bay and clearly could not afford to alienate Hanoi, the host government. On the other hand, Moscow was unhappy with Vietnamese misuse of Soviet aid and was moving to improve its own relations with China, with which Vietnam had been on very bad terms since the late 1970s. The Soviets appeared to be applying cautious pressure on Hanoi to improve its relations with Beijing and agree to a Cambodian settlement that would involve a Vietnamese military withdrawal and a coalition government including the resistance groups as well as the pro-Vietnamese government, and would be acceptable to China, ASEAN, and the U.S.

Relations with the U.S. were still difficult. In 1986, Hanoi reneged on two pledges that it had apparently given: to resolve fully the issue of American personnel still considered missing in action during the Vietnam war (the MIA's) and to release to American custody several thousand Vietnamese prisoners being held for having collaborated with the U.S. during the war. In view of this behavior on the Vietnamese side, and the absence as yet of a Cambodian settlement, the U.S. continued to withhold diplomatic recognition and trade from Hanoi.

In June 1987 the National Assembly (elected the previous April) made changes in the state leadership similar to those made in the party leadership the year before, although the old guard was still in charge. Vo Chi Cong replaced Truong Chinh as president and Pham Hung succeeded Pham Van Dong as premier. When in early March 1988 Pham Hung died of a heart attack, the 75-year-old leader was temporarily succeeded by Vo Van Kiet.

The trend toward liberalization continued. Some 6,000 political prisoners were released in September 1987. Somewhat greater freedom was allowed intellectuals and Catholics. Plant managers of state factories were given more authority, and a partial revival of private enterprise was permitted.

The Hanoi leadership decided that the invasion at the end of 1978 of Cambodia, which was unpopular in Vietnam as well as Cambodia itself, was a mistake and planned to withdraw by 1990, while somehow leaving a pro-Vietnamese government in power in Phnom Penh.

In June 1988, in selecting a premier, the National Assembly passed over the reforming acting premier, Vo Van Kiet, in favor of the conservative Do Muoi, who had been responsible for the disastrous socialization of the South Vietnamese economy in 1978. This choice probably had some connection with a number of unfortunate developments that followed soon after: a crackdown on intellectual dissent, demonstrations by South Vietnamese farmers against the failure of local officials to implement a recent law returning land taken over by the state in 1978, etc. On the other hand, early 1989 saw some more favorable trends: a cut in the size of the huge army of more than one million men; the deletion of hostile references to the U.S., China, and other foreign countries (not the Soviet Union) from the preamble to the state constitution and the addition of some reformers to the cabinet.

The foreign affairs picture during this period was similarly mixed. The idea of a "new Vietnam," eager for foreign contacts, was energetically promoted by an able Foreign Minister, Nguyen Co Thach. Hanoi expressed an interest in joining ASEAN. In response to foreign concern over the state of human rights in Vietnam, some political prisoners were released and some boat people allowed to return. Official anger at the Vatican's canonization, in mid 1988, of 117 Vietnamese martyrs of the seventeenth and eighteenth centuries was not allowed to derail a policy of increased toleration of religion, including Catholicism. Disagreements and even tensions with the Soviet Union, probably including Soviet pressures for a Vietnamese withdrawal from Cambodia on the model of the Soviet withdrawal from Afghanistan, did not quite disrupt this important relationship. Hanoi continued to want recognition and aid from the U.S., which are being withheld pending a withdrawal from Cambodia and a satisfactory accounting for MIAs. On both these scores, the Vietnamese performance was ambiguous; the timetable for a Cambodian withdrawal was extended and Hanoi suspended cooperation on the MIA question in August 1988, only a month after reaching an agreement with the U.S.

The dramatic developments of 1989–90 in the Soviet Union and Eastern Europe had a considerable impact on the Vietnamese leadership. The basic reaction was one of alarm and of determination that the erosion of the ruling parties' power there would not be repeated in Vietnam. On the other hand, Hanoi hoped to avoid the opposite extreme—a bloody crackdown in the Chinese manner—by means of very cautious political and economic reforms (*doi moi*). This difficult task was soon to be complicated by a leadership succession question; General Secretary Nguyen Van Linh was elderly and ill.

Vietnamese troops completed their withdrawal from Cambodia in September 1989, mainly in the hope of improving Hanoi's international image, although several thousand reentered

Shopping in Ho Chi Minh City (formerly Saigon)

157

Cambodia shortly afterward to help defend some western towns from the Khmer Rouge.

In 1991 the divided leadership in Hanoi tried to work out a plan for improving the limping economy without diluting the ruling party's monopoly of political power. One requirement was the establishment of normal commercial relations with the industrial countries, especially the United States and Japan. The withdrawal from Cambodia helped this process, but Washington was still demanding a full accounting for MIAs.

Political opposition in Vietnam has been almost nonexistent, because of a history of severe repression. Accordingly, the regime has felt free to proceed along very much the same lines as in China: minimal political reform (in the name of "stability," but actually also for the sake of the regime's power), combined with some reasonably effective economic reform. Hanoi has moved toward a corresponding improvement in its relations with Beijing, although without settling the troublesome issue of conflicting claims in the South China Sea.

Hanoi has been distressed and harmed by the decline of its formerly important relationship with Moscow, which has cut off economic aid and withdrawn nearly all its forces from Camranh Bay, and by the failure of the hardline coup in Moscow in August 1991.

At the Seventh Communist Party Congress (June 1991), the pro-Soviet Nguyen Co Thach was dropped from the Politburo, probably to appease Beijing. Do Muoi, the hardline premier, replaced Nguyen Van Linh as General Secretary. The National Assembly, at its August 1991 session, approved the dismissal of Nguyen Co Thach as foreign minister and of military hero Vo Nguyen Giap as deputy premier, perhaps because he had criticized the invasion of Cambodia. At the end of the year, a new "draft" constitution, adopted the following spring, reaffirmed the Communist Party's right to rule and deleted certain social "rights" (housing, etc.) as unrealistic, but also guaranteed a place in the economy for free markets.

The population still appeared to be weary from the long war, disillusioned with the current leadership, and nostalgic to some extent for the days of Ho Chi Minh. In late 1991, Hanoi decided to accept the return of a large number of refugees, about half of them from Hong Kong, who had fled Vietnam and then been classified as "economic migrants" rather than political refugees in their places of destination.

Hanoi clearly wanted to improve relations with the United States, in order to facilitate trade with and aid from the United States and Japan. It became increasingly cooperative on the MIA issue. By the end of 1991, the State Department began to authorize tour groups of Americans to visit Vietnam.

While the U.S. Presidential election prevented earlier action, in late November President Bush permitted U.S. companies to open offices in Vietnam and begin the negotiation of trade deals, though actual trade remained prohibited.

Politics and Government: The political system of Vietnam, if it can be called that, remains in the hands of the *Communist Party of Vietnam*. In early 1994, Party Secretary Do Muoi, Prime Minister Vo Van Kiet, and Deputy Prime Minister Phan Van Khai were firmly in control.

In such a system, the Politburo is the highest decision body. The Central Committee is second in the party hierarchy with the Secretariat responsible for disseminating orders from above. In Vietnam, power thus rests with the party. The National Assembly of Vietnam has been primarily window–dressing with no authority independent of the party.

In 1993, however, acting with the approval of the party, the Assembly began producing "laws." Legislation is apparently approved by the party. It appears that the leadership is attempting to rationalize the means by which the country is ruled, i.e. law vs party decree.

The country is divided into almost 400 electoral districts. Each of these is now required to respond to the legislative efforts of the National Assembly by producing an evaluation at the end of each assembly session. It would not seem likely that the Party intent is to create a rival center of authority in the country. Nevertheless, as events propel the country forward, the Party may have less and less to say about how things are done.

Throughout 1994, signs pointed to the continued opening of Vietnam to the outside world. Vietnamese officials were being trained in contemporary diplomatic practice, a Fulbright program was begun, and American professors were in the

The crowded waterfront of a Mekong Delta town at market time.

Courtesy: William Garrett Stewart

Prime Minister Vo Van Kiet

**Do Muoi, General Secretary,
Communist Party**

country at several institutions teaching business and economic courses. Americans also visited Vietnamese military bases and government offices in search of additional information on American MIA's. Vietnamese were also being trained to aid them in the process of determining the fate of their own MIA's which far outnumber the Americans lost.

In January the Politburo, the highest party organ, was enlarged to 17. Analysts noted that three of the four new appointees were hard–line Marxists. Only the Foreign Minister, Nguyen Manh Cam, is university trained. However a number of change–oriented southerners were appointed to the 161–member central committee. Le Mai, Deputy Foreign Minister in charge of U.S.–Vietnam relations, is one of the appointees.

The Vietnamese government worked in 1995 to establish a bureaucracy and legal system which foreigners could work with and trust. An entire new legal code was approved in October. Debate within the party also indicated that there was concern about giving up too much authority to the rule of law. At one point during the year, a number of Vietnamese were sentenced to stiff prison sentences for organizing a conference on democracy. Things may have changed in Vietnam, but not that much.

The party was also concerned about the growth of corruption, including the growth of a sex and drugs industry. According to one estimate, there were 44 massage parlors in Hanoi. By the standards of other Asian societies, Vietnam has very little to worry about. Still, the party in Hanoi wants to nip things in the bud before they get out of hand. Another more serious problem was smuggling.

Perhaps as much as $1 billion in goods was smuggled into Vietnam in 1995.

The government also moved to clear streets of vendors who block traffic and to require cycle drivers to have a license. One decision of greater import put a halt to further conversion of agricultural land to industrial use. This was undertaken to prevent the loss of further rice–growing land. All in all, the year was one in which an archaic organization, the Communist party, struggled to cope with an ever expanding and more complicated economic environment about which it had little experience or understanding.

Foreign Relations: In July 1993, President Bill Clinton ended U.S. opposition to International Monetary Fund (IMF) loans to Vietnam. On September 14, President Clinton announced that American companies could bid on infrastructure projects funded by the international lending agencies. On February 4, 1994, Vietnamese officials welcomed the lifting of the 19-year U.S. trade embargo. Prior to this move, American companies were already in Hanoi signing deals in anticipation of the action. One year later, at the end of January 1995, the U.S. officially opened a liaison office in Hanoi. The Vietnam liaison office opened in Washington on February 1st, and full diplomatic relations were announced in July 1995. Vietnam will now be less exposed to China to the north, while both Hanoi and Washington can look forward to expanded trade. In addition, Washington will eventually have to consider reestablishing a credible military presence in Southeast Asia. Vietnam has the facilities and will eventually have the motive.

That motive may be China. The two countries fought one conflict in the late

70's, and have come to blows twice, in 1974 and 1988, over conflicting claims in the South China Sea. In 1994, relations worsened. A Vietnamese patrol boat seized three Chinese fishing boats off Bach Long Vi, an island claimed by Hanoi half way between Vietnam and Hainan island (Chinese territory). A Chinese boat opened fire the next day on another patrol, wounding two Vietnamese. In 1992, China awarded Crestone Energy a drilling contract for a block of territory less than 200 miles from Ho Chi Minh City. Other than China's historical claim, there is no modern international law which could possibly recognize Beijing's claim to this territory. In addition, British Gas and Atlantic Richfield began drilling in the same area in June under Vietnamese authorization. President Jiang Zemin visited Hanoi in November. To their credit, both sides seem willing to go ahead in areas where there is mutual benefit.

Normalization of relations with the United States was clearly a major event when the U.S. embassy opened in Hanoi on August 6, 1995. However, development of the new relationship is being held up by a number of important matters. Hanoi and Washington have not as yet concluded a trade treaty, which would cover among other things the important area of intellectual property rights. Vietnam also needs to gain "most favored nations" status as soon as possible, so that its goods can enter the U.S. as cheaply as those from America's other "best" trading partners. On the other side, American businessmen are hampered by not having access to the Export–Import Bank which provides U.S. government backed financing and insurance.

In order for the above to be realized, the Clinton Administration must certify

The northern branch of the Mekong River as it splits on its way to the South China Sea
Courtesy: William Garrett Stewart

to Congress that Hanoi meets its requirements for allowing emigration of its people. And to qualify for Overseas Private Investment Corporation programs Vietnam must meet internationally accepted labor standards. American companies lost out on several big contracts in 1995 and early 1996. The Clinton Administration could probably move ahead on the issue if it wanted to. Waivers have been granted to other countries which do not meet all the criteria. However, in this election year, a decision is not expected until after November.

Vietnam became the 7th member of ASEAN (Association of Southeast Asian Nations) in July. This provides the country with significant economic and strategic benefits. Trade with the other ASEAN six (Brunei, Indonesia, Malaysia, Philippines, Singapore, and Thailand) will grow more rapidly. Also, being a member of ASEAN provides Vietnam with some cover in its relations with China. An important example of this occurred in July when the ASEAN states spoke out with one voice at the second ASEAN Regional (security) Forum in Brunei on the issue of conflicting claims in the South China Sea. China had insisted that these claims be addressed on a bi–lateral basis. Countries like Vietnam and the Philippines, who have had run–ins with the Chinese military in the sea, much prefer the multilateral approach.

Vietnam also continued to talk with Cambodian officials about the treatment of ethnic Vietnamese located along the border just inside Cambodian territory.

Relations are not the best and they could deteriorate easily.

Culture: The Vietnamese have been influenced by the culture of the Chinese to a greater extent than all other nations of Asia, except Singapore, where there is a Chinese majority. Chinese characters were used to write the Vietnamese language until the French replaced them with an alphabetical system. The Red River in North Vietnam is controlled with dikes of Chinese design.

On the other hand, it must be remembered that during the thousand years of greatest Chinese influence, the Vietnamese were virtually confined to what is now North Vietnam. Those who later moved south to Cochin China in the Mekong Valley retained less of the Chinese influence the farther south they moved. This, plus the fact that many of South Vietnam's modern leadership came from the north and only recently moved south after the communist takeover in the region, partially explains the instability and factionalism which infected South Vietnam politics before the communist conquest of 1975.

All Vietnamese, regardless of their politics, feel that the Chinese are the main traditional threat to their national survival. This fear presumably accounts for united Vietnam's obvious hostility to Chinese efforts to increase their influence in Southeast Asia. It should also be remembered, however, that the Chinese have not been eager in recent years to involve themselves in conflicts to any greater ex-

tent than appeared to be absolutely necessary.

South Vietnam is religiously divided between Buddhists with a variety of practices that are quite distinctly Vietnamese, and Roman Catholicism, brought to the area by the French colonists. This division is reflected in the political and military experiences in the South—the Catholics, more aggressive and better educated along Western lines, supported a conservative nationalism for the most part, but the Buddhists favored a brand of "pacifism" which, whether intended or not, assisted the Viet Cong materially and morally. Substantial ethnic Vietnamese communities are now found in many United States cities. The economic opportunities open to these people have been eagerly seized and Vietnamese children are almost uniformly excellent, hard–working students in public schools. Good Vietnamese restaurant food is available in most larger U.S. cities.

Economy: There traditionally have been three layers in the Vietnamese economy: the bottom one based on rice growing, the middle based on mining in the North and rubber plantations in the South and the third added by the war, based on large–scale Soviet and Chinese aid in the North and substantial American aid in the South. The socialist economy of the North developed the most impressive industrial system in Southeast Asia, although the cost of paying for it, particularly in view of destruction by U.S. bombing, kept living standards at a very low level.

Unlike that of the North, the economy of the South was largely free enterprise rather than socialist, and there was much less industry. Living standards probably showed greater differences between the classes in the South than in the North, but it is highly probable that in general, most people in the South lived better than those in the North. Land reform measures and the introduction of a new variety of rice developed in the U.S. resulted in a dramatic increase in rice production in the last decade.

Economic and social conditions in the South, needless to say, deteriorated badly at the close of the war; widespread shortages of food and prevalence of disease were made worse by a lack of basic services.

In 1995, Vietnam appeared as if it was on the verge of becoming another "Asian tiger." The term, refers to the rapidly growing economies of Asia: Singapore, Taiwan, South Korea and Hong Kong. Malaysia and Thailand are the new "cubs." In Ho Chi Minh City, fine restaurants, new high–rise buildings, television, and lots of new cars were plentiful.

From 1987 to 1994, the country experienced a real boom. This was based on the

Communist Party's policy of *doi moi*, or restructuring, which ushered in a series of market reforms. Many restrictions on the private sector were removed. One result is that Vietnam is currently the world's fourth largest exporter of rice, behind Thailand, the U.S., and India. Inflation was under 6% in 1993, and about 16% in 1994. Excess labor from closed state enterprises was absorbed by almost five million new jobs in the private sector. However, in 1995, per capita income was still only about $250. Foreign trade continued to expand to about $8 billion two–way with only a small deficit.

At the end of the year, it appeared that Hanoi may be siphoning off resources needed by the private sector to help state enterprises. For example, textiles made in state concerns are given preference for export. These companies also benefit from better access to foreign currency loans. Foreign companies are even being forced to form joint ventures with local state owned businesses. The next Party Congress should take place in the summer of 1996. Many fear that it will signal an all out attempt by the party to re–establish socialism, thus making the future for investors and local capitalists very bleak.

The Future: The *Communist Party* still runs the country, but with a new constitution and a National Assembly that has been given functions associated with an independent legislature. There should be no mistake that the party will try to hold on to power as long as possible. The problem is that change in Vietnamese society is likely to pick up to the point that the old political apparatus for control will be irrelevant to events around it. The use of tanks in the midst of an economic boom will not work. At some point, management of Vietnamese society and the economy will be beyond the party's abilities.

The end of the U.S. embargo, full diplomatic relations, and the flood of foreign investment and personnel into the country will of course hasten the pace of change. Not all of this will be good. The environment will suffer and many individuals will not benefit from the initial stages of economic growth and development. In short, Vietnam is rapidly becoming the equivalent of an old West "boomtown," where fortunes will be made and government goes along for the ride. This condition will persist until appropriate governmental structures and functions are developed. When they are, Vietnam will be on its way toward a modern, orderly yet dynamic society. However, it will be without the *Communist Party*.

The bustling port of Haiphong.

Courtesy: Embassy of the Socialist Republic of Vietnam

161

The Island Nations of the Western Pacific

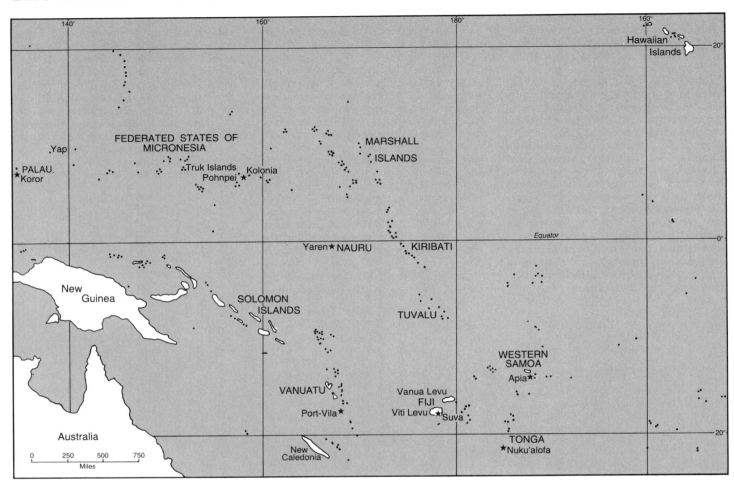

"... the seas bring us together, they do not separate us ..."

From the preamble to the Constitution of the Federated State of Micronesia

Scattered like brilliant pieces of jade across an area covering more than 3 million square miles of the Pacific Ocean lie a number of island states which have achieved independence or have become self–governing; they have been under British, French, U.S., Australian or New Zealand administration either as colonies, protectorates, or UN trusteeships. They range in population from Fiji's 805,000 to Nauru's 9,400 inhabitants. Most islanders are ethnically Polynesian, Melanesian or Micronesian, although some Asian groups such as Indians, Chinese and Vietnamese have settled in the islands in the last century.

On the majority of the islands the terrain is generally low, sometimes only a few feet above sea level (of coral origin) or mountainous (of volcanic origin) covered by lush vegetation and bordered by legendary white beaches. Many, however,

bear the ugly scars and rusted armaments brought to them by the savage engagements waged throughout the region during World War II; gentle wavelets brush the bows of hulking battleships sunk during those years, while palm trees sway in the cooling breezes which moderate the tropical climate. World–renouned for their beauty, the islands are subject to fierce typhoons from June to December.

Long before the era of Christianity, Asian peoples migrated into the area. Spanish explorers plumbed the region for gold and spread Christianity among the people, a belief which was often blended with their traditional dieties. Spain simultaneously laid claim to much of this area of scattered islands.

In the latter 1800's, as part of the German program to establish an overseas empire in competition with an already widespread and successful colonization by other European powers, German control was eventually imposed over most of the Spanish–claimed region. After World War I, Japan, which had joined the victorious Allies, was rewarded with possession of the former German–held islands

north of New Guinea, but during World War II an island–by–island struggle by Allied troops wrested the area from the Japanese, and the islands came under control of the United States, Great Britain, France, Australia and New Zealand, with the Dutch reclaiming their former colony of the Dutch East Indies—now most of which forms Indonesia. Over the years the islands achieved independence (see individual nation entires).

Some exports of the islands are quite specific, as in the case of Nauru with its dependence on phosphate deposits, but others generally produce in varying quantities basic products of a tropical climate: coconut and palm oil, fish, copra, fruits and—in the case of Fiji—sugar and some gold. Timber is also an important export for both Fiji and the Solomon Islands. Another prime source of income which all are striving to develop is tourism.

The Solomon Islands, Tonga, and Vanuatu are members of the (British) Commonwealth of Nations. Nauru and Tuvalu are special members, i.e., they may participate in all functional Commonwealth meetings and activities, but do not have the right to attend meetings of the Commonwealth Heads of Government.

The poor condition of the economies of these small states have accentuated tensions with the West and especially with the United States, whose tuna boats fish aggressively in the South Pacific. The former Soviet Union had been promoting contacts with the island states, especially Vanuatu, which is the most leftist, but the breakup of the USSR has at least temporarily put a halt to them. There are also tensions with France caused by its persistence in testing nuclear weapons in its part of the South Pacific and the delay in granting independence to New Caledonia.

The states of this region, including Australia and New Zealand, have formed an organization called the South Pacific Forum. In 1985 they signed a South Pacific Nuclear–Free Zone Treaty barring such weapons from the region's territories, but not banning transit of its waters by nuclear–armed or nuclear–powered ships.

Following World War II, the United Nations established a trusteeship over three primary archipelegos north of the equator: the Carolines, the Marshalls, and the Marianas (except for Guam, a U.S. possession since the end of the Spanish–American War in 1898.) The U.S. was the trustor, and the Department of the Interior took jurisdiction over these islands from the Navy in 1951.

In 1975 the Northern Marianas (again, except for Guam) was given separate status as a commonwealth. The rest of the territory was divided into the Marshall Islands (in the East), the Federated States of Micronesia (in the South), and the Republic of Palau (in the Southwest).

In January 1986 the Unites States, having held the role of trustor for the UN's Trust Territory of the Pacific Islands, approved a Compact of Free Association for them; it consists of two agreements included in the same act of Congress—one between the U.S. and the Federated States of Micronesia and the other between the U.S. and the Marshall Islands. The Compact provides for extensive cooperation in numerous areas such as law enforcement, narcotics control, economic and technical assistance, resolution of nuclear–cleanup programs, health care, fishing rights, etc. With the enactment of the Compact, the Trust Territory of the Pacific Islands essentially ceased to exist. The FSM and the Marshall Islands are now independent republics and members of the United Nations. The Republic of Palau is also a part of the Compact, but its dependence on the U.S. is far more pronounced. The Compact of Free Association is subject to many varying (and more often vague) interpretations.

The islands as a whole have considerable strategic importance, at least to the extent that the United States has wanted to make sure that they did not become Russian naval bases, and there are a number of U.S. bases in the islands. The Eniwetok and Bikini atolls in the Marshalls were the site of H–bomb tests in the 1950's and are still considered contaminated. There is considerable local discontent, especially over the nuclear and missile testing issues.

Palau, because of its nearness to important shipping routes linking the western Pacific and the South China Sea with the Indian Ocean, is being considered for development as a major port complex and military base; these are not welcome to the inhabitants. Palau's president, Haroo I. Remeliik, was assassinated on June 30, 1985.

Contrary to the wishes of many voters, who are anti–nuclear and suspect of the U.S. seeking bases in Palau as a possible replacement to those in the Philippines, the government of Palau managed to get a vote accepting a "compact of free association" with the U.S. in August 1987. In effect, Palau receives economic aid from the U.S. in exchange for an American option on bases.

The agreement was invalidated by the Palau courts, however. Negotiations for a new agreement foundered on economic disputes. President Lazarus Salii died in August 1988, an apparent suicide. The voters of Palau in February 1990 refused a revised version of the "compact of free association." However, on October 2, 1994, Palau formally proclained its independence from the United States in return for over $500 million in assistance from Washington.

Typical island scene, this one in Micronesia   Courtesy of Marianna H. Rowe

The Republic of FIJI

**President Ratu Sir Penaia Ganilau
(d. December 1993)**

Area: 7,055 sq. mi. (330 islands) of which about 97 are inhabited).
Population: 805,000 (estimated).
Capital City: Suva (Pop. 70,000 estimated).
Languages: English (official), Fijian, Hindustani.
Principal Religion: Christianity.
Main Exports: Sugar, copra, fish, lumber.
Currency: Fiji dollar.
Former Colonial Status: British Crown Colony.
Independence Date: October 10, 1970.
Chief of State: *Ratu* Sir Kamisese Mara, President.
Head of Government: Major General Sitiveni Rabuka, Prime Minister.

In 1994, two of the major opposition parties, the Fijian Nationalist Party and the Fijian Association Party, undertook separate moves to unseat Prime Minister Sitiveni Rabuka and his Fijian Political Party. Sakeasi Butadroka, Nationalist Party leader, accused the Prime Minister of failure to consult the Great Council of Chiefs on major government decisions, including a proposed Hong Kong business migrant scheme, the lifting of Sunday observance laws, and the proposed use of the term "Fijian" for all Fiji citizens.

Under the proposed plan, up to 28,000 Hong Kong Chinese will be permitted to come to Fiji. They will be required to pay a non–refundable application fee of $30,000 and $100,000 which will be placed in a national investment fund. Information Minister Ratu Josefa Dimuri stated that this demonstrated that the government did not intend to sell the country cheaply.

At the end of February, 1995, Prime Minister Rabuka appeared to be in firm control of the government.

Foreign Relations: Fiji is attempting to raise the level of its foreign relations with its neighbors. The country's central location, among the Pacific island states, places it in a geographic advantageous position. In 1994 a memorandum of understanding was completed on fisheries and handicrafts with Tuvalu. Fiji also offered Kiribati a one year accommodation without charge if it would set up an embassy. Visa fees for students from the smaller Pacific island states have be abolished. Fiji is a member of the Pacific Forum but has thus far declined membership in other, more sub–regional groupings such as the Melanesian Spearhead Group. Fiji is broadening its horizons with a new "look North" policy which will focus more on Asia. The country already has well developed ties to the West with Australia and New Zealand. India recently closed its embassy after the ambassador was asked to leave. In 1994, Fiji had two peace keeping battalions in the Sinai and Lebanon.

The Republic of KIRIBATI
(pronounced Kiri–baas)

Beretitenti **(President) Teburoro Tito**

Area: 338 sq. mi. (34 small islands).
Population: 71,300 (estimated).
Capital City: Bairiki (on Tarawa).
Languages: English (official), Gilbertese.
Principal Religion: Roman Catholic (48%), Protestant (Congregational) 45%.
Main Exports: Fish, copra.
Currency: Australian dollar.
Former Colonial Status: British Colony as the Gilbert Islands.
Independence Date: July 12, 1979.
Chief of State: Teburoro Tito (pronounced See-Toe), President (since October 1994).

The Republic of the MARSHALL ISLANDS

President Amata Kabua

Area: 68 sq. mi. (31 small islands).
Population: 48,500 (estimated).
Capital City: Majuro.
Language: English.
Principal Religion: Christianity, mostly Protestant.
Main Exports: Copra, copra oil, agricultural products, handicrafts.
Currency: U.S. dollar.
Former Political Status: Part of the UN Trust Territory of the Pacific under U.S. administration.
Independence Date: October 21, 1986.
Chief of State: Amata Kabua, President, but chief political leader since 1979.

The year was relatively calm for the Republic. In April 1994, President Kabua reshuffled the national cabinet. The significant changes involved the foreign minister, Tom Kijiner, who will become Minister of Health and Environment. Phillip Muller, Minister of Education, becomes foreign minister.

Both men have been key cabinet officials. Kijiner served as foreign minister during the time when the islands moved from United States control to independence. The Republic now has embassies in China, Fiji, Japan, the U.S., and the United Nations; with consulates in California and Hong Kong.

The Chinese are using the Marshall Islands to circumvent the limit on the amount of garments that it can export to the United States. China and the Marshall Islands agreed on a joint venture in December 1993 to build a garment factory. It will produce almost one million pieces a year and will employ Chinese workers initially. Marshallese will eventually take over all of the production jobs.

The Federated States of MICRONESIA

President Bailey Olter

Area: 271 sq. mi (about 600 islands, the largest of which are Pohnpei, Truk, Yap, and Kosrae).
Population: 110,000 (estimated).
Capital City: Kolonia (on Pohnpei).
Language: English, although other indigenous languages are spoken.
Principal Religions: Mostly Roman Catholic and Protestant.
Main Export: Copra.
Currency: U.S. dollar.
Former Political Status: Part of the UN Trust Territory of the Pacific under U.S. administration.
Independence Date: November 3, 1986.
Chief of State: Bailey Olter, President (since May 1991).

ISSN: 0892 2098
THE MARSHALL ISLANDS JOURNAL 50¢ on Majuro
Volume 22, Number 38
Friday, September 20, 1991

MARSHALLS JOINS UN

Majuro, Sept 18 The Republic of the Marshalls Islands was officially admitted to the United Nations today in an historic vote taken among its members at the international organization's headquarters in New York City.

nition of the Marshall Islands as an sovereign nation, has finally achieved one of his most cherished goals. The President left Majuro on Wednesday for the UN, where he will deliver a formal speech before the General Assembly

France, and China have veto power over applications for membership.

Britain, which had been disputing the right of the two freely associated states to membership in the U.N. on the basis of legal arguments claiming that the

on membership and voted for approval of the application.

One last minute problem threatened to derail the application. According to U.S. Ambassador William Bodde, "Only a few days before the Security Council was to vote on the Marshall's membership application, the delegate from the Soviet Union informed the United States that the Russian Parliament would have to approve the application before the So-

"The culmination of our struggles"

"We believe that the admission of the Republic of the Marshall Islands as full member of the United Nations represents the culmination of our struggles and the transformation that our country has undergone during the past 100 years. Admission to the United Nations also confirms before the world community the full restoration of our sovereignty.

The Republic of the Marshall Islands will now be able to use this world forum to fully participate in discussions and resolutions of problems affecting us as well as the rest of the world. The Republic of the

The Republic of NAURU

Former President Bernard Dowiyogo

Area: 8.2 sq. mi.
Population: 9,400 (estimated).
Capital City: There is no capital city as such, but most of the government offices are located in the Yaren District of the island.
Language: Nauruan (official); English is widely spoken and used in government and commerce.
Principal Religions: Protestant (65%), Roman Catholic (30%).
Main Export: Phosphates.
Currency: Australian dollar.
Former Political Status: UN trusteeship under Australia, New Zealand, and the UK.
Independence Date: January 31, 1968.
Chief of State: Lagumot Harris, President (since November 1995).

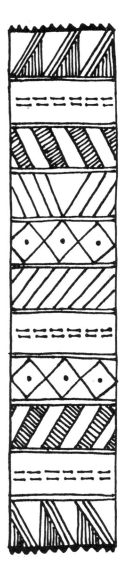

Micronesian tatoo design

The Republic of PALAU

President Kuniwo Nakamura

Area: 364 sq. mi. of land on approximately 200 (mostly tiny) islands.
Population: 15,000 (estimated).
Capital City: Koror (Pop. 10,501, estimated).
Language: Palauan (official), but English is widely used in government and commerce.
Principal Religion: Predominantly Roman Catholic and Protestant.
Currency: U.S. dollar.
Former Political Status: The last remaining entity in the UN Trust Territory of the Pacific, it was largely responsible for its domestic affairs. The U.S. remained the UN-designated trustee for Palau, responsible for its international relations, until the country declared its independence.
Independence date: October 2, 1994.
Chief of State: Kuniwo Nakamura, President.

166

SOLOMON ISLANDS

Prime Minister Solomon Mamaloni

Revolutionary Army (BRA) from Papua New Guinea (PNG) over the last year may have prompted the announcement. In March 1994, the PNG government paid the Solomon Islands $500,000 for damages incurred from an illegal border violation in 1992, which took the lives of three people.

The new force will be separated from the Ministry of Police and National Security, and will be used to monitor exports by sea and for other national security matters including border patrol.. Under an agreement signed at the end of 1994, the force will be trained in Port Moresby, PNG. In peace time, it will be used for civil work projects and disaster relief.

The Kingdom of TONGA

His Majesty the King of Tonga

Area: 10,640 sq. mi.
Population: 350,000 (estimated).
Capital City: Honiara (Pop. 25,000, estimated) on the island of Guadalcanal.
Languages: Over 100 indigenous tongues, with a Melanesian pidgin used for simplified communication. English is used in government and commerce.
Principal Religion: Nominally Christian, with many denominations and indigenous beliefs.
Main Exports: Fish, timber, copra, palm oil.
Currency: Solomon Islands dollar.
Former Political Status: British protectorate.
Independence Date: July 7, 1978.
Chief of State: Queen Elizabeth II.
Head of Government: Solomon Mamaloni, Prime Minister (since November 7, 1994).

On November 7, 1994, Solomon Mamaloni was elected Prime Minister. He defeated Sir Beddeley Devesi, 29 votes to 18 in a secret ballot election in the national Parliament. This is the third time for Mamaloni to be chosen Prime Minister.

The government faced a minor political crisis in March 1994 when Michael Miana, Minister of Tourism and Culture, was charged with 28 counts of misconduct. He is the first cabinet officer to face such charges.

Prime Minister Solomon Mamaloni announced that a newly reorganized national reconnaissance and surveillance force will be in operation by 1998. Recent border incursions by the Bougainville

Area: 283 sq. mi. (171 islands).
Population: 104,000 (estimated).
Capital City: Nuku'alofa (Pop. 32,000 estimated).
Languages: Tongan, English.
Principal Religion: Christianity.
Main Exports: Coconut oil, copra, bananas, other fruits and vegetables.
Currency: Pa'anga.
Former Political Status: British Protectorate.
Independence Date: June 4, 1970.
Chief of State: His Majesty King Taufa'ahau Tupou IV.
Head of Government: His Royal Highness Prince Farafehi Tu'ipelehake, Prime Minister (since December 1965).

TUVALU

Area: 10 sq. mi. (nine islands).
Population: 9,400 estimated).
Capital City: Funafuti (Pop. 3,000, estimated).
Languages: Tuvaluan, English.
Principal Religion: Christianity, mostly Protestant.
Main Export: Copra.
Currency: Tuvaluan and/or Australian dollar.
Former Political Status: British Protectorate as the Ellice Islands.
Independence Date: October 1, 1978.
Chief of State: Queen Elizabeth II.
Head of Government: Kamuta Laatasi, Prime Minister (December 10, 1993).

Tuvalu has a new Prime Minister, Kamuta Laatasi, after he defeated Bikenibeu Paeniu seven votes to five on the vote of the 12 member parliament. Two earlier attempts to elect a prime minister had ended in a tie vote in September. Mr. Laatasi will also have the foreign affairs and economy portfolios.

The Republic of VANUATU

Area: 4,750 sq. mi. (82 islands).
Population: 172,000 (estimated).
Capital City: Port Vila (Pop. 21,000 estimated).
Languages: English and French.
Principal Religion: Nominally Christianity interlaced with indigenous beliefs.
Main Exports: Copra, cocoa.
Currency: Vatu.
Former Political Status: British Protectorate as the New Hebrides.
Independence Date: July 30, 1980.
Chief of State: Jean-Marie Leye, President (since March 1994).
Head of Government: Maxime Carlot Korman, Prime Minister (since December 1991).

In December the coalition government of Vanuatu led by Prime Minister Maxime Carlot Korman faced a severe crisis. The coalition, composed of the Prime Minister's *Union of Moderate Parties* and a segment of the *National United Party* had a majority of two in the parliament when two senior ministers resigned. Mr. Cecil Sinker agreed to come back into the cabinet thus averting the crisis. The Prime Minister now has a majority of two in the 46 member parliament.

The crisis was provoked over the government's handling of a labor strike which had gone on for several weeks.

In December 1993 the People's Republic of China signed an agreement with the government to finance up to 75% of a $3.6 million dollar hydroelectric dam on the northern island of Mallicolo. China will also provide some forty technicians for the project. China also helped Vanuatu build its new parliament buildings and maintains an ambassador to the country. Japan is helping to build a second hydroelectric dam on the Sarakata River on Santo.

Gross domestic product (GDP) increased by 4% in 1993, while exports fell in 1994. In an attempt to preserve resources, the government banned the export of timber in June 1995. The country's major trading partners are Bangladesh, 34%; European Union, 27%; Japan, 19%; and Australia, 6%. The national budget for this year was announced on December 9, at $49 million, up from the 1994 budget of $45 million. Education is the largest item in the budget.

WESTERN SAMOA

**His Highness
Sasuga Malietoa Tanumafili II**

Area: 1,097 sq. mi. (Two large islands—Savai'i and Upolu—and seven smaller ones).
Population: 198,000 (estimated).
Capital City: Apia (Pop. 30,000 estimated) on Upolu.
Languages: Somoan, English.
Principal Religion: Christianity.
Main Exports: Coconut oil and cream, taro.
Currency: Tala.
Former Political Status: UN trusteeship administered by New Zealand.
Independence Date: January 1, 1962.
Head of State: His Highness Sasuga Malietoa Tanumafili II.
Head of Government: Tofilau Eti Alesana, Prime Minister (since April 1988).

The Samoan coast

The Dependencies

View from the Peak on Hong Kong Island looking towards the North Point

The active interest of the United States and European nations in ruling colonies in the countries of Southeast Asia was dramatically lessened by two elements of World War II: Japanese military conquest, and the economic drain of the war against Germany and Japan. Shortly after the end of the war two colonial wars erupted, the first against the French in Indochina and the second against the Dutch in Indonesia. The necessity for the West to yield to nationalistic pressures made it clear that the age of colonialism in Asia was over.

Near China, two areas of European rule remain: Hong Kong and Macao. These remain as colonies with largely Chinese populations. Hong Kong will pass to Chinese control in 1997 and Macao in 1999.

British Dependency
Hong Kong

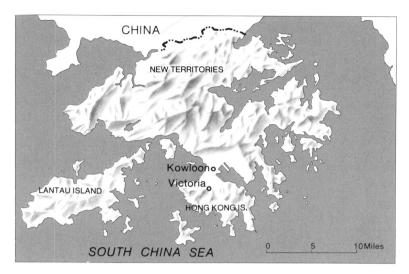

Area: 398 square miles.
Population: 5.7 million (estimated).
Administrative Capital: Victoria.

The British Crown Colony of Hong Kong consists of three parts. The first is the island of Victoria (or Hong Kong Island) on the north side of which the city of the same name is located. The second part is the small area known as Kowloon, at the tip of the peninsula jutting from the Chinese mainland toward Victoria. Between Victoria and Kowloon lies one of the world's busiest and most beautiful harbors. The third part is composed of the New Territories, which extend northward from Kowloon to the Chinese border, and also include some islands in the waters around Victoria. Kowloon is connected by rail with the Chinese city of Guangzhou (Canton).

Most of the area of Hong Kong consists of hills and low mountains, but there are enough level lands in the New Territories for large quantities of food to be harvested; Hong Kong is actually dependent for much of its food and water on the mainland of China. The population is almost totally Chinese, many of them having arrived since 1949 in order to find greater safety, freedom and economic opportunity than was allowed on the troubled mainland of China. The climate is subtropical and monsoonal in the summer, but relatively cool in the winter.

Realizing the potential value as a naval base, although not seeing at first the commercial possibilities of Hong Kong, the British annexed it from the Manchus in 1842, after the so-called Opium War. Under orderly and effective British administration, and sharing in the increase of British trade with and investments in China during the nineteenth and early twentieth centuries, Hong Kong experienced rapid growth as a port. Kowloon was annexed in 1860, after another Anglo-Chinese war. The New Territories were added in 1898 in order to provide agricultural land and living space for the growing population but were held on a 99-year lease.

Given their large population, Victoria and Kowloon could not survive without the New Territories. The flow of refugees from the mainland has been stopped. Public housing has been built but many "squatters" still remain without permanent housing.

During the damaging Japanese occupation of Hong Kong from 1941–45, and the Communist takeover in China in 1949, Hong Kong's "trade" with the mainland of China was increasingly confined to the import of food, water, and consumer goods. The mainland economy now earns roughly $1 billion a year from trading with Hong Kong. The colony is able to pay this bill and still grow economically because of its excellent port facilities and commercial relations with the rest of Asia, its established business firms, and its very efficient, but rather poorly paid, labor force. In recent years, especially in the 1960's, foreign capital, including that from America and Japan, has poured into Hong Kong, building apartments, erecting office buildings and light industrial plants in particular.

Because of the effect of the "Great Cultural Revolution" (see China) and communist gains in nearby Macao, Maoists in Hong Kong decided in 1967 to inflict a major political defeat and humiliation upon the British. It appears probable that the Maoist leadership in Beijing did not give a specific order for the operation, and did not want to face the confusion and economic losses that would result from an actual seizure of Hong Kong. But Beijing probably felt that it had no choice but to give public support, mainly in the form of propaganda, to the actions of its enthusiastic followers in Hong Kong.

Had the latter cooperated with the communist–led unions in Hong Kong, which are strong, things might have gone badly for the British. Instead, the Maoists distrusted the unions as being interested in bread and butter, not ideological issues, and also because they were supposed to be controlled by the sort of party leaders who on the mainland were the targets of the Cultural Revolution.

A series of demonstrations in late May 1967, followed by a sporadic campaign of terrorism and occasional incidents created by Mao enthusiasts at the Chinese border, disrupted life in the colony somewhat and caused a limited falling off in trade and tourism, but actually did almost nothing to shake British control of the colony. In fact, the campaign tended to alienate public opinion among the Chinese population of Hong Kong from the communist cause and push it for the first time onto the side of the British.

China was very careful about involving itself directly in the Hong Kong situation; it did not ship any significant quantity of explosives to the terrorists, and its troops at the border created almost no trouble for the British. There was some disruption of deliveries of food and water to Hong Kong, but this seemed to be more the result of the general confusion on the mainland than of any decision in Beijing to put any direct economic pressures on the colony.

In recent years Hong Kong has become the third largest financial center and the fourth largest container port in the world.

Under an agreement announced in September 1984, after two years of negotiations, sovereignty and administrative control over Hong Kong will pass to China in 1997. Beijing promises to leave the existing economic and social systems essentially unchanged for at least fifty years after that as well as to permit a degree of self–government. Although there will be no way to compel Beijing to honor this pledge if it chooses not to do so, most of the population of Hong Kong—who have nowhere else to go—appear to have resigned themselves reluctantly to a future under the Chinese flag. White collar and professional workers are emigrating in considerable numbers, however. Some local Chinese capital has already left, but new short–term investment of U.S. and Japanese money is still being made.

Beijing has shown an increasing desire to influence events in Hong Kong even before 1997, yet without harming the economy, whose complex workings it really does not understand. It objects to various efforts by the British government of Hong Kong to move toward representative government, such as indirect elections for some members of the Governor's Legislative Council in September 1985, as tending to reduce China's ultimate freedom of action and confront it in 1997 with a situation in Hong Kong that it will find unacceptable. This attitude in turn has created additional uneasiness in Hong Kong.

There has been considerable development of light industry, which does not require much imported energy and generates sizable exports, especially of textiles and garments. The British colonial government has followed a policy of "positive non-interventionism," rather than planning and regulating the economy as is the policy of most other countries of the region. In recent years, there has been a considerable flow of investment between Hong Kong and China in both directions, so that their futures are interlinked in the economic sphere as they are in the political sphere.

With the participation of some Hong Kong Chinese, Beijing drafted a Basic Law, which was published in draft form in 1988 and will regulate Hong Kong's government after 1997.

Initially, the British appear to have been reluctant to tinker too much with China's long term view of what Hong Kong should look like. However, with the appointment of a former Conservative Party MP, Chris Patten, to the post of Governor of Hong Kong in 1992, the British have apparently decided to take a stronger hand in determining the future of the colony's government prior to their withdrawal in 1997. Even before Governor Patten's appointment, the British had taken some steps to strengthen the democratic process in Hong Kong. In September 1991, elections were held for 18 of the 61 seats on the Legislative Council (Legco). Sixteen of these seats were won by pro–democratic candidates. This election gave a considerable boost to the

pro–democracy movement in Hong Kong though it did not make the Chinese on the mainland happy. In late 1992 Governor Patten appeared to be pushing for further changes which the Chinese objected to. The basic disagreement between the British and the Chinese has to do with the type of government Hong Kong is to have in the future. The Chinese in Beijing have in mind an executive–dominated government for Hong Kong, where the legislature plays the role of an adviser. The British propose a strong, elected legislative assembly.

The talks between the two sides did not produce any results during the rest of 1993. In December, Beijing ended the talks because Governor Patten had tabled a bill in the Hong Kong Legco to provide for elections in 1994 and 1995. The Chinese had not given their consent. China argues that Patten's proposals violate the Basic Law and the Sino–British Joint Declaration on Hong Kong. The Basic Law provides for Beijing to set up a preparatory committee in 1996 to oversee the transition.

At the end of February 1994, Legco adopted phase one of Governor Patten's democratic reforms, in spite of the fact that China had threatened to scrap the changes when it takes control of Hong Kong from Britain in 1997. Under the reforms, the voting age is lowered to 18 from 21.

Appointed local council seats were replaced by elected single–member–district seats for the 1994 and 1995 elections. The 1994 elections for 346 district board seats were held on September 18. The pro–democracy *Democratic Party* won 32% of the seats. The pro–Beijing *Democratic Alliance* won 14%. The remainder went to independents. The results showed a significant improvement for the pro–China party over the 1991 elections.

Other events throughout the year suggested that China had abandoned the "one country, two systems" formula for everything but the economy. In September, the Chinese parliament, National

People's Congress, passed a resolution stating that it would scrap all legislative structures created under Governor Patten's reforms. One month later, the suggestion was made that a provisional Legco would be established on July 1, 1997, to replace the Legco elected for a four–year term in 1995.

There were other indications of what is to come as well. Lu Ping, Director of China's Hong Kong and Macau Affairs Office, stated that all judges would have to be reappointed when the colony is turned over to Beijing. In addition, Beijing has indicated that the five–judge Court of Final Appeals, set up under the Basic Law to govern Hong Kong after 1997, will only have one overseas judge. Furthermore, Beijing will scrap the Bill of Rights in 1997, which among other things allows for citizens to sue the government for violations of civil rights.

There is also evidence that even the media is knuckling under to Beijing in anticipation of 1997. At the end of the year, Asia Television pulled the Raymond Wong show, News Tease. Wong was very popular and well known for his blunt criticism of the mainland. This is not the first time for television to cower in front of Beijing. Rupert Murdoch pulled the BBC from his Star TV broadcasts into China. In another incident, TVB, a rival of Asia Television, pulled a documentary on the private life of Mao after Beijing protested.

One would think that no government would be stupid enough to "kill the golden goose." Perhaps Beijing cannot help itself. And, the argument could be made that Hong Kong is no longer indispensable with the rise of Shanghai and the new gold coast. The counter argument is that Beijing will have to clean up its act throughout all of China if it wants to keep the outside investments coming. Hong Kong should be a model instead of a target for China. This should be obvious. However, failing communist systems cannot be judged by Western definitions of rationality.

French Dependencies
New Caledonia

Area: 8,550 square miles.
Population: 150,000 (estimated).

This island group is located east of Australia. Its economic importance is as a major exporter of nickel. It has a limited degree of self–government, but it was not scheduled to become independent before 1989 at the earliest.

The indigenous Kanakas (or Kanaks) who are Melanesians, are outnumbered by the combined European, Asian and Polynesian settlers. The majority wants a con-

tinuation of French rule, but a militant group of the Kanakas demands independence—which Paris fears might destabilize French Polynesia to the east—and has taken to violence. President Mitterrand visited the island in early 1985 in an atmosphere of crisis, and offered it limited independence in association with France. This proposal seemed to please neither side.

In elections held in September 1985, the Kanaks, who are becoming increasingly radicalized, won majorities in three

of the four regions, although pro–French elements (Europeans and Asians) won an overall majority in the territorial assembly.

The new French government of Premier Jacques Chirac in 1986 canceled the previous political concessions pending the outcome of elections. A referendum held in September 1987 was boycotted by most of the Kanaks, and accordingly the vote was 98% in favor of continued existence as a French territory (rather than as an independent state). Pro–independence demonstrations by Kanaks were then suppressed by French police.

In June 1988, a new French government worked out an agreement with both sides; following a year (1989) of direct French rule, there would be a period of limited self–government and accelerated economic development, followed by a referendum on independence in 1998.

Although highly controversial, this agreement was approved in a referendum held in both France and New Caledonia in November.

French Polynesia

Area: 1,545 square miles.
Population: 148,000 (estimated).

Scattered over a wide area in the South Pacific, this group of islands includes the famous tourist attraction of Tahiti. The islands have limited self–government. The most controversial issue in recent years has been French nuclear tests as recently as 1985 which caused an accidental nuclear explosion in 1979 that produced a tidal wave and charges of serious environmental contamination.

New Zealand Dependency
Cook Islands

Area: 90 square miles.
Population: 18,500.
Prime Minister: Sir Geoffrey Henry.

These islands, located about 1,700 miles northeast of New Zealand, have a predominantly Polynesian population. They have had internal self–government since 1965, but New Zealand continues to control defense and foreign relations. The northern islands are relatively poor; the southern islands are rather prosperous.

The Cook Islands is one of the world's smallest nations, with 18,500 people, spread over one of the largest sea areas in the world. The country is known as a tax haven and has a reputation for rough and tumble politics. Unfortunately, the country also has a foreign debt of approximately NZ$100 million. In April 1995, the Prime Minister accused the Central Intelligence Agency of funding the opposition *Democratic Party* and a new newspaper, the Cook Island Press. The government was recently linked to an US$1.1 billion fraud involving Cook Island financial instruments.

Internal government is controlled by the *Cook Island Party (CIP)* which won re–election in March 1994. It holds 16 seats in the parliament (Legislative Assembly), the *Democratic Party*,(3) and the *Alliance,* (2). Prime Minister Sir Geoffrey Henry first came to power in 1983. Elections are for a maximum period of five years.

United States Dependencies
Guam

Area: 212 square miles.
Population: 115,000 (estimated).

The United States acquired Guam, which is the southernmost of the Marianas, from Spain in 1898 as a result of the Spanish American War. The population is predominantly Micronesian and Catholic. Guam has self–government but is not yet a Territory or Commonwealth, like Puerto Rico. Its residents are U.S. citizens but do not vote in American national elections. Guam has been the site of a major U.S. air base since it was recaptured from the Japanese during World War II. Now that the U.S. has lost its naval base in the Philippines, it is considered as a possible alternative site.

The lush jungle on Guam cannot erase the traces of World War II
Photo by Cdr. Thornton W. Wilt

American Samoa

Area: 76 square miles.
Population: 34,000 (estimated).

The inhabitants of these seven islands, located just east of Western Samoa, are mostly Polynesian. They enjoy limited self–government under the jurisdiction of the Department of the Interior. The main occupations are farming and fishing.

The U.S. has recently launched a major effort to improve the economic well-being of the territory by stimulating private enterprise to take over government–administered enterprises ("privatization").

Portuguese Dependency
Macao (Macau)

Area: 6 square miles.
Population: 450,000 (estimated).

Portugal's only remaining overseas territory, Macao, is divided about equally into Macao proper, which has a common land frontier with the Chinese mainland, and two nearby islands. The terrain is mostly flat. The offshore waters are muddy with silt carried by the Pearl River. The climate is subtropical, with a summer monsoon and a relatively cool winter. Except for a small community of Portuguese (officials, soldiers, police, missionaries, businessmen, etc.) and other Europeans, the population is overwhelmingly Chinese.

Portugal acquired Macao in the mid–16th century for use as a base from which to trade with nearby Canton by an agreement with the Ming dynasty of China. It became prosperous in this way in the 18th century, but during the 19th century it was rapidly overshadowed by Hong Kong. It was not occupied by the Japanese during World War II, however, as was Hong Kong. From its earlier days of prominence, Macao has retained some beautiful old buildings and something of a Mediterranean flavor. It has a reputation, partly justified but also somewhat exaggerated, as a center of opium and gold smuggling and assorted vice. Gambling is unquestionably a major feature of the economy, and auto racing and bull-fighting have recently been introduced as well.

In late 1966, local Maoist enthusiasts took offense at some clumsy Portuguese official actions and decided to inflict a political defeat on the Portuguese. Peking approved of their decision, but did not necessarily originate it. Massive and violent demonstrations proved too much for the small Portuguese garrison and police force, even though it was fairly clear that Chinese troops would not move in.

The Portuguese were compelled to agree to nearly all of the demonstrators' demands by early 1967, the effect of which was to leave the Portuguese nominally in control of the colony, but also to give the local Maoist organization a virtual veto over any act of the colonial administration. The situation would probably have been even worse for the Portuguese if the far stronger British administration in Hong Kong had been simultaneously compelled to yield to the similar demands of local Maoists there; the resolute British performance helped to shield Macao from further pressure, at least for the time being.

The new government of Portugal after 1974 wanted to return Macao to China, but Beijing would not accept it, because of the disturbing effect that such a transfer would have on Hong Kong. Once the Sino–British agreement was reached on Hong Kong in 1984, however, negotiations began in 1986 between Lisbon and Beijing for the reversion of Macao to Chinese control. It was agreed in April 1987 that reversion would take place in 1999, along lines similar to those already worked out for Hong Kong.

Selected Bibliography of Key English Language Sources

General

Aikman, David. *Pacific Rim: Area of Change, Area of Opportunity.* Boston: Little Brown, 1986.

Barnett, A. Doak. *China and the Major Powers in East Asia.* Washington, DC: Brookings Institution, 1977.

Clyde, Paul H. *The Far East: A History of the Western Impact and the Eastern Response (1830–1970).* 5th Ed. Englewood Cliffs, NJ: Prentice–Hall, 1971.

Dibb, Paul. *Siberia and the Pacific: A Study of Economic Development and the Trade Prospects.* New York: Praeger, 1972.

Encyclopedia of Asian History. 4 vols. New York: Scribner, 1988.

Kapur, Ashok, ed. *Diplomatic Ideas and Practices of Asian States.* New York: Brill, 1990.

Kelly, Brian. *The Four Little Dragons.* New York: Simon and Schuster, 1989.

Kihl, Young W., ed. *Asian–Pacific Security: Emerging Challenges and Responses.* Boulder: Lynne Rienner, 1986.

MacFarquhar, Roderick, ed. *Sino–American Relations, 1949–1971.* New York: Praeger, 1971.

Nemetz, Peter N., ed. *The Pacific Rim: Investment, Development, and Trade.* 2nd Ed. Univ. of British Columbia Press, 1990.

Phillips, David. *New Towns in East and South–East Asia: Planning and Development.* Oxford Univ. Press, 1987.

Pye, Lucian W. *Asian Power and Politics: The Cultural Dimensions of Authority.* Harvard Univ. Press, 1985.

Reischauer, Edwin O. *East Asia: Tradition and Transformation.* Boston: Houghton Mifflin, 1973.

Scalapino, Robert A. *Major Power Relations in North–East Asia.* Lanham, MD: Univ. Press of America, 1987.

Taylor, Robert H. *Asia and the Pacific.* 2 v. New York: Facts on File, 1991.

Vogel, Ezra F. *The Four Little Dragons: The Spread of Industrialization in East Asia.* Harvard Univ. Press, 1991.

Zagoria, Donald S., ed. *Soviet Policy in East Asia.* Yale Univ. Press. 1982.

Southeast Asia

Altschiller, Donald, ed. *Political Change in Southeast Asia.* New York: H. W. Wil0son, 1989.

The Cambridge History of Southeast Asia. 2 v. Cambridge Univ. Press, 1992.

Esterline, John H. *How the Dominoes Fell: Southeast Asia in Perspective.* Lanham, MD: Univ. Press of America, 1990.

Fitzgerald, Stephen. *China and the Overseas Chinese.* Cambridge Univ. Press, 1972.

Lim Tek Ghee. *Conflict over Natural Resources in South–East Asia and the Pacific.* Kuala Lumpur: Oxford Univ. Press, 1990.

Lyon, Peter. *War and Peace in Southeast Asia.* New York: Oxford Univ. Press, 1969.

Neher, Clark. *Southeast Asia in the New International Era.* Boulder: Westview Press, 1991.

Schlossstein, Steven. *Asia's New Little Dragons: The Dynamic Emergence of Indonesia, Thailand, and Malaysia.* Chicago: Contemporary Books, 1991.

Steinberg, David, ed. *In Search of Southeast Asia.* Rev. Ed. Harvard Univ. Press, 1987.

Tillman, Robert A., ed. *Man, State and Society in Contemporary Southeast Asia.* New York: Praeger, 1971.

Von Der Mehden, Fred R. *South–East Asia 1930–1970: The Legacy of Colonialism and Nationalism.* New York: Norton, 1974.

Zasloff, Joseph J., ed. *Indochina in Conflict: A Political Assessment.* Boston: D.C. Heath. 1972.

Australia

Carroll, John, ed. *Intruders in the Bush: The Australian Quest for Identity.* Oxford Univ. Press, 1982.

Dibb, Paul, ed. *Australia's External Relations in the 1980's: The Interaction of Economic, Political, and Strategic Factors.* New York: St. Martin's Press, 1983.

Finkelstein, Dave. *Greater Nowheres.* New York: Simon & Schuster, 1990. (Travel, social life and customs)

Grattan, Clinton Hartley. *The Southwest Pacific to 1900: A Modern History.* Univ. of Michigan Press, 1963.

———. *The Southwest Pacific since 1900: A Modern History.* Univ. of Michigan Press, 1963. (Australia, New Zealand, The Islands, Antarctica)

Grey, Jeffrey. *A Military History of Australia.* Cambridge Univ. Press, 1990.

Gunther, John. *Inside Australia.* New York, Harper & Row, 1972.

Harris, Alexander. *Settlers and Convicts, or, Recollections of Sixteen Years' Labour in the Australian Backwoods, by an Emigrant Mechanic.* Foreword by Manning Clark. Zion, IL: International Scholarly Book Services, 1969.

Keneally, Thomas. *Australia: Beyond the Dreamtime.* New York: Facts on File, 1987.

Molony, John N. *The Penguin Bicentennial History of Australia: The Story of 200 Years.* New York: Viking, 1987.

Osborne, Charles, ed. *Australia, New Zealand and the South Pacific.* New York: Praeger, 1970.

Oxford History of Australia. Oxford Univ. Press. 1986. v. 4, 1901–1942; v. 5, 1945–1985.

Simpson, Colin. *The New Australia,* New York: Dutton, 1972.

Ward, Russel Braddock. *Australia Comes of Age.* New York: St. Martin's Press, 1989.

China

Barnett, A. Doak. *China's Economy in Global Perspective.* Washington, DC: Brookings Institution, 1981.

Butterfield, Fox. *China: Alive in a Bitter Sea.* New York: Times Books, 1982.

Chang, Parris H. *Power and Policy in China.* Rev. Ed. Pennsylvania State Univ. Press, 1978.

Cheng, Chu–Yuan. *Behind the Tiananmen Massacre.* Boulder: Westview Press, 1990.

———. *China's Economic Development.* Boulder: Westview Press, 1982.

Clubb, O. Edmund. *Twentieth Century China.* Rev. Ed. Columbia Univ. Press, 1971.

Fairbank, John King. *China: A New History.* Harvard Univ. Press, 1992.

———. *The United States and China.* 4th Ed. Harvard Univ. Press, 1979.

Garside, Roger. *Coming Alive: China After the Cultural Revolution.* New York: McGraw–Hill, 1981.

Harding, Harry. *China's Second Revolution: Reformation After Mao.* Washington, DC: Brookings Institution, 1987.

———. *A Fragile Relationship: The United States and China Since 1972.* Washington, DC: Brookings Institution, 1991.

Hinton, Harold C. *An Introduction to Chinese Politics.* 2nd Ed. New York: Holt, Rinehart and Winston, 1978.

Hucker, Charles O. *China to 1850: A Short History.* Stanford Univ. Press, 1977.

Johnson, U. Alexis, ed. *China Policy for the Next Decade.* Oelgeschlager, Gunn and Hain for the Atlantic Council, 1984.

Lardy, Nicholas R. *Foreign Trade and Economic Reform in China, 1978–1990.* Cambridge Univ. Press, 1992.

Leys, Simon. *Broken Images: Essays on Chinese Culture and Politics.* New York: St. Martin's Press, 1980.

———. *The Burning Forest: Essays on Chinese Culture and Politics.* New York: Holt, Rinehart, and Winston, 1986.

———. *Chinese Shadows.* New York: Viking Press, 1977. (Essays of a Traveler)

Michael, Franz. *China Through the Ages.* Boulder: Westview Press, 1986.

Moser, Leo. *The Chinese Mosaic: The Peoples and Provinces of China.* Boulder: Westview Press, 1984.

Ogden, Suzanne. *China's Unresolved Issues: Politics, Development, and Culture.* 2nd Ed. Englewood Cliffs, NJ: Prentice–Hall, 1992.

Pye, Lucien W. *China: An Introduction:* 3rd Ed. Boston: Little, Brown, 1984.

Schaller, Michael. *The United States and China in the Twentieth Century.* 2nd Ed. Oxford Univ. Press, 1990.

Schram, Stuart. *The Political Thought of Mao Tse–tung.* Rev. Ed. New York: Praeger, 1969.

Shaw, Yu–ming, ed. *Power and Policy in the PRC.* Boulder: Westview Press, 1985.

Spence, Jonathan D. *The Gate of Heavenly Peace: The Chinese and Their Revolution.* New York: Viking Press, 1981.

Stacy, Judith. *Patriarchy and Socialist Revolution in China.* Univ. of California Press, 1983.

Tuchman, Barbara W. *Stillwell and the American Experience in China.* New York: MacMillan, 1971.

Zagoria, Donald S. *The Sino–Soviet Conflict, 1956–1961.* Princeton Univ. Press, 1961.

Hong Kong

Cameron, Nigel. *Hong Kong: The Cultured Pearl.* Oxford Univ. Press, 1978.

———. *An Illustrated History of Hong Kong.* Oxford Univ. Press, 1991.

Cheng, Joseph Y. S., ed. *Hong Kong in Search of a Future.* Oxford Univ. Press, 1984.

Davis, Michael C. *Constitutional Confrontation in Hong Kong: Issues and Implications of the Basic Law.* New York: St. Martin's Press, 1990.

Jao, Y.C., ed. *Hong Kong and 1997: Strategies for the Future.* Hong Kong: Univ. of Hong Kong, 1985.

Roberts, Elfed Vaughan. *Historical Dictionary of Hong Kong and Macau.* Metuchen, NJ: Scarecrow Press, 1992.

Indonesia

Abeyasekere, Susan. *Jakarta: A History.* Singapore: Oxford Univ. Press, 1987.

Andaya, Leonard Y. *The World of Maluku: Eastern Indonesia in the Early Modern Period.* Honolulu: Univ. of Hawaii Press, 1993.

Booth, Anne, ed. *The Oil Boom and After: Indonesian Economic Policy and Performance in the Soeharto Era.* Singapore: Oxford Univ. Press, 1992.

Bresnan, John. *Managing Indonesia: The Modern Political Economy.* Columbia Univ. Press, 1993.

Cribb, Robert B. *Historical Dictionary of Indonesia.* Metuchen, NJ: Scarecrow Press, 1992.

Frederick, William H., ed. *Indonesia: A Country Study.* 5th ed. Washington, DC: 1993. Sold by the Supt. of Documents.

Hardjono, Joan, ed. *Indonesia: Researches, Ecology, and Environment.* Singapore: Oxford Univ. Press, 1991.

Jenkins, David. *Suharto and His Generals.* Cornell Univ. Press, 1984.

Lubis, Mochtar. *Indonesia: Land under the Rainbow.* Singapore: Oxford Univ. Press, 1990.

Pearson, Scott R. *Rice Policy in Indonesia.* Cornell Univ. Press, 1991.

Ricklefs, Merle Calvin. *A History of Modern Indonesia: c. 1300 to the Present.* 2d ed. Stanford Univ. Press, 1993.

Roff, Sue Rabbitt. *Timor's Anschluss: Indonesian and Australian Policy in East Timor, 1974–1976.* Lewiston, NY: Edwin Mellen Press, 1992.

Schlossstein, Steven. (see **Southeast Asia**)

Vatikiotis, Michael R. J. *Indonesia under Suharto: Order, Development, and Pressure for Change.* London: Routledge, 1993.

Japan

Barnett, Robert W. *Beyond War: Japan's Concept of Comprehensive National Security.* New York: Pergamon Press, 1984.

Burks, Ardath W. *Japan: Profile of a Post–industrial Power.* Boulder: Westview Press, 1982.

Curtis, Gerald L. *The Japanese Way of Politics.* Columbia Univ. Press, 1988.

Curtis, Gerald L., ed. *Japan's Foreign Policy after the Cold War: Coping with Change.* Armonk, NY: M. E. Sharpe, 1993.

Frost, Ellen L. *For Richer, For Poorer: The New U.S.–Japan Relationship.* New York: Council on Foreign Relations, 1987.

Hane, Mikiso. *Modern Japan: A Historical Survey.* Boulder: Westview Press, 1986.

Ito, Takatoshi. *The Japanese Economy.* MIT Press, 1992.

Koppel, Bruce M., ed. *Japan's Foreign Aid: Power and Policy in a New Era.* Boulder: Westview Press, 1993.

Lincoln, Edward J. *Japan: Facing Economic Maturity.* Washington, DC: Brookings Institution, 1987.

———. *Japan's Economic Role in Northeast Asia.* University Press of America for the Asia Society, 1987.

Lockwood, William W. *State and Economic Enterprise in Japan.* Princeton Univ. Press, 1965.

Nakane, Chie. *Japanese Society.* Univ. of California Press, 1971.

Okazaki, Hisahiko. *A Grand Strategy for Japanese Defense.* University Press of America for Abt Books, 1986.

Reischauer, Edwin O. *Japan, the Story of a Nation.* New York: Knopf, 1970.

———. *The Japanese.* 3rd Ed. New York: Knopf, 1980.

———. *The Japanese Today: Change and Continuity.* Cambridge, MA: Belknap Press, 1988.

Richardson, Bradley M. *Politics in Japan.* Boston: Little, Brown, 1984.

Sansom, George B. *Japan: A Short Cultural History.* Rev. Ed. New York: Appleton–Century Crofts, 1962.

Thayer, Nathaniel B. *How the Conservatives Rule Japan.* Princeton Univ. Press, 1969.

Van Wolferen, Karel. *The Enigma of Japanese Power.* New York: Vintage Books, 1990.

Vogel, Ezra F. *Japan as Number One.* Harvard Univ. Press, 1979.

Korea

Amsden, Alice H. *Asia's Next Giant: South Korea and Late Industrialization.* Oxford Univ. Press, 1989.

Bandow, Doug, ed. *The U.S.–South Korean Alliance: Time for a Change.* New Brunswick, NJ: Transaction Publishers, 1992.

Clark, Donald N. *The Kwangju Uprising: Shadows over the Regime in South Korea.* Boulder: Westview Press, 1988.

Das, Dilip K. *Korean Economic Dynamism.* New York: St. Martin's Press, 1992.

Han, Sungjoo. *The Failure of Democracy in Korea.* Univ. of California Press, 1964.

Henderson, Gregory. *Korea: The Politics of the Vortex.* Harvard Univ. Press, 1968.

Hinton, Harold C. *Korea Under New Leadership: The Fifth Republic.* New York: Praeger, 1983.

Jacobs, Norman. *The Korean Road to Modernization and Development.* Univ. of Illinois Press, 1985.

Kihl, Young W. *Politics and Policies in Divided Korea: Regimes in Contest.* Boulder: Westview Press, 1984.

Koh, Byung Chul. *The Foreign Policy Systems of North and South Korea.* Univ. of California Press, 1984.

Lee, Manwoo. *The Odyssey of Korean Democracy: Korean Politics, 1987–1990.* New York: Praeger, 1990.

Lowe, Peter. *The Origins of the Korean War.* New York: Longmans, 1986.

Macdonald, Donald Stone. *The Koreas: Contemporary Politics and Society.* Boulder: Westview Press, 1990.

Matray, James I., ed. *Historical Dictionary of the Korean War.* Westport, CT: Greenwood Press, 1991.

Mazarr, Michael J., ed. *Korea 1991: The Road to Peace.* Boulder: Westview Press, 1991.

Nelson, M. Frederick, *Korea and the Old Orders in Eastern Asia.* Univ. of Louisiana Press, 1945.

Rees, David. *Korea: The Limited War.* New York: St. Martin's Press, 1964.

Savada, Andrea Matles, ed. *South Korea: A Country Study.* 4th ed. Washington, DC: 1992. Sold by the Supt. of Documents.

Scalapino, Robert A. *Communism in Korea.* 2 vols. Univ. of California Press, 1972.

Steinberg, David I. *The Republic of Korea: Economic Transformation and Social Change.* Boulder: Westview Press, 1989.

Taylor, William J., ed. *The Korean Peninsula: Prospects for Arms Reductions under Global Detente.* Boulder: Westview Press, 1990.

Woo–Cumings, Meredith. *Race to the Swift: State and Finance in Korean Industrialization*, by Jung–en Woo. Columbia Univ. Press, 1991.

Laos

Dommen, Arthur J. *Laos: Keystone of Indochina.* Boulder: Westview Press, 1985.

Stuart–Fox, Martin. *Historical Dictionary of Laos.* Metuchen, NJ: Scarecrow Press, 1992.

Macao

Cremer, R. D., ed. *Industrial Economy of Macau in the 1990s.* Hong Kong: UEA Press, 1990.

————. *Macau: City of Commerce and Culture.* Hong Kong: UEA Press, 1987.

————. *Macau: City of Commerce and Culture: 2d ed.: Continuity and Change.* Hong Kong: API Press, 1991.

Guillen–Nunez, Cesar. *Macau.* Oxford Univ. Press, 1984.

Roberts, Elfed Vaughan. (see **Hong Kong**)

Malaysia

Andaya, Barbara Watson. *A History of Malaysia.* Macmillan, 1982.

Bedlington, Stanley S. *Malaysia and Singapore: The Building of New States.* Cornell Univ. Press, 1978.

Chin, Kin Wah. *The Defence of Malaysia and Singapore: The Transformation of a Security System.* Cambridge Univ. Press, 1983.

Gould, James W. *The United States and Malaysia.* Harvard Univ. Press, 1969.

Gullick, John M. *Malaysia: Economic Expansion and National Unity.* Boulder: Westview Press, 1981.

————. *Rulers and Residents: Influence and Power in the Malay States, 1870–1920.* Oxford Univ. Press, 1992.

Hua, Wu Yin. *Class and Communalism in Malaysia: Politics in a Dependent Capitalist State.* Totowa, NJ: Biblio Distribution Center, 1983.

Kaur, Amarjit. *Historical Dictionary of Malaysia.* Metuchen, NJ: Scarecrow Press, 1993.

Pye, Lucian W. *Guerrilla Communism in Malaya.* Princeton Univ. Press, 1956.

Schlossstein, Steven. (see **Southeast Asia**)

New Zealand

Bateman New Zealand Encyclopedia. David Bateman Ltd., 2nd Ed. Auckland, N.Z., 1987.

Encyclopedia of New Zealand. 3 vols. Wellington, N.Z.: Government Printer, 1966.

Grattan, Clinton Hartley. (see **Australia**)

Hawke, Gary Richard. *The Making of New Zealand: An Economic History.* Cambridge Univ. Press, 1985.

Mulgan, Richard G. *Democracy and Power in New Zealand: A Study of New Zealand Politics.* 2nd Ed. Oxford Univ. Press, 1989.

Osborne, Charles, ed. (see **Australia**)

The Oxford History of New Zealand. Oxford Univ. Press, 1981.

Sinclair, Keith. *A History of New Zealand.* Enl. Ed. Baltimore, MD: Pelican Books, 1980.

————, ed. *The Oxford Illustrated History of New Zealand.* Oxford Univ. Press, 1990.

Sturm, Terry. *The Oxford History of New Zealand Literature.* Oxford Univ. Press, 1991.

The Philippines

Bonner, Raymond. *Waltzing with a Dictator: The Marcoses and the Making of American Policy.* New York: Times Books, 1987.

Brands, H. W. *Bound to Empire: The United States and the Philippines.* Oxford Univ. Press, 1992.

Broad, Robin. *Unequal Alliance: The World Bank, the International Monetary Fund, and the Philippines.* Univ. of California Press, 1988.

Chapman, William. *Inside the Philippine Revolution.* New York: Norton, 1987.

Davis, Leonard. *Revolutionary Struggle in the Philippines.* New York: St. Martin's Press, 1989.

Dolan, Ronald E., ed. *Philippine: A Country Study.* 4th ed. Washington, DC: 1993. Sold by Supt. of Documents.

Hawes, Gary. *The Philippine State and the Marcos Regime: The Politics of Export.* Cornell Univ. Press, 1987.

Jones, Gregg R. *Red Revolution: Inside the Philippine Guerrilla Movement.* Boulder: Westview Press, 1989.

Karnow, Stanley. *In Our Image: America's Empire in the Philippines.* Yale Univ. Press, 1989.

Kerkvliet, Benedict J. *Everyday Politics in the Philippines.* Univ. of California Press, 1990.

Robinson, Thomas W., ed. (see **Taiwan**)

Steinberg, David Joel. *The Philippines: A Singular and a Plural Place.* 2d ed. Boulder: Westview Press, 1990.

Wurfel, David A. *Filipino Politics: Development and Decay.* Cornell Univ. Press, 1988.

Youngblood, Robert L. *Marcos Against the Church: Economic Development and Political Repression in the Philippines.* Cornell Univ. Press, 1990.

Singapore

Bedlington, Stanley S. (see **Malaysia**)

Bellows, Thomas J. *The People's Action Party of Singapore.* Yale Univ. Press, 1970.

Chen, Peter S. J., ed. *Singapore Development Policies and Trends.* Oxford Univ. Press, 1983.

Chew, Sock Foon. *Ethnicity and Nationality in Singapore.* Ohio University Center for International Studies, 1987.

Chin, Kin Wah. (see **Malaysia**)

LePoer, Barbara Leitch, ed. *Singapore: A Country Study.* 2nd Ed. Washington, DC, 1991. Sold by the Supt. of Documents.

Li, Tania. *Malays in Singapore: Culture, Economy, and Ideology.* Oxford Univ. Press, 1989.

Mirza, Hafiz. *Multinationals and the Growth of the Singapore Economy.* New York: St. Martin's Press, 1986.

Mulliner, K. *Historical Dictionary of Singapore.* Metuchen, NJ: The Scarecrow Press, 1991.

Salaff, Janet W. *State and Family in Singapore: Restructuring a Developing Society.* Cornell Univ. Press, 1988.

Taiwan

Clough, Ralph. *Island China.* Harvard Univ. Press, 1978.

Copper, John Franklin. *Historical Dictionary of Taiwan.* Metuchen, NJ: Scarecrow Press, 1993.

Robinson, Thomas W., ed. *Democracy and Development in East Asia: Taiwan, South Korea, and the Philippines.* Washington, DC: AEI Press, 1991.

Thailand

Keyes, Charles F. *Thailand: Buddhist Kingdom as Modern Nation–State.* Boulder: Westview Press, 1987.

LePoer, Barbara Leitch, ed. *Thailand: A Country Study.* Washington, DC, 1989. Sold by Supt. of Documents.

Schlossstein, Steven. (see **Southeast Asia**)

Smith, Harold E. *Historical and Cultural Dictionary of Thailand.* Metuchen, NJ: Scarecrow Press, 1976.

Wyatt, David K. *Thailand: A Short History.* Yale Univ. Press, 1984.

Vietnam

Davidson, Phillip B. *Vietnam at War: The History, 1946–1975.* Oxford Univ. Press, 1991.

Duiker, William J. *Vietnam: A Nation in Revolution.* Boulder: Westview Press, 1983.

Hoang, Van Chi. *From Colonialism to Communism—a Case History of North Vietnam.* New York: Praeger, 1965.

Hosmer, Stephen T. *Viet Cong Repression and Its Implications for the Future.* Boston: D.C. Heath, 1970.

The Pentagon Papers. New York: Bantam Books, 1971.

Pike, Douglas. *Viet Cong*. MIT Press, 1966.
⎯⎯⎯⎯ . *Vietnam and the Soviet Union: Anatomy of an Alliance*. Boulder: Westview Press, 1987.
Vandemark, Brian. *Into the Quagmire: Lyndon Johnson and the Escalation of the Vietnam War*. Oxford Univ. Press, 1991.

Pacific Islands

Craig, Robert D., ed. *Historical Dictionary of Oceania*. Westport, CT: Greenwood Press, 1981.
Grattan, Clinton Hartley. (see **Australia**)
Osborne, Charles, ed. (see **Australia**).

Sahlins, Marshall David. *Islands of History*. Univ. of Chicago Press, 1985.
Stanley, David. *Micronesia Handbook: Guide to an American Lake*. Chico, CA: Moon Publications, 1985.
⎯⎯⎯⎯ . *South Pacific Handbook*. 4th Ed. Chico, CA: Moon Publications, 1989.

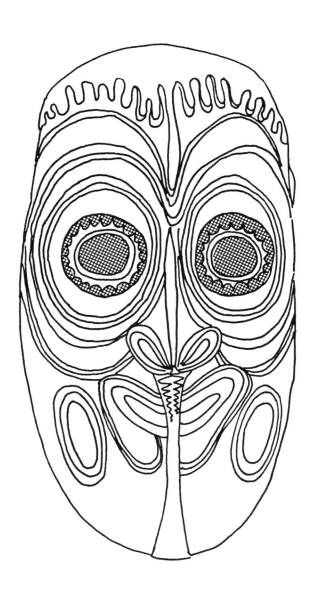